National Theatre Connections 2012

PLAYS FOR YOUNG PEOPLE

Victim Sidekick Boyfriend Me

Journey to X

Little Foot

Prince of Denmark

Socialism is Great

The Grandfathers

Alice by Heart

Generation Next

So You Think You're a Superhero?

The Ritual

with an introduction by

ANTHONY BANKS

Methuen Drama

Methuen Drama

1 3 5 7 9 10 8 6 4 2

This collection first published in 2012 by Methuen Drama,
an imprint of Bloomsbury Publishing Plc

Methuen Drama
Bloomsbury Publishing Plc
50 Bedford Square, London WC1B 3DP
www.methuendrama.com

Victim Sidekick Boyfriend Me © Hilary Bell 2012
Journey to X © Nancy Harris 2012
Little Foot © Craig Higginson 2012
Prince of Denmark © Michael Lesslie 2012
Socialism is Great © Anders Lustgarten 2012
The Grandfathers © Rory Mullarkey 2012
Alice by Heart © Steven Sater and Duncan Sheik 2012
Generation Next © Meera Syal 2012
So You Think You're a Superhero? © Paven Virk 2012
The Ritual © Samir Yazbek 2012
Introduction copyright © Anthony Banks 2012

Resource material copyright © National Theatre 2012

ISBN 978 1 408 15724 4

A CIP catalogue record for this book is available from the British Library

Available in the USA from Bloomsbury Academic & Professional,
175 Fifth Avenue / 3rd Floor, New York, NY 10010.
www.BloomsburyAcademicUSA.com

Typeset by Country Setting, Kingsdown, Kent
Printed and bound in Great Britain by CPI Group (UK) Ltd, Croydon CR0 4YY

Contents

Introduction

Ten Plays About the World

On the opening night of the 2005 National Theatre Connections Festival there was dancing in the streets as London discovered it was to host the Olympics in 2012. The following morning, the city suffered a terrorist attack on its public transport system. During those extraordinary twenty-four hours we started to imagine a special Connections Festival which would premiere ten new plays about the wider world, performed by thousands of young actors across the country – a generation exploring stories from beyond the borders of the UK through the art of making theatre.

The National Theatre's Connections programme has been flourishing for seventeen years, and this is the first time a starting point has been given to its ten writers. The aspiration is, as always, to create an enticing collection of short new plays by leading writers for enthusiastic actors aged from thirteen to nineteen to perform at home and in professional theatre venues across the country, during the festival and for years to come.

The 2012 Olympics presents an opportunity to bring different voices from around the world into Connections, and this year the plays have been researched and developed in many different parts of the globe. They are stylistically varied and are suitable for all the age groups within the teenage spectrum. Our stories span the previous and next Olympics host countries, China and Brazil, and travel to Russia, India and South Africa. A political drama from Ireland with a very human heart sits alongside a sporting comedy which takes place not just all over the world, but in other galaxies too! There's an American take on a favourite English novel, an antipodean crime drama, and, coinciding with celebrations of Shakespeare in 2012, a response to one of his most famous plays.

Victim Sidekick Boyfriend Me

CAST SIZE 16 *plus ensemble*

AGE SUITABILITY 13–19

Hilary Bell is one of Australia's leading playwrights. She developed her script in Sydney, with the help of the young actors from ATYP – the Australian Theatre for Young People.

A Girl commits a crime without punishment or remorse. Her Sidekick is ordered to serve a prison sentence. The Victim's Boyfriend offers his unconditional forgiveness. Rather than receiving the court's punishment, the Girl is welcomed into the home of her Victim's friends and family. At first she takes this for granted, but as she's affected by their kindness her conscience is aroused – to the point where she craves a chance to atone. But what are they really doing? If it's not as simple as mercy, if they're not using her to fill the victim's place, then perhaps they're exacting a punishment far more intricate and sustained.

Journey to X

CAST SIZE 10

AGE SUITABILITY 14–19

Nancy Harris is from Dublin, where her comedy *No Romance* was recently a huge hit for the Abbey Theatre, the National Theatre of Ireland. Her play is about a nation's opinion on a sensitive subject, and although based on knowledge of cases and stories from Ireland, could be set in many countries around the world.

A group of friends have formed a new band and are scheming to raise money to get to London to audition for the world's biggest talent contest. Their costumes, songs and fundraising techniques may divide opinion but one of the girls has a far more important choice to make. Their journey for fame and fortune is really a journey for something far less glamorous – something their country doesn't approve of, something their parents wouldn't condone. In a culture of instant fame and talent-show 'stories', the importance of life and friendship come to the fore.

Little Foot
CAST SIZE 5 *plus chorus*
AGE SUITABILITY 13–19

Craig Higginson's play *The Girl in the Yellow Dress* was a huge success in 2010, and toured internationally. Craig has developed his Connections play with young people in his home town of Johannesburg, where he is also literary director of the Market Theatre.

Deep within some South African caves, a group of friends dare each other to spend the night and explore the mysteries of the nearby area known as the 'Cradle of Humankind'. As the young friends venture deeper into the sepulchre of the oldest human remains, relationships within the circle of friends become strained. With truths revealed and loyalties strained, these modern teenagers find themselves stripped back to their primordial instincts. Surrounded by a chorus of ancestral voices, the group unravels. Just how far will modern humans go to exact revenge? This poetic play draws on Greek tragedy and South African folklore to create a powerful portrayal of modern relationships.

Prince of Denmark
CAST SIZE 10 *plus ensemble*
AGE SUITABILITY 15–19

Michael Lesslie has responded to Shakespeare's play *Hamlet* with a prequel. Set about ten years before the death of old Hamlet, the story stands completely apart from Shakespeare's play, though it borrows characters, riffs on themes and reverberates with the rotten state of Denmark in a way which will be intriguing both for those who haven't yet experienced *Hamlet* and those who have. Michael played Hamlet when he was at school so he was able to imagine the younger prince and present his story in a way which resonates with young people today.

Prince of Denmark presents a generation of teenage characters we rarely see in European historical plays about royal families. Apathetic and broody, they loll around Elsinore castle, killing time by sword-fighting with each other. The swagger and poise of their ambition in the late 1500s is not dissimilar to ambitious young men who hunger to run the universe half a millennium later.

Socialism is Great
CAST SIZE 12 *plus ensemble*
AGE SUITABILITY 13–19

Anders Lustgarten is a playwright and a political activist. He has studied Chinese culture and language extensively, and is fluent in Chinese. Thanks to the support of the British Council, Anders was able to spend a month travelling around China, interviewing dozens of young people. It was the conversations he had with these young people, and with a group of Chinese teenagers he spent time with in Manchester's China Town, that fuelled the themes and stories in his play.

A new generation of the Chinese Republic faces the reality of their parents' ideals – shifting between the revolutionary young men and women who took to the streets to celebrate Socialism and their children who take to the street to sell iPhones. Set in one of the world's most populous countries, the play focuses on three separate encounters between two young girls in a factory, two schoolboys debating British culture, and a girl and boy who both pretend to be other people. The propaganda of the East meets the propaganda of the West in a play about love, work and power.

The Grandfathers
CAST SIZE 9
AGE SUITABILITY 15–19

Rory Mullarkey is from Manchester and has travelled extensively around Russia and Eastern Europe. He took a train to Archangel in the north of Russia, where national service is still obligatory, to research his play about young conscripts in the army. He also spent time with teenage recruits on a British army base in Surrey. The generosity, frankness and honesty of the soldiers' tales ignited his play.

National service in the UK ended fifty years ago, but young people across the world are still conscripted into the armed forces. *The Grandfathers* follows nine young recruits as they are trained to become defenders of their nation.

Alice by Heart

CAST SIZE 7 *or more*
AGE SUITABILITY 13–19

Steven Sater and Duncan Sheik tapped into the teenage heart-beat across the world with their smash-hit rock musical version of *Spring Awakening*. For Connections, they've chosen to revisit Lewis Carroll's *Alice in Wonderland*.

In the throes of adolescence, determined Alice Parsley convinces her seriously ill friend Alfred to follow her one last time down the hole and play White Rabbit to her petticoated heroine. Mad as it all is, there's so much she still wants from him. And yet, how late it's getting! A rock musical about growing up and letting go of the past.

Generation Next

CAST SIZE 9 *plus dancers*
AGE SUITABILITY 15–19

Meera Syal is a much-loved performer, who last appeared at the National Theatre in the hit comedy *Rafta Rafta*, and is well known on television for *Goodness Gracious Me*. Although Meera has written novels, screenplays and the book for the musical *Bombay Dreams*, this is her first play for the stage.

Generation Next takes place in a community centre where two young British Punjabis are about to get married. The same wedding occurs in three different generations: in 1979, 2005 and 2035. Couples fight, friends disagree, and there are always too many aunts and uncles to remember. As time speeds forward, conflicts shift and traditions change.

So You Think You're a Superhero?
CAST SIZE 24 *plus ensemble*
AGE SUITABILITY 13-14

Paven Virk returned to her home town of Coventry to talk to some thirteen-year-olds about their views on sport, the universe and what makes a good joke funny. She then tested out her play with the Chichester Festival Theatre Youth Theatre, who helped her sculpt it into the fast-paced, athletic piece of lampoonery it has now become.

The prestigious Sports Academy has a secret sporting superhero lined up for the Olympics. When Teen TV goes under cover to find out more, any hopes of Olympic success are put in jeopardy.

The Ritual
CAST SIZE 7
AGE SUITABILITY 13-16

Conexões, a version of Connections, has been running in Brazil for the last six years. We wanted to celebrate our relationship to their programme by jointly commissioning one of Brazil's leading playwrights, and engaging one of their most talented youth theatres, Vizinho Legal, which involves young people who live in *favelas* on the outskirts of São Paulo, to workshop the play. Their ideas and feedback were vital in Samir Yazbek's creation of his episodic thriller. Mark O'Thomas has translated the play with great care and sensitivity.

The Ritual is about a secret organisation with a set of rules its members must follow, instructing them that they must engage only in relationships which are devoid of affection or emotional investment. This intense psychological thriller tracks their weekly endeavours to follow the ritual, and explores the extremes people are prepared to go to, in order to remain one of the group.

*

We're very grateful to the many young people who have helped in the genesis of these ten plays, and also to the actors from the National Youth Theatre who have travelled to the NT Studio in London for script readings in the final stages of the plays' developments. Ruth Little has given invaluable script guidance, and the collection would not have come about without the passion and enthusiasm of the writers who have given their ideas and their plays with such generosity and enthusiasm. We hope young people on- and offstage will relish creating productions of these plays throughout 2012, and for many years to come.

Anthony Banks
National Theatre, 2012

Victim Sidekick Boyfriend Me

Hilary Bell

Characters

Girl
Sidekick
Boyfriend
Youth Group (**A**, **B**, **C** *etc.*)
Dance Troupe (**1**, **2**, **3** *etc.*)
Cavers (**X**, **Y**, **Z** *etc.*)
Medieval Re-enactors
Victim

The cast size is flexible, depending on the number of available actors. For instance, the Youth Group can be comprised of anything between two and twenty people, and the lines divided up among many or few. The Girl, Boyfriend, Sidekick and Victim are the only constants.

One

Girl, Sidekick.

Girl 'I have struggled. It's been agony, and there was a time when if I'd had a gun I would've killed you. You drove me to doubt everything I believed in, to see the world as a dark and wicked place.

'But my faith forced me to look into my heart. Buried deep under the grief and rage and crushing pain, I found a small spark of light. It's mercy.'

Sidekick Show me.

Girl 'I found mercy there. I forgive you.'

Sidekick Wow.

Girl Wow what?

Sidekick Seems like a nice bloke.

Girl 'Forgive' me? For what?

Sidekick It's the boyfriend, right?

Girl I didn't do anything.

Sidekick No, I know.

Girl How dare he?

Sidekick I wish I got a letter like that. I wish someone would forgive me.

Girl Have it, it's yours.

Sidekick Hey . . . listen . . . We're going to stand by each other, aren't we?

Girl I wasn't even there.

Sidekick I only did what you told me to.

Girl Jump off a bridge.

Sidekick If you've got a good reason . . .

Girl   I wasn't there, I didn't know her, I didn't do anything.
So how can anything happen to me?

Sidekick   It won't, don't worry.

—

But I sent the texts.

Girl   Then your mum better get you a good lawyer.

Sidekick   Lawyer?

Girl   I love how you believe anything I say.

Sidekick   You will stand by me, though, right? You'll tell
them you wrote the texts and forwarded them to me?

Girl   All this fuss over a nobody, a blip, what's the
difference if she's here or not?

Sidekick   I was just following orders. You'll tell them if it
comes to that?

Girl   I'm not getting involved, this is your problem now. I
did nothing. That is the whole point, you can't get in trouble
for doing nothing.

Sidekick   You said to act like she wasn't there, if she said
anything, like we didn't hear her.

Girl   It's called a joke.

Sidekick   If she phones don't pick up, don't answer if she
asks a question.

Girl   Anybody's fault it's hers, for having no sense of
humour.

Sidekick   You got me to spread the word.

Girl   Spread the word to do nothing: exactly!

Sidekick   But if anyone's going to get in trouble . . .

Girl   It'll be you. Your laptop, your account, your phone,
you you you.

Sidekick   Your words.

Girl   No, you wrote them, you typed, you texted, you.

Sidekick   You said them. Your friends. Your idea in the first place.

Girl   Well, she's certainly making up for the lack of attention now. Can we talk about something else?

Sidekick   It's serious, girl. We could be in it pretty deep.

Girl   Why does everyone keep telling me that? What's it got to do with me?

Two

Girl, Sidekick, Boyfriend.

Sidekick   They asked what it's got to do with you and I said nothing.

Girl   Did you say 'Nothing' or did you not say anything?

Sidekick   You got to say something or it's contempt of court. I said 'Nothing.' 'It's got nothing to do with her.'

Girl   You shouldn't have opened your mouth.

Sidekick   Get in even more trouble then.

Girl   You do, not me. You.

Sidekick   I couldn't get in any more trouble.

Girl   You bloody could, look what I'm facing! You only got a year, I could be in for five!

Sidekick   A year I'll be eighteen, I'll be fully an adult. That's the rest of my childhood.

Girl   I'll be middle-aged in five years, what are you whining about? You've got to make sure it doesn't happen, you've got to do something.

Sidekick   My counsel said I was weak.

Girl   Everyone was involved, all the boarders: are they going to put a hundred kids on trial?

Sidekick   Only the ringleader. You're strong and I'm weak.

Girl   What?

Sidekick   He called you intelligent, said you're powerful and charismatic – he should've been your lawyer, not mine. Except he also called you a villain.

Girl   This is a nightmare, stuff like this doesn't happen to me. It's not like I was doing anything different from what I always do. – What about you, can't you do something?

Boyfriend   I've forgiven you.

Girl   Something useful.

Boyfriend   Do you know what that means?

Sidekick   I think it's awesome.

Girl   Not if it doesn't help.

Boyfriend   We have a relationship now. I didn't want it, I never asked for it. But like it or not, we're connected for ever. Some people have told me I've let Shona down, mustn't've loved her. But that's their stuff. If I wallow in hatred, I'm letting you destroy me too.

Girl   That's really nice and everything, and no offence but, you know, so what?

Boyfriend   I went to the judge.

Girl   You what?

Boyfriend   I told him I forgave you.

Girl   . . . And?

Boyfriend   I asked for clemency.

Sidekick   What does that mean?

Girl   You mean like letting me off?

Boyfriend   I said I didn't see who it would help, locking you away – not me, because I've overcome my need for revenge; not you – become institutionalised, reoffend; and her . . . well it won't help her now.

Sidekick   What about me?

Boyfriend   Too late sorry.

Girl   And what did he say?

Boyfriend   He listened. Considering I'm her fiancé –

Sidekick   You were getting married?

Boyfriend   Next month.

Sidekick   Congratulations.

Girl   But what did he say?

Boyfriend   He heard me.

Girl   Meaning what?!

Boyfriend   The justice system won't pursue you.

Girl   You're saying I'm let off, I'm free.

Boyfriend   Yes.

Sidekick   You mean . . .

Girl   Oh my God.

Boyfriend   Your name will be removed from all the documents.

Girl   Yes!

Sidekick   Wow, that's fantastic.

Girl   What did you just stand there for, saying nothing all that time? Why didn't you tell me soon as you walked in? Enjoy watching people suffer, do you?

Boyfriend   No, do you?

Girl   I'll enjoy watching that detective's face who's been coming round to our house. I might even pay him a visit at the station.

Sidekick   Will you visit me?

Girl   Oh great, that's right, if you're in gaol where am I going to live?

Sidekick   Her parents kicked her out, she's been staying at my place.

Girl   I guess your mum won't let me have your room since you're not using it? No.

Boyfriend (*to* **Girl**)   Your parents seem nice.

Sidekick   They're really nice.

Girl   You think so? They're the ones who dobbed me in. And they made it clear I wasn't wanted at home. That's why I've been staying with her.

Sidekick   They said you're welcome home once you've paid your debt to society.

Girl   Hear that? This is my parents! Whatever happened to unconditional love?

Sidekick   You've got that great room with the balcony lined up next term.

Girl   You think I'd go back to boarding school? Did one of those teachers come to my defence?

Sidekick   Then where will you stay?

Boyfriend   I know somewhere.

Girl   . . . Where?

Boyfriend   Friends of mine and Shona's.

Girl   What sort of friends?

Boyfriend   Good people.

Girl   You mean your Fellowship.

Boyfriend   Her peeps, they'll look after you.

Girl   Please don't say that unless you want to make us laugh.

Boyfriend   Our Youth Group runs a shelter. She was over there all the time, helping out, before she went away to school. It's a place to crash, a hot meal.

Girl   This had better not be some elaborate plan to convert me, because if they try any Jesus stuff –

Boyfriend   No.

Girl   Fellowship freaks, I'll never live it down.

Sidekick   Swap places, I'll go.

Girl   Only till I get a better offer, understood?

Boyfriend   Sure.

Girl   If you let it get around –

Sidekick   So her friends must've forgiven you too.

Boyfriend   All of them, not just the Youth Group. Yes, they have. That's because Shona inspired love in people.

Sidekick   If they do convert you, say a prayer for me.

Girl   Oh, not you too.

Sidekick   I'm scared.

Girl   Price of getting caught.

Sidekick   Come and see me?

Girl   Look at him, what a dork. Imagine the two of them kissing . . . Urgh.

Sidekick   Hey . . .

Girl   Look how he stands, look at his clothes.

Sidekick   Be careful.

Girl   What do you mean?

Sidekick   It's suspect. Why would her mates, her bloody fiancé, get you off?

Girl   Lucky for me, they're trying to get into Heaven.

Sidekick   I'm just saying, watch out.

Girl   I only hung around with you because you believed whatever you were told. Now what am I supposed to like about you?

Sidekick   No one gets off that easy.

Sidekick *is led to an isolated area, where she remains.*

Boyfriend   Coming?

Three

Girl, Boyfriend, Youth Group.

Everyone (*but* **Girl**) *sings – guitar and tambourine number.*

> The road we all travel,
> Is hard on the feet.
> It's covered in gravel,
> There's dust and there's heat,
> And sometimes you just
> Can't take all the dust,
> You wanna cry out, 'Lord, I'm beat!'
>
> But turn around,
> He's there beside you.
> Turn around,
> To love and to guide you.
> Turn around,
> To shelter and hide you from the sun.
> Just turn it around.

The people you meet
As you travel along,
They offer temptations
With laughter and song,
And sometimes you think,
'It's just one little drink,
One little risk, one little wrong.'

But turn around,
You're going straight now.
Turn around,
Shrug off that weight, now.
Turn around,
It's never too late to take your life,
And turn it around.

Boyfriend
It isn't too late to take your life . . .

All (*except* **Girl**)
And turn it around.

Boyfriend   There's a spare mattress, and you don't have to worry about chipping in for groceries until you're able.

Girl   Yay.

Youth A   Hi, I'm Shona's cousin. It's so great you could join us.

Girl   Yeah, right hi and all that. Look, just so you know –

Youth B   Chillax, we're not going to put Jesus-juice in your food.

Youth C   We don't want anything except to help you find peace in your heart.

Youth D   If we can't do that, we've failed.

Girl   I'll let you know.

Youth E   You seem a bit wound up, are you okay?

Youth F   Have a drag on this. We call it the Peace Pipe. It'll help you kick back.

Girl   No thanks.

Youth G   You like singing?

Girl   No.

Youth H   You might get to like it if you try . . .

Youth I   Can't beat music for unwinding. Do you play anything?

Girl   No, and I'm not banging on a tambourine.

Youth I   I was going to offer to teach you a few chords, but that's cool.

Youth J   How long you staying?

Girl   I'm out of here soon as I get the chance.

Youth A   So how did you know Shona?

Girl   —

Youth B   *Did* you know Shona?

Girl   Not at all.

Youth C   That's a shame. What a beautiful soul.

Youth D   Like a big candle, and when she looked at you it was like she lit your candle, so before you knew it the room would be full of light.

Youth E   You should've heard her sing.

Youth F   She wrote that song we just played.

Girl   No kidding.

Youth D   What are we going to do without our big candle, how will we see our way in the darkness?

Youth G   The memory of her. We'll use that to light the way.

Youth E   That's where she sat, where you are.

Youth H   Her face glowing.

Youth I   Her beautiful voice.

Youth J   So we're just going to have to sing twice as loud, folks. Sing so she can hear us.

Boyfriend   If you join in, maybe she'll hear us.

Youth F   Will you sing? Come on, just one song, sing with us.

Girl   Why?

Youth F   What do you mean, why?

Girl   Why would you want me to sing?

Youth E   It's our way of inviting you in, blending our voices in praise.

Girl   Why would you want me to smoke and sing and to stay with you? What's this about?

Youth H   It's not about anything but sharing our love.

Youth I   We're trying to make you feel welcome.

Boyfriend   Don't you feel welcome?

Girl   . . . Because, you know, my friend's in gaol thanks to her.

Youth A   We don't traffic in blame.

Youth B   We're sorry about your friend, and we're sorry about Shona. But there's a lot to be glad about too, a lot of good in the world.

Youth C   And that's what we try to focus on.

Boyfriend   You're not in gaol – there's something to smile about.

Youth J   We don't presume to judge our fellow creatures, that's the Lord's job.

Youth D   Ours is a faith of forgiveness.

Youth E   One life's been destroyed, why ruin another?

Youth F   It's not like we're ignoring what happened, we're never going to forget her, but it's what she would've wanted: move forward, don't dwell on the past, effect change positively, through love.

Youth G   Okay?

Girl   Sure. Great. Okay. If you say so.

They commence their song again.

Girl (*sotto*)   Though I'm starting to envy my friend.

Boyfriend   Yeah, I reckon gaol's the soft option.

Girl   Oh –

Boyfriend   The harmonies are pretty gruesome, I've been working on them but some of these guys, they're all heart and no talent.

Pause.

Girl   Why did you talk to the judge?

Boyfriend   We all agreed; we decided to take it into our own hands.

Girl   Who knew she had, like, friends?

Boyfriend   Shona had many, many friends. You'll meet them.

Girl   Well, whatever, change the subject, too depressing.

Boyfriend   I'm sorry about your family kicking you out.

Girl   They're the ones who'll be sorry, when I publish my tell-all memoir.

Boyfriend   Maybe you can find it in your heart to forgive.

Girl   What I can't forgive is this song.

Boyfriend They pick up the guitars first thing in the morning and don't put them down till bedtime. Hope your better option comes along soon!

Girl It's not like I'm planning to hang around in here all day.

Boyfriend What else are you going to do?

Girl —

Boyfriend You can close the door if it gets too much. The room with the mattresses is right through there.

Girl Mattress*es*? I'm sharing a room?

Boyfriend A lot of kids pass through here, looking for refuge until things blow over. There's a high turnover, so if you get a problem-person you can take comfort knowing it won't last long.

Girl I can't share a room.

Boyfriend Better than sharing a cell.

Girl What do you want, eternal gratitude? You going to keep bringing it up? You've scored your brownie points for getting me off, don't pretend this is all for my sake.

Boyfriend Where are you going?

Girl Somewhere else.

Boyfriend No, wait.

Girl I can't stay here.

Boyfriend Wait – I've got a room.

Girl —

Boyfriend We shared a place, me and Shona.

Separate rooms of course.

So there's a spare bedroom.

Girl You want me to take it?

Boyfriend It's empty.

Yes. I want you to.

Girl Well, if it's just sitting there . . .

Four

Girl, Boyfriend, Youth Group, Modern Jazz Troupe.

Dancer 1 This one goes out to you, baby. We'll never be the same without you, but you live on in the beat, in the breath, in the music.

The **Troupe** *performs a dance routine. It features an absence – e.g., empty chair, empty spotlight. As they dance:*

Dancer 1 Hey, look at what she's wearing.

Dancer 2 That's her robe.

Girl It was in the wardrobe, that's my room now . . .

Dancer 2 It's her costume, we made them for the Chinese spectacular.

Girl Take it, I don't care.

Dancer 1 No – no, it fits you.

Dancer 2 It looks great on you. Do a turn and see how it billows out.

Girl Piss off.

Dancer 2 Just try it, we designed it specially to billow out.

Girl No!

The dance continues.

Boyfriend I think they want you to join in.

Girl Get lost.

Boyfriend Can't you dance?

Girl   That is not what I call 'dancing'.

Boyfriend   Guess that means you can't.

Girl   And you can.

He dances with the absent place. Intense, emotional.

Boyfriend   Aren't you going to laugh?

Girl   —

Boyfriend   Either laugh at me or dance with me.

She steps in. He dances with her and is aggressive, almost brutal. It's a charged centre in the **Troupe***'s campy choreography. By the end, she has filled the empty place.*

Boyfriend   Thanks, guys. She'd have loved it.

Dancer 1   She was here, she was right here.

Dancer 2   In the rhythm's backbeat, in the breath of the horns.

Dancer 3   The wail of the guitar, that was all her pain and suffering.

Boyfriend   Yes.

Dancer 4   The dust motes in the spotlight.

Dancer 5   The sound of bare feet hitting boards.

Dancer 6   She's the sweet high note that wrings the heart.

Boyfriend   Yes.

Girl   I didn't know she danced.

Dancer 7   Oh yeah, dance was her life.

Dancer 6   She didn't say much, but when she danced she told you everything –

Dancer 5   – about what it means to be alive.

Dancer 4   Some people's souls are a colour or a sound, hers was a gesture.

They perform a gesture.

Dancer 3   Hers was an in-breath.

They inhale.

Dancer 2   Hers was a stag leap.

They do a stag leap.

Girl   Must leave a bit of a hole.

Dancer 2   It forces you to be more creative. There's a gap – what can we do with that gap? How can we make it work for us?

Dancer 3   In some ways, the routine's actually better.

Girl   But you miss her.

Dancer 3   —

Come over here.

Listen, before you go beating yourself up, there's something you should know about Shona. My dad's doctor, he heard it from someone at his hospital that she had a pretty appalling wasting disease. She didn't know it, they hadn't worked up the courage to tell her. But it did not bode well for her future. She was facing a difficult, and short, life.

Dancer 1   A life without dance.

Dancer 2   So don't feel too bad about what happened, okay?

Dancer 3   You might've even done her a favour.

Beat.

Girl   Can we do it again?

Dancer 1   And!

Jazz hands –

Isolations –

Grapevine –

Stag leap!

*The **Girl** ends up in the **Boyfriend**'s arms.*

A beat, and they disengage.

Five

Girl, Boyfriend, Youth Group, Modern Jazz Troupe, Cavers.

Headlamps in darkness.

Girl   This is amazing!

Boyfriend   Turn your light on.

Girl   It's incredible, I've never done anything like this.

Caver X   Everybody okay back there? Team leaders, quick roll-call.

Lightning speed:

Caver Z   Yoda.

Caver Q   Here!

Caver Y   Arthur.

Caver R   Here!

Caver Z   Anakin.

Caver S   Here!

Caver Y   Merlin.

Caver T   Here!

Caver Z   Lord of the Sith.

Caver U   Here!

Caver Y   Lancelot.

Caver V   Here!

Caver Z   Princess Leia

Boyfriend   That's you.

Girl   Oh – here!

Caver Y   Guinevere.

Caver W   Here!

Caver Z   Youth Group.

Youth Group   Here!

Caver Y   Jazz Troupe.

Dance Troupe   Here!

Caver Z   All here.

Caver Y   All here.

Caver X   Good. Now we're about to embark on a fairly tricky section. I've got her map, but since she never had a chance to test it we can only hope it's accurate. Shona was a top caver, I have complete faith in her route. However, I urge you all to exercise caution. New girl, that means you.

Girl   Yep, alright!

Caver X   Normally I'd never allow a novice on a high-risk adventure, but we're doing this for Shona and we can't afford a broken link in the chain. So, new girl, when they say Leia that means you. Right?

Girl   Right! Let's go!

Boyfriend   Hang on.

Caver X   Anything from the team leaders?

Caver Z   I'd suggest you put your wetsocks on because the next section is pretty slippery and damp.

Caver Y   And look out for bats.

Caver X   And of course don't leave a thing behind. That means breadcrumbs, drink-bottle lids, faeces containers. Okay, proceed.

As they crawl:

Girl   I just can't imagine it.

Caver V   What?

Girl   Shona, doing this.

Caver V   Leia was a fanatic. She made the maps, taught us knots for descending pitches: your figure-of-nine loop, your bowline, your Italian hitch, your Alpine butterfly . . .

Boyfriend   Where are your elbow pads, did you forget them?

Caver V   What? Oh – oh, great.

Boyfriend   You don't want to open up all those lacerations, they've only just healed.

Caver V   And I've been practising my knots for months.

Girl   She never told me she was into this kind of stuff.

Boyfriend   You never spoke to her.

Caver T   I thought you knew her.

Girl   Not well enough to talk to.

Caver W   Really? Leia was very outgoing.

Caver U   Maybe she did something to upset you?

Girl   No –

Caver T   She might've been different there.

Caver S   Boarding school can change people.

Caver U   Yeah, she probably provoked you.

Caver W   Did she provoke you?

Caver X   Leia!

Girl   Yes?!

Caver X   You alright back there?

Girl   I'm alright . . .

Caver X   Okay, folks, have a sip of water before we ascend the pitch.

Caver W   What are you going to do about your elbows?

Caver V   I'm heartbroken, I've been looking forward to this for months, practising my knots . . .

Girl   Here.

Boyfriend   You need your elbow pads.

Girl   I've got long sleeves.

Caver V   Are you serious?

Girl   Take them.

Caver V   Thanks.

Caver X   Okay, people, let's test for oxygen.

Strikes a match – it fizzes out.

Hmm. Danger Will Robinson! But that's how we like it. So now, everyone breathe deeply and calmly, and when I say 'go', wriggle through this passage as fast as you can and up to the next chamber – there'll be more oxygen there.

Headlamps on. Ready? GO.

Girl   Oh God, oh God, I'm going to hyperventilate.

Boyfriend   Don't talk, you'll waste your breath.

Caver X   Stop talking back there!

Come on teams, come on, come on! You can make it!

I'm already up here, see my light?

Nice fresh air, just a few metres.

Wriggle wriggle wriggle, come on, faster!

Girl *coughs violently.*

Caver X   Drag her through! Get her to the air!

Boyfriend   Shona, you alright?

Girl   What?

Boyfriend   I mean –

Girl   'Shona'?

Boyfriend   Take some breaths.

Girl   I'm fine.

Boyfriend   I'm going ahead.

Girl   He's angry.

Caver W   He's just upset.

Caver T   He loved her.

Girl   Didn't everyone?

Caver T   Not everyone.

Caver V   Look, Leia, to tell you the truth, it's not all bad.

Caver W   She was a fabulous caver, but as a person . . .

Caver S   She had an air rifle, and she took pot-shots at birds. Bet you didn't know that. Harmless pigeons in her back yard.

Caver T   And once I happened to look at the mail on her kitchen table: she was a member of the Nuclear Re-Armament Party. I couldn't believe it.

Caver V   I believe it.

Caver W   Like I said, a great caver.

Caver V   Not that we would ever, ever have wished such a thing.

Caver W   God, no.

Caver V   I guess all we're saying is . . .

Caver W   It's not the end of the world. Right?

Girl   No . . . Yes, but still –

Caver V   He'll get over it.

Six

Girl, Boyfriend, Youth Group, Dance Troupe, Cavers, Medieval Re-enactors.

A party.

The **Girl** *observes everyone having a good time, then goes to her room.*

The **Boyfriend** *joins her.*

Boyfriend   Everything okay?

Girl   I was going to leave tonight.

Boyfriend   Move out?

Girl   I should've guessed, all the signs – but it came as a complete shock. Not until you called me Shona . . .

Boyfriend   Oh, that.

Girl   I felt sick. I didn't want to see any of you again – especially you.

Boyfriend   What are you talking about?

Girl   To bring me in, put me in her room, make me part of the dance routine, the caving, give me her team name, the jousting thing just now with the medieval guys, I thought –

Boyfriend   What?

Girl   You know.

Boyfriend   No, tell me.

Girl   . . . But now I get it: you want me to take her place.

—

Why are you laughing?

Boyfriend   No, I'm just . . .

Girl   Is that funny?

Boyfriend   I'm surprised.

Girl   I don't blame anyone: why should you like me?
A few months ago I'd've wanted revenge.

Boyfriend   And now?

Girl   If it helps you, using me to fill her place, then I'll stay.

Boyfriend   That's very nice of you.

Girl   You're smiling again.

Boyfriend   You make me smile.

Girl   . . .

They're big shoes to fill but I want to try. Tell me about her –
here in her room, with all her stuff. What was she like? I think
maybe we could've been friends.

Boyfriend   No.

Girl   I've been avoiding it, but –

Boyfriend   Too depressing, change the subject.

Girl   I want to know.

Boyfriend   I'm finished with talking about Shona.

Girl   We need to, and there are some things I have to tell
you, too. Like what happened.

Boyfriend   It's over.

Girl   Not 'what happened': what I did.

Boyfriend   Forget about it.

Girl   I can't forget, it's become this weight –

Boyfriend   Stop.

Girl   Please, it'll make me feel better.

Boyfriend   You don't get off that easy.

Girl   —

Boyfriend   Let's go back in.

Girl   What did you say?

Boyfriend   They're holding dessert for us, come on.

Girl   Wait –

Boyfriend   Yes?

Girl   Are you angry?

Boyfriend   Why would I be angry?

Girl   Because you should've been married by now.

Boyfriend   Perhaps it wasn't meant to be.

Girl   Don't say that.

Boyfriend   Perhaps she had to go so that –

Girl   No.

Boyfriend   – someone else could come along.

Girl   You don't believe that.

Boyfriend   You know, Fate.

Girl   Is that what you think?

Boyfriend   We're only mortals, can't see the whole picture.

Girl   I thought you loved her.

Boyfriend   I'm eighteen, what do I know?

Girl   We know some things, like right and wrong.

Boyfriend   Is it that simple?

Girl   Sure, isn't it?

Boyfriend   I'm just saying maybe, in the grand scheme of things –

Girl   That what?

Boyfriend   Sometimes –

Girl   —

Boyfriend   —

Girl   Maybe.

Boyfriend   Let's go back.

Girl   Or we could stay here.

Boyfriend   Get up.

Girl   What's wrong?

Boyfriend   Nothing, get up.

Meanwhile . . .

The **Sidekick** *is released.*

A quiet transition. She moves away, starts a new life.

Seven

The party is in full swing. The **Girl** *finds the merriment increasingly stifling.*

Girl   Hello – ?!

Can I say something?

—

You all know it was me. My words, my friends, my idea. Me.

I knew what I was doing. I never thought it'd end that way, but when it did I didn't care.

You've all been really kind. You've done everything you could to make me feel okay about it. But you know what's weird? The nicer you are the worse I feel.

You've all forgiven me. But it isn't enough, I have to do something too. I want to pay for what I did.

Silence. Then everyone applauds.

Fellowship Youth   That was really brave.

Caver   Yes, what a beautiful speech.

Medieval Re-enactor   It takes a lot of courage to look at yourself like that, unflinchingly.

Dancer   Thank you. But we're not letting you pay: this one's on us.

Boyfriend   Dance with me.

Then the party swings back into action.

Girl   No, no wait –

*Jazz dance routine starts up, involving everyone but the **Girl**.*

Girl   I don't think you understand.

Dancer   We're here for you, baby.

Girl   You're not listening.

Medieval Re-enactor   What's to say?

Girl   I can't go on like nothing happened.

Caver   Sure you can.

Girl   I'll go back to the judge –

Medieval Re-enactor   Your name's been wiped from the records.

Fellowship Youth   They won't know what you're talking about.

Dancers   Jazz hands –

Isolations –

Grapevine –

Boyfriend   Who wants more cake?

All (*except* **Girl**)   Me!

Eight

Girl *observes* **Sidekick**, *who now has a baby.*

Sidekick *goes about a mundane routine:*

Picking up the baby and comforting it back to sleep.

Putting on her glasses as she sits down to study.

Receiving a text, smiling, sending a brief one back.

The unremarkable moments of a life.

Over these silent actions, we hear:

Sidekick's Voice   'My crime was weakness, and it ended really badly.

I can't make up for it, but I can get on with things. I walked into hell because I owed it to her family, her boyfriend, her friends. Times I thought it'd swallow me. Then one day I came out the other side.

I'm married now. I've got a job. I've got a new life and I don't want you in it.

I did tell you to be careful. Even dim and gullible me: even I could see you wouldn't get away with it.

Please don't contact me again.'

The **Girl** *is about to make her presence known . . .*

When the **Sidekick** *turns off the light and exits, leaving the* **Girl** *in the dark.*

Nine

The **Girl** *lights a candle.*

Girl   Shona. They said you lit the place up. This is for you. In memory of you.

I'm sorry.

She sets it down: a tiny shrine.

Boyfriend   'Sorry'.

Girl   I'm sorry.

Boyfriend   That's really nice and everything, and no offence, but you know −

Girl   They're my words.

Boyfriend   But you know: so what?

Girl   I said them to you.

Boyfriend   Go ahead, apologise, no one's stopping you. What good will it do? It doesn't mean anything.

Girl   I thought it would help.

Boyfriend   Who?

Girl   Me.

Boyfriend   What about Shona? What about me and her friends? It doesn't change anything for us.

Girl   Is there nothing I can do then.

Boyfriend   No. Never. Not ever.

Girl   Not even if I want to.

Boyfriend   Not a single thing.

Girl   −

I see.

Boyfriend   Good.

She attacks him. They struggle.

Boyfriend   Hurting me, do you think that's going to get you punished? We're a very forgiving lot, I'm afraid, we'll let you get away with anything.

He controls her.

A long beat.

Girl   Oh –

Oh God.

Yes, I do, I see, I understand.

*The **Group** is there.*

Boyfriend   We looked at what they'd give you – a few years, tops.

She's worth more than that.

So we took it into our own hands.

Caver   You wanted a short cut, we gave it to you.

Dancer   No one will ever ask you about it, and if you confess who's going to take you seriously?

Medieval Re-enactor   Once, you'd have been fine with that, because you were heartless.

Fellowship Youth   Not any more.

Girl   I can't sleep.

All   Good.

Girl   Then there was never any friendship?

Boyfriend   Friendship?!

*Tight focus on **Girl** and **Victim.***

Girl   No forgiveness.

Victim   Forgiveness? What have you done to earn that?

Girl   Nothing.

Victim   You keep thinking you understand, but you're so far away from knowing anything.

Girl   Yes.

Victim   Do you even know what forgiveness is?

Girl   It's a feeling.

Victim   You know about feelings now, do you?

Girl   They were lying the whole time but their kindness reached inside me and shifted everything around. I should hate them. It hurts, to feel.

Victim   Just because you suffer doesn't mean you're atoning.

Girl   No.

Victim   Doesn't mean you'll find peace.

Girl   They've made sure of that.

Victim   You'd have been out by now, starting your life. Like this, you won't ever be free.

Girl   They won't let me mention you, they act like you don't exist.

Victim   I don't any more.

Girl   —

Victim   I won't lie to you, I'm not kind: I'll never forgive.

From now on, I'm silent.

Everyone disappears but the **Boyfriend** *and the* **Girl**.

Girl   But if you can suffer, you can feel other things too.

Boyfriend   Here. Your stuff.

Girl   Some, you don't even know what they are. They make you heavy, or they pinch your lungs . . .

Boyfriend   Have a nice life.

Girl   Or make you a bit lighter.

Boyfriend   No.

Girl   Some do.

Boyfriend   Not for you, nothing will lighten you.

Girl   Some you can't help, they just surprise you. You don't even want it, you don't feel right, cast about for what to call it –

Boyfriend   We don't want to see you again.

Girl   But I've found the name, and I have to say it.

Boyfriend   Go away.

Girl   I have to tell you.

Boyfriend   . . . What are you doing?

Girl   Holding your hand.

Boyfriend   No.

Girl   It came into my heart and I can't help it.

Boyfriend   Make it go away.

Girl   I can't.

Boyfriend   You don't have the right.

Girl   Is it wrong?

Boyfriend   Yes, yes, it's wrong! The murderer doesn't deserve it, does not have that privilege –

Girl   It's what I feel.

Boyfriend   I won't let you.

Girl   I can't stop it.

Boyfriend   You have to, kill it!

Girl   I forgive you. I forgive you. For what you've done, for how you'll keep on making me suffer, I forgive you.

Don't cry.

Don't cry.

It's alright.

Don't cry.

Victim Sidekick Boyfriend Me

*Notes on rehearsal and staging, drawn from a workshop
with the writer at the National Theatre, November 2011*

The Workshop

In November 2011 Hilary Bell, Deborah Bruce and a group
of drama teachers and youth theatre directors taking part in
Connections 2012 met at the National Theatre Studio to
explore approaches to Hilary Bell's *Victim Sidekick Boyfriend Me*.
This exploration was to take the form of a practical workshop
facilitated by Deborah Bruce using actors from the National
Youth Theatre.

The day's workshop was to use exploration, discussion and
experimentation to tease out ways of approaching the play.
Deborah was also keen to address any specific questions or
problems that the directors might have. A number of key
issues that came up in the discussion were: approaches to
using lots of people to tell the story; approaches to physicality;
approaches to a play that was open to many different
interpretations. The day would involve ensemble work, close
text work, and work which would tackle themes of the play.

The workshop began with a read-through of the play so that
all present started from the same place. Deborah said that
before directing a scene she would always begin with a table-
read with the cast to establish what's happening and where
the gear changes happen. It is very important for her to have
lots of discussion of a scene before she puts it on the floor.

The Play and the Writer

After the initial read-through Hilary talked about how she
came to write the play. As a writer she likes to work within
tight parameters, and here she wanted to write a play with a
large cast but one that allowed for flexibility in numbers, and
she wanted to have song and a dance.

In approaching the play Hilary asked a hypothetical question – if you had the opportunity to get off scot-free for something you had done wrong, who wouldn't do so? She felt that this was an interesting idea to pose to young audiences, given that in our culture young people can get away with things very easily.

Hilary looked at a number of different stimuli when writing the play. She re-read a play called *The Visit* by Swiss playwright Friedrich Dürrenmatt. *The Visit* is about a central character who has done something awful but sails through life not having to face up to the consequences of his actions until one day his victim returns and throws his life into chaos. She also watched again a film called *Quiz Show* (1994) which is about a man who had got away with something up to a point.

She had been heavily influenced by a documentary which she saw in Australia about a man whose son had been murdered and the murderer had been sent to jail. Upon his release, the only person there to meet him at the gate was the father of the victim. This man let the murderer come and live with him and rehabilitated him. Hilary was interested in the idea of whether this act was a true act of forgiveness or if something more sinister was involved. An interesting question occurred to her – could you use forgiveness as a substitution for existential punishment? She thought it was interesting that a stranger can do something to you that can affect the rest of your life.

While writing the play Hilary knew that there would be a question about what had happened to the victim, but she didn't necessarily want the play to be about this or for the audience to be constantly trying to work it out. She then decided that the girl would be bullied to the point of committing suicide. She was interested in the idea of 'being sent to Coventry' (when a group decides to punish someone by pretending they don't exist) as this is essentially a form of existential punishment.

A Discussion with Deborah

Deborah Bruce talked about some of the things which initially struck her about the play – firstly, the fact that the stage directions were very stylised: '*The* **Group** *is there*' rather than '*The* **Group** *enter*' or '*The* **Group** *arrive*'. This gives you permission to be really experimental with the style of the piece.

She also advised that directors shouldn't try to spend too much time trying to figure out a back-story for two central characters. What's fascinating about their play is the journey they are on in the moment.

Characters who we don't learn a lot about, such as A, E and X, offer directors and actors a very interesting place to focus energy and creativity in terms of working out who they are. The level of work required for those groups and the young people playing those characters is interesting and offers rich opportunities for creativity as they will be great to flesh out. Also, so many characters are acting – with the exception of Girl and Sidekick, all are pretending to be someone or something else, which is quite unusual in a play for young people. You are not quite able to see where they are in the moment. Deborah was shocked when she realised they were disingenuous and that offers interesting possibilities in terms of how the audience react to the play. It doesn't have to be clear that the Boyfriend is playing a long game. Hilary feels that this is especially interesting from an audience's point of view.

Deborah felt that with this piece it is essential that a director finds out where the gear changes are. There is an opportunity to find a lovely relationship between stillness and speed and the juxtaposition of speed and pace.

Lastly she was struck by the fact that the last five lines of the play take it to a completely different place. Had the play ended five lines earlier, you would have felt satisfaction that the girl would punish herself. The fact that she pushes through and manages to forgive the others pushes the play even further. The natural place to stop would have been that their punishment had come full circle and for them to have wreaked vengeance on the girl.

Hilary felt that as a writer there is a responsibility to leave the audience with something – not just despair. So when writing the end of the play she thought about the character having reached a point of empathy where she had never been before. She wondered what effect that might have on the girl. It can make you hurt, but it can make you care about other people. So the girl forgiving the group would make her someone who had travelled further than expected – not just from cold-heartedness to empathy, but on to forgiveness. Hilary felt that the character of the girl should have gone on a journey. She is horrid at the start but isn't completely rotten by the end.

This relates to one of the central themes of the play, which is the nature of rehabilitation. Does rehabilitation work? Does it come from within or from outside yourself? Is there such a thing as a 'horrible person'? Can people transform? What kind of person would forgive the murderer of someone they loved?

It was suggested by one of the directors that the whole play could exist as a metaphor for an internal journey. While this could be true, Deborah advised that even if you are doing stylised work it is important to talk and think about your intentions. Sometimes you can see work that is all style but has a vacuum at the centre. When dealing with these themes there is a responsibility, especially when working on the play with young people. People go on a journey and learn that empathy is important. It would be dangerous not to acknowledge that people can be rehabilitated.

In terms of marking gear changes, Hilary feels that an important moment to mark in terms of the girl's journey to discovering empathy is the point where she gives her elbow pads to another one of the cavers. It is the first point in the play where she explicitly thinks about another person's needs.

Some Questions Considered

- Why is the Sidekick always visible? The reason the Sidekick is always visible is that she presents the alternative process of rehabilitation that the girl might have gone on if she had owned up.

- Why don't any of the characters have names except for Shona? Hilary felt that when you name a character you give them a background, a class, parents and a back-story. She wants to leave that work to the actors. The play exists in a theatrical reality which is not literal.

- Why are there dancers? Hilary wanted there to be a song and a dance in the piece.

- Why are there Cavers? Hilary wanted to push the girl to a place outside her comfort zone, a place where she would never normally go.

- Why are there medieval re-enactors? Because Hilary felt they were funny and silly.

- Would it be possible to change the religious group from Christians if working with young people from other religious backgrounds? So long as the religious group would believably have forgiveness as part of their philosophy.

- How did the play get its title? Hilary normally finds it very easy to come up with a title, but in this instance one didn't present itself. Ultimately she thought about the four people who were affected the most by the act that took place.

- Had she visualised the play in a certain way? In Hilary's mind, she had always seen the play taking place in an empty space, but the play is a blueprint and open to interpretation.

Useful Exercises

YOUR STORYTELLING

This is an exercise that can be done with young people about using the themes of the play to invest something of yourself into the action.

Deborah asked the group to split into pairs and tell a story from their experience of something they had done in the past that they were ashamed of and wouldn't like to represent them.

People were to share their stories with their partner on the condition that no one would have to share with the group.

Four people were then asked to tell their partner's story to the entire group, but to do this in the first person, using the story as a starting point and embellishing it as much as they liked. There was no set order and they had to use their sense as a group to figure out when to start and finish. They could also use things about how their partner had told the story when performing. Watching the exercise, audience members commented on how you thought more about the speaker's pain even though they had been (were playing) the perpetrator.

For the next level of the exercise, four different people were asked to tell the same story but from the perspective of the victim. For the audience it was very revealing how the exercise switches your empathy. The exercise suggests that there is no such thing as truth, only perspective, and that there are different versions of people depending on perspective. Empathy can also be affected by acting style.

This exercise is very useful when dealing with the themes of the play because the play is about a number of different people affected by an event, and at different points in the play every character is seeking to present themselves as a victim. It also raises questions such as: how can you be prejudged in a courtroom? What is the truth of the play? There are different ways to hear the same story. A director has a responsibility to interrogate these questions with the young people in this play.

It is important when doing this exercise that it remains an acting exercise not a therapy group. You should always have the performers act out a story and not tell a story that actually happened to them. Their stories should only be shared with the consent of the young people.

VISUAL PICTURE EXERCISE

It is always worth reminding a performer how much work an audience does in terms of reading the narrative of a play. Firstly, select a volunteer. Place them on a chair in the middle of the stage. Give four volunteers a piece of paper which only they should look at. On these pieces of paper write the name or nature of a character (e.g., 'friend', 'saboteur', 'oppressor' etc.) and ask the four volunteers to position themselves on stage in relation to the central (seated) character. A still image is then created. Ask the spectators to analyse the still image. The exercise illuminates that a number of different narratives and stories can be taken from a very simple stage picture.

Make changes to the picture. What happens if one actor suddenly looks away? Looks at the ground? Makes eye contact with another character? It changes the narrative drastically. Who is the most powerful person in the picture? How does eye contact change the picture? The stories are very richly told.

Young people often don't realise that the smallest changes in what they do, even if they are playing a small part, can change a story drastically.

Next relate the exercise to words in the play.

ENSEMBLE EXERCISE: BONDING THE COMPANY

This exercise demonstrates that everybody in the company has a responsibility for the overall outcome. It will not work unless everybody contributes to its success.

Take a space in the room. One person walks, and after a while stops, at which point two people start walking, then after a while they stop, and at that point three people stop, then four stop, then back to three, two, and one. The exercise won't happen exactly first time. It is about having awareness of what's going on in the room, sensing the rest of the group and using peripheral vision. Don't be afraid to breathe and have a form of communication that isn't literal. Shut out decision-making.

Try to make this an organic exercise. Always be active, and always be conscious of success. Allow yourself to be affected by and to affect the pace of walking. Atmospheres which are generated could include: suspicious, tentative, bold, etc. The whole group should get into the same rhythm before they stop.

The exercise is surprisingly compelling and can show how in tune a group are with one another. If it takes place at every rehearsal it will allow a group to become more and more in tune with one another.

One way to advance the exercise is to ask young people to acknowledge what they are doing in their head, then liberate themselves from it. For example, if you are someone who naturally hangs back, try being brave with the exercise. If you are someone who volunteers, then hold back a bit. See what happens if you push yourself to be in a different head space. Challenge people to go out of their comfort zone. Invite participants to challenge a meaningless thing about themselves.

Ideally the atmosphere decision happens in silence and the group will work towards making it happen organically. Stop worrying about everyone else or worrying about having to check each other.

This exercise could be very useful for exploring ensemble movement for the play. It is an exciting way of looking at how groups can move in unison – it could be a holding form for scene changes, or shifting focus. It could also act as a good starting point for developing a style.

Try the exercise in relation to the text. If the girl is the first person who moves and the last person who moves and always stays in character, and if she moves in a high-status way the first time and a low-status way the last time, how does that illuminate her journey in the play? Give the rest of the group playing cards to tell them the status they should play. Ask the girl to remain in character all the time and take everything that happens personally. Explore the feeling of empowerment moving within a group.

FORM, STORM, REFORM EXERCISE

'Form, Storm, Reform' is another exercise that can be used to explore ways in which a group can move as a fluid unit. A group creates a tableau – perhaps by giving the young people a playing card each from which to create an image based on their status within the group. Decide on a person to be the trigger for creating the tableau. Ask the performers to move around the room. Once that person decides to create the image, the rest of the group falls in accordingly. This section of the exercise is 'form'.

You then decide upon a 'trigger' for the tableau to fall apart or dissipate and for its formers to spread around the room: this is known as 'storm'. You then decide on another 'trigger' which might be one of the groups deciding to create a similar or a different image in another part of the room. The group then creates a second tableau (reform).

This exercise can be really interesting in terms of finding movement dynamics within a group. Use ways to apply the narrative from the play to this exercise. What happens if the girl is the trigger for 'storm'? Does it heighten the idea of the group trying to exclude her? How might this exercise be used to explore how the different types of groups move? If you have a small number of actors playing all the groups in the play, this might be an interesting way to differentiate between them.

From a workshop led by Deborah Bruce,
with notes by Des Kennedy

Journey to X

Nancy Harris

Characters

Joey, *fourteen*
Penny, *fourteen*
Sarah, *fourteen*
Louise, *fourteen*
Tara, *fourteen*
Vince, *sixteen*
Ellis, *sixteen*
Liam, *sixteen*
Bruce, *fifteen*
Davy, *fifteen*
Some Dancers

Time: now

A Note on Staging

This play is inspired by the current Irish law regarding abortion. At the time of writing it is illegal to have an abortion in both the north and south of Ireland, but travelling overseas to seek a termination is permitted. However, for the sake of universality and clarity, I would request that groups use their own accents when performing the piece.

Scenes should move fast and fluidly from one to the next – almost running into each other. Props are suggested but only as needed.

Locations can be conjured as swiftly and imaginatively as possible, using lights and sound.

All music mentioned in the piece is meant to be suggestive, rather than prescriptive, and is open for groups to change and reimagine as they wish.

Dialogue

. . . an unfinished or unarticulated thought.
/ an overlap in dialogue.
( ) a word that is not spoken but is conveyed in the playing.

One

The departures lounge at an airport.

The usual cacophony of airport noise – flights being called, etc.

Penny, **Tara**, **Louise**, **Sarah** and **Joey** *run on trailing little compact suitcases on wheels behind them.*

They all wear sunglasses and talk over each other at great speed.

Penny   Where is it? /

Tara   Here.

Joey   Don't see it. /

Louise   It's the wrong terminal.

Tara   It's not the wrong terminal.

Louise   It's Terminal Two.

Tara   It's Terminal One.

Louise   How do you know?

Tara   It's on the ticket.

Louise   Where?

Tara   On the fucking ticket. /

Louise *looks at the e-printout.*

Louise   I can't see it.

Sarah *(re sunglasses)*   I can't see anything.

Tara *grabs the ticket off* **Louise**.

Tara   There. It says it there. Area H, Terminal One.

Penny   Can't see Area H.

Sarah   I actually can't see a thing.

She takes off her glasses. Looks around.

Do we look stupid?

Louise   Yes.

Joey   No. We're rocking the look.

Sarah   That woman over there's giving us evils.

Tara   Well give her the finger

She gives some woman the finger.

Joey   She's just jealous.

Sarah   Of what?

Joey   Our kick-ass charisma.

Penny   There's no way they could've closed it, is there?

Tara   We've ten minutes to go.

Penny   They said leave an hour.

Joey   They always say that – *hey*, there's your sister.

Sarah   Where?

Louise   Over there at check-in. *This* is Area H.

They all start to wave over shrieking and giggling.

Sarah   Stop. Don't.

Louise   Why?

Sarah   She said not to.

Tara   She's walking us through.

Sarah   She said she'll get us to the gate but she's not talking to us, she's not sitting with us and she doesn't want to look like she knows us.

Tara   Oh.

Sarah   She thinks we're embarrassing.

Tara   . . . Bitch.

Sarah   Yeah.

Joey   Forget her – we're here. (*To* **Sarah**.) Put on your glasses.

Sarah   It's too dark – I keep falling.

Joey   You wanna be famous, you have to act like you're famous. Channel Beyoncé, Channel Lady Gaga.

Louise   Channel your arse.

Joey   Put 'em on.

Sarah *puts the sunglasses back on. They look at one another.*

Louise   We do look stupid.

Penny *looks up at one of the display boards.*

Penny   Look – Zurich, Berlin, Moscow. Imagine we went to Moscow.

Sarah   Do they do it in Moscow?

Louise   The Russians are feminists.

Sarah   I meant the show.

Penny   They have it everywhere – it's a franchise.

Louise   They have it in Italy.

Tara   They have it in Kazakhstan.

Joey   The one in Spain's called *Factor X*.

Louise   That's original.

Penny (*pointing to the board*)   Delhi. Imagine we went to Delhi.

A phone goes.

Louise   Fuck, my phone. Oh god –

Louise *pulls it out. Looks at the others, worried.*

Penny   Don't panic. She'll just think you're in class.

Tara   What did you say about tonight?

Louise   That I'm at yours. What did you say?

Tara   That I'm at yours.

Louise   Jesus, Tara.

Tara   What?

Louise   Couldn't you have thought of something better?

Tara   You thought of it too. I thought you'd say you were at Penny's. You're always at Penny's.

Louise   What if your mum calls my mum? /

Joey *takes the phone off* **Louise**. *Turns it off.*

Joey   Ladies, please. Put the phones away. We're here. We're flying, baby. Nothing they can do about it now.

Tara (*looking back at check-in*)   Eh, Sarah – your sister is either waving at us or having a seizure.

Sarah *tilts her glasses to see.*

Sarah   She's waving. She just doesn't like lifting her arms. She thinks it makes her look heavy.

Joey   It does sort of make her look heavy.

Sarah (*waving back*)   We should go over. She's getting angry – I can tell from her cheeks.

They start to gather together, all except **Penny**.

Joey   Okay – everyone got everything? Passports, tickets, tampons.

All Girls   Yes!

Joey   Now heads up, shoulders back, walk with purpose, walk with poise. Remember who you are. Remember who you're going to be. One, two, three.

They swish off giggling. All except **Penny** *who stays looking at the departures board.* **Louise** *turns back.*

Louise   Penny, come on – we've to check-in the bags.

Penny *keeps looking at the board. The sound of a plane taking off.*

Two

Then music – something pop.

It suddenly stops.

A classroom, break-time, several weeks earlier. Everyone is in uniform.

The girls are taking notes.

Tara *is looking up flights on something – computer or iPhone.*

Joey *comes on and faces the audience as though he is giving a lecture.*

Joey   Fame is a fickle mistress. She gives with one hand. She takes with the other. And like all insatiable sirens she must be handled with care.

Tara   Easy-jet's doing them for £79.99.

Louise   One-way or return?

Joey *(carrying on)*   Groups is without question the hardest category.

Tara   That's one-way. /

Joey *(raising his voice a little)*   Because even if selected, it's the one least likely to win.

Sarah *(to **Tara**)*   No way! It's a budget airline.

Tara   It's cos we're going last minute.

Joey *clears his throat, looking for attention.*

Joey   The reason for this is threefold. The first is that audiences like individuals better. And groups – being groups – divide loyalty. The second is that there is usually only one significantly talented member in any pop group – the rest are mere props to make that one look member look good. Dancing puppets, if you will. The third is that . . . well, most pop groups are crap.

Bruce   That's not a fact.

Joey *turns.*

Joey   I thought we said no interrupting.

Tara   Yep, £79.99 one way, £159 return.

Louise   They can piss off.

Tara   If we'd booked a month ago, it'd be cheaper.

Louise   Well, we didn't know a month ago, did we?

Penny   Look up someone else.

Bruce   They have auditions here too, you know.

Joey   Not this year.

Louise *shoots* **Penny** *a look, then covers.*

Louise   And we want to have an adventure.

Sarah   We want to go to Harrods.

Tara   And Madame Tussauds.

Penny   And the Tower.

Joey (*continuing his lecture*)   Now. If we are going to get this right we have to set a tone. There are three crucial components to any successful pop group.

Bruce   Is everything you do divided into threes?

Joey   The first is a name. The second is a look. The third is a story.

Penny   What about a sound? It's supposed to be a singing competition.

Joey   Everyone knows it's not a singing competition.

Louise   What is it?

Joey   A popularity contest.

Sarah   Well, that's us fucked.

Joey Not necessarily. People like underdogs.

Louise You're saying we're dogs?

Joey Yes.

Tara Cheers.

Joey It's part of the story.

Sarah What story?

Joey The group story. A lot of really famous people were unpopular as teenagers.

Sarah Like who?

Joey All of them practically.

Tara Michael Jackson – freak. Angelina Jolie – freak

Joey It's what gave them their determination to succeed. Anyway, that's story. We're not on the story yet. We're on the first part.

Louise What's the first part?

Sarah Names.

Joey You need a name. Something catchy. Any thoughts?

Louise The Suffragettes.

Everyone gags.

Penny That's shite.

Louise Cos we're women with purpose.

Joey It needs to be sexy.

Louise Psycho Sisters.

Joey Pop, Louise, pop. It's light. It's fluffy.

Louise Well someone else think of it then.

Penny I'm crap at this.

Sarah Me too.

Joey   Try putting two distinct yet suggestive images together. So they paint a picture.

Penny   Like?

Joey   Like Spice Girls or Sugababes. Food is good.

Tara   Ugh.

Joey   Or animals – Pussycat Dolls. Cats are very popular.

Louise   Cos I wonder what they make people think of.

Suddenly **Liam, Vince** *and* **Ellis** *burst into the room.*

Vince   Alright, ladies.

The girls get up, embarrassed.

Joey   Hey!/

Ellis   This the auditions, is it?

Penny   You can't come in here.

Vince   Says who?

Tara   We booked the room.

Liam   Too bad.

Bruce   We're in the middle of something.

Liam   So we hear.

Louise   And it's private.

Joey   There's a sign on the door. 'Rehearsals in Progress'.

Vince   Didn't see it. Sorry.

The boys start to size up the girls, circling them.

Liam   So come on then. Show us your stuff.

Louise   Get lost.

Vince   What? We're not here to take the piss.

Liam   No, we want to give you a hand.

Ellis   We want to be judges.

Liam   Yeah, I'm Simon Cowell, now show us your tits.

The boys laugh.

Vince *looks over and sees* **Penny***, starts to walk towards her.*

There's something suggestive and aggressive about it.

Vince   Hey Penny. How you doing?

Penny   Just get out, Vince.

All Boys   *Oooh!*

Vince   That how you talk to the judges, is it?

Penny   You're not a judge.

Liam   Hey, Penny, you know your boyfriend's outside?

Penny   What?

Ellis   Want us to give him a message?

Penny   He's not my – boyfriend.

Vince   Yeah, we heard he dumped you. Too bad.

Sarah   They weren't even really going out.

Vince   That why he's moved on so quickly, is it?

Louise   What?

Liam   Heard he got it on with Sandra Morris Saturday.

Vince   Yeah, they got all hot and heavy at her party. You obviously weren't doing it for him any more, Penny.

Louise   Will you just get out, Vince?

Vince   What? We're just saying.

Louise   She's not interested.

Vince *looks at* **Penny***, who is clearly uncomfortable.*

Vince   He was probably only after one thing anyway.

Louise   Shut up –

Ellis   Dirty scut.

Liam   All the same, men. Never trust 'em.

Louise   Maybe she was only after one thing too.

Sarah   Louise!

Vince   That right?

Vince *puts a hand on* **Penny**.

Vince   Show us your moves, Penny.

Ellis   Yeah, show us what you showed him, eh?

Penny *pushes him off her.*

Penny   Get lost, Vince.

Liam *grabs a notebook from* **Sarah**.

Sarah   Hey. /

He starts to read it.

Liam (*reading*)   'Think of name.' That's as far as you've got?

Ellis   Genius. You guys are gonna be huge.

Joey   Look, will you just leave us alone? We're actually working here.

Vince   And who are you, faggot? Lead singer?

Joey   I'm the manager.

Vince   Well manage this.

He pushes **Joey**. *He falls to the ground.*

Penny   Hey. /

Bruce   Watch it Vince.

Vince *turns on him.*

Vince   Or what? What are you gonna do?

Bruce *backs off.*

Bruce   Nothing. I just /

Ellis (*suddenly excited*)   Hey, hey. I've a name for yous. I've a name. Guantánamo Babes – get it?

Vince   Guantánamo Babes?

Ellis   Yeah. Get it?

Liam   No.

Ellis   Cos looking at them is like fucking torture. Ha!

They high-five.

Vince   Yeah, man. I'd rather go water-boarding.

Tara   You can't *go* water-boarding, imbecile. It's not surfing.

The bell goes.

Vince   Whatever, mingers. Come on, this is bullshit.

The boys leave.

Bruce (*shouts after them weakly*)   Losers!

Joey *gets up off the ground, looks at* **Penny**.

Joey   You okay?

Penny (*visibly rattled*)   Yeah, totally. You?

Joey   Used to it now. Like water off a duck's arse. Is there dirt on my jacket?

Louise   You're good.

Tara (*to* **Penny**)   You're so much better than Sandra Morris, you know.

Penny   I don't care. He can do whatever he likes. Nothing to do with me any more, is it?

She picks up her bag and leaves.

Three

A park bench. Evening.

Sarah, **Penny**, **Louise**, **Tara**.

Penny *stands away from them, on the phone.*

The others are singing the first verse of 'I Kissed a Girl' by Katy Perry. Nicely.

All
   I kissed a girl and I liked it
   Taste of her cherry chapstick

They stop.

Sarah   Do you use chapstick?

Tara   Nah. You?

Sarah   Vaseline makes your lips softer.

Louise   I hate that song. We're not singing that, are we?

Tara   Here. Which would you choose – if you had the choice, right? Being really really famous and having an amazing body and being super rich and loved by everyone and taking planes to work and everyone wanting to be your friend and fall in love with you and all that?

Louise   Yeah.

Tara   But being dead by the time you were twenty-one.

Sarah   Okay.

Tara   Or being really really poor and having to work really hard your whole life in a boring job and married to a boring person but living until you were really old.

Sarah   Like how old?

Tara   Ninety.

Louise   Depends. What's the job?

Tara   Something boring.

Sarah   Would I be sick?

Tara   Sick?

Sarah   My nana was really sick when she was ninety – used to wet herself and shake and didn't know who any of us were. I wouldn't want to go like that.

Tara   No, you wouldn't be sick and you'd have your memory.

Louise   But I'd be poor.

Tara   Yeah.

Sarah   But married.

Tara   In a loveless marriage.

Sarah   Still married, though.

Tara   And you'd be fat.

Louise   You never said fat.

Tara   Well, I'm saying it now. You'd be old and fat and in a loveless marriage but you'd have had a long life.

Louise   Or I could be rich and thin and fancied by everyone?

Tara   And going out with whoever you want.

Sarah   But dead in seven years?

Tara   Which would you choose?

Beat.

Sarah   Dead in seven years.

Louise   Really?

Sarah   Definitely.

Louise   Why?

Sarah   Seven years is a long time.

Louise   Not that long.

Sarah   They'd be seven great years.

Penny *hangs up the phone, walks over to the girls.*

Penny   Is he here yet?

Sarah   Nah.

Penny   It's nearly eight.

Sarah   He said just to wait.

Penny *sits down.*

Louise   I hate this place at night.

Penny   There's a guy over there in the bushes.

They look.

Don't look.

Sarah   What's he doing?

Penny   What do you think? Don't look.

Louise   They want you to look. They get off on it.

Tara   I heard if you just walk up and scream in their face they run away.

Sarah   Yeah, they're real cowards most of them, my mum says.

Penny   Still. Don't look over.

Louise   What did she say on the phone?

Penny   I need someone to come with me.

Louise   We're coming with you.

Penny   Has to be a parent or a legal guardian.

Tara   No it doesn't.

Penny   If you're from here. If you're under sixteen. Otherwise they won't do it.

Sarah   Well, you'll have ID.

Louise   If he ever turns up.

Penny   It's not like a passport or something though, is it?

Tara   Provisional licence. Might work. I mean, if you're there and you have the money, they're not going to make you go home.

Penny   . . . It's five hundred quid.

Tara   Five hundred quid!

Penny   Five hundred and thirty-five. If you're from here.

Sarah   Where are we going to get five hundred and thirty-five quid?

Louise   . . . Cake sale?

They look at her.

I'm taking the piss.

Sarah   That's crazy. We can't. I mean we can't just – get five hundred quid.

Penny   We have to.

Tara   From where?

Louise   We can sell something.

Sarah   Sell what?

Tara   That's. I mean that's a lot of – god.

Penny   I know.

Beat.

Louise   You could always ask him.

Penny   No.

Louise   But if you needed –

Penny   No. I'm not asking him.

Silence.

Sarah (*taking out her picture*)   I look really ugly in this photo.

Tara   I look shit in mine too.

Sarah   Do you think he could airbrush it for us?

Louise   It's a fake ID, not a bloody *Vogue* cover. No one's gonna see.

Beat.

Sarah   Hey, Penny, if you had the choice right of being really old and fat and having no money or being really gorgeous and famous but dying in seven years – which would you choose?

Penny   What are you talking about?

Tara   That's not the question.

Louise   Yes it is.

Sarah   Which would you choose?

Penny   I don't understand.

A rustling in the bushes.

Tara   Oh god, there's something in the bushes.

Louise   What?

Tara   I saw it rustling.

Sarah (*squeals*)   It's him.

They turn away backs to the bushes.

Penny   Quick. Don't look. Just don't look. There's more of us than there is of him.

Sarah   I really don't want to see it.

Louise   There's probably nothing to see. (*Raising her voice.*) Which is why he's hiding in the bushes.

Penny   Just keep talking and pretend he's not there.

Louise   We've all got our phones.

Sarah (*shouting*)   We've got our phones, you sick perve. If you come near us we're calling the police?

Tara   Yeah.

Sarah   Yeah.

Louise *turns and looks back.*

Sarah   What's happening? Has he got his trousers down?

Louise   It's a dog, you idiots.

Sarah   A dog?

Louise   Jack Russell. Ran up there.

They turn around. They laugh, relieved.

Sarah   Oh. (*To* **Penny**.) But you said.

Penny   Maybe we scared him off.

Tara   My heart there for a minute.

Penny *looks around, nervous.*

Penny   I wish he'd just hurry up and get here, I'm freezing.

Louise   Hate this place at night.

Four

A burst of music.

Some dancers take to the stage and deliver a very brief, highly choreographed dance routine. It's fast and furious, then stops abruptly. Lights down.

Lights up on **Joey** *and the girls. They are in a deserted classroom huddled round a laptop. Over their uniforms the girls wear oversized T-shirts with giant glittery 'X's on them.*

Everyone seems unhappy. Except **Bruce**.

Louise (*pointing at the laptop screen*)   You want us to do that?

Bruce   Cool!

Joey   Not exactly that.

Bruce   No, you should. Definitely do that.

Tara   I can't do that – I've got scoliosis.

Joey   I'm not saying we should do that.

Tara   If I did that my spine would snap.

Louise   Bullshit.

Joey   I'm just showing you.

Sarah   Why?

Joey   For inspiration. They got through last year.

Tara   But they're not even singing.

Louise   Forget it – I'm not standing onstage and grinding my crotch like some *Playboy* bunny.

Bruce   No one would mistake *you* for a *Playboy* bunny, Louise.

Louise *turns on him savagely.*

Louise   What does that mean?

Bruce   Nothing. I was just . . .

Louise   What?

Bruce   Nothing.

Tara   They didn't get through last year. I watched the whole thing.

She takes out her iPhone.

Joey   I'm just saying we could step out of our comfort zone more.

Louise   Is that why we're wearing these?

She pulls at the big oversized T-shirt.

Joey   I had nothing to do with those.

Sarah   Hey – I spent all Saturday making these.

Louise   It shows.

She points to the 'X's.

Sarah   I glued these on myself and everything.

Tara   What are they?

Sarah   They're supposed to sparkle.

Louise   They're horrible.

Penny   They're not horrible, Louise, come on –

Louise   We look like we've survived a nuclear holocaust and this was all that was left to wear.

Sarah (*to* **Joey**)   You said we needed to find a look. Something unifying.

Joey   You do.

Louise   What's unifying about a big fat 'X'?

Sarah   It stands for –

Louise   I get what it stands for. I just think it looks shite.

Sarah   It works if we stand in a line. Look.

She pulls them into an unhappy line.

See?

Tara   No.

Sarah   The colours all talk to each other.

Tara   And what are they saying?

Louise   Mine are saying this is tragic.

Bruce   Why can't they wear their own clothes?

Joey   Because. They need to stand out.

Louise   What's the difference between stepping out of your comfort zone and doing something you think is crap?

Joey   We should challenge ourselves.

Sarah   Yeah. Like if we're going to go over there, if we're going to properly make the effort, we should like . . . properly make the effort. You know?

Louise   That's incredibly profound, Sarah. I'm taking mine off before Vince comes in here.

She pulls the T-shirt off.

Sarah   I don't care what Vince thinks.

Louise   You're not the one they call Pig's Vomit. All this morning walking up from the bus I had the three of them behind me – 'Pig's Vomit, Pig's Vomit. Give us a tune.'

Penny   Dickheads.

Joey turns to the computer.

Joey   Look, let's just watch one more. There was a group last year who –

Tara *holds up her phone, excited.*

Tara   Here. Look. Ryanair are having a sale.

Louise   What?

Tara   Flights for 99p if we go on the Friday.

Louise   We have to go on the Friday.

She holds up the phone.

Tara   Well then. Says it here.

Penny   99p? Are you sure?

Tara   That's good, isn't it? I mean, that's really cheap.

Joey   Hell yeah. We won't get better than that.

Bruce   You should book them.

Tara   Duh!

Bruce   I meant they'll sell out quickly. Those ones always do.

Louise   Well, let's do it then.

Louise *looks at* **Penny**, *who seems a little pensive.*

Louise   Penny, should we do it?

Penny   . . . Yeah. Course.

Louise   You sure?

Penny (*brave face*)   Definitely. Book.

Tara *goes to the laptop, starts to type.* **Sarah** *gives a little squeal.*

Sarah   I can't believe we're actually doing this.

Tara (*looking at the screen*)   Hang on.

Joey   What?

Tara   We don't have a credit card.

Joey   Oh.

They look at each other.

Shit.

Five

The park. Evening. The girls are in their uniforms.

Joey, **Sarah**, **Penny**, **Tara**, **Louise**.

Tara *and* **Sarah** *are panting as though they've been running.*

Joey, **Louise** and **Penny** *look at them.*

Penny   What did you do?

Tara   I just – she just /

She stops talking, tries to breathe.

Sarah (*excited*)   That was unbelievable. I can't believe – she was screaming. Could you hear her screaming?

Penny   Who was screaming?

Sarah   She had Tara's arm and she was screaming and screaming and Tara was shouting 'Run', so I did. I just ran.

Penny   What happened?

Tara *doesn't say anything. Just tries to breathe.*

Sarah (*more excited*)   I didn't even know why we were running – but she had this look – Tara – on her face – like something was wrong and that I shouldn't – so I just jumped off the bus and I legged it.

Tara   Does anyone have any water?

Louise *hands her a bottle.* **Tara** *drinks.* **Sarah** *looks around, excited.*

Sarah   I've never nicked anything before.

Penny   Nicked?

Louise   You nicked something? What did you nick?

Penny   Jesus, Tara.

Tara   It wasn't like that.

Sarah   Yes, it was.

Tara   No, it wasn't. Shut up.

Beat.

Tara   Her bag was open.

Joey   What?

Tara   Her bag was open.

Penny   Tara –

Tara   We were sitting on the bus, alright. As normal. Just chatting about the credit card and whether my mum would notice if we used hers or whether she'd just think it was my brother again. And she lets him off everything cos you know she's scared he'll try and – you know – again if she says a word. And we were saying that even if we could use her card and even if we had that sorted there's still the matter of the hostel and the bus into London and the five hundred and thirty-five. And we were just talking about that and what we were going to do – when I looked over and saw –

Sarah   The old lady.

Tara   Sitting opposite. And she's reading a book

Sarah   She was reading the Bible.

Tara   It wasn't the Bible, it was Marian Keyes. But she was reading it. Totally involved.

Sarah   And muttering to herself.

Tara   Yeah, she was clearly a bit (*mental*) cos I saw that she'd left her bag open. Like it was just sitting there wide open on the seat and all her stuff was falling out of it, tissues and mints /

Sarah   And bookmarks with pictures of saints.

Tara   Shut up.

Sarah   I'm just saying.

Tara (*gives her a look*)   And her purse was just lying there in the middle of it all and there was this big wedge of cash in it. Just there. Just – out in the open. Like anyone could've – you know.

Sarah   I didn't see that. I was looking more at her talking to herself but /

Tara   There was a load of it. She must have just been to the bank or something. And I didn't plan it.

Sarah   No, she definitely didn't plan it.

Tara   Like I didn't really think about it even. I just – did it. I reached over and I put my hand inside her bag. Like, really really quietly and no one was noticing. And I had my fingers round some of the notes and everything was totally fine –

Sarah   Until she looks over and starts screaming.

Tara   Yeah, she just – grabs my hand out of nowhere and I tried to pull away but I had the money and I couldn't get her off.

Sarah   It was mad.

Tara   And the bus had stopped and the doors were open, but because she was screaming so much the driver was trying to close them.

Sarah   So we had to jam ourselves in them.

Tara   And push ourselves through. And right up to the last second she was clinging on to my hand and trying to pull back the money.

Sarah   So Tara pushed her.

Tara   I didn't push her. I just gave her a little – shove/

Sarah   But she fell back and she's all screaming and Tara's all 'Run'.

Tara   And by that time the bus had stopped properly and the driver had got out and he was shouting something after us but I didn't look back, cos if I looked back I would've panicked so we just legged it and legged it and the woman kept screaming and screaming but we just kept running and running and running until we got . . . here.

Sarah (*excited*)   Thieves.

Silence.

Joey   Cool.

Penny   Joey.

Joey   How much did you get?

Penny   Joey!

Tara *pulls something out of her top.*

Tara   Hundred and fifty.

Louise *whistles approvingly.*

Louise   Wow.

Sarah (*excited*)   I know.

Tara   All in tenners.

Louise   That's brilliant.

Penny   It's not brilliant.

Sarah (*chastened*)   No, I know. It's awful . . . But it kind of feels brilliant.

Louise   It's fucking amazing. A hundred and fifty.

Tara *holds the money out towards* **Penny**.

Tara   Here.

Penny   What are you giving it to me for?

Tara   It's for you.

Penny   I didn't ask you to do it.

Tara   Yeah. But I just thought . . .

She takes the money back.

Look I said I didn't plan it, it just happened.

Joey   She saw a chance and she took it. Fair enough.

Penny   What if that was your mum sitting on the bus and someone nicked her money?

Tara   My mum doesn't go round with that kind of money.

Penny   Yeah, but what if it was?

Louise   Look, it wasn't okay. It was just some mad old woman. She probably has loads of it. She was probably married to some millionaire and he's kicked the bucket and now she just goes around on buses with a load of money in her bag.

Joey   Maybe we should all get on some buses. We'll have the whole lot by tomorrow.

Penny   No.

Joey   Joke!

Penny   What if that was her pension or something?

Tara   She wasn't that old, Penny.

Penny   Did she see your uniform?

Tara   What?

Penny   Did she see the crest on your uniform?

Tara   I don't know.

Penny   Well, Jesus, Tara, if she saw the crest she could report you.

Sarah   I don't think she saw the crest.

Penny   And they have cameras on buses.

Tara   Stop freaking me out. Why are you freaking me out?

Penny   I'm just saying.

Tara   Look, if we're going to break the law one way –

Penny   We're not breaking the law.

Sarah   Aren't we?

Penny   No. You're allowed to go.

Beat.

Tara   I just – I just thought. I mean it's not every day that you see someone's bag just open with a load of money in it. And we need money and I thought if we need money and she's got all this money then –

Joey   *Carpe diem.*

Tara   What?

Joey   Look. It's fine. No one got hurt – and we got a hundred and fifty quid and actually, you know, there's a really important lesson here.

Penny   About what?

Joey   About the fact that sometimes good people have to steal. I mean look at Robin Hood. Look at Jay-Z.

Tara   Look, if you want we can just pay this guy for our IDs with it and keep the rest for –

Penny   He's not coming.

Tara   Who?

Penny   The guy.

Louise   He's behind. He'll get them to us by Thursday.

Sarah   My sister says he's a real perfectionist.

Silence.

Tara (*looks at the money*)   I thought you'd be pleased.

Penny   I am – pleased. I just . . . feel bad. For the woman.

Joey   Don't feel bad. Think of it this way. When she sees us up there on her screen, singing our hearts out and making everyone else look crap, she'll be telling all her friends that we robbed her. She'll be putting it on Facebook. They robbed me. Those youngsters, they completely fucking fleeced me. Imagine if Beyoncé robbed your purse. You'd be upset at the time but now – you'd be selling your story to the *Sun*. You wait and see, this is probably the most exciting thing to happen to her in years.

Tara *looks at* **Penny**. *She holds out the money.*

Slowly **Penny** *takes it.*

Six

A pitch. After school.

The sound of shouting, a fight.

Vince, **Liam** *and* **Ellis** (*maybe more*) *on bicycles, circling the girls. They've clearly just nicked something from them.*

Louise   Give it back.

Sarah   Give it to her, Vince, now.

Vince *looks at the wedge of cash in his hand.*

Vince   Jesus. How much is here?

Ellis   Three hundred.

Louise   Vince, I swear.

Ellis   You swear you'll what, Pig's Vomit?

Vince   What are you girls doing with three hundred quid?

Liam   They were counting it. They were sitting there on the pitch counting it out. Then they wrapped it all up in an elastic band. Like Tony fucking Soprano.

Sarah   Please. We need that.

Ellis   For what?

Liam   Paying off the judges.

Vince   Paying them to listen to you.

Ellis   Paying them not to puke.

Penny   Just give it back, okay, Vince. It's ours, not yours.

Vince   That right?

He looks at her.

Okay. Fair enough. Here.

He holds the money out towards her.

She takes a step towards it, reaches. He throws it at **Ellis**. **Ellis** *catches it.*

The boys laugh.

Vince   Better luck next time.

Penny *turns and looks at* **Ellis**.

Louise   Ellis, I swear if you don't hand that over right now –

Penny   Just give it to me, okay? Please.

Ellis (*mimicking*)   Please. Why? What's in it for us?

Penny *moves towards* **Ellis**.

Ellis *throws the money at* **Liam**. **Liam** *catches.*

Liam   Yeah, what are you going to do for us in exchange, Pen Pen?

Louise   Why don't you just go back to the septic tank they grew you in, Liam?

Liam   Why don't you?

Tara   Look, just give her back her money and we won't tell.

Vince   Is that a threat?

Tara   No, but . . .

Vince   Not a big fan of threats, us.

Penny   You don't know what we had to do for that?

The boys all roar.

Liam   What did you have do for it?

Penny   I didn't mean –

Liam   No, go on, tell us. What did you have to do for it?

Liam *throws the money at* **Vince**.

Vince *catches.*

Vince   Get down on your knees did you, Penny?

Louise   Hey.

Vince *throws the money at* **Ellis**. **Ellis** *catches.*

Vince   Lie on your back and spread your legs did you, Penny?

Louise   Vince, I'm warning you.

Liam   Hear you're good at that.

Ellis   Yeah!

Louise   I mean it.

Vince *cycles towards* **Penny**. *Then stops and looks at her. She is visibly shaken.*

Vince   Davy says you're *very* good.

Ellis *throws the money at* **Vince**. *He catches.*

He looks at **Penny**.

He holds up the money. Taunting.

Vince   How are we going to spend this, then, lads?

Louise   That's it.

Suddenly **Louise** *runs at* **Vince** *and knocks him off his bike.*

Penny   Louise –

Louise   Don't speak to her like that.

Vince   Get off me, you mad cow.

Louise   Don't ever speak to her like that again. Do you hear me?

She pushes him to the ground. A vicious scuffle.

Ellis *and* **Liam** *laugh as she climbs on top of him.*

Vince   What are you doing? Are you trying to kiss me or something?

Ellis   Go on then, Pig's Vomit.

Louise *pins him to the ground.*

Vince   I don't fancy you, Pig's Vomit.

Suddenly she lunges in and bites his arm.

Vince   What are you – AGGGGGH!

He screams in agony.

AGGGGH! Get off me.

Louise *sits up. There is blood all over her mouth.*

Louise   Give her back her money, Vince. Now.

Vince   She bit me.

He looks at his arm. It is covered in blood.

Shit. She just – she just took a chunk from my/

Ellis   Gross.

Liam   Aw look at her face.

Vince *looks at his arm. Shock.*

Vince   She just bit me.

Ellis   That's nasty, man.

Louise   I said give it to her. Or I'll do it again.

She moves towards him, menacing.

Vince (*scared*)   Okay. Okay. Here.

He drops the money on the ground. **Penny** *picks it up quickly.*

Louise *gets off* **Vince**. *He looks at his arm.*

Vince   Shit. We weren't gonna do anything. We weren't – we were just messing?

Ellis   You gonna cry, Vince?

Vince   No.

Liam   Run home and say some bird tried to eat you?

Vince   Get lost.

He stands up a little shakily. He looks at his arm covered in blood.

Liam   Oh man. That is – a proper chunk, she took.

Vince *moans, looks a little faint.*

Vince   I think – I think I'm gonna be sick.

The girls watch as **Vince** *stumbles away and starts being sick.*

Louise *wipes the blood off her face.*

Ellis *and* **Liam** *look at her, impressed.*

Louise   What? What are you looking at? WHAT?

Liam   . . . What the hell do you birds need that money for?

Seven

Music. Loud, pulsing.

A spotlight on **Joey**.

Joey   I want to win because my favourite uncle Jerry always said it's not about winning, it's about having the determination to succeed . . . god rest his soul.

He nods solemnly.

Kidney failure.

A spotlight on **Sarah**.

Sarah   I want to win because when I was little a group of boys tied up my fox terrier Twinky and poured a can of petrol over him and set him on fire in the street and we were all watching from the top window but there was nothing anyone could do.

A spotlight on **Louise**.

Louise   I want to win because last year my dad had an accident in the garden and can't use his legs properly any more and I am sick of the way that women are continually objectified by society and I think we have something else to offer as a pop group that is not about wearing hot pants.

Tara   I want to win because my mother is dead.

Music stops. Lights up on everyone, normal, a deserted classroom.

Joey *shakes his head.*

Joey   Your mother is not dead.

Tara   You said something sad.

Joey   Something sad but true.

Tara   I don't have anything sad but true.

Bruce   Is that true about your dog?

Sarah   Twinky. Yeah.

Louise   That's horrible.

Sarah   We had to put him down.

Bruce   That's awful.

Joey   Yeah, well, it is awful but it's not *that* awful.

Sarah   It was pretty awful at the time.

Joey   Yeah, but it's not like her whole family were killed in a car crash or she's a survivor of genocide. It's a dog.

Sarah   Yeah, but it was my dog. And what did he ever do to anyone?

Joey   I don't think any of you are getting this.

Penny *starts to walk away.*

Penny   This is a waste of time.

Bruce   No, this is good. If I were the judges I'd feel sorry for you.

Penny   It's pointless. All we have to do is go in there and sing a few lines.

Joey   They'll have researchers. We should have something ready.

Penny (*getting upset*)   I don't want to have something ready. I'm sick of this.

Tara   Come on, Penny – I'll think of something better. It's just a story.

Penny   We have a story. We have a really good story. Only if we actually told it, they wouldn't let us on the show.

Bruce   What story?

Joey   Look, we're all in this together.

Penny   No, we're not.

Joey   If we don't all pull our weight/

Penny   We are not all in this together.

Louise   Penny. Come on, calm down.

Penny   I'm in this on my own. And Vince and Liam and Ellis, the way they look at me, the way they talk like I'm some kind of disease.

Louise   They talk to everyone like that. They're rodents.

Penny   Yeah, but they're right. I mean it's my fault we have to do this. It's my fault we have to go away.

Bruce   Why is it her fault you have to go away?

No one says anything.

Bruce   I thought you were going over to audition.

Sarah   We are going over to audition.

Bruce   So what else are you doing over there?

Joey   Nothing.

Bruce *looks around. He can tell that they are keeping something from him.*

Bruce   Tell me what it is.

No one says anything.

Is it bad?

Louise   Bruce, just leave it will you.

Bruce   What? Come on. Why does no one ever tell me anything? No one ever tells me a thing. I'm always here on the outside. Not being told. And do you know what that's like? It sucks. It completely sucks. I'm just some support act to you, aren't I? You're the stars in the big sell-out show and I'm the support. That's how you see me, isn't it? You didn't even ask me to be in the group. Well, I'm sick of it. I am here, you know. I am a person and you are supposed to be my friends and I would actually like to know what is going on. What are you really doing over there? What's the story?

He looks around. The group stay silent.

The very faint sound of a plane overhead.

Eight

Penny's *bedroom. Evening.*

Louise   We've figured a way. Sarah's sister is seeing her boyfriend in London this weekend so she'll walk us through check-in. Then she's going to put Sarah and Joey on her card as long as Sarah doesn't tell their folks she's back with the boyfriend, they think she's shopping. Then Tara's got her mum's Visa and she's pretty sure that she won't notice cos her brother tried to top himself and that's all they care about. And my dad's just got his statement so I figure if I book for

you and me, that'll buy us a month and even if he does say
something, we can always –

Penny No.

Louise I have the card. Here.

She takes it out.

Louise I mean flights aren't 99p any more, but –

Penny I've figured out a way too. And we won't have to
skip school and use the credit cards and find the money and
go to another country – we can . . . we can do it ourselves.

Louise What do you mean?

Beat.

Penny Are you my best friend?

Louise Yeah.

Penny So if I asked you to do something for me you would
do it?

Louise Yeah. Course.

Penny Like . . . if I asked you to hurt me you'd do it?

Louise Hurt you?

Penny If I asked you. If it was really really important to me.

Louise Hurt you how?

Beat.

Penny In the old days people used to use coat hangers.

Louise What?

Penny Or knitting needles.

Louise Are you mental?

Penny They still do some places. Where it's illegal. That's
what they do.

Louise   You'd bleed to death.

Penny   Women do it.

Louise   And they bleed to death. They mash up their insides so that nothing in there works properly and they die. Jesus, Penny – have you lost it?

Penny   Well then . . . you could hit me. You could hit me really really hard. You could do that couldn't you?

She stands and lifts up her T-shirt.

Penny   Go on. Punch me. Punch me really hard.

Louise   Penny . . .

Penny   Go on. You did it to Vince. Pretend I'm Vince. Think about what an ass I am and all those days I've called you Pig's Vomit. Really hurt me. Like just really really smash me up.

Louise   You have lost it.

Penny   Go on.

Louise   No.

Penny   I want you to.

Louise   You don't.

Penny   I do.

Louise   No.

Penny   I do. I want you to. I want you to do this.

Louise *doesn't do anything.* **Penny** *hits her.*

Penny   Just do it, will you?

Louise   Penny.

Penny *hits her again.*

Penny   I said do it.

Louise   Stop.

Penny *hits her again.*

Penny   Come on.

Louise   No.

Penny   I deserve it.

Louise   You don't deserve it.

Penny   I do. I do deserve it. Just do it. Come on. Do it.

Louise *stands helpless as* **Penny** *hits her one last time.*

Penny   Please.

Beat.

Please.

Beat.

Please.

She looks at **Louise**, *desperate.*

Penny   Please . . . It'll be so much easier.

Nine

Penny *and* **Davy**. *The pitch after school.*

Penny *sits, pensive.*

Davy *bounces or kicks a ball, nervous.*

Penny   Did Louise make you come?

Davy   Said she'd bite me if I didn't.

They smile.

He's such a wanker, Vince. I hope he needs stitches. I hope his arm's infected and he gets gangrene and they have to cut it off.

Penny   They won't.

Davy   But I hope they do.

Beat.

Davy I never told him anything you know.

Penny *looks away.*

He keeps bouncing the ball.

Penny So how's – stuff?

Davy Good. We lost Saturday.

Penny I heard.

Davy So that was crap.

Penny Yeah.

Davy But we're going to France this summer.

Penny Oh?

Davy Yeah. You been to France?

Penny No.

Davy Me neither. But that'll be good. Playing in France.

Penny Yeah. Brilliant.

He stops.

Davy I don't want to be a . . . you know.

She looks at him. Realises what he's saying.

Penny Oh. Yeah, no, I know.

Davy I mean, I do someday.

Penny Me too.

Davy But not now.

Penny No.

Davy Really not now. I mean – shit, you know.

Penny Yeah.

Davy Couldn't believe it when she told me first. Was up all night crying.

Penny Really?

Davy No. Well, sort of. I mean – weren't you?

Penny I guess.

Davy Couldn't sleep all last night. I was so – I wanted to tell my mum.

Penny I know.

Beat.

You didn't, did you?

Davy No. No, but . . . imagine.

Penny I know.

Davy I can't. I mean, it's your choice. It's up to you. But I can't. I just – like I have to say it now – so you know.

Penny I know.

Davy I want to do my exams. I want to go to France. I don't want to be a –

Penny I know.

They sit in silence.

I want to go to France too. Not with you, like – not to play football or anything. I meant – someday. I'd like to go to France someday. I'd like to go everywhere you can go in the world. Someday.

Davy Yeah. Me too.

Penny I'd like to be an explorer. Why don't they have explorers any more?

Davy They don't need them. They've explored everywhere.

Penny Well, I'm still going. Want to see it for myself.

Davy Yeah. Well, I'll let you know if France is good.

Beat.

Penny   Are you with Sandra now?

Davy   Sort of. Not really. Sort of.

Penny   Okay.

Davy   Sorry.

Penny   No. Look. You can do what you – I just . . .

Beat.

He sits down beside her and takes out an envelope. Gives it to her.

Davy   Here.

Penny   What's this?

Davy   Three hundred. That's how much Louise said you needed. She said you were desperate.

Penny   . . . How did you get it?

Davy   Don't ask.

Penny   Did you steal it?

Davy   Seriously. Don't ask. (*Smiles.*) But if I don't come in next week tell the cops to talk to my brother.

Penny   He'll kill you.

Davy   Doesn't know yet.

She smiles.

Beat.

Will it hurt?

Penny   They say it won't.

Davy   Is it an operation?

Penny   Yes.

Davy   Do they give you a needle?

Penny   Yes. But I'm going to stay awake.

Davy   And you can't do it here?

Penny   Nope.

Davy   But you're allowed to go over there?

Penny   Yep.

Davy   That's allowed?

Penny   They don't stop you.

Beat.

I mean. They used to stop you. Years ago. If they found out.
But they changed the rules cos of a girl called X.

Davy   Her name was X?

Penny   In the newspapers.

Beat.

She was fourteen. She'd been raped. Said she'd kill herself if
they made her have the child so . . .

Davy   Why did they call her X?

Penny   To protect her identity. Maybe. Or to cross her out.
Maybe. Make like she didn't exist. I don't know.

Davy   God.

Penny   Imagine. No name, just an . . .

She draws an 'X' in the air.

Penny   Anyway, now they let you go.

Davy   So is it a bad or a good thing – what you're doing?

Penny (*shrugs*)   Louise thinks it's a human right.

Davy   My mum thinks it's murder . . . She'd kill me if I had
a kid though.

Penny   Mine too.

Davy   She'd really –

Penny   Mine too.

Beat.

Penny   I wish it wasn't up to me. I wish it wasn't my . . .
I wish I could just close my eyes and wake up tomorrow and
everything could be like it was. A few weeks ago. Before. You
know?

Davy   . . . Yeah.

Beat.

It's better though, isn't it? Doing it there.

Penny   How do you mean?

Davy   Cos it's there. It's not here. You can go and do it and
no one will know. And then when you come back, it'll be over
and you can just – forget all about it. Like it never happened.
You know?

Penny   . . . Yeah.

Davy   That's definitely better.

She looks at the money.

Is it enough?

Penny   Yeah. It's enough.

Davy   Cos I don't think I can get any more. But I don't
want Louise coming after me next.

Penny   She won't.

Beat.

I really liked you.

Davy   Yeah. I know.

Penny   Like I wouldn't have – I'd never have – just so you
know. It was because I – really . . .

Davy   Yeah. No. I know.

He starts to bounce the ball.

Here. Louise says you're going to audition when you're over there.

Penny   Gonna try. It was Joey's idea. When in Rome.

He doesn't get it.

Davy   Don't you need to be sixteen to audition?

Penny   We're getting ID.

Davy   Cool. You nervous?

Penny   A bit.

Davy   Where are you staying?

Penny   We don't know yet.

Davy   What are you singing?

Penny   We don't know yet.

Davy   What's the group called?

Penny   We don't know yet. We'll figure everything out when we get there.

Davy   London's mad.

Penny   I know. Hope we don't get lost.

Davy   You've a really good voice.

Penny   Thanks.

Davy   No, you do. You're really good – everyone says.

Penny   My mum always said I'd be a singer when I grew up.

Davy   Maybe you will . . . You'll see loads of famous people in London.

Penny   It's just a big stadium.

Davy   No, but it's full of them. They're like flies to shit. My brother saw Eminem there on the side of a road. Just staring. (*Suddenly perking up.*) Hey, maybe she'll be there. That judge.

Whatshername – with the hot body. Do you think she'll be there?

Penny   I don't know.

Davy   It would be mad if she was – like if you got to see her. In the flesh.

Penny   I don't think she's on it any more.

Davy (*getting excited*)   Oh man. If she's there –

Penny   She won't be –

Davy   But if she is – if she is – will you give her a message from me?

Penny   A message?

Davy   Yeah.

Penny   . . . Okay.

Davy   Cool.

She waits.

Penny   . . . What?

Davy   What?

Penny   What's the message?

Davy   Oh. Just like – say hi. From me. You know. Word. Word from Davy.

Penny   'Word from Davy'?

Davy   Hi from Davy.

Penny   'Hi from Davy'?

Davy   Yeah. Yeah. And tell her she's hot. Tell her she's smoking. Tell her I think she's smoking hot.

Penny   Okay . . . I'll tell her.

Davy   Cool. That's – yeah. Cool.

He bounces the ball, pleased.

I hope you do see her. I hope you get through. That'd be . . .
What would happen if you did – you know – if you guys
actually got through to the actual show?

Penny   They'd probably find out our real ages and
disqualify us.

Davy   Oh.

Penny   But Joey thinks the publicity would be worth it and
we'd get another deal so . . .

Davy   Cool.

He laughs and kicks the ball. **Penny** *watches.*

Penny   If you had to choose between being super rich and
famous but only living for seven more years, or being poor
and invisible but living till you're ninety – which would you
choose?

Davy   Being rich and famous.

Penny   Really?

Davy   No question. Wouldn't you?

Penny   I don't know. I mean, how would you feel when the
seven years were coming to an end and you knew that that
was it? You'd made your choice. There's no going back.

Davy   Wouldn't think about it.

He smiles.

I'd just keep partying.

Penny *looks at him.*

Penny   Yeah . . . yeah.

Fade.

Ten

Music.

Penny, **Tara**, **Louise** *and* **Sarah** *sing the first verse of 'Call Me' by Blondie. When they get to the key change in the chorus, it falls apart.*

Sarah (*normal*)   Shit – sorry!

Lights up. The park, night. They are in the middle of rehearsing.

Tara   It was me.

Sarah   No, it was me. I always go too high at that bit.

Tara   I lost the words.

Joey   That was better.

Sarah   I just get nervous.

Louise   Well, you can't get nervous Saturday – you'll sink us all that way.

Joey   No one is going to sink. It's sounding good.

Tara   I think we should do Rihanna.

Sarah   Or Abba. Abba's easier.

Joey   Abba's prehistoric.

Penny   Or a ballad – they always love a ballad.

Joey   This is good. Trust me.

Louise   But what if she gets nervous?

Joey   She won't get nervous. This is a rehearsal, you're allowed to mess up in rehearsal.

Sarah   Yeah, Louise. That's the point.

She looks at her ID.

Sarah   Here. Is that what I really look like?

Tara   Shut up.

Sarah   No, really – do I really look like that?

Tara   Yes.

Sarah   I think he's made my eyes smaller.

Louise   Why would he make your eyes smaller?

Sarah   I don't know. I just thought I'd look more –

Tara   Like Natalie Portman?

Sarah   No.

Tara   Jessica Alba?

Sarah   Get lost.

Penny   What if they know this is fake?

Tara   It looks real.

Penny   Yeah, but what if they know? Will they make me go home?

Joey   We'll deal with that when we have to.

Louise   I can't believe this time tomorrow we'll have been there a whole day.

Beat.

Penny   I wish someone could come with me.

Louise   We'll be right outside in the waiting room.

Penny   They won't let you sit in the waiting room. It gets too busy.

Tara   Well, we'll just stay in the street then.

Sarah   We'll sing if you want. So you'll know we're nearby.

Penny   No, please. Don't sing.

Tara   It'll be over before you know it.

Sarah   Yeah, and afterwards we'll go somewhere nice. The park.

Tara   Or the river. Have a picnic.

Beat.

Penny *tries to smile.*

Penny   . . . What do you think it is?

Joey   What?

Penny   The 'X' factor? What do you think the 'X' actually is?

Joey   They can't put a name on it.

Penny   Why?

Louise   Because. They don't know how. That's the point. It's unnameable. That's why it's an 'X'.

Penny   But is that because there isn't a word for it? Or because no one can be bothered to think of what it is?

Sarah   It's because it's invisible.

Penny   An 'X' isn't invisible, it's like a big mark.

Joey   Yeah, because the people who have it are marked out to be famous.

Sarah   It's that certain *je nais sais quoi.*

Tara   Stop.

Sarah   What?

Tara   Doing that French accent. You sound stupid.

Sarah   No, I don't.

Louise   You both sound stupid.

Joey   Shhh – what's that?

Tara   What?

Joey   I heard something. Over there.

Sarah   Oh god. It's him.

Joey   Who?

Penny   There's a guy. In the bushes We saw him last time.

Louise   We saw a dog last time.

Sarah   God, imagine if he just jumped out now with a knife and stabbed us all to death.

Tara   Sarah!

Sarah   Be just our luck to get murdered before we even got on the telly.

Louise   He's not interested in murdering us, he just wants to pull down his pants.

Joey   Some people really should get out more.

Louise   Or less.

Penny   Let's just go – this place gives me the creeps.

Sarah   I thought we were going to practise.

Joey   We are going to practise.

Tara   We can't practise with some freak-show listening in the bushes.

Joey   Course we can. Have you seen the people that audition for this? Now, from the top.

Louise   Seriously?

Joey   Practice makes perfect. We only have another few hours. On the count of three – one, two, three.

They start to sing again, as the lights fade and a cacophony of airport noises swells around them.

Eleven

An airport departures lounge.

Joey, **Louise**, **Tara**, **Penny** *and* **Sarah** *run on in sunglasses with their suitcases.*

They talk over each other at great speed.

Louise   You are such an idiot.

Sarah   Sorry.

Tara   What were you thinking? /

Joey   I said to pack light.

Louise   Fifty quid – what the hell did you put in there?

Sarah   I don't know.

Penny   You knew they charge for extra weight.

Sarah   It's cos we never decided on an outfit. If we had decided on an outfit this wouldn't have happened.

Joey *flings open the suitcase.*

Joey   How does one person have so many clothes?

Sarah   I got panicked.

They look at the bag.

Tara   We're going to have to put them on.

Louise   What?

Tara   We're going to have to wear stuff, so the bag gets lighter.

Louise   I'm not putting on her clothes.

Sarah   What's wrong with my clothes?

Tara   It's either that or pay the fifty.

Louise   Cheapskates. My dad says they'd charge you for an oxygen mask.

Joey   Come on, they're closing the gate. Everyone grab something and shove it on.

They scramble to put on things – socks over shoes, tops over T-shirts. Hats, whatever she has in there.

They keep piling them on over the following.

Sarah   I'm sorry.

Penny   It's okay.

Sarah   Everyone's looking.

Tara   Who gives a shit?

Sarah   I wanted us to feel like celebrities.

Joey   Well, we're off the A-list now.

Louise   What did you bring this for?

She holds up the T-shirt with the glittery 'X'.

Sarah   I thought I might wear it.

Louise   I thought you might burn it.

Tara   Just put it on. We haven't time.

Louise *throws it at* **Penny**.

Penny   You're so immature sometimes, Louise.

She puts on the T-shirt casually. **Sarah** *looks up at the Departures board.*

Sarah   Hey, there's a flight to New York. Maybe we could sneak on that instead.

Tara   Or what about Munich?

Joey   Or Paris.

Penny   Or Buenos Aires.

They keep dressing.

Tara   Imagine – they're in assembly now.

Penny   They're definitely going to know something's up. All five of us out.

Joey   Bruce is covering.

Penny   What are we going to say Monday?

Joey   Monday's years away. We could be famous by Monday.

Louise   We'll think of something.

Sarah   Here, if you had to lose a part of your body in an accident – which would you choose? Your legs, your arms, or your face?

Louise   Why are you asking this now?

Sarah   It just came into my head.

Tara   Well, shut it. We don't have time for this.

She closes the bag.

Here. Try it now.

Sarah *picks it up.*

Sarah   Feels lighter.

Joey *tries.*

Joey   Yeah. We might just get away with that.

Tara   Look at the state of us.

Joey   It's fine, it's a look. All it takes is the right attitude and you can get away with anything.

Sarah *looks over.*

Sarah   Oh shit. My sister's waving. They really are closing the gate.

Joey   Okay. Come on. Glasses on. Heads up. Shoulders back.

They all put on their shades. Put their heads up, shoulders back.

Joey   Imagine that you're walking into a sea of paparazzi.

They do.

Are you ready?

Louise   For what?

Joey   Whatever's coming next.

They pick up their bags and walk into the crowd. The lights begin to fade.

At the very last minute **Penny** *stops. She turns and stands for a beat looking at the Departures board. The X on her T-shirt glitters in the light. Then she moves off.*

The roar of a plane taking off. Deafening.

Blackout.

Journey to X

*Notes on rehearsal and staging, drawn from a workshop
with the writer at the National Theatre, November 2011*

The Play and the Writer

When I was first commissioned by NT Connections to write
for their 2012 season, I was working in Dublin at the Abbey
Theatre on another play called *No Romance*. In that play a
character made a brief reference to the Irish abortion law by
making a joke about how if abortion was ever legalised in
Ireland, one particular low-budget airline would lose a lot of
money. While potentially controversial in a country where
abortion is illegal, the comment was not greeted with shock or
outrage by Irish audiences, but usually with a laugh.

This made me think. If audiences are able to laugh at a joke
like that, it must mean that the subject of travelling overseas
for an abortion is one that we can talk about. And yet we
don't seem to. We simply have a law that says it is acceptable
to go elsewhere for a termination, but not to have one on our
own soil.

This got me thinking about what that then means in practice
for women and in particular young teenage girls who find
themselves pregnant and having to make that choice and
subsequently that journey. It got me thinking about the prac-
ticalities involved in such a journey in terms of organisation,
cost and travel. It got me thinking about the cover stories that
would have to be made up to explain to family, friends and
teachers where they were going. And it got me thinking about
girls I knew when I was a teenager who had to make both
that choice and that journey. And how they never really
talked about it afterwards.

Ireland isn't the only country where abortion isn't talked
about. It isn't talked about much in the UK either, though it
is legal. And whatever one's views on the subject, or wherever
you're from in the world, the fact is, deciding whether or not

to have an abortion is never a choice that any woman *wants* to have to make.

It was 'the X case' – referred to briefly in the play – which ultimately led to the current Irish law granting women the right to travel, and has become part of our political and social history in Ireland. However, the letter 'X' seemed to me a potent and striking symbol for the conflict at the heart of this play. An 'X' has a dual meaning – it can mean marked out as someone or something special, as it does in *The X Factor*. Or it can symbolise being crossed out, in the sense of being invisible or non-existent. Penny, the protagonist in *Journey to X*, feels both marked out *and* crossed out by her situation. The boys in the school know there is something different or special about her because she has been sexually active and she knows she is different from her friends because she is pregnant. But if she makes the journey to London and has the termination, when she comes back home to a country where what she has just done is not permitted, it will be, as Davy puts it, 'like it never happened'. Even though it did.

This struck me as a very tough, confusing and lonely thing for anyone, especially a teenage girl, to have to experience. And yet countless teenage girls have done so. So I wanted to write this play – to tell an ordinary story about ordinary people in a situation that could potentially happen every day, about something that nobody seems to talk about.

Nancy Harris, November 2011

The Universal and the Specific

The directors starting work on *Journey to X* agreed that this shouldn't be approached as an 'issue play' or a polemic, but an accessible, fast and fluid play about friendship, solidarity and growing up that, with humour and pathos, deals with thorny and complex subject matter.

During the first meeting of the group at the directors' weekend many present voiced their concern about the 'Irishness' of the play. Should it be performed in an Irish accent? Where in

Ireland should it be based? Nancy Harris was keen to point out that the play was inspired by events and politics in Ireland, but is not *about* Ireland, but *a place where abortion is illegal* and the directors shouldn't be overly concerned about whether it would 'translate' to wherever the producing company is based. Telling the characters' stories is the most important thing.

Very few place names are mentioned in the text and in the opening Location Notes Nancy writes 'for the sake of universality and clarity, I would suggest that groups use their own accents when performing the piece'. The character names she has chosen are similarly not specific to Ireland or indicative of a particular place; so these should not be changed. The writer suggested that this 'universal' approach should be considered when staging the play: locations 'conjured as swiftly and imaginatively as possible', with minimal props – just those needed for the clarity of the story. Don't get too elaborate and encumbered with detail.

The Production

For the play's opening scene in the airport it was suggested that really all the *mise en scène* required were the few props mentioned in the stage directions, and that little else was needed to tell the story effectively. Similarly for the creation of the classroom at the beginning of Scene Two, it might be beneficial to take an impressionistic approach, not attempting to re-create a complete classroom onstage, but just a few items suggestive of a room in a school; and for the bushes in Scene Three, an evocation of an uncomfortable, scary place where the friends are trying to keep themselves busy, all struggling to ignore their potentially precarious position, knowing that having to stay here for the ID cards is more important than the actual physical representation of the bushes.

Just how little can you get away with, what tells the story? Naturalism may not be the most advantageous approach to take when approaching the design of this play as it might hinder 'fluidity' and pace which the writer and facilitating director agreed are key to a successful production of this play.

It was suggested that the use of specific mid-scene sound effects and ambient sound should also be kept to a minimum, particularly if it risks interfering with the flow of the scenes. Avoid anything that might distract the focus from the dialogue (flights being called at the airport for example).

A note on music. The song choices are flexible and not prescriptive, except for 'I Kissed a Girl' at the top of Scene Three (since the lyrics are alluded to during the scene). Nancy was certain that productions should make the live musical elements as good as the actors can make them – certainly there should be no attempt to sing 'badly'.

The Characters

The central characters are young and learning as they go, but blanket pejorative character descriptions like 'deluded' should be avoided when starting to layer characters in rehearsal. Avoid criticising or negatively evaluating the characters; to begin with a word like 'honest' will be much more helpful and fruitful than 'naïve'. Hopefully this will help avoid an actor's temptation to *play* naïve instead of *being* naïve – to see the character making genuine attempts to achieve goals, not merely being in a singular state of stumbling callowness.

The boys and girls have *aspirations*, they want to do well, to succeed, and it is important that we support and 'root for' them. They may make wrong or bad decisions, but actors should try to avoid judging them – the fault should be seen to lie in the action or method, not innately in the character. The play deals with fidelities and vulnerabilities, young people coping with life as best they can, and at times they are motivated to do desperate things in times of desperation – Louise biting Vince, Tara stealing the money on the bus. Such spontaneous incidents should be seen in the light of the action of the rest of the play.

The group discussed how these young people have a degree of self-absorption, seeing only the now: what impacts on them at this moment, disregarding the 'wider picture', often acting impulsively and immediately, before concern of consequence becomes a factor, perhaps motivated into doing something 'bad' in order to achieve something 'good'.

'Teenagers live in the present . . . it's an accumulation of limited experience.' (Nancy Harris)

The central characters are a close-knit group of friends. This is a world without visible adults, and we perceive the rest of the world through their eyes. Friends have become family; they know each other well and all want to do something good, for each other and for self-betterment, but are frequently tripped up. What keeps them together, what is the common bond? What are the characters' reasons for staying together? The actors should try and identify the characters' ambitions and driving aspiration and the *obstacles* that impede them during their individual journeys.

Try not to get emotional or sentimental when building characters, but concentrate on telling their stories; it's what the characters do that helps define them. In Scene One, for example, what are the characters doing? Charlotte Gwinner, who was leading the workshop, encouraged the group to 'chase the detail': Louise is organising, looking out, making sure things are getting done; Tara, with lots of bravado, mouthy, 'gives some woman the finger', but still keeps an eye on the clock; Joey, seemingly quite comfortable being the only boy in a group of girls discussing poise and tampons. What clues could these details have for developing characters?

Draw up time-lines for the different characters, starting some time before the opening of the play, plotting when significant moments occur, when the characters are at points of complication, when they encounter obstacles that hinder their progress, how they tackle the obstacles. Also mark moments of clarity, unravelling, denouement and big decisions. Charlotte suggested that full-on, from-birth character histories might not necessarily be helpful. When do the big events happen and in what order? Penny sleeping with Davy, discovering she's pregnant, telling her friends (and in what order), who is not told and why (parents, Bruce), considering the available options, deciding on abortion and going to London, the *X-Factor* cover story, booking the flights, when does Davy find out about the pregnancy?

The character time-lines might prove particularly helpful when plotting what leads to Louise attacking Vince. This doesn't come out of nowhere: what are the factors and what does this say about her character? Is she seeing things clearly at this moment, or does she just snap? Surrounded by her friends, is it a collective group strength that bolsters her, or a sense of righteous unassailability? Does she feel she has right on her side in the light of Penny's 'condition'? Is this an inevitable explosion after all the injustice of the bullying and name-calling? Many group members thought the fact that Louise bites Vince instead of slapping or kicking him may say a great deal about her state of mind at this moment in the play: 'feral', 'animalistic', 'instinctive' and 'primitive' were among the descriptions offered for her choice/impulse to bite.

Finding a Key Line for the Characters

It may help when working through the time-lines to *select a key line in each scene for each character*. What does it tell us about the character at that point in their journey, about their priorities? For example:

Joey: 'I'm the manager' (Scene Two). This gives us a good idea where Joey's energies are at this point. His speeches have been leading up to this declaration, but his bubble is swiftly burst when Vince pushes him and he takes some time to recover.

Some key lines could be telltale signals for characterisation: in the workshop, when discussing a key line for Sarah in Scene Three, some members of the group proposed that when Tara pops the 'live-fast-die-young' question, it's significant that Sarah is reassured by 'But married . . . Still married, though,' but she is also the first to choose the option 'dead in seven years'. What might this say about her?

For Louise in Scene Four, when the girls are trying on their *X Factor* T-shirts: 'I'm taking mine off before Vince comes in here' and 'Forget it – I'm not standing on stage and grinding my crotch like some *Playboy* bunny' were suggested as possible key lines. Is she afraid of Vince or does she like him? Does she find the notion of the *Playboy* bunny degrading or is she worried about looking silly?

For Penny in Scene Four, 'Definitely. Book.' was regarded as the key line: she has made a decision and this is the springboard into the next phase of action – without her approval the travel plans wouldn't get much further at this stage. The punctuation is important, these are two distinct separate statements followed by full stops: this is Penny making a decision, having remained relatively quiet for so long. This is her public admission that it's time to do something definite.

Single-sex Casting and Physicality

Over the weekend a number of companies with few male actors discussed the implications/complications of having girls play the roles of the boys. It was agreed that the characters' genders were important and shouldn't be changed. It is fine to have girls playing the boys' roles – but as boys, not feminising the roles. Don't be tempted to change Vince to Valerie.

Towards the end of the workshop the group worked on how Scene Two could be directed with a single-sex cast. The female cast experimented with posturing and the centring of the boy characters, and played with keeping the characters mobile, fidgety, predatory and restless, taking up a lot of stage space. The male actors played the female characters as much less animated, less mobile, and considered the way the girls might sit – in particular their proximity to one another. Charlotte Gwinner advised actors to be careful of moments of physical contact: consider if and when breaking the physical barrier might be appropriate and for which characters. Who would feel comfortable touching someone else?

Though the physicality of the characters was a good starting point, Charlotte wanted to make clear that the actors must also have unambiguous objectives, clear actions in conveying what their character wants to achieve in the scenes. Mannerisms and posturing might help to embellish the characterisations but clarity of intention and psychological action was primary, what they wanted and how they went about getting it was more helpful in telling the story than creating caricatures. The agreement at the end of this exercise was to be wary of stereotypes.

Rhythm and Language

Charlotte impressed upon the directors the importance of actors learning the lines together, running the lines together, familiarising themselves with the flow and rhythm of the script, keeping it alive and vibrant, making each moment in the 'now' and not getting ponderous. Nancy has inserted additional symbols and a useful dialogue key at the beginning of the text to assist with the construction of the dialogue, particularly helpful in sections that need to be pacy and energised. Decide where the need to speak happens in the preceding line(s), since the use of the '/' indicates a very quick following line: locate where the thought and connected breath take place to fuel this line. The cast should be talking to each other, so listening is very important.

Particular care should be taken to observe and adhere to *punctuation*. Be clear when statements are clearly separated ('Definitely. Book.') and when there is a lack of punctuation and what effect this has on the pace of the dialogue. For example, Bruce's speech at the end of Scene Seven and Louise's at the beginning of Scene Eight are both ten lines long, but one speech has eighteen marked sentences, the other only four and a half. What might this suggest about the energy and rate of delivery? Pay close attention to the length of the lines: what effect does this have on the flow of the dialogue? Compare Penny and Davy's staccato awkwardness in Scene Nine with Tara's excited speeches in Scene Five.

Avoid extraneous hesitations and pauses. Nancy has included clear beats in her stage directions. Consider what the beats (or bouncing the ball in Scene Nine) marked in the script might represent; as well as beats Nancy also includes ellipses (. . .) and dashes (–), and actors should be sure what they indicate: discomfort, tiredness, an unspoken thought, hesitancy, fear. Use and don't ignore what Charlotte called the 'architecture of silences' in the text, but try to avoid adding to them.

Many of the scenes start (and end) with what Charlotte described as a 'coiled spring' that launches into the next phase of the action, and many of the scenes open with a question being asked or answered. The actors should be sure about what has happened prior to the beginning of the scene. Using the time-lines mentioned above might help with this. All the scenes start in mid-action, not on an empty stage: things are already happening, so new scenes should launch with a strong impetus, not take time gathering momentum.

Though it was a concern for some members of the group, the writer and facilitating director advised that directors should not be tempted to edit the swearing or potentially offensive language but stay faithful to the text.

Penny's Story

What is Penny's 'situation' at any given moment? Her progression through the play should be carefully monitored. What state of mind is she in at the beginning of the play? Don't forget that the beginning of the play is almost the end of the story, so the choices made here for all the characters should be informed by events in the other scenes. How much does she say (not much)? What does she say (she knows flight details and regulations)? How involved is she with the other members of the group (quite detached)? Questions like these will all help to inform and concentrate Penny's character at this point in the play. Her story is about to unfold for the audience, but she's already lived it. The directors agreed that the positioning of Penny on stage at the end of the first and last scenes is of considerable significance and should be given particular attention.

'There is nothing Penny can do, she's overwhelmed, caught for a moment in the huge reality' (Nancy Harris).

Consider in what ways Penny might be different in Scenes One and Eleven. Will any change in the audience's perception be informed by what they have learned about her? Has she finally made the decision to go? What is the effect of an open ending?

A time-line of Penny's pregnancy might be helpful. Was this her first sexual experience? (The consensus was 'yes'.) Who has she told? Who doesn't know? How pregnant is she? (Eleven weeks at the end of the play was the writer's suggestion.) What are the time lapses between the scenes? What Penny is experiencing is cumulative, snowballing, and what has gone before and its possible resonance and repercussions shouldn't be ignored.

Things happen to the whole group because of what Penny has done: on the less harmful side, they're booking flights and all going to London, Sarah's making T-shirts and her sister's sourcing fake identity cards. It's become quite an adventure; but how might it affect Penny thinking that Louise attacked Vince or that Tara has robbed an old lady on a bus *for her*? Is her predicament the catalyst for her friends' uncharacteristic actions? Is it her fault that these things are happening to her and her friends? Has she caused all this? Even if she wanted to change her mind and reconsider having the abortion, are her friends now so involved and caught up in it all that she doesn't have a choice? The key lines that were suggested during workshop are:

'It's my fault we have to do this. It's my fault we have to go away' (Scene Seven).

'I deserve it' (Scene Eight).

Consider what are the other characters' proximities to, or involvement in, Penny's predicament, and what are their degrees of separation? Louise and Joey, for example, have different levels of immersion in Penny's dilemma . For Joey in Scene Two it seems to be all about *X Factor*. Are the girls feeling the same way? Is Penny's well-being still the primary motive or has the sense of adventure taken over?

Be quite sure what is motivating characters' actions throughout the play – what's on their priority list. Are the group thinking about Penny when practising their 'sad but true' stories? Penny's reaction to it all is quite unambiguous – 'This is a waste of time' – and her feelings are more visible when responding forcefully to Joey: 'We are not all in this together … I'm in this on my own.' It would be useful to decide what 'this' in this line actually means for each of the characters at various points in the play.

From a workshop led by Charlotte Gwinner,
with notes by Phil Sheppard

Little Foot

Craig Higginson

Author's Notes

Location

The play is situated in a valley north-west of Johannesburg, loosely referred to as the Cradle of Humankind. The area contains underground caves in which our oldest human and pre-human remains have been found – along with the remains of many extinct animals. The area is now a National Park, but some of it extends into privately owned farms and smallholdings, many of which have caves and areas of interest to palaeontologists and archaeologists.

Little Foot and the Chorus

Here, the Chorus consists of hominins. They wear masks. The masks should not be naturalistic. Little Foot could be played by a smaller child or puppet. The Chorus start off as a traditional Greek Chorus, speaking with one voice. They are then split down the middle into two opposing forces and become individualised. By the end, they have degenerated from Chorus into crowd.

The Chorus should consist of at least six people. They are *Homo habilis* hominins, our direct ancestors, who are over one million years old. Little Foot is a more ancient hominin, *Australopithecus*, a less direct ancestor who is over two and a half million years old. *Homo habilis* lived in caves and could control fire – and so were able to keep predators at bay. *Australopithecus* lived before our ancestors controlled fire or used stone tools and were more vulnerable to predators. It is believed they nested in trees in an attempt to escape predators. *Australopithecus* eventually became extinct.

Design

The play has been written so that hardly any set is required. Most of the action takes place in caves, underground. There should be shadowy lighting or complete darkness. Sometimes scenes are only lit by a torch or a lamp. This means that the words and the act of listening become extremely important. The Chorus should provide a soundscape, sighing with the wind and echoes of the caves.

The Symbolism of the Cave

This will require some research. In different cultures across time, the cave can stand for our ancestral origin/home, as well as the womb, the egg (or the place of development or evolution, out of which there is birth or rebirth), the Underworld or Hell. It can stand for an alternative world (perhaps a dystopia), a shadow of the real world (see Plato) or it can provide an image of the world itself (in this play, the main cave even has its own version of a sun). The cave can also stand for the brain or the human mind, or the location of the unconscious.

Political Context

Little Foot is set in post-apartheid South Africa. All the characters were born after the end of apartheid.

Craig Higginson
Johannesburg, 2011

Characters
in order of appearance

Chorus
Little Foot
Braai
Mercedes
Rebecca
Wizard
Moby

One

Darkness. The **Chorus** *appear. They are lit only in silhouette. They wear masks – stylised, non-naturalistic apemen masks. During the following they will begin a slow movement, a rhythmic swaying.*

At the centre, a small hominin appears and is illuminated. This is **Little Foot***. He is represented by a puppet or a masked child.* **Little Foot** *opens his mouth to speak, but no sound comes out. The* **Chorus** *start whispering – a hostile sound. The light on* **Little Foot** *fades.*

The **Chorus** *break apart. Two figures are revealed, a glowing fire between them. They are in a circular earth clearing. They are* **Mercedes** *and* **Braai***. They are about seventeen years old.* **Braai** *is smoking a cigarette. It is dusk. Darkness grows gradually during the scene. Neon lamps and torches will be switched on as the light fades.*

Braai Where is he?

Mercedes Late as usual. There was some girl he had to look after.

Braai What's wrong with her?

Mercedes She's over from England. Her mother works with his mother. He's showing her around.

Braai Wizard as tour guide? (*He is amused.*) What's she like?

Mercedes I haven't seen her.

Braai Well, what did he say about her?

Mercedes I've hardly spoken to him since she arrived.

Braai He'd better not bring her with.

Mercedes Why not?

Braai It wasn't the deal. It's only supposed to be the three of us. Before we go our separate ways.

Mercedes We did that a while ago. Didn't you notice?

Braai But you and me are still together, aren't we?

Silence.

Mercedes   It's more likely he'll bring Moby Dick.

Braai   But you asked him not to.

Mercedes   That won't matter. Moby tags along.

Silence.

Braai   We should phone him. Make sure he's coming.

Mercedes   I told you. There's no reception.

*A beautiful girl enters. She is **Rebecca**, from England. She is a couple of years older than the other two. She looks at them for a moment – startled.*

Rebecca (*calling to* **Wizard** *and* **Moby** *– who are some distance behind*)   I've found them, I think. (*To* **Mercedes** *and* **Braai**.) Sorry, you gave me such a –

Braai   And who are you?

Rebecca   Rebecca. Wizard's friend.

Mercedes   Rebecca from England.

Rebecca   That's me.

Wizard *enters, followed by* **Moby**.

Wizard   Hello, happy campers. We've been driving about for two hours, trying to find you. (*To* **Mercedes**.) We couldn't make sense of your directions. We kept getting out and calling. Didn't you hear us? We decided to climb this mountain before giving up.

Mercedes   But you've been here before.

Wizard   A long time ago.

Braai   You brought friends.

Wizard   Is that alright?

Braai (*to* **Rebecca**)   You want a drink?

Rebecca *walks over to* **Braai** *and takes the cigarette from him. She takes a drag.*

Rebecca   Later. Thanks.

Moby *and* **Mercedes** *nod at each other.*

Mercedes   Moby. You came.

Moby   Wizard said it would be okay.

Mercedes   I'm sure he did. (*To* **Wizard**.) We aren't going to have much food. If there are five of us.

Wizard   I don't eat. (*Referring to* **Moby**.) And neither does he.

Mercedes   That's not the point.

Wizard   Listen, I'm sorry. I tried to call. Your phone was off.

Braai   There's no reception.

Mercedes   Between these hills there's a blind spot.

Rebecca   I'm sure we can leave if you –

Mercedes   Don't worry. Any friend of Wizard's is a friend of ours.

Braai   Except for Moby Dick.

Moby (*trying to laugh this off*)   Thanks.

Braai   Jokes. (*To* **Wizard**.) Did you tell her about the caves?

Wizard *is looking for the beers.*

Wizard   If I don't eat, am I allowed to drink?

Mercedes   Braai brought the beer. There's enough for a month.

Braai   Wizard, did you explain to Rebecca? About the dare?

Wizard   No.

Rebecca   What dare is this?

Wizard   About three years ago, we came here. The three of us. To visit the caves.

Braai   Wizard had some kind of panic attack.

Wizard   Apparently.

Mercedes   Ever since, Braai's said Wizard would be too scared to go down there and spend the night.

Wizard   So that's why I'm here.

Braai   I'm here to see if he'll be brave enough.

Rebecca (*to* **Braai**)   I think if Wizard *had* explained, I wouldn't have come.

Braai   You're here now.

Mercedes   For better or worse.

Moby   Actually, Wizard was too busy trying to explain you three.

Braai   And how did he do that?

Moby   He made Mercedes sound like one of those parcels that get passed around the circle. Each time getting more –

Rebecca   I think the word he used was 'unwrapped'.

Mercedes   What?

Rebecca   Sorry, Mercedes – no offence.

Wizard (*to* **Mercedes**)   I said you were with Braai, then me, then Braai again.

Moby   Like 'pass the parcel', you said.

Braai (*to* **Rebecca**)   Wizard was never with Mercedes. She was with me. Then, this one time, Wizard kissed her. She repented and came back.

Silence.

But there's no hard feelings – hey, Wizard?

Wizard   I hope not.

Rebecca   I'm sure it's none of my business.

Braai   If you stick around, it might become your business.

Mercedes   I'm not a parcel. I make my own decisions.

Wizard   Exactly. Tell them how you kissed me back.

Moby (*to* **Rebecca**)   Don't worry. They love each other really.

Silence. By now, they have all settled into the space.

Rebecca   You mentioned caves. Where are they exactly?

Braai   Ask Mercedes. This is her uncle's place. She knows all about it. She does tours in the holidays.

Rebecca   Tours of the caves?

Mercedes   I work at a place nearby. The Cradle of Humankind. All I do is talk. To make the caves sound interesting. Things are only interesting if you make them sound interesting. Nothing is that interesting in itself.

Wizard   We've hurt her feelings.

Mercedes   I don't like being referred to as a parcel.

Wizard   Sorry. I was only trying to make you sound – interesting.

The others laugh.

I'm sorry, alright?

Mercedes   Whatever, Wizard.

Rebecca (*to* **Mercedes**)   The caves. How do you make them sound interesting?

Mercedes   You're trying to change the subject.

Rebecca   No – I'm genuinely interested now.

Braai   It was in these hills that the oldest human remains were found.

Mercedes   Pre-human remains, actually.

Braai   There are hundreds of caves right under us. All connected.

Mercedes   Only some of them are.

Braai   That's where the bones have been found. That's where we're spending the night.

Rebecca   We're actually sleeping down there?

Braai   If we go to sleep. I'm hoping to stay up.

Mercedes   And do what?

Braai   That depends on you, baby.

Mercedes *smiles, relenting slightly.*

Rebecca   I must say, you have the strangest names. Wizard, Mercedes, Braai, Moby.

Braai   Braai means to cook meat. To barbecue. Actually, it comes from Brian.

Rebecca (*ironic*)   A pretty name. Brian.

Moby   I'm Richard.

Braai   Dick. Moby the Dick.

Rebecca (*to* **Wizard**)   And you?

Wizard   I hate my name.

Mercedes   Our names are our disguises.

Moby   They hide our true natures.

Braai   We're really vampires.

Mercedes   We hang from the roofs of caves, upside down, like bats – and only come out about now, at dusk –

Braai   To drink the blood of English virgins.

Rebecca   Oh, then I'll be alright.

They laugh.

Braai   She has a sense of humour, Wizard. Well done.

Mercedes   She'd have to. To be with Wizard.

They laugh again.

Rebecca (*to* **Mercedes**)   So if this is your uncle's farm, where's his house?

Mercedes   Over the hill and far away.

Rebecca   Can't I sleep there tonight?

Mercedes   He isn't there. It's all locked up.

Rebecca   We could break in.

Mercedes   The staff have guns. We might get shot.

Rebecca   I keep forgetting. We're in Johannesburg. Everyone seems to get shot – eventually.

Moby   Don't say that.

Rebecca   Why not?

Moby   Wizard's dad died like that.

Rebecca   Sorry.

Wizard   Well, it does prove her point, doesn't it?

Silence.

Moby   My mom's a novelist.

Wizard   Unpublished.

Moby   She says we're still at the start of something. We're finding our – shape.

Mercedes (*indicating*)   On the other side of that hill, there's this – wasteland spreading. Barbed wire. Tin shacks. Rubbish dumps. Barking dogs. Burned-out trees. Gunshots at night.

Wizard   And people sweeping their yards. Feeding their chickens. Watching TV. Doing homework.

Braai   Shagging.

They laugh.

Wizard   When it grows dark, you'll see the city shining along the horizon. A dirty orange glow across the sky. But above us, there'll be like a thousand stars. Far more than you'd expect above a city. If you scratch the surface of this place, you soon find the wilderness underneath.

Braai   We haven't been tamed, you see.

Rebecca   And you call this place the Cradle of Humankind?

Mercedes   Ja.

Rebecca   Because of the old bones in the caves?

Mercedes   We're sitting above the world's oldest and richest graveyard.

Rebecca   So the bodies were – buried there?

Mercedes   Not exactly. The caves under us connect to the surface through these narrow shafts – these long sink holes, dropping down. For millions of years, our pre-human ancestors – along with a whole lot of other now extinct creatures – have been falling down these shafts and been preserved in the caves.

Rebecca   Creepy.

Mercedes   They say over a third of the world's pre-human fossils have been found in this valley. Here and somewhere in East Africa is where they think humans evolved.

Braai   Tell her about Little Foot.

Mercedes   Why?

Braai   He was this little guy. Famous. He was – what? A million years old?

Mercedes   Well over two million.

Braai   They found his skeleton in a cave not far from here.

Rebecca   And why's he famous?

Mercedes   Partly because he's so old. But also because his remains were like more or less intact when they found him. Usually, only bits survive. Fragments. Like a puzzle. Forensics at the site of a murder. They had to work out everything about him. How old he was, how he died, how –

Rebecca   And how did he die?

Mercedes   Well, he was around before we'd moved into the caves. Before we could even control fire. They think we lived in nests. In the trees. To get away from the predators. Some people argue that Little Foot fell down a shaft. That he was fleeing something. Some wild beast, or something.

Braai (*teasing her*)   But Mercedes doesn't believe that theory, does she?

Mercedes   Shut up, Braai.

Rebecca   So what happened?

Mercedes   Little Foot must've known where the shafts were, don't you think? This was his environment. He knew exactly where everything was. And there was no sign on him of an attack – like claws or teeth marks. I reckon he was put down there on purpose. Maybe chucked down a shaft and left to die.

Rebecca   How awful.

Wizard   I'm sure she's making half of this up.

Mercedes   When they found him, his head was rested on his arms. Like he was waiting to be saved.

Braai   But no one came for him, did they?

Mercedes   Well – obviously not.

Rebecca   Poor Little Foot. And we're going there tonight? To where they found him?

Mercedes   We're going to caves of our own.

Rebecca   And I've got no – choice?

Braai   If you want to stay with us, you'll have to come down with us.

Wizard (*to* **Rebecca**)   Don't worry. It should be fun.

Rebecca *and* **Wizard** *look at each other. She gives him a quick kiss.*

Moby   They've been doing that since I picked them up.

Braai   He doesn't mess about, does he?

Mercedes   Some would say he messes about far too much.

Moby *takes a photograph of* **Wizard** *and* **Rebecca**. *The camera flashes.*

Wizard   Can't you guys give us some peace?

Blackout.

Two

Darkness. The **Chorus** *emerge, a shadowy presence. They hold long sticks in one hand and breathe with one breath, like a large beast that has been running.*

The five are in a spacious underground cave. There is loud music. They are dancing, their torches flashing. The **Chorus** *surround them, providing a wall. Sometimes, a torch will cross a masked face – but the characters do not see the* **Chorus**. *Neon lamps light the space.*

Braai *is passing round beers.* **Rebecca** *gravitates towards* **Wizard**. **Wizard** *dances with her. They hold on to each other.* **Wizard** *then notices the others – watching them – and they separate. They all dance together for a while, in a united group. Then the music stops abruptly. The five characters collapse to the floor.*

The **Chorus** *close in on them during the following. There's a restless movement growing among them, a swaying from side to side. The* **Chorus** *speak as one animal, in unison.*

Chorus
Who are we? We are the old bones
Filled with the cave's darkness.
We breathe with one breath
And speak with one speech.
Can you feel the cave's darkness
Echoing through your bones?
Everywhere you go, we will follow.
Everything you are, we have been.
We invented your appetites.
We learned how to weep.
It was in these cave walls
That laughter was heard for the first time,
And murmurs of tenderness
As two bodies found each other,
A tongue without language
Touching a tongue without language
Inside the dripping rock.

Torches light up, probing the darkness. **Rebecca** *is lying in* **Wizard**'s *arms.*

Mercedes   This is the main cave. See that hole in the roof? I've always thought of it as an eye, looking down. I once witnessed the full moon flooding in. Everything looked like it was made of bone.

Rebecca   What's that smell?

Mercedes   Bat droppings.

Rebecca   Fantastic.

Braai   Hey, Wizard. Any panic attacks?

Wizard   I've never felt better, thanks.

Moby   You know, this reminds me . . .

Silence.

Isn't anyone going to ask me what it reminds me of?

Wizard   What does it remind you of, Moby?

Moby   That nightmare you used to have.

Wizard   What nightmare?

Moby   When you came here before you – maybe that's why you freaked out.

Rebecca   What was the nightmare about?

Moby   He was stuck in this cave. More like a series of caves, actually.

Rebecca (*to* **Wizard**)   And what happened?

Wizard   I can't remember. But I'd have to go from cave to cave. Sometimes I was running away from something. Sometimes I was looking for something. But I could never stop. Or rest. And I never arrived anywhere.

Rebecca   I wonder what it means.

Moby   Wizard tried to explain it once.

Wizard   I did?

Braai   It means he doesn't know his arse from his elbow.

Mercedes   He doesn't fit.

Rebecca   Does anyone?

Silence.

Wizard   So – this is it, isn't it?

Moby   What?

Wizard   The last time we'll all be alone together. By next month, I'll be at my Gran's.

Moby   But we'll keep in touch.

Silence.

Rebecca   Where's your grandmother's place?

Wizard   Sussex. In some village. But I'm going to art school in London. St Martins – or maybe Goldsmiths.

Braai   Fart school, more like.

Wizard   And Braai will be in the post office. Licking stamps.

Braai   I'm going to be a quantity surveyor.

Mercedes   I'm studying Law in Cape Town. Mainly on the beach.

Rebecca   What about you, Moby?

Moby   My mom works at the university here in Johannesburg. I have to go there so she gets a remission in fees. I'd like to be a psychologist.

Wizard   We can hook up, Rebecca. You know – in England?

Rebecca (*teasing him*)   Can we?

Silence.

Moby   My head's kind of – spinning.

Mercedes   It's the air down here.

Braai   The fermented bat droppings.

They listen to the silence.

Mercedes   Sometimes, you hear whispering in the dark. I don't know what it is. The wind above us. The blood in our ears.

Rebecca   I thought I heard something earlier. A murmur starting up.

Braai   It's the bat shit – that's all. It can make you mad.

Wizard   Don't worry, Rebecca. I'll protect you.

Rebecca   You will?

Mercedes   I wouldn't rely on him, if I were you.

Wizard   Thankfully, she isn't you.

He kisses **Rebecca***.*

Mercedes   Do you two have to slurp like that?

Wizard   Her mouth tastes nice.

Mercedes   It's disgusting.

Moby   Imagine if we had to live here for ever. Stay here for ever.

Braai   Surrounded by bat crap? No thanks.

Mercedes   During the day, if you shine a torch on the roof, you see hundreds of them hanging upside down. The bats. Like little packages. In brown wrapping paper. But they've already left for the night. They'll only come back at dawn. When we're asleep.

Torchlight probes the cavernous space. A camera flash goes off. It is **Moby** *– taking another photograph of* **Wizard***.*

Wizard   Moby, I wish you'd stop doing that. (*To* **Rebecca**.) He keeps taking photos of me and putting them on the internet.

Rebecca   Why?

Wizard   No idea.

Rebecca   Why, Moby?

Moby   Moby has no idea either.

Braai   Moby's weird. But we put up with him.

Rebecca   I think he's nice.

Wizard   You think everyone's nice.

Rebecca   Aren't they?

Wizard   They aren't who they think they are.

Rebecca   You're funny, Wizard.

Moby *takes another photograph of* **Wizard**.

Wizard   For God's sake, Moby. Can't you give me some space?

Moby   Moby gives you all the space you want.

Wizard   Believe me – you don't.

Moby   He does.

Wizard   I never even asked you to come here tonight.

Moby   Didn't you? But you were happy for me to steal my mom's car for the night. Was I supposed to just drop you off?

Wizard   I'm not going to argue about it.

Moby   I hope she doesn't notice.

Rebecca   I thought she was on holiday somewhere.

Moby   She'll see the mileage. She notices stuff like that.

Wizard   But Moby, I told you Mercedes didn't want you here.

Mercedes   Why did you do that?

Wizard   Because it's the truth.

Mercedes   Yes – we invited you. Not your entourage. (*To* **Rebecca**.) No offence, Rebecca.

Rebecca   Don't worry about it.

Mercedes (*back to* **Wizard**)   But, as usual, you couldn't do anything by yourself. You had to get Moby to drive you. And bring Rebecca – to make you feel good about yourself. (*To* **Rebecca**.) Sorry, Rebecca – no offence.

Rebecca (*becoming more offended*)   None taken.

Wizard   Why would I want to come here alone? You and Braai seem so – weird these days.

Mercedes   What are you talking about?

Wizard   Kind of hostile. Don't deny it.

Braai   I'm not hostile. I just think you're a two-bit runt.

Wizard   Don't call me a two-bit runt.

Braai   Well, you are a two-bit runt.

Moby   Please – let's not fight.

Braai   I like to fight. It makes me feel alive.

Mercedes   At least it's honest.

Wizard   Since when have you been honest?

Braai   Since when have you – runt?

Wizard   Caveman.

Braai   Runt.

Mercedes   You two – for God's sake.

Moby   Braai's just jealous.

Braai   Of what?

Wizard   Anyone with opposable thumbs.

Moby *laughs.*

Braai (*to* **Moby**)   I don't know what you're laughing at, Moby Dick.

Wizard   You, Braai.

Braai (*to* **Moby**)   You think he's your friend? He isn't your friend.

Wizard   Of course I am.

Braai   Then why do you call him a fag behind his back?

Wizard (*laughs*)   Don't worry, Moby. He's making this up.

Braai   Why would I make that up?

Wizard   I don't know. Why would you?

Braai (*to* **Moby**)   He says you're in love with him.

Moby   But I'm not.

Braai   That's why you took those photographs. Of him swimming and sleeping and all that. That's why you put them on the internet.

Moby (*to* **Wizard**)   Please tell me you didn't say that.

Wizard   I didn't.

Moby   I don't know what –

Wizard (*to* **Braai**)   Moby and I have been friends long before you even met me. You think he's going to believe you?

Braai   Admit it, Wizard – you even laugh at the way he laughs. The way he dresses. Walks and talks. Listen to what you call him: Moby the Dick, Moby's Dick, Whale Dick, Whale Willy, Free Willy, Willer Wonker, Wonky Willy.

Wizard   You also call him that.

Braai   But all those names come from you.

Moby (*believing* **Braai**)   I don't believe this.

Wizard   All Mercedes and me did was kiss, Braai. Alright? It was a kiss. Can't you get over it?

Braai   Never.

Wizard   We were drunk. We didn't know what we were doing!

Braai   You knew exactly what you were doing!

Mercedes   Stop shouting – both of you.

Braai   You kissed her because you could.

Mercedes   This is getting –

Wizard   She doesn't care about you. She never will. Even now she's waiting for something better to come up. And believe me, Braai, it will.

Braai   I'm going to break your neck.

Wizard   You'd need opposable thumbs for that.

Braai *attacks* **Wizard**. *They roll around on the ground, trying to hit at each other. Eventually,* **Braai** *pins* **Wizard** *down. He twists* **Wizard***'s arms back.*

The **Chorus** *slowly gather around during the following, their masked heads dimly visible, peering forward.*

Braai   Moby. My bag. In my bag. There's a rope.

Moby   What?

Braai   Get it.

Moby   Please –

Braai   Are you really going to stand up for him? Even now? When you know he calls you a freak?

Moby   He wouldn't.

Braai   Why not?

Moby   Because we're – the same.

Wizard   And what's that supposed to mean?

Moby   You know exactly what it means, Wizard.

Wizard   I'll never be anything like you.

Moby   We can be honest –

Wizard   Shut up, freak. Can't you get a life?

Braai (*to* **Moby**)   The rope.

Moby *goes to the bag and takes out the rope.*

Braai   Help me. Wrap it round his wrists.

Rebecca (*to* **Mercedes**)   Can't you do something!

Mercedes *says nothing. She is shining her torch on* **Wizard** *–
looking amused.* **Rebecca** *tries to push* **Braai** *away from* **Wizard**.
Braai *grabs hold of her and twists her arm back too.*

Braai   Come on, Moby. Help me here.

Moby *kneels down and starts to wrap the rope around* **Wizard***'s
wrists.*

Moby   I don't know why I'm doing this.

Braai   Of course you do. Make it tight.

Wizard   It hurts.

Braai   A double knot. So he can't get out.

Moby *knots the rope tightly, hurting* **Wizard**. *Then he and* **Braai**
stand back. **Braai** *still has* **Rebecca***'s arm twisted back.*
Mercedes *has continued to help by shining her torch on* **Wizard***'s
hands. Now she directs the bright beam between* **Braai** *and* **Wizard***'s
face.*

Rebecca   You're hurting me.

Braai   Am I?

Rebecca (*to* **Mercedes**)   Please tell him to let me go.

Mercedes   Don't worry. We're only having a laugh.

Rebecca   Well, no one's laughing.

Wizard   Braai, this is stupid.

Braai   I'd stop calling me that.

Rebecca   Brian – let me go!

Braai *pushes* **Rebecca** *roughly to the ground. Then he steps forward
and kicks* **Wizard** *hard in the stomach. The* **Chorus** *start humming
– distantly.*

Moby   What's that noise?

Braai   What?

Moby   That – listen.

They listen. **Rebecca** *is still on the floor.* **Wizard** *is groaning. The* **Chorus** *hum louder.*

Blackout.

Three

The **Chorus** *are still humming. They are holding more sticks – one in each hand – and standing in a wall, downstage. The sound they make is like that of disturbed bees. During this speech, the* **Chorus** *may suggest different caves or different creatures – depending on what* **Little Foot** *is experiencing. They can use their bodies and their sticks.*

Chorus 1
Under the mountain are thousands of caves.

Little Foot *appears. The* **Chorus** *gravitate towards him. They move in a slow dance, stamping and clashing their sticks.*

Chorus 2
In one cave, Little Foot finds a giant termite,
All amber, with bulging jaws and hairy limbs.

Chorus 1
In another, there's a bright blue kingfisher.
It shrieks and makes a stab at Little Foot.

Chorus 2
Some caves, Little Foot knows to avoid.

Chorus 1
From the wasps' cave, he hears the dry scuffling of paper.

Chorus 2
From the leopard's, he feels the dark blood pumping.

Chorus 1
From the adder's, there's the velvet flicker of black lightning.

Chorus 2
But none of the caves accepts Little Foot.
Even the cave of the hare blinds him with its moon whiteness.

Chorus 1
The cave of the hedgehog reeks with pine needles and urine.

Little Foot *keeps moving from cave to cave. He runs, limping, through the different caves, sometimes being tripped up by a body or a stick.*

Chorus 2
Some caves Little Foot has to swim through.
He swims naked with the dolphin until
It runs its razor teeth across his skin.

Chorus 1
He swims through the caves of many fish.

Chorus 2
Some fish are filled with rainbow fire.

Chorus 1
Others are bulbous and gloat like toads.

Chorus 2
Some caves have to be plunged into, like the otter's.
This is a cave rippling with golden-green light.
The otter's cave bubbles and is beautiful at its centre.

Chorus 1
But other caves are rotten at the core, overflowing
With maggots and rust-coloured slime.

Little Foot, *in an attempt to get away, suddenly finds that he can fly.*

Chorus 2
In some caves, Little Foot can fly.

Chorus 1
The owl's cave is grey with broken bones,
Regurgitated food and ash.

Chorus 2
Little Foot flies through it without breathing.

But the **Chorus** *hit him down again. He starts to move forward.*

Chorus 1
In one cave, a boy is painting his dreams against the wall.

Chorus 2
In another, two milky bodies meld and kiss.

Chorus 1
In one, a stooped figure comes towards him, a rock its fist.

The **Chorus** *hit him down again.* **Little Foot** *struggles but can no longer get up. The* **Chorus** *shuffle towards him, closing in.*

Chorus 2
Little Foot moves through the caves more and more quickly.
Until he's flashing through them.

Chorus 1
Flashing through the darkness and the light.

All
Until he wakes up screaming.

Little Foot *is lying with his head rested on his arm, his legs twisted back, no longer moving. The* **Chorus** *is humming, assembled around him. The sound grows in menace as they raise their sticks, and then it stops abruptly as the light cuts out.*

From here, the **Chorus** *will be like a large bull – stamping, snorting, grunting, poised to charge forward.*

Light grows to reveal the five human characters. **Wizard**'s *body is in the same position as* **Little Foot**'s. *The legs are twisted back. He groans and struggles.* **Rebecca**'s *hands have also been tied behind her back.* **Mercedes** *still holds a powerful torch, mostly directed at* **Wizard***, but sometimes turning towards whoever is speaking.*

The **Chorus** *are watching. Sometimes they moan or mutter, almost inaudibly.*

Braai (*to* **Wizard**)   We were supposed to be friends.

Rebecca   I'm going to scream.

Braai   Shut up.

Rebecca *screams.*

Moby   Maybe we should gag her.

Braai   Has anyone got an old sock?

Rebecca *screams again.* **Braai** *kicks* **Wizard**. *The* **Chorus** *groans.*

Rebecca   Help!

Braai *kicks* **Wizard** *again. The* **Chorus** *groans louder.*

Braai   Every time you make a sound, I'm going to hurt your boyfriend, alright?

Rebecca   Okay – I'll stop.

The **Chorus** *are whispering and muttering more excitedly now.*

Moby   There are other people. In the caves. Coming towards us.

Mercedes   Those are echoes. It's only us.

Moby   It's other people.

Rebecca   Help!

Mercedes   The walls are fragile. Don't shout.

Rebecca   For God's sake – let me go! Help!

Braai *walks towards her. He tears a strip off her blouse and stuffs it into her mouth.*

Braai (*to* **Rebecca**)   You need to calm yourself, alright?

Silence.

Wizard   So what are you going to do with us?

Braai *kicks* **Wizard** *again – very hard. The* **Chorus** *are growing increasingly restless. Some of them are enjoying this. Others appear to disapprove.*

Braai   I hate you, Wizard. You know that?

Wizard   Yes.

*The **Chorus** grow quieter during the following, peering in again, listening to every word.*

Moby   Wizard. Always the coolest guy in class. The best-looking. The one the girls talk about. He forgets how well I know him.

Wizard   You know nothing about me, Wonker.

Moby   Do you even know why he's called Wizard? I do. I came up with the name myself. I did it to help him out.

Wizard   You're just a freak.

Moby (*to* **Wizard**)   I was even there when you pissed yourself during that tennis lesson.

Wizard   What tennis lesson?

Moby   The teacher was showing us how to serve. We were huddled, in this group – and Wizard, he was too shy to ask to go to the toilet. I think we smelt the piss first. Or maybe we saw the dark puddle spreading. We all said – gross! And stood back, to watch the puddle – growing towards us.

Braai (*laughing*)   Sick.

Moby   They used to call him 'Whizz' – which meant to piss – or the 'Whizz Kid', because even then he was too clever for his own good. I can still see him standing there. Leaking. And the tears coming down his face.

Wizard   It wasn't –

Moby   Wizard pissed away his whole childhood. He wet his bed until he was at least fourteen. He once told me he was too afraid to go to sleep. In case he pissed himself. So he'd lie in bed all through the night, waiting for the first birds to sing. For a few years, he even started wearing nappies at school. The teacher told us when he was off sick once that he had a problem. A defective valve, or something. We mustn't tease him. But that only encouraged them. Soon everyone was laughing at him – to his face.

Wizard   You know it wasn't – like that.

Moby   Even after the nappies went, he'd cry for days at a time. For no reason. Even when the others had forgotten, and moved on to someone else.

Wizard   Ja – on to you.

Moby   His mother took him to a psychologist. The psychologist blamed her. Said he hadn't entered latency, or some such thing. So his mom took him away again. We all know Wizard's dad was killed when he was small. Murdered for his wallet. Shot in the back as he was running away – whimpering.

Wizard   You've got no right. To talk – like this.

Moby   Poor Wizard. He was a pathetic sight. A blubbering joke. I was the only one who stood up for him.

Braai   And what thanks did you get?

Moby   None at all.

Braai   He doesn't deserve your loyalty.

Wizard   You call this loyalty?

Moby   So I started to call him Wizard. To turn his name into something positive. With a bit of magic in it. But Wizard originally comes from Whizz. Whizz the nappy-wearer. He was a sight for sore eyes. A mommy's boy. A wet. A drip.

Braai   Ja, wetting himself wherever he went.

Wizard *is sobbing. They watch him – the two boys amused.*
Mercedes *is still shining her torch on them.*

Mercedes   I think we should leave him alone now.

Blackout.

Four

The **Chorus** *are dimly visible, holding sticks.* **Little Foot** *lies in light where we left him, his legs twisted back – at the centre of the group. During the following the* **Chorus** *will move around him, with growing speed and intensity. As the different* **Chorus** *members pass* **Little Foot***, they prod at him. He flails about, trying to defend himself. If he starts to get up, they knock him down. The image is like someone at a public stoning.*

Sometimes a Chorus member will try to defend **Little Foot***, but the Chorus member is always pushed aside or beaten back by a stick.*

Chorus 1
From the cave's darkness came fire.

All
From the cave's darkness came fire.

Chorus 2
A painting on the wall. A drum. A dance.

Chorus 3
An arrow. An axe. The first war.

Chorus 4
The wheel. The brick. The temple.

Chorus 5
The spectacle. The sacrifice. The slaughter of children.

Chorus 6
Books. Ships. Compasses.

Chorus 7
Flags. Fences. Locks.

Chorus 8
Silks and spices. Botanists and novelists.

Chorus 9
Canons and guns. Slaves and masters.

Chorus 10
Fields of wheat. Gold.

Chorus 2
A swastika. An atom bomb.

Chorus 3
A footprint on the moon.

All
War. A war to end all war.

Little Foot *is still.*

Chorus 1
From the cave's darkness came fire.

All
From the cave's darkness came fire.

Little Foot *lets out a terrible animal cry.*

Darkness.

Neon lamps light up to reveal **Mercedes** *and* **Rebecca** *alone.*
Rebecca *is tied up but no longer gagged. Nothing happens.*
Mercedes *lights a cigarette.*

Mercedes   You want some?

Rebecca   No.

Mercedes *puts the cigarette in* **Rebecca**'s *mouth anyway.*
Rebecca *is forced to inhale.*

Mercedes   You don't have to be scared of us.

Rebecca *says nothing.*

Mercedes   We aren't bad people.

Rebecca   If you were a good person, you wouldn't have to
tell me. I'd know.

Silence.

Mercedes   You don't know Wizard like we do.

Rebecca   Maybe I know him in a better way.

Silence.

Mercedes   They'll soon be back. They're probably best friends by now. Wizard would've talked them out of it. You should have more faith in us.

Their neon lamp flickers and goes out.

Mercedes   The battery's dead.

Rebecca   Do we have another lantern?

Mercedes   The boys took it.

Rebecca   What about your torch?

Mercedes   Moby has it. But we've got cigarettes. A lighter. And a phone that doesn't work.

Rebecca   Fantastic.

Mercedes *turns on her phone to give them some more light. They wait. There is a murmuring along the corridors. The* **Chorus** *is stirring – gathering themselves for another violent act.*

Rebecca   That sound gives me the creeps.

Mercedes   You'll get used to it.

They wait. The sound continues.

Mercedes   Why did you come here?

Rebecca   What?

Mercedes   To South Africa.

Rebecca *says nothing.*

Mercedes   All I want is to get away from this place.

Rebecca   I'm beginning to understand how you feel.

Mercedes   Wizard told me, you know. On the phone yesterday. All about your birth mom. He said you were adopted. And were coming here to meet her for the first time.

Silence.

Mercedes   Were you disappointed?

Rebecca   What?

Mercedes   In her. Your birth mother.

Rebecca   It's none of your business.

Mercedes   You can't have connected very well. Otherwise, why hang out with Wizard? Why come here? You should be together. Going out for pizzas, walking the dog, catching up for what you've like – lost.

Rebecca   What's lost is lost.

Mercedes   But are you at least pleased you came here?

Rebecca   Delighted. I'm tied up in a cave. Surrounded by bats and crazy people. I should've stayed in Milton Keynes.

Mercedes   Wizard said you were born here.

Rebecca   Did he?

Mercedes   Maybe it's fitting, then – that you should die here.

She laughs. The **Chorus** *make a moaning sound. There's another groan from far off, echoed and distorted.*

Rebecca   What was that?

Mercedes   Nothing. We have to keep talking.

Rebecca   What if they're hurting him?

Mercedes   We don't have any light. They could be anywhere. And it's a maze down here. Stop stressing. They're only trying to freak us out.

Rebecca   I wish you could try again with the rope.

Mercedes   When Braai comes back, he'll cut the knot.

Rebecca   You know he won't.

Silence.

Mercedes   When Little Foot was still alive, living in his nest, this whole area – it was still subtropical bush. Not grassland. There were like these giant and long-limbed hyenas. And sabre-toothed tigers, lions and leopards.

Rebecca   I'm not in the mood for one of your history lessons, Mercedes.

Mercedes   There was also this huge eagle that would carry children off – its claws going right through their skulls.

Silence.

Rebecca   You're still in love with him, aren't you?

Mercedes   Braai?

Rebecca   Wizard.

Mercedes *says nothing.*

Rebecca   When we were together last night. Wizard and me. He also told me all about you. About him and you. You didn't just kiss. That day when it was his birthday and you got drunk at his house. He said you did a whole lot more than that.

Silence.

Maybe when Brian comes back, I'll tell him. That you did it all weekend – and that you've done it again since. How would you like that?

Mercedes   Please don't. Braai can get a bit – unhinged.

Rebecca   Really? I hadn't noticed.

Mercedes   When he heard about that one kiss, he threatened to put a knife in Wizard's throat. I almost believed him. For a moment, even Wizard did.

They hear a scream.

Rebecca (*managing to get to her feet*)   That was Wizard. We have to help him. Wizard!

The **Chorus** *echo her.*

Chorus   Wizard, Wizard, Wizard.

Rebecca *starts stumbling forward in the darkness.* **Mercedes** *follows her, using her lighter for light.*

Rebecca   Wizard! We're over here! Wizard!

Chorus   Here, over here. Wizard.

Mercedes   Please stop yelling. It can be very fragile down here.

Rebecca   I don't believe that.

Chorus   Fragile. Leave that. Down here.

Rebecca   Help me, please!

Chorus   Please help. Please help.

A torch beam probes the darkness. **Mercedes** *reignites her lighter.*

Rebecca   What's that?

Mercedes   Them.

Rebecca   Hello?

The **Chorus** *is still present as an echoing whisper throughout the following.*

Rebecca   Who's that?

Moby   We are the living dead.

Chorus   Living dead.

Mercedes   Thank God.

Moby   Is that them?

Braai   Is that you?

Mercedes   We're over here.

Chorus   Over here.

Braai   Where are you going?

Mercedes   Our lamp went out.

Braai   Ours too. We only have this torch left.

Moby *and* **Braai** *are in the cave, but there's no sign of* **Wizard**.

Rebecca   Where's Wizard?

Braai   We let him go. He ran straight for the ladder and climbed up. He's probably halfway back to Jo'burg by now.

Mercedes (*to* **Moby**)   He came in your mom's car, didn't he?

Moby   He's got the keys in his pocket.

Mercedes   Typical.

Rebecca   You mean – he just left?

Braai   And he left you. (*Trying to frighten her.*) With us.

Chorus   With us.

Mercedes (*to* **Rebecca**)   You want to know what Wizard's like? That's what he's like.

Rebecca   I don't believe that.

Braai   It *is* hard to believe, isn't it?

Rebecca   It's you I don't believe. We heard something – like a cry in the dark.

Chorus   Cry in the dark.

The **Chorus** *become more agitated for a moment.*

Braai   That noise – it was only me and Moby. Fighting over the torch. I called it my flame-stick. Didn't I, Willy Wonker?

Moby (*quietly*)   We have to leave. Before our last torch conks out.

Mercedes   He's right.

Rebecca   But what about Wizard? I want to make sure he's alright.

Braai   Then you'd better come with us.

Chorus   Come with us.

The **Chorus** *are still muttering.*

Blackout.

Five

Wizard *is standing alone in a cave. He's still tied up. There's a single neon lamp. It flickers and then the light goes out.* **Wizard** *is plunged into complete darkness.*

Wizard   Hello?

The **Chorus** *start to emerge from different directions. They grow dimly visible, in silhouette. Their sticks are glowing or on fire.*

Through the following, the **Chorus** *remain quite still, forming the walls of the cave. They are barely audible – more of a whispered echo that fades away.*

Little Foot *enters. He is limping, broken, bloodied.*

Wizard   Who are you?

Little Foot *peers at him. He opens his mouth to speak. Again – he makes no sound. He sticks out his tongue. It is crimson with blood.*

Wizard   Little Foot?

The **Chorus** *are all around.* **Little Foot** *looks at them.*

Wizard   Are you afraid of them?

Little Foot *looks back at* **Wizard**.

Wizard   Please can you help?

Wizard *and* **Little Foot** *stare at each other.* **Little Foot** *lifts off his mask. There is a skull underneath. All of the* **Chorus** *members then lift off their masks. There are skulls underneath. Their tongues are all crimson with blood. The light grows around them.*

Blackout.

Rose-coloured light grows back gradually. It is dawn, at the campsite.
Mercedes, **Braai** *and* **Moby** *are sitting around the dead fireplace.*
During this scene, it will slowly get lighter – until it is a bright morning.

Braai   What are we going to do?

Moby   I'm trying to think.

Mercedes   Braai, this is completely your fault.

Braai   You were also part of it.

Moby   We have to come to a group decision.

Braai   It's her I'm worried about. Rebecca. We have to
shut her up.

Moby   God, Braai. Listen to yourself.

Braai   But she'll tell the truth.

Mercedes   And we won't?

Braai   People go to prison for this.

Moby   We'll say it was a game. A joke that went wrong.

Braai   She'll say it wasn't. She'll show them the rope. The
bruises on his stomach.

Moby   You didn't kick him hard enough for that.

Mercedes   Of course he did.

Braai   We'll say Rebecca's exaggerating. It'll be our word
against hers. Three against one.

Mercedes   They'll believe her. Not us. Remember how
you threatened to stab him during that biology lesson?
Everyone knows how much you hate him.

Braai   And everyone knows how much Moby – Moby will
back me up.

Moby   Come on, Braai. Haven't we done enough?

Braai   We have to stick together. Otherwise, we're lost.

Moby   Don't you see? That's exactly why we're lost.

Braai   We can blame – the air down there. We couldn't breathe. We went mad. It wasn't us.

Mercedes   It was. That was us.

Moby   We killed him.

Silence.

Mercedes   We don't know that.

Silence.

We don't even know he's down there. Maybe he's –

Rebecca *enters.*

Rebecca   The car's still there. Moby never left last night.

Silence.

That's good news, isn't it?

Moby   What's going to happen to us?

Rebecca   Can someone please explain what's going on?

Mercedes   Tell her, Braai.

Braai   Shut up. There's nothing to tell.

Moby   It wasn't like we said, Rebecca. We didn't let Wizard go in the –

Rebecca   You mean he's still . . . Then we have to go and get him.

Mercedes   We – can't.

Rebecca   Why not?

Braai   Can't you shut up?

Moby   Last night, when we were walking with him in the caves, we pushed him into this – chamber. When we went in there, he was gone. We looked everywhere. It was like he'd vanished.

Rebecca   Didn't you call him?

Moby   He didn't answer.

Rebecca   He must've hidden. And later escaped.

Mercedes   It was dark. He was tied up. How would he find the ladder – let alone climb it?

Moby   Near where he disappeared, we found a place where the ground had fallen in. As if there was another cave underneath. And its roof had collapsed.

Rebecca   You think he fell into another cave? Maybe he's alright. He probably lost consciousness. We could dig him out.

Mercedes   We'd have to get rescue teams for that.

Rebecca   Then what are we waiting for?

Mercedes   Wizard's got the keys. My bike's at my uncle's –

Rebecca   Then let's go. There must be a phone there.

Moby   We wanted to get our story – straight.

Braai   It was a joke, right? A joke that went wrong.

Rebecca   What?

Moby   No, Braai. You know you wanted him dead. For a moment, we all did.

Rebecca   I never did.

Mercedes   And neither did I.

Braai   Didn't you? Remember how you shone the torch.

Rebecca   Don't think for a moment I'm going to protect you. Any of you.

Mercedes   What about me? We shared a – smoke.

Braai   Shut up. Both of you. I'm trying to think.

Wizard *arrives.*

Wizard   Good morning, happy campers. Am I interrupting something?

They stare back at him with disbelief. **Wizard** *seems strangely euphoric.*

Rebecca   Wizard!

Rebecca *goes to him.*

Wizard (*to* **Rebecca**)   You look like you've seen a ghost.

Rebecca   Wizard. Thank God you're alright.

Wizard   My real name's Edward.

Rebecca   Edward?

Wizard   Horrible, isn't it?

Braai   Edward!

Wizard *ignores him.*

Rebecca   What happened?

Wizard (*to* **Rebecca**)   I don't know. I woke up in a cave. Some sound all around. Everywhere was light. I walked with – something. I thought it was Little Foot.

Rebecca   Little Foot?

Wizard   I suppose I imagined it.

Braai   Still the same old Wizard.

Wizard   He showed me where the ladder was.

Mercedes   And the ropes?

Wizard   I was sweating so much, they must've slipped off.

Silence.

When I came back, into the world, I saw the moon sinking down and the sun coming up. I climbed that hill and waited. Then I watched you – crawling out. So small you seemed, picking your way between the rocks. It was – kind of fascinating.

Mercedes   We thought something terrible had happened.

Wizard   Are we going to pretend it didn't?

Silence.

(*To* **Rebecca**.)   When I was down there, in the cave, I thought a lot about – us.

Braai   I think I'm going to be sick.

Mercedes   Shut up, Brian.

Rebecca *is smiling at* **Wizard**.

Wizard   Come. Let's get away from here.

Rebecca   Right now?

Wizard   Yes.

He and **Rebecca** *start to gather their things.*

Mercedes   Wizard?

Wizard *stops.*

Mercedes   I'm glad to see you again.

Wizard   Are you?

Silence.

When I was down there, I wondered. Did you two bring me here on purpose? Had you planned that – all along?

Mercedes   Of course not. We –

Braai *says nothing. He can't meet their gaze.*

Wizard   It doesn't matter. It happened – that's all. But I feel – different now. Better. Not so – ashamed.

Mercedes   People don't change that easily.

Wizard *looks at* **Rebecca**. *She smiles at him. He smiles back.* **Mercedes** *watches them.*

Wizard (*to the others*)   Goodbye.

No one speaks. **Wizard** *and* **Rebecca** *decide to leave.*

There is a long silence. **Mercedes**, **Moby** *and* **Braai** *don't look at each other.* **Moby** *fiddles with his camera. He photographs something random – like the dead fireplace.*

Moby   What are we going to do?

Braai   Go home, I suppose.

Moby   Do you mind if I come with? Wizard's got my keys.

Braai   We came on my bike.

Moby   Right.

Braai   I'll call you a cab, if you like.

Moby   Thanks.

Silence.

Braai   When I get home, I'm going straight to sleep. Aren't you tired?

Moby   Very tired. Yes.

Braai   Mercedes? You?

Mercedes *simply stares ahead.*

Braai   Mercedes?

Mercedes *says nothing.*

Braai   Mercedes?

Light fades back to darkness.

Little Foot

*Notes on rehearsal and staging, drawn from a workshop
with the writer held at the National Theatre, November 2011*

Background to the Play

Craig Higginson knew he wanted to write about the valley of
caves named the Cradle of Humankind, located around forty
miles outside Johannesburg. He explained that this is an area
of land rich in fossils, accounting for more than a third of the
hominid fossils in the entire world. One of the most famous
finds was the remains of an ancient ancestor hominin 2.5
million year old – *Australopithecus*, or Little Foot as he was
nicknamed. Also present in the world of the play is the chorus
of *Homo habilis* hominins who are our direct ancestors, but at
over one million years old less ancient than Little Foot.

It is believed that Little Foot was the inferior species of the
two and became extinct because unlike *Homo habilis* hominins
they couldn't control fire, use stone tools or adequately
defend themselves from predators. Both Little Foot and the
Chorus should appear very different from one another and
have contrasting qualities of movement.

Although the play features the inhabitants of the past it is set
in post-apartheid South Africa. The principal characters are a
new generation of South Africans even though they are part
of the violent landscape born out of a fascist society. Craig
stresses that although there is an inherited violence they are
aspiring to a new society, an almost American style of living
with a hunger for material goods.

The play is ultimately about our ancestry and our identity.
Craig wishes to undermine an audience's complacency and
encourage them to ask questions. His play isn't about the
pursuit of Darwinism, but about human nature itself. It's the
best and worst of our history, our desire for light and dark –
everything that makes us human.

Characters

Originally there was a sense that all the principal characters had a premeditated plan to attack Wizard. Craig's concern was that if the characters were too malevolent at the top of the play then the audience would be alienated from them. The wearing of masks and use of nicknames disguises the inner emotions and intentions of the characters, creating more mystery. Craig has suggested some concerns about costume and design in the text, but insists that they are just indications; he expects each production to evolve ideas and make the characters their own.

Due to the South African mentality and culture of violence, when something bad happens, it is sadly in the realm of reality for the young people living there. This has a bearing on the characters when they contemplate that Wizard may actually be seriously hurt or dead at the play's end and that they may be responsible for this.

It is crucial that the lack of parental figures is really felt: this helps to inform the close but compensatory relationships within the group. Rebecca has hinted that the reconciliation with her mother hasn't gone particularly well and her new relationship with Wizard occurs in the wake of this. Mercedes is also displaced and presently staying at her uncle's with no connection to her parents. She is also particularly sensitive about Wizard's father having been killed, and she pretends to not know about Rebecca's unsuccessful reunion with her mother until alone with her. There is a serious lack of role models, leaving the young people to fend for themselves and find their own moral compass.

Craig imagines that the main characters have been at high school together, except for Rebecca who is new and has known Wizard for a matter of days, as their mothers are friends. Moby's relationship with Wizard goes a little further back as they have been to junior school together too. There has been some kind of homosexual tryst between the two which Moby tries to share with the group in order to attack Wizard; he refers to it in his line: 'Because we're – the same' (p. 134).

Blackouts

Darkness should be the natural lighting state for this production, so that lights come up to present images or scenes to the audience. Craig recommends using cross-fades to redirect the audience's attention to another area of the stage or character, but warns that the audience shouldn't be left in darkness between scenes. This is a lazy way of indicating the passing of time and directors should look to the Chorus to denote these shifts. They can also transform from one image to another, divert attention and alter locations.

Casting Specifics

Although the race of each character is not specified, how the cast is composed will alter the production. Be sensitive to the South African history: casting choices will have meaning and implications that may be controversial and provoke the audience, but hopefully not in a stereotypical way. The use of 'Ja' is specific to South Africa and a useful signifier of the play's setting, but the natural accents of the cast may betray it, since Craig does not expect the characters to speak in South African accents.

Establish the world of the play for yourself. What is important is the distinction between the established groups of friends and the newcomer Rebecca. There is the possibility of using natural accents and a more regional accent for Rebecca or the reverse of this. Make decisions with confidence in dictating the rules of your production.

Jeremy Herrin, leader of the workshop, stressed the importance of consistency and suggested that there could be practised ways of saying certain words that serve to unite the group. When the audience observes something in direct contrast to what has gone before and with a completely different rhythm to everything else that has featured, it clearly reads as 'other'. Jeremy likens it to the playing of a king: the actor in that role doesn't play the high status – it is the job of everyone else to demonstrate that.

Exercises for Use in Rehearsals

Divide the company into equal-numbered groups and allocate each one a principal character. Then ask them to make four lists with the following headings:

- What the character says about themselves.
- What other characters say about them.
- Facts.
- Things the character says about others.

The purpose is to find out all the solid information the text provides about any given character and realise what remains unknown or unspecified. At this stage you have licence to invent and create details to complete the back-story for a character and make them three-dimensional.

You may also begin to determine the following:

- What is the character's objective (both in the entire play and from scene to scene)?
- Write the character's back-story.
- What does the character add to the play? What's their function?
- What are the challenges for the actor playing the character?
- Identify a clear point of change for that character.

THIS IS YOUR LIFE EXERCISE

Within their assigned character groups, one person takes a central position as that character, with everyone else forming a circle around them. Then one person from the circle edge comes in to join them, playing another character from the play that either appears, is mentioned or has been imagined in their created back-story. They then improvise a scene together, and when that scene is resolved another person from the edge of the circle steps in, and so it continues. Once these improvisations are exhausted the smaller groups should reconvene as a whole company again and feedback their improvisations, or bravely attempt new, unrehearsed ones.

Chorus Work

The Chorus should be given as much status as the principal characters. Yes, their role is to support the story, but they also offer a great theatrical opportunity. Within their moments of theatricality it's important to respect the story and the text itself. Jeremy recommends that the focus should be on getting the Chorus to work together as a unit.

Begin with the entire Chorus walking around the room breathing in and out collectively. Then as a group get them to stop, then begin walking together once there is a general consensus to do so. This exercise is all about feeling a common impulse. When the group gains confidence in stopping and walking as a group, add in the option of raising the right arm above the head and another option on exhaling to make a 'huh' sound.

This exercise can then evolve into the group walking as a close unit of people with those at the front leading. The group may then start to move sideways, feeling which direction to lead from. Chairs and other obstacles can also be placed in the room to test the group's physical awareness of the space as well as one another.

There is also the plateau exercise where a centre point is marked out on the ground. We imagine there is a plane balancing on that central marker and then, beginning with just two actors stepping on to it, the task is for them to maintain the balance. One by one each remaining member of the group joins them on the plane, but every step taken could potentially knock everything off balance and so needs to be treated with caution.

If the actors can work effectively on this exercise, they can move on to creating arresting shapes and images. Craig is wary of the temptation to move in an illustrative way where the Chorus speak and then immediately create a literal version of that speech. He encourages more abstract ways of moving, and Jeremy suggests splitting the company into smaller groups and getting them to think of three words which they associate with the play. Then from those three words the groups create three accompanying images and concentrate on making the transitions between them as clear as the words themselves.

If they were to be paused midway into the next word, the audience should still get an idea of the word that they were travelling into. The rest of the group should watch and try to guess the original words chosen. To take the exercises further, encourage the groups to distort their chosen images and attempt to make them abstract.

Revert to asking the group to work around the space as individuals, but this time ask them collectively to say 'Us', working on the sharpness of the start and end of the word. Integrate this with moments of walking and pausing as a group, encouraging the actors to form a tableau at a time of their choosing as an added option.

When working on text as a Chorus, establishing a rhythm and identifying hot words will really help to add flavour and exciting dynamics. Interpret the words as a group to ensure there is a consistency of attitude line by line. It's really important to counter bad Chorus traditions and avoid sounding like monotonous robots. Approach all Chorus text as if it was a monologue – you don't want to prepare the audience for a long speech. Each line should feel spontaneous.

Be specific and allocate natural inflections for the cast members. In the words of Jeremy Herrin, 'Throw jazz at it!' and make bold decisions like delivering certain lines on the offbeat. Don't be afraid to establish rhythms, lulling the audience into a false sense of security only to subvert it later . Another piece of advice is to see the images being talked about. Precision will only be achieved with practice, but good vocal warm-ups will make a huge difference.

Make the Chorus specific to the group of actors, as there is freedom within the written text and plenty of scope to split lines, add echoing, percussion and general soundscapes. In fact each mention of music is open for interpretation, and the music does not have to be naturalistic in any way. Similarly the representation of Little Foot should be experimented with. Craig encourages directors and designers to think inventively about each sighting of Little Foot. Each appearance could be in a different form – e.g., in shadow, as a puppet, an actor, a ray of light, a voice. Refresh and alternate the image and stay ahead of the audience's expectations.

From a workshop led by Jeremy Herrin,
with notes by Monique Sterling

Prince of Denmark

Michael Lesslie

Characters
in order of appearance

Laertes
Reynaldo
Osric
Ophelia
Hamlet
Rosencrantz
Guildenstern
Horatio
Player
Marcellus
Several Courtiers
Several Guards
Several Players

All the characters are in their late teens and can be played by either male or female actors.

Setting

Various locations in Elsinore in the same temporal and political setting as Shakespeare's *Hamlet*, medieval Denmark focalised through Elizabethan England.

Dialogue

' – ' indicates that the line is to be interrupted.
' . . . ' indicates that the line trails off.

Scene One

Early evening, the underbelly of Elsinore. Clanging sounds from the forges nearby, the fervour of preparation for war. **Laertes** *bursts bitterly on to the stage, quickly followed by* **Reynaldo**, *wary and watchful. They both speak in urgent whispers.*

Laertes   But when was this?

Reynaldo   Last night, my lord. And every night for the last –

Laertes   From Hamlet, you say?

Reynaldo   My lord, they bear the king's seal. Either his father is sending –

Laertes   But have you read them, Reynaldo? Any of them, have you –

Reynaldo   My lord! My duty to your father –

Laertes (*firmly*)   I said have you read them? This is a matter of state.

Reynaldo *nods.*

Reynaldo   Poetry, my lord.

Laertes   Oh God.

Reynaldo   Some dozen lines apiece. Confused, mired in paradox –

Laertes   And her replies?

Reynaldo   My lord, she proves elusive.

Laertes   This cannot come to good, Reynaldo. I cherish my sister more than the mortal earth, but she is a girl, and as such, she cannot be trusted to vouchsafe her own fortune. As for Hamlet . . . our army prepares for England and its prince writes verse? No. We do not elevate great ones to have them meddle in our affairs, they are above us to serve us, gilt pinions to our iron wheels. Should the pinion turn against the teeth that hold it, the whole machine will crack. Bring me my sister. And look you, be secret.

Bang! **Laertes** *and* **Reynaldo** *spin round, drawing swords. A bumbling, be-hatted* **Fool** *tumbles onstage.*

Reynaldo   Who goes there?

Laertes   Stand and unfold yourself!

Fool   If you desire my formal nomination –

Laertes (*together with* **Reynaldo**)   Osric.

Reynaldo (*together with* **Laertes**)   Osric.

Osric   Trepidatious woe, Laertes! Your sister is over-suitored! She spurns my cupidinous epistles with the obstinacy of –

Reynaldo (*aside*)   My lord, I will to your command.

Laertes (*aside*)   Be quick. Please.

Exit **Reynaldo**.

Osric   What's to be done? The fair Ophelia!

Laertes   Take heart, my lord. You have land, wit, charm . . . land . . . .

Osric   But not enough! I need not remind you of the promise you've made, Laertes. Thanks to my family, your father is newly lodged in court, servant to the king's brother. One day, you could be steward.

Laertes   This is democracy. I could be king.

Osric   Not if you betray those who support you. Your tenure in Elsinore is still vulnerable, you know. You promised me her favour.

Laertes   And I shall deliver it, I swear. Indeed, I believe that servant there may just now have disclosed to me the source of my sister's disdain.

Osric   Disdain?

Laertes   Distemper. She is coming here presently. Leave us a while, I will dig her to her depths. Woman's affection runs differently to ours, Osric. It is impractical, chaos in miniature, unmannable till it choose to be manned. But Ophelia is a sister first, a girl second. She knows her duty. (*Glancing offstage.*) Quick, here she comes. Meet me on the battlements this evening, the first watch, I'll tell all. Now go!

Osric *bows elaborately and hurries offstage as* **Ophelia** *hurries on from a separate entrance, with* **Reynaldo** *following close behind.*

Ophelia   My God, Laertes, was that Osric?

Laertes   A paean to manhood if I ever saw one.

Ophelia   A talking mushroom! I never knew a man with such a capacity to repulse and bore at the same time, it's like being tortured with wet fruit. Honestly, I don't understand why you still speak to him.

Laertes   His father is the richest landowner in Denmark. Were it not for his kindness, we would still be in the city, futureless and –

Ophelia   Alive! I am bored, Laertes! Father is established, you have a hope in court, and what do I do? Sew and wait.

Laertes   You're a lady in waiting. That's your job.

Ophelia   Anticipation. Hardly a future worth looking forward to.

Laertes   Our mother would have been proud, Ophelia. To see you here.

Ophelia *hesitates.* **Laertes** *smiles.*

Laertes   You look so like her, you know.

Ophelia *looks down. Gently, he strokes her face.*

Laertes (*quietly*)   How much do you love me, Ophelia?

Ophelia   I cannot say.

Laertes   Why not?

Ophelia   Because love can't be put into words, Laertes.

Laertes   Not even poetry?

Ophelia *looks up.*

Laertes   It lies in action, then. In loyalty.

He holds her stare.

Why didn't you tell me? You're my sister.

Ophelia   I'm me.

Laertes   Part of a greater whole to which you are subject.
Don't be deluded into whorish aperture by a slip of high
attention, Ophelia, Hamlet's blood and flesh, same as the rest
of us.

Ophelia   He's a prince.

Laertes   And we are low! All we have is our name. If you
open your legs to this degenerate prince, you'll ruin us all.

Ophelia   He loves me.

Laertes   You haven't even spoken to him! You've never
been alone in a room!

Ophelia   Not yet.

Beat.

Laertes   When? Tell me.

Ophelia   There's a play tonight for the Norwegian king.
We're going to meet afterwards, by the third watch.

Laertes   Where?

Ophelia   In my chamber.

Laertes   You can't, Ophelia!

Ophelia   I have to! He's the prince, it's treason if I don't
agree.

Laertes   It's treason if you do, to a father, to a family who loves you.

Ophelia   Who expect me to wait for the rest of my life? I could be queen.

Laertes   Are you mad?

Ophelia   Not a jot. I saw something last night, Laertes. During the entertainments, I stole out of court to take some respite and walked down to the brook.

Laertes   The brook? Ophelia –

Ophelia   There was someone there. In the water, a woman, naked, white as the moon.

Laertes   She's dead, Ophelia. You have to let go.

Ophelia   No, listen. I hung back behind the trees, my breath freezing in the air, and . . . I watched. She was cleaning herself, Laertes. As though she were guilty.

Laertes   So? It was a drab, what's that got to do with –

Ophelia   It was the queen.

Beat.

Laertes   The queen was in her chamber last night. I heard Father tell the king.

Ophelia   No. I went to her chamber straight afterwards, it was empty.

Laertes   But Father swore. Why would he lie?

Ophelia   I don't know. He's been confused. I'm worried, Laertes. I have to tell Hamlet.

Laertes   Why?

Ophelia   What if she hurts herself? If we warn him, he might be grateful. Besides, I can't back out now, I've sent the reply.

Laertes *thinks.*

Laertes   How does he receive your letters?

Ophelia   A servant passes them to one of his friends. Guildenstern, I think.

Laertes   Not Rosencrantz?

Ophelia   I can't tell. The lanky one.

Laertes   Reynaldo, come. I shall write out a letter in Ophelia's hand. Will you deliver it to this Guildenstern?

Reynaldo   I shall, my lord.

Ophelia   But –

Laertes   You are a girl, Ophelia. You must remember that the cost of your giddy passions is a sacrifice of judgement from which we men are thankfully exempt. You are to meet him outside the castle walls, somewhere you won't be seen.

Ophelia   Where?

Laertes   The shelter on the cliff.

Ophelia   But the winds there are freezing!

Laertes   Not if you're wrapped up. You must trust me, Ophelia, for our mother's sake. All I ask is discretion.

Ophelia *nods.* **Laertes** *kisses her forehead.*

Laertes   Reynaldo, quick, we don't have much time.

Laertes *hurries offstage.* **Reynaldo** *starts to follow.*

Ophelia   Wait.

Reynaldo *turns back.*

Ophelia   I asked you not to tell anyone. (*Beat.*) Watch him for me, Reynaldo.

Reynaldo   Why should I take orders from a girl?

Ophelia   Because as a girl I have feminine means of payment. Tell me what he writes, please.

Reynaldo *smiles and bows.*

Reynaldo   My lady.

Exeunt.

Scene Two

Early evening, the halls of court. **Hamlet** *bursts on to the stage, impassioned and furious, followed anxiously by* **Rosencrantz** *and* **Guildenstern.** *Behind them, teams of* **Youths** [*or* **Courtiers**] *practise ceremonial fencing in preparation for the evening's festivities. One* **Bookish Fencer** *is particularly inept.*

Hamlet   God's blood, what a fool!

Guildenstern   Quiet, my liege!

Rosencrantz   My good lord, please! The very walls here are ears –

Hamlet   What a kingdom, so taken with hearing that it forgets how to see! Why are you afraid of him, friends? He's just a man!

Rosencrantz   To you, my lord, he may be a man. To Guildenstern and I, he is your father.

Guildenstern   The king.

Rosencrantz   You walk with a freer rein than we do.

Hamlet   Then let me be its sovereign! Surely each of us has the right to break off our parents' chains, Rosencrantz, be we prince or nobleman or anything else on the earth?

Rosencrantz   So long as we know the consequences of that break.

Guildenstern   In your case, sire, Wittenberg.

Hamlet   Go to! My father won't send me away, my mother wouldn't let him.

Guildenstern My lord, I have never seen him so
distempered. Your outburst before the court just now was
indecorous, to say the least.

Hamlet Then perhaps in its ugliness it struck of truth!
Decorum is the anaesthetic of our age, Guildenstern, a paint
that distorts the thing it coats until every object is
unrecognisable as its own being. I meant what I said before
the king, and it is right that those who elect him hear of his
failings.

Rosencrantz But what failings, my lord, has he
committed?

Guildenstern Look how humbly the Norwegian king
bows. Surely such servility signifies honour, not debasement?

Hamlet Honour?

Guildenstern Did you not see?

Hamlet No, Guildenstern, I didn't. For whilst that slave-
king of Norway toadied himself to his brother's killer, I could
not tear my eyes from the rear of the room, where young
Fortinbras, silent, aflame, stood strewing both his uncle's
servitude and my father's honour with the same wrathful
loathing. My father murdered his on the day I was born,
friends. As my mother risked very death to bring me into this
world, our king was in another country, winning a bet on
which he'd wagered the whole nation's future. All for your
honour, Guildenstern. And after he had slain old Fortinbras
and set up this substitute Norway in his place, did he return
to his country to celebrate with his newborn son and birth-
torn queen? No. He continues on to Poland, where thousands
more sons and fathers and uncles are made to die for his
honour. And now, finally, after more than a decade of war,
when even his own old bones rebel against his bellicose
command, does he come home? Of course he doesn't. As
though Denmark were burning purgatory, he immediately
announces a campaign for England, an island of drunks and
drabbers so deluded by the sight of their own borders that

they think they rule the world, which in fact cares no more for them than the warm beer and cold conversation they produce. Again, all for honour. The more countries my father conquers in the name of today's honour, friends, the more enemies he bequeaths us in the future, enemies like young Fortinbras, charged with the fury of filial vengeance. That's far more dangerous than any impulse for honour.

Guildenstern   So what would you suggest, my lord?

Hamlet   That he take a leaf from my uncle's book. Claudius. As much a friend to Denmark as King Hamlet is scourge of the rest of the world. The only man who stayed behind to hold my mother's hand as she screamed for assurance. One who commands the love of the country he lives in, capable of making the whole populace laugh with a single smile. What does foreign victory matter when the people you fight for don't recognise your face, or the sound of your voice? Where was Claudius during last night's warlike entertainments? Walking outside the castle walls, no doubt warming the hearts of people that love him. That, friends, is a true king.

Rosencrantz   Be careful what you advise, my lord. If your father does send you away, he'll have no choice but to depose you as his most immediate heir and nominate Claudius in your place. Not only will you lose your chance of becoming king, you'll be stuck in Wittenberg.

Guildenstern   And moreover, we'll be stuck with you.

Rosencrantz   And Wittenberg is dull! A place for monks and midwives, not princes.

Guildenstern   Or their noble friends.

Hamlet   So much the better! Were it not for the fair Ophelia, friends, I would dearly desire such an exile. For in Wittenberg, we may no longer be noble. There we may be taken for what we are, separated from role and royalty. Why, a peasant may approach us and shake our hands as equals, made honest by his ignorance.

Rosencrantz   I fail to see the attraction.

Hamlet *suddenly yells and runs at the* **Bookish Fencer**, *who backs away, hesitant.* **Hamlet** *laughs and turns back to* **Rosencrantz** *and* **Guildenstern**.

Hamlet   Real life, Rosencrantz! In Wittenberg, this fencer here would have run me through without a moment's hesitation as though I were just another man. How can we know what we're capable of when we're shackled by such general licence? We only discover our true selves when our whole future lies at stake.

Enter **Reynaldo**.

Hamlet   But enough of this, here's matter more compelling. How did she receive my last poem, Reynaldo? Did she smile when she read it? Or did she frown? Speak freely, such signs are all a lover may live by.

Reynaldo   My lord, I cannot tell. But sure, her haste in writing this reply suggests a reciprocation of the sentiment laid out therein.

Reynaldo *holds out a letter.* **Hamlet** *takes it.*

Hamlet   Oh, Ophelia! There is our true model of freedom, friends! A spirit of fire, unbridled by the demands of the world! Pure energy straining at the body that holds it.

Reynaldo   Indeed, my lord.

Hamlet *reads*.

Hamlet   The cliffs? Why would she want to meet there? The winds alone might throw us over the edge.

Reynaldo   I believe for privacy, my lord.

Guildenstern   Oh ho! It seems your virginal target may not be as innocent as you presumed.

Hamlet   Quiet.

Rosencrantz   Her family is newly come to court, my lord. You don't know what sordidness these city girls contain.

Hamlet   She is pure, Rosencrantz, I'll wager my life. (*To* **Reynaldo**.) Tell her I'll meet her wherever she desires.

Guildenstern   My lord, you cannot mean it?

Hamlet   I can and do.

Rosencrantz   But you heard the king. After your outburst in court, he ordered that you be confined to your chamber as soon as the entertainments are done. You'll never be able to escape, let alone to board that servant girl.

Hamlet   I had forgotten. Let me think, let me think. (*Getting an idea.*) Ah! A troupe of tragedians are playing this afternoon, are they not?

Guildenstern   They are, my lord. They've come from the city to perform Dido and Aeneas.

Hamlet   I've seen these players before. One of them is my age, the one who plays the prince. Reynaldo, bring him here.

Exit **Reynaldo**.

Hamlet   Good friends, I serve a greater master than the king. The heavens have dictated that men be free to love and live in full pleasure of their gifts. Ophelia is one such gift, celestial light fallen to earth, and in the eye of the Lord I am as much man as prince. I will meet her tonight whether my father likes it or not.

Enter **Reynaldo** *with a* **Player**.

Hamlet   How goes it, noble friend?

Player   Well, my lord. I'm a little nervous, perhaps.

Hamlet   Don't be. The audience you perform for today are courtly, so stunted by decorum they'll clap at your every pause, no matter what you might have said before it. Tell them they're murderers and villains and they'll rise to their feet in rapturous approbation.

Player   I wouldn't be so sure, my lord. In the city last week we performed a tale of a husband's murder, and in the middle of the villainous speech, a new widow leapt up in the stalls, white as bone, and proclaimed the play her exact biography. She was arrested on the spot.

Hamlet   It doesn't surprise me. True-played fiction is far more incisive than any accusation of fact, for the malleable tale will turn a guilty imagination on itself, thus destroying its last hope of defence. But look you, here's matter more urgent. After the play tonight, would you be willing to perform a further role? It must be secret, do you understand?

Player   Sire?

Hamlet   The king has ordered that I am to be interred in my chamber after the play. Matters of the heart compel me to defy him. If you consent to my plan, after the performance, I shall visit you in your dressing chamber on the pretence of congratulation. Then, in secret, we shall exchange clothes, and in my guise you will hurry to my chamber as though I were willingly submitting to imprisonment. Once there, spend the evening as you will, but be sure to try the floorboards. These two loyal friends of mine will stand guard and attest that your footfalls proclaim my presence within, whilst I hurry away to my loving enterprise.

Guildenstern   But my lord –

Hamlet   I'll return by cover of dark, when the castle's corridors are all asleep. Forgive the secrecy of my mission, friend, but I cannot tell you more lest I ruin a good lady's name. Do you understand?

Player   The role of prince is one I am used to, sire. I will not let you down.

Hamlet   Thank you. Now quick, to your rehearsals, lest your absence provoke suspicion.

Exit the **Player***.*

Rosencrantz   My lord, as your servant, I tell that you this is unwise.

Hamlet   And as your schoolmate I beg you to help. You will conspire with me in my love, will you not, old friends?

Rosencrantz *and* **Guildenstern** *exchange glances.*

Guildenstern   My lord, we shall.

Hamlet   But swear it.

Rosencrantz   Why do you want us to swear, my lord? We have agreed already.

Hamlet   Indulge me.

Rosencrantz (*together with* **Guildenstern**)   We swear.

Guildenstern (*together with* **Rosencrantz**)   We swear.

Hamlet   A quadruple promise, each on behalf of the other. Now come, let's test this plan further.

Exit **Hamlet, Rosencrantz** *and* **Guildenstern. Reynaldo** *watches them go. As he does, the* **Bookish Fencer** *approaches him.*

Bookish Fencer   You were ordered to return that letter minutes ago. But you stayed. You listened.

Reynaldo (*surprised*)   So did you, it seems. This is politics, Horatio, not philosophy. Go back to your books.

Exit **Reynaldo. Bookish Fencer** (**Horatio**) *watches him go.*

Scene Three

Night, the battlements. Enter **Laertes** *alone, seething.*

Laertes   Disguised as a player, he says? So, not content with debasing my sister, with ruining my family and stealing from me the only being precious enough to sustain a belief in the gods, this lecher lord is yet so embarrassed by his lust that he must carry out our humiliation in disguise! As a tawdry player! God's blood, his shame confirms his base intentions!

This is no prince, this is a tyrant, one who views his subjects as fairground rides for venal entertainment! If he knew the nobility of soul my mother contained he would weep before he dared whisper to her youthful image, let alone board it, and yet this whore-maker will be king! Taken by the whole nation as the measure of a man! What then will happen to Denmark? I have seen him in court, glowering and mumbling to himself as though his troubles would defy the comprehension of mortal men, and we imitate our monarchs as pets their masters. Thus will Denmark be reduced to a nation of cowards, brooding solipsists so paralysed by soliloquy as to be blind to their social duty. And all for nothing. For convention. Why must this player be king? Why Hamlet and not another? My natural capacities are as strong as his. Stronger, my friends might say. Is it man's duty to accept the future handed down to him, or to arm himself against the will of fate and carve out his own fortune? What would happen, say, if Hamlet were removed from Denmark? If he were to fall from the cliffs this very night? Then the direct succession would be interrupted, and the king's brother would become heir. Claudius, my father's lord. And sure, I have seen that when the presumed line is thus disturbed, men's minds are opened to the true possibility of their limitless election. A meritocracy may be born. Then, who is to say that a peasant could not be king? Who is to say not Laertes? And would Denmark be better off? All for a push! I must act. Hamlet, make your peace. Your audience tonight will pay you handsomely for your player's costume. (*Glancing offstage.*) But hold, my tongue, for here comes a weapon in my plan.

Enter **Osric**.

Osric   Laertes, what news? Did you discover the source of your sister's sang-froid?

Laertes   Do you think me honest, Osric?

Osric   I think you a gentlemen.

Laertes   Then my gentility compels me to be abrupt. You have a rival.

Osric   A rival?

Laertes   One of the players newly come to court, an old passion of my sister's from our city days. In faith, he is a robust man, a fulsome specimen of virility.

Osric   Then I am lost!

Laertes   Is that all? Is that all you will summon for the love of my sister? Why, I was going to suggest a route to your usurpation of this adulterer, but it seems Ophelia was right. You do lack the stomach of a man.

Osric   She said that?

Laertes   That was the prelude.

Osric   Go on.

Laertes   She said that you were a handsome fellow –

Osric   True enough.

Laertes   But a coward. A spineless, mewling babe too timid to beg his mother for milk, let alone to defend a young girl's honour. Sure, she said, she would give herself to you in the beat of a heart if she saw proof of the manly fire I assured her raged within. But now I see she was right. I shouldn't have bothered devising our plan at all.

Osric   What plan?

Laertes   No, it is of no use.

Osric   I pray you, Laertes, tell me!

Laertes   How can I, in good conscience? When I've seen how cheaply you esteem her?

Osric   I promise you, I love her more than all the jewels in Denmark! More than all the dirt in my fields!

Laertes   Enough to fight for her?

Osric   Of course!

Laertes   Enough to kill?

Osric   Why would I have to kill?

Laertes   This player plans to board her tonight, Osric. If he succeeds, all is lost. For, sure, once a woman has tasted of an actor's passion, there is no return.

Osric   Then what's to be done?

Laertes   My sister thinks you a tadpole. A strapling. What better way to disprove her than with a display of might? Eliminate your rival, Osric.

Osric   Eliminate him?

Laertes   If you are a man. Listen close. Out of our dear friendship, I have contrived that my sister will meet this lover in a secluded shelter on the cliff. We shall go there tonight, you and I, and lie in wait. When you see him press her innocent flesh, rush forward and with a blood-stilling cry of, 'I will protect you!', send this paddling player to his doom. Thus will you in one swoop claim your manhood and my sister's affection.

Osric   But what if he sees us, Laertes? What if he turns and fights? I have no skill in combat.

Laertes   You have your brain, Osric. And so the element of surprise.

Osric   That's true. My brain is a formidable weapon.

Laertes   And besides, you have heard of my skill with the rapier?

Osric   Who hasn't? You are given out as the light of Denmark.

Laertes   Well then. I shall be waiting in the shadows, ready to protect you should any mischance occur.

Osric   But this is murder, Laertes. If we're caught, we could be put to death.

Laertes   Not if the deed is performed with a noble motivation. And what more noble than protecting an angel from her defilement? You shall profess to the judge that you found her locked in struggle with the amorous youth. She won't contest your claim, it would only serve to dishonour her. Thus you shall become at once hero to the court, creditor to your love, and my dear brother. A crime of impunity, Osric, for my sister's heart. You only have one chance. What do you say?

Osric   In faith, I do not know. But sure, Laertes, you are a good friend.

Laertes   Then why hesitate further? Go, quick, and get you ready. We shall meet at the cliffs by second watch, when I shall give you further reason for our bloodless endeavour.

Exit **Osric**.

Laertes   So be it. I can no more allow this buffoon to have my sister than I can the carnal prince. And he has a claim on me in court, which his arrest will eradicate. It is not on my conscience. The lives of these lords will clear the way for the country's rightful future, and my own just ascension. If the cost of greatness is others' blood, I am willing to pay. Until tonight.

Exit **Laertes**.

Scene Four

Night, the halls of court. Enter **Ophelia** *and* **Reynaldo**.

Ophelia   And Laertes knows of this?

Reynaldo   My lady, I told him of the intended disguise. What more he has planned I cannot gather.

Ophelia   'Tis well. My brother is a faithful and a decent friend, and my girlish ignorance demands that I put trust in his more sound judgement. Tell Laertes I will meet Hamlet on the cliffs, as we agreed.

Exit **Reynaldo**.

Ophelia   These scheming boys! In such courtly company I don't even trust my own blood. What's to be done? (*She thinks. Getting an idea.*) Ah! What ho, Horatio?

Enter **Horatio**.

Horatio, you are an honest man, are you not?

Horatio   As far as this world might allow.

Ophelia   What think you of Reynaldo, then? Is he to be trusted?

Horatio *hesitates*.

Horatio   He is as trustworthy as any courtier in Denmark, my lady.

Ophelia   Your hesitation speaks bibles. Any nobleman would have been smooth as ice. You can be relied upon, Horatio, I know it. Will you take an urgent message from me to the Lord Hamlet? But do not write it down, I pray you. It seems that in Denmark words thus made flesh can become executioners to their own authors.

Horatio   What would you have me say?

Ophelia   Tell him to meet me at the same hour, but by the brook under the castle walls. There's a willow there that my mother loved. I shall wait for him under its shade.

Horatio *hesitates*.

Horatio   Madam, you know that in this election of Hamlet over your own blood, you are risking great misfortune.

Ophelia   Good Horatio, if I cannot act on my instinct of love, what kind of a person will I be? My brother says that to live is to carve for oneself. Is life then the preserve of men? No, in such boyish times, we women must be loyal to ourselves before we may be loyal to others. I shall meet with the Lord Hamlet, let the consequences fall.

Trumpets sound offstage.

The play's about to start, we must go in. Oh, I am so nervous, Horatio! What if I disappoint him?

Horatio   My lady, I have never seen a more suited pairing.

Ophelia   Thank you, honest friend. Now quick, take him the message.

Exeunt **Horatio** *and* **Ophelia** *in separate directions.*

Scene Five

Night, the court. Enter **Hamlet** *and* **Horatio**, *conferring.*

Hamlet   The brook, you say? These changing messages bespeak treachery.

Horatio   You must trust me, my lord.

Hamlet   Why?

Horatio   Because I am a scholar. One whose value is set in his own mind, not a prince's advancement. As my brain is my Elsinore, I have nothing to gain from you but the approval of my own conscience.

Hamlet (*surprised*)   No one speaks to me like that.

Horatio   The more reason to believe me. But keep this amendment to yourself, my lord. There are others in your company whose interests open them to more promiscuous loyalty.

Enter **Rosencrantz** *and* **Guildenstern**.

Guildenstern   Bookworm! Stop bothering the prince!

Rosencrantz   The audience is returning, my lord, we must take our seats.

Hamlet   Is that an order, Rosencrantz?

Rosencrantz *and* **Guildenstern** *laugh uproariously.*

Guildenstern (*pointing to one side of* **Hamlet**)   I'll sit here, my lord.

Rosencrantz (*pointing to other side*)   And I here.

Trumpets sound. Enter **Laertes**, **Osric**, **Ophelia**, **Reynaldo**, **Courtiers** *and* **Guards**, *including* **Marcellus**. **Marcellus** *steps forward, militaristic.*

Marcellus   My lords, ladies and gentlemen, the rulers of Norway, and the King of Denmark!

Trumpets sound and **Marcellus** *gestures to the audience. All save* **Hamlet** *turn and bow, but* **Hamlet** *remains upright, looking around at the obsequious nobles. They all straighten and sit.*

Guildenstern   Such a noble carriage!

Rosencrantz   Such a royal bearing!

Guildenstern (*whispering*)   I take it we continue as planned, my liege?

Rosencrantz (*whispering*)   You still head for the cliffs?

Hamlet   I do, good friends. There is no change.

Rosencrantz   Good. Then on with Pyrrhus!

With a flourish, warlike music starts up and **Players** *rush on to enact a cacophonous scene of battle. From their chaos emerges the* **Player**. *The action he describes is acted out onstage.*

Player
    And lo! 'Mid the bowels of Trojan carnage
    The rugged Pyrrhus, he whose sable arms,
    Black as his purpose, did the night resemble
    When he lay couchèd in th' ominous horse,
    Hath now this dread and black complexion smeared
    With heraldry more dismal, head to foot.
    Now is he total gules, horribly tricked
    With blood of fathers, mothers, daughters, sons,
    Baked and impasted with the parching streets

That lend a tyrannous and a damnèd light
To their lord's murder; roasted in wrath and fire,
And thus o'ersized with coagulate gore,
With eyes like carbuncles, the hellish Pyrrhus
Old grandsire Priam seeks. Anon he finds him,
Striking too short at Greeks. His antique sword,
Rebellious to his arm, lies where it falls,
Repugnant to command. Unequal matched,
Pyrrhus at Priam drives, in rage strikes wide,
But with the whiff and wind of his fell sword
Th' unnervèd father falls.

Hamlet   Dead?

*The **Player** freezes. The nobles turn to **Hamlet** in surprise.*

Rosencrantz   My lord?

Hamlet (*quietly, to the **Player***)   I'm sorry. Go on.

*The **Player** looks out to the king for approval, then continues.*

Player

                         Then senseless Ilium,
Seeming to feel this blow, with flaming top
Stoops to his base and with a hideous crash
Takes prisoner Pyrrhus' ear. For lo, his sword
Which was declining on the milky head
Of reverend Priam seemed i' th' air to stick.
So as a painted tyrant Pyrrhus stood,
And like a neutral to his will and matter,
Did nothing.

Rosencrantz (*whispering*)   My lord, you have turned to very
bone.

Hamlet (*whispering*)   To the play, look you!

Player
But as we often see against some storm
A silence in the heavens, the rack stand still,
The bold winds speechless, and the orb below
As hush as death, anon the dreadful thunder

Doth rend the region, so after Pyrrhus' pause
A rousèd vengeance sets him new a-work
And never did the Cyclops' hammers fall
On Mars's armour, forged for proof eterne,
With less remorse than Pyrrhus' bleeding sword
Now falls on Priam.

Hamlet *stands abruptly, unsettled. The* **Player** *stops again.* **Hamlet** *starts to back towards the exit.*

Guildenstern   My lord?

Hamlet   I am sorry. I am shaken by this speech, truly. (*To the* **Player**.) This is an excellent performance, friend. I will hear its conclusion later, as we have agreed.

Exit **Hamlet**. **Rosencrantz** *and* **Guildenstern** *glance up to the king and follow.*

Scene Six

Night, the howling cliffs. Enter **Osric**.

Osric   Oh, I do not like this plan! And sure, the action of the play did provoke my spirit in much the same manner as it did the noble prince. My God, murder? Or coward? Which character do I take? I confess I have no great devotion to the deed, and yet Laertes hath given me satisfying reasons. 'Tis but a player gone. Forth, my arm, he dies.

Enter **Laertes**.

Laertes   What hour now?

Osric   I think it lacks of twelve.

Laertes   No, it is gone. They should have been here some time ago.

Osric   Perhaps her conscience prevents her departure. Let's go in.

Laertes   Be strong, Osric! True nobility lies in self-determination, not in whimsying yourself to the fortunes of others. This is your only chance.

Osric   Be you near at hand, then. I may miscarry it.

Laertes   At your elbow, I. Be brave.

Osric   As an ox.

Voice (*offstage*)   My lord –

Osric   Help!

Laertes (*drawing his sword*)   Who goes there?

Enter **Reynaldo**.

Reynaldo   Your servant, my lord.

Laertes   What are you doing? I told you to keep guard by the castle gates!

Reynaldo   My lord, so I did.

Laertes   And did she leave as I intended?

Reynaldo   She did, my lord. But on the way, as though aware of her observer, she bled into the darkness and vanished from my sight.

Laertes   When was this?

Reynaldo   My lord, an hour past.

Laertes   An hour?

Reynaldo   That's not all, my lord. As I left, it was given out at court that Prince Hamlet has defied the king's order and stolen out of the castle.

Laertes   Hamlet?

Osric   What's that to us?

Laertes   Nothing. But how came this discovery, Reynaldo?

Reynaldo　My lord, I do not know. But the king was incensed. He has dispatched Marcellus and a crowd of guards, they are coming here even now.

Laertes　Here?

Reynaldo　Directly.

Laertes　This coincidence bodes ill, Osric. Our shadowy enterprise will not benefit from such an audience. Reynaldo, head Marcellus off and tell him that you saw Hamlet moving east. Divert his party along the cliff whilst we search for my sister.

Osric　But where will we find her?

Laertes　By the brook, I'll wager my life. Come, quick!

Exeunt **Laertes** *and* **Osric**, *then exit* **Reynaldo** *in a separate direction.*

Scene Seven

Night, the brook. **Ophelia** *sits by a willow staring at the water in the audience below. After a pause, she reaches down to touch her reflection.*

Ophelia (*singing quietly*)
　　She is dead and gone, lady,
　　She is dead and gone,
　　At her head a grass-green turf,
　　And at her heels –

Voice　Ophelia?

Ophelia *jumps. Enter* **Hamlet**, *disguised as the* **Player**.

Hamlet　It's only me. Don't be afraid.

Ophelia　I'm not.

Hamlet *smiles awkwardly.*

Hamlet　So. Now we are alone.

Ophelia   Should I curtsey?

Hamlet *shakes his head. Pause.*

Hamlet   Those poems I sent –

Ophelia   They were beautiful.

Hamlet   They didn't even rhyme.

Ophelia   I'm here, aren't I?

Hamlet   I'm the prince. You don't have a choice.

Ophelia   Yes, I do.

Hamlet *smiles.*

Hamlet   Why did you change the meeting place?

Ophelia   My mother used to come here. Before she died.

Hamlet   I'm sorry.

Ophelia   People say she lost her mind. But looking at my father . . . I think she made the sanest choice she could.

Hamlet *hesitates, then sits down next to* **Ophelia**. *Pause.*

Ophelia   What happened to you in court, Hamlet?

Hamlet   I don't know. That speech . . . People say that plays are made to awaken the truths lying dormant in their audience. My father . . . I don't know him, Ophelia. He is no more father to me than he is to one of his conquered subjects. And he is ruining Denmark with his wars, I know it, I know it in my heart. Watching then my double stand as Pyrrhus, streaked with blood and raising his righteous sword above the tyrannical old king, it was as though the gods themselves had climbed down from Olympus and were charging me to earn my name of greatness.

Ophelia   You think you should usurp your father?

Hamlet   No. But then, if I feel it is right, why shouldn't I? Why force myself to obey these ancient roles, son to father and father to son?

Ophelia   It was only a play, Hamlet.

Hamlet   One still worth the telling some dozen centuries later. Perhaps if I am to merit such a permanent commemoration, I must do something equally terrible. Am I a man or a prince, Ophelia? Pyrrhus, striking for himself in ancient Troy, or the player performing him, no more in charge of my own life than a mechanical actor reciting his lines?

Ophelia   What do you feel?

Hamlet   Myself! Look at you. You are a servant and a woman, but I know you have that within which surpasses any role.

Ophelia   How?

Hamlet   I have seen you smile. It is no more the smile of a girl than it is of a flower, or a cat, or any other earthly being to which we may draw comparison. It is the smile of Ophelia alone, irreplicable as the sun. But then, who's to say that up in that sky, elsewhere in time, there are not hundreds of other Ophelias and thousands of other Hamlets each as capable of smiling, or passion, or murder as we? Look there in the water at your pale reflection. Why is that Ophelia not as real as you are, staring back at us as though we are but temporary reflections of her more solid self? Then is our sense of our own uniqueness as mistaken as an actor's pride in his author's words, and our actions no more good or bad than the performance of a play. What then does it matter whether I kill the king?

They stare at the water.

Ophelia (*quietly*)   If that were Ophelia, she would be drowned.

Hamlet   In another story, maybe she is.

Ophelia   If there are hundreds of Ophelias up in that sky, Hamlet, it doesn't matter to me. Because each one will see the world with her own eyes, and so, to her, all its treasures will be wonderfully unique. What then does the truth matter? Here, in my world, I know that I love you now, and always will. What the reflections of me might feel is of no concern.

Pause.

Hamlet   My father wants to send me to Wittenberg.

Ophelia   What do you want, Hamlet?

Hamlet   Just you.

Ophelia   Then take me.

Hamlet *looks up at* **Ophelia**. *Gently, they kiss.* **Hamlet** *presses her back. Enter* **Laertes** *and* **Osric**, *aside.*

Laertes (*aside*)   Just in time, Osric! Quick, draw your sword!

Ophelia *hesitates.*

Ophelia   Wait. There's something I have to tell you. Last night, your mother –

Osric *rushes forward brandishing his rapier.* **Hamlet** *and* **Ophelia** *break apart, startled.*

Osric   Unhand her, slave!

Ophelia   Osric?

Osric   Indeed I am Osric, one whose nobility compels him to run this peasant through! Have at you!

Osric *lunges at* **Hamlet**, *who ducks out of the way.*

Hamlet   What are you doing?

Osric   My duty, vile player! You are no more fit to board this girl than I am to clean your hovel of a dressing chamber!

He lunges again. Again, **Hamlet** *narrowly avoids the blow.*

Hamlet   Dear God, you fool, don't you recognise me? I am Hamlet the Dane!

Osric *freezes. He looks at* **Hamlet** *for the first time and turns deathly white.*

Osric   But . . . But I thought –

Hamlet   Your thoughts are of little consequence. Give me the rapier.

Osric *immediately surrenders the rapier and falls to his knees.*

Laertes (*aside*)   What? No more?

Osric   My lord, I profess I was acting out of duty. Had I but comprehended that it was Your Royal Highness attempting to seduce this gentle maid, I would of course have never dared to intervene.

Laertes (*aside*)   So much for love.

Osric   Please, my lord, don't report this to the king!

Hamlet   Don't worry, treasonable rogue. Just leave us alone, and tell no one what you have seen.

Osric   Thank you, my lord!

Laertes (*aside*)   This cannot stand.

Laertes *rushes forward.*

Is that all?

Ophelia   Laertes?

Hamlet   It seems this brook isn't as secluded as we may have hoped.

Laertes   Osric, for shame! He is defiling your love!

Osric   He is a prince.

Laertes   And you are a man! Take charge as one.

Hamlet   Who is this, Ophelia?

Laertes   I am Laertes, your victim's brother, Hamlet, and one who does not care whether you are a prince or a slave. Your abuse demands that I defend her honour.

Hamlet   I do not seek to ruin it, noble youth. I love her.

Laertes   I love her! More than any prince could ever love! On my brother's authority, I order you to step away from her right now.

Hamlet   I care no more for that than the claim of a king. I am as free a man as you, Laertes, there is no authority on earth that can compel me but my own conscience.

Laertes   Then it is your conscience I challenge. If you are indeed as free a man as I, fight me for her.

Hamlet   Fight you?

Laertes   I'll wager your love against mine you won't surpass me in three hits.

Ophelia   I am not yours to wager, Laertes.

Hamlet   Three?

Ophelia   Hamlet, no! He is the most praised swordsman in all the city.

Hamlet   What's that to me? I'm undefeated in court.

Ophelia   Because no one will let you lose! Please, Hamlet, you don't know your own skill. Don't try to match him.

Laertes   Come, Hamlet. Are you a royal coward or a real Dane?

Hamlet *looks between them, then down at* **Osric***'s rapier.*

Hamlet   I accept.

Ophelia   No!

Hamlet   I must stand for you myself, Ophelia. As a man, not a prince. Otherwise how can I know if I deserve you?

Laertes   You'll surrender her if I win?

Hamlet   And if I do, you'll leave us alone.

Ophelia   But –

Laertes   Swear it.

Hamlet   I swear. (*To* **Osric**.) You will play the judge?

Osric   I shall, my lord.

Hamlet   Then come. The best of three hits.

Laertes   Let us play!

Ophelia   No!

They raise their rapiers and start to fight. Eventually, **Laertes** *hits* **Hamlet**.

Laertes   One!

Hamlet   No!

Laertes   Judgement?

Osric   A hit, I do declare it!

Hamlet   Again!

Ophelia   Hamlet –

They fight. **Hamlet** *hits* **Laertes**.

Hamlet   Mine?

Laertes   It is true, I do confess it. Come then, Hamlet, let's play the last. For my sister's love!

They fight. Just as **Laertes** *gains the upper hand,* **Marcellus**, **Horatio**, **Rosencrantz**, **Guildenstern**, **Reynaldo** *and* **Guards** *burst onstage.*

Marcellus   Put up your sword!

Hamlet   Good fellows, leave him be! He tries a wager to which I have sworn.

Marcellus   We cannot, my lord. Your father insists that you come with us immediately.

Hamlet   My father? How does he know I've gone?

Rosencrantz (*together with* **Guildenstern**)   I don't know.

Guildenstern (*together with* **Rosencrantz**)   I've no idea.

Marcellus   He is incensed, my lord.

Laertes   Will you back out now?

Hamlet   Let us play out this bout, Marcellus. Please.

Marcellus   My lord, I cannot. These swords are unprotected.

Hamlet   Then the greater the victor's honour. Come Laertes, let us play!

They fight, dodging the **Guards** *who try to stop them. In the midst of the chaos,* **Laertes** *trips* **Hamlet**, *takes his rapier and levels it at his throat. The* **Guards** *all freeze.*

Laertes   Hold off, all of you!

The **Guards** *stand back, hesitant.* **Hamlet** *and* **Laertes** *stare at each other, breathing heavily.*

Laertes   You agree to the terms? You will abandon her?

Hamlet *looks from* **Ophelia** *to* **Laertes**, *caught. He nods.*

Hamlet   Put up your sword.

Laertes *does.* **Hamlet** *stands.*

Hamlet   Hold him, Marcellus.

Marcellus *rushes forward and takes hold of* **Laertes**.

Laertes   What are you doing?

Hamlet   Oaths stand between equals, Laertes. Your courtier's terms can't hold me.

Laertes   But you swore! As a man, you –

Hamlet   I am no man, I am the Prince of Denmark! I may do as I please!

Laertes   You lying dog!

Laertes *breaks free from* **Marcellus** *and rushes at* **Hamlet**.

Hamlet   Help, treason!

Immediately, **Horatio** *rushes forward and knocks* **Laertes** *to the ground. The others catch up and restrain him.*

Laertes (*struggling*)   But he swore! An oath on his honour, a betrayal before God! Are you going to let this stand, friends? This is tyranny! The tyranny of his father and his father before him! Of men who care for nothing but the preservation of their own power! Why must we live as dogs to such false masters? I say, no more! If we act together, now, we can end it all. All of you who want to live as free men, I order you as your fellow to stand back and let me take my rightful action!

Hamlet   And as your lord, I order you to hold him fast.

The courtiers look between them. No one moves.

Laertes   Come, friends. Are we such cowards?

Hamlet   No. You are subjects. Take him in.

Marcellus   My lord, please, you must come too. The king has ordered that you go to your chamber immediately and prepare for Wittenberg.

Ophelia   Wittenberg?

Hamlet   I'll lead the way. Do not report this youth's actions to the king, he cannot be blamed.

Ophelia   Hamlet?

Hamlet *turns.*

Hamlet   I am sorry, Ophelia. It seems that some authorities have reason to be upheld. I am the prince, still. Will you wait for me?

Ophelia   Do I have a choice?

Hamlet   That depends. Who do you serve? Onwards, loyal Danes.

Exeunt all but **Ophelia** *and* **Horatio**.

Ophelia   Good God, Horatio. What's to be done? I pray that none of these men are ever king.

Horatio   Perhaps your wish will come true. Who knows
what story lies in wait?

Cannons sound offstage.

Young Fortinbras departs. Let's go in. For my own part, I can
say that whoever comes to power, there shall be no escape
from bloodshed. For when human rivalries are thus laid
down, private tempers wreak havoc upon the earth, though
all public reasons give them pause. The rest, Ophelia, is
always violence. Come, let's follow the prince.

Exeunt as cannons boom out to silence.

Finis.

Prince of Denmark

*Notes on rehearsal and staging, drawn from a workshop
held at the National Theatre, November 2011*

How the Play Came to be Written

When Anthony Banks suggested writing a prequel to *Hamlet*
using only the younger characters, I hesitated: trying to add
anything to so monumental a text seemed presumptuous, and
the idea of plugging gaps in a plot invigorated by its
ambiguity felt reductive.

On re-reading *Hamlet* with the project in mind, however, I
was struck by two things: firstly, how one of Hamlet's central
dilemmas – whether to take action or to live for ever in his
own mind – is crucial for so many young people today; and
secondly, how the conception many of us have of ourselves
as brooding Hamlet-heroes in our own personal tragedies
underlies the individualism of today's world.

This made me think about the offstage lives of the other
characters. I realised that, within the elective monarchy of
sixteenth-century Denmark, people like Laertes might have
been infuriated by Hamlet's inherited centrality both in the
court and the dramatic action. By giving these supporting
players the lead roles each of us craves and by exploring their
reactions to Hamlet's solipsism, I thought I could bring to life
the conflicts that an individualistic world view causes when it
is held by everyone in society.

My fears about the reductiveness of writing a prequel were
allayed when I saw that another of Hamlet's worries is living
up to the role into which he was born – whether he can act
as his own agent or is an avenger automated by duty.
Addressing this anxiety in a story in which the audience
already knows the outcome of the characters' actions would
allow me to question the very notion of self-determination,
and so give the play a life distinct from its source.

Once I'd agreed on a prequel and a young cast, the faux-Elizabethan idiom seemed the only option – these characters would one day speak in Shakespearean English, after all, but as yet would still be green, and so only able to approximate the brilliant later language. After working within the strictures of naturalistic dialogue, it was a real thrill to be able to have characters actually articulate ideas in elaborate rhythms.

Most of all, though, what excited me about the NT's proposal was the opportunity to approach a play many think of as oppressively serious in an irreverent, fast-paced, fresh way. I hope the pleasure I had writing it translates to the experience of watching it.

Michael Lesslie

The Key Theme

The young men in the play are fascinated by violence. Where teenagers now might have 'Call of Duty', these characters have fencing. It's important that they are excited by swords, that they can't resist getting involved. This is necessary for the realisation at the end of the play that the danger is now real and without noticing they have entered the adult world.

Ways to Begin Work: a Play Map

Try sticking the script on the wall with all the pages in a line. Then put some Post-It notes to mark where the scenes fall. This shows that the play echoes a five-act structure.

There are thirty pages in the script; a good rough guide is two hours' rehearsal per page of script for a well-rehearsed production, so for this play that would mean around sixty hours. If you have less time, as some youth theatres will, you should still start from this ideal. See how you might be able to make it work – e.g., with parallel rehearsals, and more work done away from the room. The play needs to feel like a compelling narrative, so spending time running the play at the end would be of great use.

The 'map' of the play can be further developed to include a breakdown of the key action in each scene as well as making a note of its location. Here are examples from the workshop:

SCENE ONE   *Underground.* Reynaldo tells Laertes about Hamlet's letters to Ophelia. Osric tells Laertes he's after Ophelia. Laertes tells Ophelia he knows what is going on.

SCENE TWO   *In Grand Hall.* Hamlet tells his friends about neighbouring countries and Rozencrantz and Guildenstern say to be careful.

SCENE THREE   *Outside.* Laetes suggests to Osric that he kills the Player (who will be with Ophelia).

SCENE THREE   *Corridor.* Ophelia changes the location and tells Horatio.

SCENE FIVE   *Back in Grand Hall.* Hamlet discovers the change of plan.

SCENE SIX   *The Cliff.* Reynaldo tells them to go to the brook.

SCENE SEVEN   *The Brook.* Hamlet and Ophelia decide whether or not to run away together. Duel and agreement. Hamlet is sent away.

You can then follow individual character journeys through the play to understand more fully their functions and through lines.

Characters

The words are your way into the characters in this play. Unlocking the text will unlock the characters.

Laertes begins the play in a bitter outburst. This letter has been the straw that broke the camel's back. Get the actor to work out exactly where this resentment has come from. This crisis begins and motivates the whole play.

There was a question in the workshop about Laertes and Ophelia and whether their relationship is incestuous. It was suggested that nothing particularly strange is going on. He has lost his mother and is protective of his sister – that is all. He is quite controlling but it comes from a place of fear for her and their position in court.

It is useful to note that Hamlet stays in control of the whole play until the very end – think about what this means for the actor's performance.

Rosencrantz and Guildenstern are a double act. Think of who they're like: Laurel and Hardy; Bill and Ted; which Inbetweeners are they? There is a lot of space to have fun with them.

Exercises for Use in Rehearsal
suggested by Kate Godfrey, NT Voice Department

This play uses complex language which must be spoken well to achieve its full effect. A few thoughts which may be of use:

When working through a section the tendency of young actors is to rush through their words. Rather than simply suggesting they 'slow down', try drawing attention to the characters' use of words. For example, in the first scene, Laertes uses the words 'cherish' and 'mortal' to speak about his sister – draw this to the actors' attention and see how it affects their work.

Much of the language in the play is rhetorical. This often involve comparisons, for example, 'Our army prepares . . . and its prince writes verse.' Get the actor to make these two different things clear. What does the preparing army look like? What does a poet prince look like? See how this affects the performance.

Images are useful. If an image is described, interrogate it. For example: 'like being tortured by a wet fruit'. What kind of fruit? What does it smell like? Get the actor to visualise or paint the picture for you, then bring them back to the text and see how it enhances what they do.

If the word is not understood or commonly used, look it up. Translating it into something you understand will inform and enhance the playing of it. Getting everyone in a group to say a tricky or difficult word can also help give ownership of it and dispel any fear there might be.

If a long word is not being committed to, try asking the actor to take out the consonants and just make the vowel sounds. Repeat it with them a couple of times, then go back to the word. This can open up the word to the actor.

A common rhetorical structure is a statement followed by examples. For example, in Scene One 'Woman's affection runs differently to ours, Osric. It is impractical, chaos in miniature, unmannable,' etc. Get the actor to read through the list putting 'A woman's affection runs' before each listed item. This will help clarify the thought.

If a list is used, as is often the case in rhetoric, ask the actor to add 'first', 'second', 'third', etc. This again will help make the structure of the argument clearer for the actor and audience.

In Hamlet's speech in Scene Two he mentions many characters we do not see in the play. Try casting actors in the 'missing parts' so that there is a face to the name, and have fun with it. What movie star could it be? This will help make it clearer.

The play-within-a-play is written in iambic pentameter – this means it is written with the rhythm of a heart beat. Get your actor or group to run on the spot for twenty seconds, then take their pulse and count with a tick in time with it. Then as a group make a 'dee' sound in time to the beat, before progressing on to making a 'dee-dee' heartbeat sound. Once the group has got into a rhythm return to the script and read it using the heartbeat as a rhythm. How does this rhythm affect the passage? Is it clearer?

This section is also one of the most complex in the play. It's important that everyone understands what is going on. As a group, read slowly through the passage and come to a consensus about what is going on. There is a great deal of action described – try acting it out as you go to make it crystal clear.

Another idea to make this section clear is to read around the room, with each reader stopping when they get to a comma. Once you have done this for a sentence, read the whole sentence without break. This helps make it clear.

THE INTERROGATION EXERCISE OR 'WHAT?'

This exercise has two stages:

First – get the actor to keep repeating the same sentence, adding on one word at a time, then finishing with the question 'What?'. For example:

- That what?
- That he what?
- That he take what?
- That he take a what?
- That he take a leaf what?

Though time-consuming, this exercise has very good results, making the actor interrogate the language and coin it in a fresh way.

Second – let the actor work through their text but the director interrogates what they are saying, not after every word but when they hear that the thought is not connected. This makes the actor wring every bit of meaning out of their language.

Stage Combat Tips
inspired by a workshop led by Fight Director Alison de Burgh

The National Theatre takes health and safety very seriously, and swordfighting should not be undertaken on stage without the professional expertise of an Equity Registered Fight Director.

There are many ways to create the style and feeling of the world of the play without even drawing your sword. Here is a list of helpful tips and ideas to ensure authenticity and for use with actors:

- The sword is always worn on the left.

- If you don't have a proper sword belt you can use a normal belt worn as loosely as possible.

- Your left hand never grips the sword – this is thought uncouth – but you can rest the heel of your hand on it. Think about showing off the rings on your fingers.

- Try walking around with the sword, get used to it. Try sitting down elegantly without bashing the sword. What works?

- You always draw with your right hand.

- When drawing, think that you are taking your right hand forward away from your body as if flicking water from your fingers.

- If you are wealthy you will have worn a sword since you were very young, so as an actor you need to learn to be at ease with it.

- When you are standing with your sword your chest should be up and your feet in the ballet third position.

- When you are listening to your fencing master with your sword unsheathed, rest the tip on the ground with your right hand resting on the handle and your left hand on top of your right.

- When you draw and are ready to fight 'en garde' there is no official position – you can try and out-pose your partner. In the Elizabethan world your left hand is forward, rather than later when it is held back.

- Don't worry about your leg work: when in doubt, walk.

A suggestion for making cheap rapiers to work with is to use bamboo, cut to 36 inches, with tape round each end so that it cannot split. You can then cut a plastic bottle and tape it on to make a hand protector.

Remember that there is no such thing as a safe weapon. If it were safe it would not be a weapon. Even a bamboo cane can be lethal if it is not used with due care and attention.

Safety things to remember:

- Pretend your partner is radioactive – always keep a force-field distance between your sword and their body.
- Never point your tip higher than your partner's heart.
- When blades are crossed ensure the crossed section is only two inches.

Ideas for Staging and Production

THE PLAY-WITHIN-A-PLAY

This section poses particular challenges in terms of style. The writer has been very open in terms of how you respond. There are many options depending upon your stylistic approach: projection, physical theatre, shadow puppets, toy soldiers. This could also be a good section in which to include more cast members.

You could experiment with the way the speech is delivered. It was observed in the workshop that it is easier to listen to one voice than a chorus, but there is probably a middle way in between choral and individual delivery.

THE SETTING

When NT Learning produced *Prince of Denmark*, the design concept mainly comprised images of sixteenth-century European royal courts with a few dashes of twenty-first-century detail. Companies should feel encouraged to envisage Elsinore in the way that best suits their production. There are limitless options – you could go fully period, more eclectic as does Baz Luhrmann, or very contemporary.

In terms of the swords, they could be other types of weapon, but it is crucial that they look 'in place' with the landscape you create, and that they are truly dangerous weapons of war, carelessly abused by adolescents play-fighting with each other.

MUSIC

Anthony Banks used dance and court music of the period to get himself into the world and feeling of the period. There are many options for the use of music – in particular how it either supports or juxtaposes the period of the play. It is up to the individual production to find something that works for them.

Additional Suggestions

Prince of Denmark was commissioned by National Theatre Learning and staged at the NT in 2010 with a young cast and a young technical team directed by Anthony Banks. When rehearsing, the acting company did a gym session before each rehearsal. This was to help achieve the athletic energy of both the characters and the play. This could be set as an exercise in a rota, with each actor in turn running a gym session at the start of a rehearsal.

Highlighting their own words is popular with actors. Maybe you should suggest they highlight what they are responding to – this is probably more helpful.

A thought that was useful for the NT Learning company was that the play happens behind closed doors. It is a family drama with the kind of arguments that happen in all families.

To read or not to read? Though the play uses *Hamlet* as its inspiration, this is a standalone piece. There is nothing wrong in reading *Hamlet*, but it is not necessary in order to perform this play. There is a danger if you read *Hamlet* that you would make assumptions. Everything you need to be able to act in or direct the play is in the text.

Troy (film) and *King Priam* (opera) are particularly interesting to look at in relation to the play-within-a-play. Looking at the use of chorus in productions such as Katie Mitchell's *Iphigenia at Aulis* and Jonathan Kent's *Oedipus* may also be of use.

From a workshop led by Anthony Banks,
with notes by Jonathan Humphreys

Socialism is Great

Anders Lustgarten

Notes on Chinese Language and Pronunciation

Chinese is a tonal language. It has four main tones: high, rising, falling-rising and falling. Tones are hard to master and for that reason I've left them out of the text, even though the language is incomprehensible to Chinese people without them.

The Chinese is in italics. A phonetic guide to how to pronounce it is in brackets.

Anhui (on-hway): province of China.

Cao ni ma! (tsow knee ma): Chinese swear words. Google them if you need to!

Dong fang hong, taiyang sheng (more or less pronounced as it looks): the start of the Cultural Revolution anthem 'The East is Red': 'The East is Red, the sun is rising.'

Hao hao hao (how how how): sort of the Chinese equivalent of 'okay', it literally means 'good good good'.

Henan (huh-nan): province in interior China. Since it began to introduce market forces in the 1980s, China has polarised into the richer industrialised provinces on the coast and the poorer agricultural provinces inland, of which Anhui and Henan are two. Many young people now leave the rural areas at least temporarily to make money in the big cities and factories.

Mao Zhuxi Wan Sui! (mao jew-she won sway): ten thousand years of Chairman Mao (common Cultural Revolution slogan).

Mei you pianzi, mei you mianzi (may yo pee-en-tse, may yo me-en-tse): 'no money, no face' – the social status or reputation that comes with correct behaviour or actions.

Sange (sohn-ger).

Sha bi (shar bee).

Shanzhai (shone-jai): culture of copying and reproducing goods and images in China, sometimes just to make money but often with satirical humour or subversive intent.

Ta ma de (ta ma dur).

Wei Renmin Fuwu! (way run-mean foo-woo): Serve the People (common Cultural Revolution slogan).

Xiaomei (she-ow-may).

Zhang (jahng) / *Li* (lee) / *Cai* (tsigh): common Chinese surnames.

Zhongguo: (jong-gwo) China.

Characters

Li
Zhang
Zhang's Dad
Lotus
Johnny
Girl
Sange
Xiaomei
First Girl
Second Girl
Li's Dad
Crowd

Drumroll, then a steady drumbeat. Massed ranks of kids march slowly on to the stage in perfect lockstep, a single co-ordinated unit. They halt in the middle of the stage. Pause, then the drumbeat quickens and they perform a dance of welcome, perhaps like the drummers from the Beijing Olympics opening ceremony. The impression should be of power, energy and most of all of a unified group moving as one. Just as the dance seems to be reaching a peak, a mobile phone goes off loudly. Instantly all the kids reach for their phones, shout 'Wei?' (pronounced 'Way?', the usual phrase to answer a call in China) and start fifty different random conversations, heading chaotically offstage in multiple directions.

An elite private boys' school in Beijing. **Zealous Li** *on an expensive laptop.* **Pigface Zhang**, *in pricier clothes, enters.* **Li** *hides one window and reads from another.*

Li 'A country with a corrupt and greedy ruling elite, where the people have few rights and little power, with a crumbling infrastructure and a hated government.' Wow. Britain sounds like a dump.

Zhang Why do you care? You're not going. (*Peers at screen.*) The *People's Daily*? Why are you reading Commie bullshit?

Li Your dad edits the *People's Daily*.

Zhang Which is why I know it's bullshit. Just cos Daddy writes it doesn't mean he believes it. Off.

He shoves **Li** *off.*

Zhang Freak.

Li It's for homework.

Zhang Buy a copy.

Li *Your* homework.

Zhang (*scans laptop*) Goddamn it. That *ta ma de* little gamer still hasn't taken me beyond Level 8.

Li Is it not like that, then, Britain?

Zhang Their trains *are* rubbish. So expensive and always late! Not like here.

Li   Your coursework's due.

Zhang   Daddy couldn't believe how in the Dark Ages Britain was. Little shabby stations and seats with the stuffing coming out of them? Embarrassing. He asked the station guard, wasn't he humiliated China's left his country so far behind?

Li   What did the guy say?

Zhang   They don't speak Chinese in Britain. Yet.

Li   What was your dad doing there?

Zhang   Building diplomatic relations. Now piss off.

Li   Your coursework's due.

Zhang   So?

Li   So, do you want it or not?

He holds out his hand. Beat.

Zhang   Time for the scholarship boy to scrape together his fees again? *Mei you pianzi, mei you mianzi*, Li. No money, no face.

He reaches into his back pocket and pulls out a thick wad of notes, from which he peels a handful and dangles them over **Li**'s *outstretched hand.*

Zhang   Essay?

Li *pulls out an essay and hands it over. Beat.*

Zhang   Say, 'Thank you, Zhang.' (*Beat.*) Say, 'Thank you, kind, generous Master Zhang, for making up for my deadbeat dad and allowing me to get a proper education.'

Li   Don't talk about my dad.

Zhang   Or what?

Li   Just don't.

Beat.

Zhang   Don't you find it humiliating to go through this every month?

He drops the notes into **Li***'s hand.*

Zhang   What's this one for?

Li   Citizenship class. How you believe humility and respect for others are the bedrock of modern society.

Zhang   If I'm not Number One, I'll kick your arse.

Li   You came top last week, didn't you?

Zhang *goes back to his laptop. Beat.*

Li   I wish I was going to London.

Zhang   Well, you're not.

Li   What are you gonna see first? Buckingham Palace, the Houses of Parliament – ?

Zhang   David Beckham.

Li   I don't think David Beckham hangs around Chinatown, Pigface.

Zhang   What did you call me?

Li   Pigface.

Zhang   I told you not to call me that.

Li   It's what everybody calls you.

Zhang   Apologise.

Li   For what, genetics?

Zhang   Listen, scholarship boy –

Li   It's not my fault you have a face like a –

Zhang   Everybody knows there's only one reason why you're in this school.

Li   I could say the same about you.

Zhang   Because they have to let a few povvos in to look like they care about equality and all that old Communist bullshit.

Li   Because your dad is a big cheese in the Party and even though you're thicker than the Great Wall of China, they have to sort you out.

Zhang   Watch your mouth, povvo. (*Beat.*) For your information, Daddy is arranging for me to meet David Beckham.

Li   Is he? Right.

Zhang   And we're going to the big Apple shop on Regent Street and we're going to buy a hundred iPhones.

Li   Why does David Beckham need a hundred iPhones?

Zhang   Not for him. For me.

Li   Why do you need a hundred iPhones?

Zhang   To bring back here.

Li   iPhones are *made* in China, Pigface.

Zhang   The tax breaks, moron.

Li   Your dad owns the factory that makes them.

Zhang   Between the tax our *ta ma de* government slaps on them here and what they take off for foreigners in the UK, I can make a thousand yuan a unit. Easy money.

Li   You're going to the UK to buy iPhones?

Zhang   And meet David Beckham. Yes. I am.

Li *shakes his head.*

Zhang   What?

Li   You don't think that's a bit of a . . . waste?

Zhang   What else is there to do? We've got their shops already.

Li   I don't know: see the history, the culture . . . ?

Zhang   What culture? Europe's got nothing China doesn't have. We had what they used to have before they had it, and we make whatever they have now.

Li   Why are you going if you don't even respect the place?

Zhang   To prove I'm right. (**Li** *makes a noise of disgust.*) What's your problem, Li?

Beat.

Li   You know it should be me.

Zhang   What?

Li   Going to Britain.

Zhang   I don't know what you're talking about.

Li   I won that essay competition. Fair and square. The form teacher told me.

Zhang   But that's not what the school says, is it?

Li   I know I did.

Zhang   Wanna see my certificate?

Li (*pulls it out*)   No, I'd rather see your essay, which I accidentally printed off.

Zhang   Give that back.

Li   The Prime Minister of the UK is not Prince William, Pigface.

Zhang   He's the one on TV, isn't he? With all the medals on?

Li   Yeah, but –

Zhang   So *obviously* he's the leader of the country.

Li   The motto *Dieu et mon droit* does not translate as 'How much for a passport?'

Zhang   That's not what Daddy says.

Li (*reading*) 'The government is elected by popular vote, in which the leaders of political parties appear on a TV show called *Britain's Got Talent* to play the ukulele and do impressions, after which the people phone in and vote for the winner.' Can you seriously be this stupid?

Zhang (*snatching essay back*) It doesn't matter what the 'truth' is.

Li I spent weeks on mine.

Zhang It matters who wins.

Li It was really good.

Zhang I'll send you a postcard.

Li Let me go.

Zhang You're joking. Why would I do something like that?

Li Because I know more about the country, I'm more interested in it, I –

Zhang Which is exactly why I made sure you didn't win. (*Beat.*) Come on, Li. The way you get ahead is you pull others back. People are just crabs in a bucket – you have to pinch them before they pinch you. And besides, who'd do my coursework?

Pause.

Li What do you want out of life, Zhang?

Zhang What do I 'want out of life'? That's a gay question.

Li No it isn't. It's normal.

Zhang Gay hippy question. Are you a gay hippy, Li?

Li It's just a question.

Zhang I want to make money.

Li You've got money.

Zhang I want more.

Li Why?

Zhang So I can get ahead.

Li   Why do you wanna get ahead?

Zhang   So I can make money.

Li   Why? What's the *point*?

Zhang (*shrugs*)   What else is there?

Li   I dunno.

Zhang   Exactly.

Li   Explore, maybe. Experiment. Discover.

Zhang   Money lets you do that.

Li   Fight. Fail. Learn.

Zhang   Why would I wanna do those things?

Li   Find out who you are. What the world is. Instead of hiding in a velvet cage all your life.

Zhang   What would you know about money? You haven't got any.

Li   Maybe that's how I know about it.

Zhang   You're just jealous. Because I've got things you'll never have.

Beat.

Li   Wasn't always about money in your family, though, was it?

Zhang   What are you talking about?

Li (*nods at computer*)   It's amazing what a Party leader's kid gets access to.

Zhang   You didn't . . . (*Frantically closes windows.*) You *sha bi*!

Li   Most of us are stuck behind the Great Firewall of China, but you little princes, you just hop right over.

Zhang   The whole point about us being allowed on these sites is cos we promise not to go on them!

Li   Proper little radical, your dad, wasn't he?

1967. A torrent of kids pour on to the stage, waving huge red Chinese flags and pictures of Chairman Mao and Little Red Books and banners with Cultural Revolution slogans on them (e.g. SOCIALISM IS GREAT, CHAIRMAN MAO IS THE RED SUN IN OUR HEARTS, ON NO ACCOUNT FORGET THE PAST. *The impression should be of joy and excitement and passion and zeal, not of 'brainwashing' or violence. At the head of the tide is* **Zhang's Dad***, aged fifteen.*

Zhang's Dad   *Mao Zhuxi Wan Sui!*

Crowd   *Mao Zhuxi Wan Sui!*

Zhang's Dad   Long Live Chairman Mao!

Crowd   Long Live Chairman Mao!

Zhang's Dad   Socialism is GREAT!

Crowd   Socialism is GREAT!

Li   What the hell happened?

Zhang's Dad   Comrades! Revolutionary students!

The crowd cheers.

Today we fight to make a new China, a China that loves all its people, no matter how poor or downtrodden or neglected. And at the same time to make China what she used to be: strong and whole and proud! What does Chairman Mao say? *Wei Renmin Fuwu!*

Crowd   *Wei Renmin Fuwu!*

Five kids rush forwards, each holding up a character from the slogan.

Zhang's Dad   Serve the People!

Crowd   Serve the People!

Zhang's Dad   On No Account Forget the Past!

Crowd   On No Account Forget the Past!

Zhang's Dad   The past of our disgrace, our humiliation by foreigners and capitalists is *over*! We are going to make a

future of equality and enough for all! A Communist future!
We are going to make it, you and me. Together. Are you
ready?

Crowd   Yes!

Zhang's Dad   Are you frightened?

Crowd   No!

Zhang's Dad   Then let's begin!

*A deafening outbreak of shouting and cheering and whistling and
chanting and flag waving and dancing. Eventually the crowd shuffles
offstage.*

Pause.

Li   Where did all that go?

Zhang   You know what happened in the Cultural
Revolution. People dying, things being smashed up. 'Ten
years of chaos', the Commies call it.

Li   They call it that *now*. They used to call it the 'Glorious
Proletarian Cultural Revolution'. So which is true?

Zhang   What do you care?

Li   My dad was at that rally. Fourteen years old. He
remembers your dad talking. How inspiring he was. Changed
his life. (*Beat.*) He went back to his work unit and he tried to
live up to the principles of the revolution. Equality,
togetherness, fighting for a better world. Trying to be like
your dad. And even when they came and beat him in the
street and broke his leg for 'revisionist tendencies', he never
gave up trying. He could've left his factory years ago, made
money like everyone else, but he won't.

Zhang   Then he's an idiot.

Li   He believed it.

Zhang   Then he's the only one.

Li   My mum calls him 'a dusty relic of the past'.

Zhang   She's smarter than she looks. Which is just as well.

Li   It was your dad that sent the people to beat him, Zhang. He was a big boss by then. (*Beat.*) I'm not angry at him. I just want to know how he gets his head around it.

Beat.

Zhang   Gets his head around what?

Li   Going from 'a China that loves all its people, no matter how poor or downtrodden or neglected', to owning a load of iPhone factories.

Zhang   It's the same thing.

Li   Making shitloads of cash is the same thing as saving China?

Zhang   Is China richer than she was before? Yes. Is China more respected than she was before? Yes.

Li   Is China more unequal and unjust than she was before?

Zhang   Is China back where she belongs in the eyes of the world? Yes, we are.

Li   Have all the good things my dad believed in been corrupted, been betrayed – ?

Zhang   Number One, Li. Number. One. That's what matters. That's what the foreigners respect.

Li   And the workers killing themselves in your dad's factories, that's the price of respect, is it?

Zhang   My daddy does not kill his workers.

Li   Look online.

Zhang (*pushing* **Li** *in the chest*)   Take that back.

Li   You can. If you want to.

Zhang   My daddy does not kill his workers!

Li   Alright, take it easy, just cos you never see him –

Zhang *shoves* **Li** *to the floor furiously.*

Zhang   *Cao ni ma!* You take that back, you turtle's egg, you son of a worker!

Li   Everyone knows you never see him.

Zhang   Daddy is a very busy and important man.

Li   That why he never comes to your open days, sports days?

Zhang (*almost shrieking*)   HE'S TAKING ME TO ENGLAND! WE'RE GOING TO ENGLAND TOGETHER! What does your filthy povvo worker father do for you, Li?

Li   He picks me up from school, Pigface. Every day.

Zhang's *expensive mobile rings. His face lights up.* **Zhang's Dad**, *played by the same actor but now as in his late fifties, walks on calling him.* **Li** *scrambles to his feet.*

Li   Have a great trip.

He exits. **Zhang** *spits after him and answers the phone with adoration.*

Zhang   Daddy!

Zhang's Dad   Listen, I haven't got much time –

Zhang   I've missed you.

Zhang's Dad   Sure.

Zhang   I can't wait till we go.

Zhang's Dad   I –

Zhang   Did you get Beckham sorted?

Zhang's Dad   There's been a bit of a . . . hitch.

Zhang With Beckham?

Zhang's Dad With me. (*Beat.*) I can't come. Problems at the factories. Ignorant worker girls can't stop hurting themselves. I need to . . . (*Beat.*) You can still go, of course. You'll have a great time. Money no object. (*Beat.*) Are you still there?

The crushing disappointment on **Zhang***'s face.*

Zhang (*quietly*) I'm here.

Zhang's Dad Look, son, I'm –

Voice (*offstage, urgent*) Director Zhang!

Zhang's Dad I have to go. I'll explain another time. School alright? Fifth year now.

Zhang Sixth year.

Zhang's Dad Well, there you are.

Voice (*offstage, more urgent*) Director Zhang!!

Zhang's Dad I have to go.

He hangs up and exits. **Zhang** *stares at his mobile, then stamps repeatedly on it.*

The kids emerge from the wings and line up in two vertical columns. They march towards each other. The column on the left carries posh shopping bags and boxes. The column on the left waves wads of cash (preferably colour photocopies of Chinese renminbi). As they meet, they exchange what they're carrying with the other column and march on across the stage and off. They leave a boy and a girl behind them.

Department store. The girl sees the boy. The boy sees the girl. The girl sees the boy sees her. She smiles to herself. He starts to approach her. She ducks away. He goes to meet her, but she doubles back. She makes to leave, then stops. Beat.

Lotus Lost something?

Johnny (*spins around*)   I was looking for . . . something special.

Lotus   In the women's clothing section?

Johnny   Yeah.

Lotus   Is that normally where you go to look for something special?

Johnny   Not usually.

Lotus   Glad to hear it. Did you find what you're looking for yet?

Johnny   Dunno. You don't know straight away, do you?

Lotus   I know. When I like something.

Johnny   Do you?

Lotus   Mostly, yeah.

Johnny   You never make mistakes? Cos sometimes you see something you like but it's not right in the end.

Lotus   I don't make mistakes.

Johnny   You have though. (*Nods at the dress over her arm.*) You shouldn't take the brown. You've got very green eyes, for a Chinese girl. You should take the green.

Lotus   Should I now?

Johnny   Yeah.

Lotus   And how do you know these things?

Johnny   Can I ask you out?

Lotus   Can you or are you?

Johnny   Can I?

Lotus   Up to you.

Johnny   Then I am.

Lotus   I have a boyfriend.

Johnny   That's alright, I'm not asking him.

Lotus (*smiling*)   That's good, I like that one.

Johnny   So?

Lotus   But I still have a boyfriend.

Beat.

Johnny   Is he the fat one?

Lotus   Which fat one?

Johnny   That fat guy watching you. Over there.

Lotus   I don't have a fat boyfriend, thanks.

Johnny   I don't blame you. I hate fat blokes. Sweaty and leery and always that little bit too close. Taking up too much space. Where fat blokes go, trouble follows.

Lotus   My brother is fat.

Johnny   Is he?

Lotus   Massive, actually. The sweetest kid in the world but massive. Sweats a lot.

Johnny   Right. Shame.

Lotus   People pick on him. Make his life a misery. It really upsets me.

Johnny   Terrible.

Lotus   I just don't know why anyone would be that bigoted. (*Beat. She smiles at him.*) I don't have a fat brother.

Johnny   Good.

Lotus   Don't have a brother at all. One-child policy and that. My parents couldn't afford the bribes for any more.

Johnny   Mine either.

Lotus   At least they got a son.

Johnny   That's what my mum says too.

Lotus   My mum hates me for what I'm not. I don't mind her hating me for what I am, but it's out of order to hate me for what I'm not. Don't you think?

Beat.

Johnny   What's your name?

Lotus (*smiles*)   See, that's where you should have started. Lotus. Lotus Liang. Yours?

Johnny   Johnny. Johnny Wong.

Lotus   No it's not.

Johnny   It is.

Lotus   Sounds like a Hong Kong film star.

Johnny   Maybe I am a film star.

Lotus   Quite young for a film star.

Johnny   Maybe I'm precocious. Started early.

Lotus   I don't know how I'd feel about dating a film star.

Johnny   What would your boyfriend feel about it? Not him, obviously, you. (*Beat.*) I'm actually not a film star.

Lotus   What are you then?

Johnny   I'm a gamer.

Lotus   A what?

Johnny   A gamer. You know, role-playing games? *World of Warcraft, Legend of Sword and Fairy*?

Lotus   Know of them.

Johnny   I play them.

Lotus (*dubious*)   For fun?

Johnny   For money. They last for years, these games, and to develop your character you get all these swords and skills and whatnot, and it takes time. And ability.

Lotus   And this is where you come in? With your ability?

Johnny   A lot of rich kids can't be arsed. To get, say, a Necromancer Sword of True Power –

Lotus   A what?

Johnny   Don't make me say it again.

Lotus   Please do. It gives me shivers.

Johnny   Really?

Lotus   No. Not really.

Johnny   Look, anyway, to get a –

Lotus   Necromancer Sword of True –

Johnny   Takes about forty hours of game time. Thirty if you're good. The rich kid can't be bothered so he dumps the job off on to me. I put the work in, get the sword, sell it on to him for five, six, seven thousand yuan.

Lotus   In real money?

Johnny   No, Lotus, in dragon's gold at the end of the rainbow. In real money. I'm working on one for this rich prick in Beijing now. Keeps bugging me about getting him on to Level 8, like you can just do it overnight.

Lotus   And this is how you earn your living?

Johnny   It is, yeah.

Beat.

Lotus   Well. I'm less unimpressed than I was two minutes ago, anyway.

Johnny   I'll take that as a compliment. What do you do, Lotus?

Lotus   I'm a pop star.

Johnny   Are you saying that because I said I was a movie star?

Lotus   I'm saying it because I am a pop star.

Johnny   Really?

Lotus   Really.

Johnny   Wow. OK.

Lotus   I have pictures on my phone.

Johnny   Pictures on a mobile phone prove everything.

Lotus   Yes, they do.

Johnny   Speaking of which – if you have a phone . . . ?

Lotus   Uh-huh?

Johnny   You must have a phone number.

She smiles. Beat.

Can I have it then?

Lotus   No. But I'll take yours.

She pulls out her mobile phone.

Johnny   *Shanzhai!*

Lotus   Oi! How dare you call my phone *shanzhai*!

Johnny   *Nookia* is not a legitimate maker of mobile phones, Lotus.

Lotus (*giggling*)   I never saw that!

Johnny   So you have a fake phone. Everyone has a fake phone. The realer the person, the faker the phone.

Lotus   Hey, this is *real* fake, not fake fake. There is a difference, you know.

Johnny   What's wrong with *shanzhai*? I love *shanzhai*!

Lotus   Do you now?

Johnny   It's the peculiar genius of the Chinese. Take something the West invented, knock it off, and make it cheaper and better and available to *everyone*.

Lotus   The peculiar genius of the Chinese, huh?

Johnny   *Crazy Stone*, that *shanzhai* film, how good was that?! More like *Mission Impossible* than *Mission Impossible* was! Like, in some ways, don't you think that fake is more real than real? Because real is stuck, right, it's limited to being itself, whereas fake can take the best of real and mix it with the best of other reals and make it something even better and a new kind of real, you know?

Lotus   Um, -ish.

Johnny   Fake is like our version of democracy. I'll never go to university, my parents don't know the right people, so if I want to get somewhere I get knock-off DVDs, *shanzhai* qualifications, a licence in someone else's name. Fake is my university.

Lotus (*impressed but hiding it*)   Alright, you can stop digging now. I'll let you off.

Johnny   I'm serious.

Beat.

Lotus   Do you wanna see the photos?

Johnny   Of what?

Lotus   Of me as a pop star.

Johnny   Go on then.

She shows him.

Lotus   This is me as Faye Wong.

Johnny   OK.

Lotus   Me as Amber Kuo.

Johnny   Yeah, I see that.

Lotus   Li Yuchun.

Johnny   Super Girl, yeah. Where's you?

Lotus   Huh?

Johnny   Where's you as you? I'd like to see you as you.

Lotus   They don't pay me to be me.

Johnny   You're a singer.

Lotus   I'm a *shanzhai* singer. (*Beat.*) They drive me to little villages or big factories where the people are too poor for the real thing and they tell them I'm whoever they want me to be off the TV and I sing for them. Maybe they even think I am the real thing, I don't know. They don't care who it really is. The songs make them happy.

Johnny   Does it make you happy?

Lotus   I want to be a singer.

Johnny   But is it you that's singing if you're being someone else?

Lotus   I thought you said you like *shanzhai*.

Johnny   I do like it.

Lotus   I thought you might . . . get it.

Johnny   I like you more. (*Beat.*) My name's not Johnny Wong. It's Tang Anjing and I come from a little village in Anhui called Black Mud Lake which is as attractive as it sounds. My dad fished and was part of the agricultural collective but the local Party chief sold off the land and built a huge paper mill upstream and now the lake stinks of rotting chemicals and dead fish and the number one industry is selling your own blood. I think I do get it, Lotus.

Beat.

Lotus   My name's not Lotus.

Johnny   I guessed that.

Lotus   It's Cai Yuling.

Johnny   'Precious Jade'. It's a nice name.

Lotus   For your granny.

Johnny   My granny's name was Stinkbox so, yes, for my granny it would have been a nice name.

Lotus   Her actual name was Stinkbox?

Johnny   If it wasn't, it should have been.

Lotus   I'm from Henan.

Johnny   OK.

Lotus   I'm not a pop star.

Johnny   Yes you are. I've seen the pictures.

Lotus   Not a real pop star.

Johnny   But you will be.

Lotus   Will I?

Johnny   I don't know. Are you good?

Lotus   Yeah, I am.

Johnny   Then you will be. (*Beat.*) Where do you really work?

Lotus   In a factory. It's horrible.

Johnny   Will you come for a walk with me?

Lotus   I'm late for my shift.

Johnny   Come for a walk with me. Cai Yuling.

Beat.

Lotus   I never knew the way to impress a boy was to be honest with him.

Johnny   It isn't, normally.

Lotus   Just with you, huh? Cos you're special?

Johnny   I dunno. This is the first time someone's been honest with me.

Lotus   Is it the first time you've been honest with them?

Johnny   It is, yeah. I dunno where it's come from. It feels a bit weird.

Lotus   Come for a walk with me. Tang Anjing.

The two of them join hands. The kids comes back on stage and form two long human chains of pairs. Each pair lifts one of the couple up and passes them down the chain at roughly the same time so their feet don't touch the ground. The couple giggle as they sway from side to side.

Johnny   When you're a singer . . .

Lotus   Yeah?

Johnny   What'll your band be called?

Lotus   The Kid Suicides.

Johnny   The Kid Suicides?! Why?

Lotus   Cos I thought about it but I didn't.

Johnny   Wow. OK. That's quite heavy.

Lotus   You like it?

Johnny   I do, yeah, it's just . . . not what I thought you'd say.

She smiles.

Lotus   Good.

They are carried offstage, laughing.

A heavy industrial factory, southern China. The grind of dangerous machines in a repetitive intimidating thump that is alienating at first but soon becomes familiar. A girl, **Sange***, seventeen, sits sullenly at a bolting machine, making the same small movement over and over and over again. Only the girls from the tide of kids come back on. They sit at* *various machines and perform similar repetitive tasks. One machine sits empty.*

One **Girl** *gets up.* **Sange** *checks her watch.*

Sange   Bathroom break isn't for another two hours.

Girl   But –

Sange   It's a five yuan fine to go to the bathroom between bathroom breaks.

Girl   But –

Sange   You want to pay the fine?

Girl (*crossing her legs*)   No, but –

Sange   Then sit down.

The **Girl** *looks at the clock, towards the bathroom, back at the clock, then squeezes her legs tighter and sits miserably down.*

Girl (*mutters*)   Bitch.

Sange   What?

Girl   Nothing.

The girls resume their labours. Pause.

Another girl enters, **Xiaomei**, *fifteen, bright and excited. She carries a small bag. She looks around her in wonder. She approaches* **Sange** *diffidently.*

Xiaomei   Hi. (*Beat. Slightly louder.*) Hi there.

Sange   What?

Xiaomei   I'm here for work.

Sange *looks her up and down.*

Sange   No you're not.

Xiaomei   Yeah I am. (*Introducing herself to the others.*) Hi, I'm Xiaomei. Hi, I'm Xiaomei. (*The others ignore her or nod cursorily.*)

They said a girl didn't turn up for her shift so I could have her job.

Sange   Well, you can't. She's a friend of mine.

Xiaomei   I'm a hard worker.

Sange   You can't just take people's jobs.

Xiaomei   Are you the floor boss? They said to find the –

Sange   I'm shift head. Who hired you?

Xiaomei   The man in the office. The one with the wandering eye?

Sange   That's not all that sleazeball has that wanders. You're too young.

Xiaomei   I'm seventeen.

Sange   No, you're not.

Xiaomei   I am, look.

She hands over an identity card. **Sange** *reads it.*

Sange   This ain't you.

Xiaomei   It is.

Sange   *I'm* seventeen. You're not seventeen.

Xiaomei   This is my ID card.

Sange   What are you, fourteen?

Xiaomei   Read what it says on the card.

Sange   Fuck the card.

Pause.

Xiaomei   I've been hired.

Sange   I can have you unhired.

Xiaomei   Why would you do that?

Sange   Because if they have an inspection and they find you're under-age, the company gets fined. And I get fired.

Xiaomei   I'm a really hard worker. (*Beat.*) Please.

Beat.

Sange   How old are you?

Xiaomei   I'm fifteen.

Sange   Where'd you get the card?

Xiaomei   I bought it. In the market.

Sange (*reading from card*)   Who's she? 'Chen Xiaomei'?

Xiaomei   She's me. Now. She is me.

Sange *gives* **Xiaomei** *back the card.*

Sange   Go home, 'Xiaomei'.

Xiaomei   No. I'm not going home. I'm here to work.

Sange   You don't want to work here.

Xiaomei (*straightforward, not dramatic*)   I paid a man five hundred yuan for a job in Dongguan but when I got here after three days' journey there was no job and the man had disappeared. I've been living on instant noodles and sleeping behind the bus shelter for three days. Last night a man tried to rape me.

Sange   So what? Everyone has these stories.

Xiaomei   My mum is dying. She needs kidney dialysis and the state doesn't care and we have no money and I've come out to earn it. I am not going home. I work here.

She drops her bag on the floor. Pause.

Sange   What's your real name?

Xiaomei   Call me Xiaomei. 'Little Pretty'. It's better than my real one.

Beat.

Sange   I'm Sange.

Xiaomei   Your name is 'Third'?

Sange   Guess what my two older sisters are called?

They smile at each other a bit.

Xiaomei   Is that my machine? (*Pointing to the empty seat.*)

Sange   She didn't even tell me she was going.

Xiaomei   Your friend?

Sange   Yeah. (*Beat.*) Come on. I'll show you how to work it.

Xiaomei   You don't have to.

Sange   I'll show you.

They move over to the dangerous machine.

Xiaomei   How long you been here?

Sange   Two years.

Xiaomei   Two years? I won't be here that long.

Sange   That's what I said.

Xiaomei   Is it a good place to work?

Sange   There's twelve to a dorm, the food stinks, the toilets are worse, the bosses are pricks and if the work bores you that's good because at least you're not scared. The mad thing is, it's better than average.

Xiaomei   Then I'm lucky.

Sange   Right, it's a cutting machine. It doesn't care if it cuts you or the metal so make sure not to give the fucker the option. Get into a rhythm – you boss the machine, don't let it boss you. Bring the metal through, blade down, cut, pass on. Bring through, blade down, cut, pass on. Do *not* lose your concentration. Want me to show you?

Xiaomei   Please.

Sange   Right.

They're both nervous. **Sange** *performs the task a couple of times to the sound of screaming metal. She leans back and breathes a sigh of relief.*

Got it?

Xiaomei   I think so.

Sange   You boss the machine, don't let it boss you. Ready to try?

Beat.

Xiaomei   Yeah. Yeah.

She takes the seat from **Sange***. She performs the operation a bit unsteadily. The metal jumps and the screaming pitch intensifies.*

Sange   Stay relaxed.

Xiaomei   I'm trying to . . .

Sange   Keep the rhythm, nice smooth rhythm . . .

Xiaomei   OK.

She does it a couple more times, becoming smoother each time.

Sange   That's it, you've got it.

Xiaomei   I've got it. (*She does it a few more times. Delightedly.*) I've got it!

She sits back from the machine, elated.

Sange   The girl's a natural. Well done, Xiaomei.

Xiaomei   Thanks, love. (*They smile. Beat.*) What's the basic wage, by the way? They wouldn't tell me.

Sange   Four hundred yuan a month. Not even enough to buy one of what we make.

Xiaomei   What are we making?

Sange   Who cares?

Xiaomei   It's just exciting, you know? Being here. I wanna know everything. Feel everything.

Sange   I remember that feeling.

Xiaomei   This is the first job I've ever had that didn't involve pigs.

Sange   You haven't met the floor boss. We make stuff for Westerners. Electronics.

Xiaomei   I've never seen a Westerner.

Sange   You won't. The factory's owned by some Communist Party big shot. The foreign bastards stay well out of it, keep their hands nice and clean. They send someone round now and again to waffle about 'human rights' and make sure we don't ask for a pay rise. I'll get back to my work now. If you think you're gonna be okay?

Xiaomei   I'm fine, I think.

All the girls resume the repetitive fluid motion of their work, as they do for the rest of the scene. **Xiaomei** *is in control of her machine. Pause.*

I'm sorry about your friend.

Sange   Who's that?

Xiaomei   The girl whose job I took. I mean, not took but –

Sange   That's alright, it's not your fault. (*Beat.*) You get to know girls and you make friends and then one day they're not there any more and you never see 'em again.

Xiaomei   What happens to them?

Sange   They get another job. They quit and go home. Something bad.

Xiaomei   Something bad?

Beat.

Sange   People kill themselves in these places, Xiaomei. The chemicals do stuff to your head.

Xiaomei   Kill themselves? Seriously?

Sange   Look out the dorm windows after shift. There's nets under them for a reason. (*Beat.*) I don't even have that girl's number.

Xiaomei   She'll come see you.

Sange   No, she won't. (*Beat.*) It's lonely here.

Xiaomei   How can it be lonely with all these people round you?

Sange   Look around.

They look around. Each of the girls is absorbed in her work, the repetitiveness and speed of the task taking up all her attention. They are alone in the same space. Pause.

Xiaomei   We should sing.

Sange   It's not allowed.

Xiaomei   We should, though. It'd help us work. Like how my granny said they used to sing Mao songs in the fields in the old days. What was that one she told me?

Sange (*giggling*) Don't.

Xiaomei   How does it go? I can't remember. '*Dong fang hong* . . .'

Sange   *Dong fang hong, taiyang sheng?*

Xiaomei   *Zhongguo* something something . . .

Sange   It was rubbish, basically.

Xiaomei   No wonder Communism failed.

Sange   Shhh! Don't say that! The bosses'll kill you!

Xiaomei (*starts doing Justin Bieber*)   Baby baby baby –

Sange   Shut up, Xiaomei!

Xiaomei   Baby baby baby, I thought you'd always be mine!

A couple of the other girls look scornfully over at her.

Sange   You'll get in trouble.

Xiaomei *keeps singing and pretty soon* **Sange** *joins in too. By the end a couple of the other girls are smiling and a couple have even started to sing a bit.*

Xiaomei
You know you love me, I know you care
Just shout whenever, and I'll be there
You are my love, you are my heart
And we will never ever ever be apart.

Xiaomei *and* **Sange** *break off after singing a verse and the chorus, laughing and flushed. Beat. The others go back to work.*

Xiaomei   Are there any boys here?

Sange   Crap ones.

Xiaomei   All of them?

Sange   There's one or two that might be acceptable. In a good light.

Xiaomei   Will you . . . ?

Sange   Will I what?

Xiaomei   You know! Introduce me?

Sange   You sure you want to be known as a girl who has boyfriends?

Xiaomei   I've come away.

Sange   Cos your parents'll find out, you know.

Xiaomei   I want to do all the things you do when you come away.

Sange   You think you're miles away from your village but there's always someone who knows someone who knows your great uncle's wife and everything gets back home. Everything.

Xiaomei   I want to do all the things you do when you come away. (*Beat.*) So can we? Go out after?

Sange   I don't go out with boys.

Xiaomei   Oh. You don't . . . go the other way, do you?

Sange   No, I do not!

Xiaomei   I mean that's cool. If you do.

Sange   I do not go the other . . . I can't afford to go out.

Xiaomei   But you've been here two years, you must have saved some money?

Sange   It's for my brother. (*Beat.*) On their fourth try, after saving up enough for all the bribes, my parents finally got a boy. You could tell they were pleased because they actually gave him a name. Little King. A name I'd hear like a curse every time I wanted anything. 'Shhh, don't run, Little King is sleeping.' 'Leave the pork for Little King.' 'Give Little King the best seat.' And now Little King wants to go to school, even though he's lazy and stupid, and so someone has to pay. And that someone is me. All my earnings go straight back home. I can't afford to go out with boys.

Beat.

Xiaomei   Why do you do it?

Beat.

Sange   Duty. Why do you do it?

Xiaomei   Because I love my mum. And I don't want her to die. And because I couldn't wait to get away. Slopping out pigs in a north wind for the rest of my life? No thanks. (*Beat.*) You know what I'm most guilty about, Sange? Most guilty about in the whole world?

Sange   What?

Xiaomei I'm glad she got sick. My mum. Or they'd never have let me go. (*Beat.*) There was a flier on the bus about learning computer skills. I'm gonna do that. Can you do that?

Sange I can't, no.

Xiaomei And one about learning English. Can you speak English?

Sange I didn't even finish kindergarten.

Xiaomei I'm going to learn English. So I can find out what Justin Bieber is saying.

Sange All the girls say that, Xiaomei. They're all gonna learn English and computing and find a boyfriend and make money.

Xiaomei (*in a comedy Chinese accent since she is speaking English*) 'I ruv you.'

Sange They all say that when they come here. I said it.

Xiaomei 'Sank you vey much.'

Sange Bright-eyed and full of hope.

Xiaomei I'm different.

Sange All saying they're different.

Xiaomei But I am different.

Sange That's what I said! *That's* why I wouldn't give you the job when you came in the door. Not because you took my mate's work but cos you reminded me of me, how I used to be! That same look in your eyes, that spark of 'I'm not going to let anyone grind me down'. I don't want you robbed of that like I was robbed of it, Xiaomei.

Beat.

Xiaomei Why does it have to be like that?

Sange It just does. It's *hard* here.

Xiaomei I'm not going to give in.

Sange   You will.

Xiaomei   I *won't*!

Sange   How do you know?

Xiaomei   I just know. I know *me*. I won't be that way and you don't have to be either.

Sange   But it's hard, Xiaomei. It's so tiring and lonely and hard.

Xiaomei   I know, Sange. But if you don't keep fighting, who'll fight for you?

Sange   No one fights for me.

Xiaomei   I will. We can fight together.

Beat. She starts singing again. This time **Sange** *and the rest of the girls all join in the verse and chorus and end in harmony.*

> You know you love me, I know you care
> Just shout whenever, and I'll be there
> You are my love, you are my heart
> And we will never ever ever be apart

Beat. They resume work smoothly and easily.

Xiaomei   I'm gonna take you out, Sange.

Sange   No, you aren't.

Xiaomei   After my first week's pay –

Sange   You won't get anything for two months.

Xiaomei   After two months then! I'm gonna take you out.

Sange (*grinning*)   Alright.

Xiaomei   We are gonna get you a proper top, for a start, one that shows you off a bit, and some nice jeans, and we are going to find some hot boys . . .

Carried away with her dream, **Xiaomei** *stops concentrating on the machine.*

Sange   Don't –

Xiaomei   And we're gonna go up to them and say –

Sange   LOOK OUT!

*The cutting machine cuts off **Xiaomei**'s right hand. The whole scene freezes. Beat. **Xiaomei** utters a single, terrible scream. **Sange** covers her horrified face with her hands. The other girls don't know where to look.*

*Beat. **Lotus** from the previous scene enters, blissfully unaware.*

Lotus   I'm sorry I'm late, but you'll never guess what –

She stops and stares at the scene in horror.

Blackout.

The main characters all on stage at once.

Lotus and **Johnny** *on the edge of a stage. A microphone on a stand a little way apart. Pause.*

Johnny   What?

Lotus   Nothing.

Johnny   You nervous?

Lotus   No.

Johnny   Is it cos your dad's here?

Lotus   No.

Johnny   Don't be nervous.

Lotus   I'm not nervous.

Johnny   He'll be fine, he'll just be proud to see you –

Lotus   I'm not nervous!

Johnny   Then why are you so quiet? You're on any minute.

Beat.

Lotus That girl lost her hand because of me.

Johnny Why are you thinking about her again?!

Lotus Because it's not right.

Johnny She didn't lose her hand because of you.

Lotus It was my machine.

Johnny No, it wasn't. It was some millionaire factory owner's who doesn't give two shits about the people who work for him.

Lotus If I'd gone to work instead of going out with you –

Johnny Then it might have been you.

Lotus It shouldn't have been her.

Johnny It shouldn't be anybody.

Lotus The worst bit is, I know what'll happen to her when she goes home.

Johnny Get ready, will ya?

Lotus I know what her parents will say.

Xiaomei, *missing her right hand, walks up the path to her father's hut. He stands in the door. They look at each other for a long moment. He slaps her in the face.*

Xiaomei's Father Failure.

He turns and leaves her standing there, head down. Beat.

Lotus That's what my dad would say.

Johnny Not after tonight.

Lotus It's not just about me, though, is it?

Beat.

Johnny I don't know anybody who cares like you. Everyone our age tries so hard to be hard and cynical and cool, like if they don't care about anything they'll never get hurt. As if any of us can stop ourselves getting hurt. I think you're kinda amazing. (*Beat.*) Except tonight it is about you, you muppet!

Lotus (*giggling*)   Tonight maybe.

Johnny   So can you get your head together please and get ready?

Lotus   Yeah, yeah, alright.

She takes a deep breath and focuses. He starts to back away. Beat.

Lotus   Anjing?

Johnny   What?

Lotus   Thank you. For getting me this.

Johnny   Head. Together. Muppet.

They smile at each other. He steps away. She takes a deep breath and steps up to the microphone. Applause. Lights up on her, then down on both of them.

A group of girls sitting in a row along a wall, listening to a lecture and taking notes. Above them hangs a sign, NICROSOFT WORB OFFICIAL TRAINING. **Sange** *enters and takes a seat at the end of the row. The girl next to her nods hello.* **Sange** *pulls out a notepad and looks for a pen but can't find one. The girl next to her hands her one.*

Sange (*whispers*)   Thanks.

First Girl (*whispers*)   Cool.

Sange *listens. Beat.*

Sange   What's he talking about?

First Girl   Word-processing.

Sange   *Hao hao hao.*

She listens. She takes a note. Beat.

What's word-processing?

Second Girl   Shhh.

First Girl   Like writing on computers and stuff.

Sange   OK.

She listens. She takes a note.

What's 'New Blank Document'?

Second Girl (*glaring at them*)   Shhh!

Sange (*loud*)   You shhh!

All the other girls turn and stare at her.

What?

Second Girl   We're trying to learn.

Sange   I'm trying to learn. Bitch.

She makes a gesture and the **Second Girl** *turns away in a huff. The* **First Girl** *is amused.*

First Girl   You work in a factory, don't you?

Sange   No. (*Beat.*) How can you tell?

First Girl   You've got that attitude.

Sange   What d'you mean?

First Girl   It's cool. Me too. Not for much longer though.

Sange   No?

First Girl   Why I'm here. Get away.

Sange   Get something better.

First Girl   Yeah. You?

Sange   Same. (*Beat.*) And this friend of mine . . .

First Girl   Huh?

Sange   This friend of mine, she . . . kinda gave me the idea.

First Girl   *Hao hao hao.*

Beat. **Sange** *takes a note.*

Sange   What's 'Print Preview'?

Second Girl   Shhh!

Sange/First Girl   You shhh, bitch!!

Beat. **Sange** *takes a note. And another. Lights down on the class.*

Zhang *on a new mobile phone. Stacks of iPhone boxes under his arm.*

Zhang   It was rubbish. For a start, it was full of Chinese. What's the point in going halfway round the world to see a load of Chinese? I could hardly see Buckingham Palace cos there were so many of them. And Buckingham Palace is shit. We've got bigger toilets than that in Beijing. All that money and that's where the Queen lives? No taste. And David Beckham is really really boring. Just goes on about football all the time. (*Beat.*) Of course I met him. (*Beat.*) I *know* his team was playing in California, but he made a special trip to see me. (*Beat.*) No, you *think* you saw him on TV, but actually you didn't, cos he was in London. With me. (*Beat.*) Well, who are you gonna believe, Huang, ESPN or me?

He moves offstage. **Li** *addresses the audience. The crowd groups behind him.*

Li   There's a *shanzhai* T-shirt that's really popular at the moment. It takes one of the old Cultural Revolution slogans:

Five kids come forward, each with one of the characters.

Crowd   *Wei Renmin Fuwu!*

Li   Meaning:

Crowd   Serve the People!

Li   And turns it into:

A sixth kid comes forward with a character and muscles his way into the line-up.

Crowd   *Wei Renminbi Fuwu!*

Li   Which means:

Crowd   Serve the Dollar!

Li   All my mates think I'm a weirdo for being interested in our past. They think the past is a dark place and why would anyone wanna go back there, to a time with no rights and no freedom? But they've got the wrong end of the stick. I don't wanna go back. I wanna go forward.

The crowd of kids starts chanting 'Wei Renmin Fuwu! Serve the People!' softly at first, but gathering in volume.

Li   How can equality and togetherness and fighting for a better world be bad things? And how did they end up giving us people like him? (*Points after* **Zhang**.) Do all revolutions have to turn out bad? I don't know. All I know is I think we can do better than this. Better than what we've got. Where money is everything and the streets are so polluted you can't breathe and we still don't know what the truth is cos they won't tell us. And even though it's not the smart thing to do, and kinda dangerous really, I'm gonna look for it. Something better. That's what I'm gonna do.

Li's Dad *appears, limping slightly.*

Li's Dad   Alright, son?

Li   Alright?

Li's Dad   Good day at school?

Li   It was good, yeah.

Li's Dad   Come on then. Let's go home.

Li's Dad *puts his arm around* **Li**'s *shoulders and they move offstage.*

Crowd   *Wei Renmin Fuwu! Serve the People! Wei Renmin Fuwu! Serve the People! Wei Renmin Fuwu! Serve the People!*

Blackout.

Socialism is Great

*Notes on rehearsal and staging, drawn from a workshop
with the writer held at the National Theatre, November 2011*

The Background to the Play

Anders Lustgarten is a political activist, and also has a PhD in
Chinese politics. He commented that in writing this play he
was primarily interested in exploring the political frameworks
people live in and how they affect ordinary people's lives.

There is a change that's been happening in China for a while,
to do with the increased role of capitalism in the lives of
people there. Anders described the concept of *Shanzhai*, which
is the subversive art and images that are circulated which use
traditional communist images, and superimpose dollar
symbols or multinational companies' logos to replace the
original symbols for communism.

One of the questions Anders wanted to explore was whether
people pursue happiness by political action, or by making
money? China has moved from the former to the latter since
the Cultural Revolution.

Anders suggested that pursuing wealth as the only route to
happiness leads to a tense and frustrated society. China is an
extreme example of this, and Anders suggested that the West
is another clear example of this. Mao's idea was that
collective political action could be a path to happiness – an
idea which got burned out by the Cultural Revolution but as
the limitations of consumerism become apparent is regaining
popularity.

Other themes in the play are the genuine and the fake; class
and wealth; the pursuit of happiness and the role of family.

Beginning Work on the Play

Anders suggested that although it isn't essential to have detailed knowledge of contemporary China to direct the play, there were some books and films that might be of interest (see below). The Chinese phrases throughout the text should be spoken with confidence and fluidity, rather than an over-emphasis on precision.

We read through the script as a group, taking one line each, so that individuals didn't feel the pressure to 'perform' a character in this initial read-through. Director Angus Jackson, leading the workshop, commented that all stage directions should also be read aloud, although often in productions stage directions don't have to be followed rigorously. The text, however, must be kept the same in all productions: we agreed this as a non-negotiable element.

One question came up about the gender of the characters in the first scene, and a director with an all-female cast requested to change the characters from two boys to two girls. Anders commented that he would have written them differently if he had imagined them as girls, but that if the director could see it working as it was on the page, he was happy for this change to be made.

We stopped after each 'section' of action, and identified the facts that had been established, including facts about the back-story and about the 'given circumstances' of the scene: in other words, things that should be established with the actors in order for them to play the scene clearly. Angus also suggested giving factual titles to each of these sections, to help clarify the structure of the play. Some examples are as follows:

SECTION ONE

It is at a private school (no school uniforms, Zhang's clothes should be what we might term 'nouveau riche') • It is in the private space of Zhang's room at boarding school • There are rich and poor students here, because of a quota system •

Zhang's father led a revolution in China in 1967. He now runs an iPhone factory. He inspired Li's dad, who was beaten at work when the priorities of the regime changed • Zhang is going to London because he has won a competition dishonestly • Li writes Zhang's homework for him • Li's ambitions are centred around self-development and his ideas about what is right • Zhang is paying someone to get to a higher level of a computer game for him • Li has got to an internet page that he isn't supposed to be able to see, because he is on Zhang's computer • iPhones are much more expensive in China, even though they are manufactured there • There are lots of 'fake' products for sale in China • Zhang seems to have little direct contact with his father • Zhang calls his father 'Daddy'. Anders commented that this is pretty normal in China, even though it may seem immature here. Rich children tend to be more infantilised, but in general children have more respect for their parents than in the West • Zhang seems to be physically aggressive • Li has the essay printed at the top of the scene (has he printed it from Zhang's laptop or beforehand? Both are possibilities).

Research facts Anders provided on this section were:

- Ninety per cent of the billionaires in China are sons and daughters of leading Communist Party officials (they are known as the '*taizidang*', or Party of the Little Princes).

- It is normal in China to pay someone else to achieve a high-level score in a game for you. Prisoners in Chinese prisons are forced to labour all day, then play computer games all night, and the prison sells their credits to foreigners for substantial amounts of money.

- There is heavy censorship of the internet by the authorities in China, so quite often if you are searching on a normal search engine, a page saying 'can't connect' will appear, which means it has been blocked. However, government officials can access these pages, which is how Li is able to reach one via Zhang's computer.

SECTION TWO

Johnny is a gamer – he is being paid by Zhang • Lotus
works in a factory • The scene takes place in the women's
lingerie department of a clothing shop (we asked why the
scene took place here, and Anders commented that possibly
Lotus wants to be someone who could shop here) • Johnny
is from a rural village • Lotus is from Henan • Lotus is late
for work by the end of the scene: in the next scene we discover
this means she will lose her job • Johnny and Lotus are from
a lower class than Zhang and Li – the scenes move down the
social scale through the play.

Research facts Anders provided on this section were:

- The areas where there are factories attract lots of young
  girls. There is a constant turnover of workers as some leave
  to go to what they consider better factories, and lateness
  means losing your job as there will be someone waiting to
  take it immediately. So the workforce is basically made of
  migrant workers. Suicide rates are high in these places.

- Things used to be very different – it was almost impossible
  (and unheard of for women) to leave rural areas.

- There is now a shortage of young women in rural China
  due to the one-child policy.

SECTION THREE

The machines in the factory are dangerous • Xiaomei is
from a pig farm, and has a dying mother • Both Xiaomei
and Sange are working for someone else • Xiaomei is the
third of three girls, and is working to pay for her younger
brother, Little King's, education • Sange explains that she
used to have the same hopes as Xiaomei does now • Sange
seems to be protective of Lotus • There are suicides here –
there are nets below the windows to stop people killing
themselves by jumping out • The factory girls don't know
what they are making, although they do know they are
Western products • The factory girls don't seem to have
rights – they are subjected to sexual harassment • They

don't get paid until they have worked for two months •
Their living conditions are poor (Xiaomei slept in the bus
station on her way here) • There was a sign advertising
English lessons on the bus • You must bribe the authorities
with money if you want to have more than one child (boys are
preferred by families having children) • You are not allowed
to sing in the factory • News about the girls would quickly
travel back to their families • The factory is really noisy •
All the girls know Justin Bieber.

Research facts Anders provided on this section were:

- The one-child policy was introduced in the 1970s to curb
  population growth. It also allowed officials to make money
  from bribes from parents who wanted more than one child,
  and resulted in many baby girls being abandoned or aborted.
  It also began the trafficking of women from the Philippines
  and other parts of South-East Asia to rural China.

- The state healthcare system in China has seriously
  deteriorated (the previous system meant that if you were
  within a work unit, you were entitled to free care).
  Smashing the 'Iron Rice Bowl', taking away free state
  education, healthcare and housing, had the effect of
  providing workers for the free market.

- Rich people hardly pay tax in China.

- These factory jobs are sought after because of the other
  possibilities of life outside the village, such as computer
  courses and English lessons. There is also slightly more
  social mobility, although it isn't enough to allow them
  to marry in a higher class, so many of the girls find it
  hard to marry – they are effectively in a female-only class
  by being factory workers.

SECTION FOUR

Zhang has been to London, has not met Beckham, and has a
new phone • Xiaomei has gone home and been branded a
failure • Sange has gone on a computer course • Li is
standing up for equality • Lotus is going on the stage •

Li's dad limps from the beatings he had as a young man   •
Zhang seems most alone by the end.

We asked the question whether the ending was redemptive or
not? Li's idea that looking at the past could help us to move
on is a redemptive one.

Rehearsal Exercises

KEEPING AN AUDIENCE'S ATTENTION

Angus suggested that in each section of a scene the cast be
asked to identify answers to the following two questions:

- *What do I want?*

- *How do I get it?*

After these have been established, they might be able to
identify an answer to this third question:

- *What is stopping me getting it?*

If these exercises are followed through in the way the scenes
are played, it will help them to have a dramatic drive,
urgency and high stakes, which will keep the audience
interested (for example, in whether the character is going to
get what they want).

For example, in Section One of the play, it was suggested that:

- Li – wants access to censored material/he is here because
  of the homework he has done for Zhang/to wind Zhang
  up (re what he tells him about Britain).

- Zhang – wants to get Li to give the impression you don't
  care about the coursework/for Li to respect you.

We agreed that Li wants to leave, but he also wants Zhang to
know that he wants to go to London (which is what keeps him
in the room). We also discussed the fact that Li doesn't want
to leave because he wants to prove his point to Zhang.

We discussed the fact that for this scene to work, the stakes should build gradually: if it is too heated at the opening of the scene, it isn't believable that both of them stay in the room for as long as they do. We discussed the fact that this seems to imply that to an extent they are used to insulting/bantering with one another – it is only when Li brings up Zhang's father that he seems to cross a line.

We discussed how hard Li would have to work to keep the essay in his hand, and how hard Zhang tries to get it back. It didn't feel quite right for Zhang to have to chase after Li too much, as this reduces his status considerably.

We agreed that Zhang avoiding eye-contact with Li was an effective way for him to maintain his status and give Li the impression that the coursework is unimportant to him.

In Section Two of the play, it was suggested that:

- Johnny – wants to get a date with Lotus.
- Lotus – wants to be wooed/wants to reinvent herself (see previous comment about the location of the scene).

We noted that it is important that Johnny believes Lotus really has a fat brother in order for her joke to work later on, and also to raise the stakes of his encounter with her, to make it clear he really wants to get her to go on a date with him.

We raised the question of how many times Lotus and Johnny have been in this situation before – for Western young people it might be a more natural encounter, so it's important that it is clear for these two that it doesn't happen often in their lives – they are navigating a new type of conversation. Having said this, the scene also seemed to play well if they both played 'hard to get'.

We discussed the push/pull rhythm of their conversation, where Lotus challenges Johnny, watches him deal with it, and then relents (an example being the 'fat brother' incident). We also discussed how nervous both of them might be, and how honest they are with each other through the scene. This ties in to one of the themes of the play, to do with 'fakeness' and how things are represented in the world. The turning point of the scene is therefore when Johnny tells Li his real name.

In Section Three, with application to specific moments in the section:

- Xiaomei – wants to get away from home/to learn.
- Sange – wants to not get fired/to protect others/to be free of the burden of her younger brother.

How they try to get these things:

- Xiaomei – tenacity, a fake ID.
- Sange – by obeying rules.

We discussed the importance that the danger of the machines was made clear by how they are handled when Sange shows Xiaomei how to use them.

Anders also commented that it was important that there was no sentimentality in the way Sange describes her family – she could almost spit the words 'Little King', because she is tough and insulated. The repetition of her work has made her numb to self-pity. He said her type of people are characteristically quite abrupt and down to earth.

In order to achieve this, Angus suggested an exercise where the actor is asked to say the speech and push against a wall as hard as they can at the same time. This introduces a very physical inner conflict.

When Xiaomei visits her father we discussed the possibility that this was an imagined scene, but agreed it was more effective played as reality.

Staging Ideas and Production Notes

We commented that overall the overlapping scenes lend themselves to simple staging, so that the action can move quickly between locations. This answered the first question about staging: can the play be done with a small budget?

SECTION ONE

We looked through the various options of positioning the desk in the first scene – whether it needs a chair, whether it should face the audience, be positioned side on, or on a diagonal. We settled on a diagonal, as it seemed to help both actors playing the scene, although we agreed other options are possibilities. We also discussed various options for how the money is transferred between the two of them, in order to keep the status difference clear. For example, Zhang might put it down on the desk rather than into Li's hand.

Later in the scene, when Zhang's father appears, suggestions included revealing him in a spotlight, or creating a sense of his location using noises of factory workers.

For the scene change direction on page 222 ('*The kids emerge from the wings* . . . ') we discussed whether the two lines of people should go upstage/downstage or left/right, and whether the pairings should remain the same across the lines throughout or could be staggered, with partners swapped during the sequence.

SECTION TWO

We noted that Johnny and Li's walk sequence should happen as they speak the lines of their conversation. We explored options of having two lines of people walking upstage, and Li and Johnny miming walking to give the sense of movement. We explored the ensemble being trees, and Anders suggested he had imagined them as people, and that they were walking down a busy street rather than in a park. He wanted to get the sense that they are somehow swept along by a human tide, but feel immune and also uplifted 'above' the other people in the scene.

We looked at options of them walking along people's hands, or on people's shoulders, so that they are elevated.

SECTION THREE

One of the questions participants raised at the beginning of the day was how you could stage the scenes in the factory – a girl getting her hand chopped off by a huge machine?

We discussed the use of a row of chairs, and choreographed actions by each girl to give a sense of her specific task.

Anders told us that the factories are built so that the girls are very close together and each has a basket on the edge of her work station into which she throws each section as she completes it. Very often component parts don't give an indication of the product that is being produced. There is a separate role for girls who collect completed parts from these side baskets, walking up and down the aisles. Anders commented it appears rather makeshift and disorganised, contrary to what he had expected.

Another point Anders shared with us in relation to this factory was that in the West workers are a costly element in the output. In China this is not the case – there are many people and they are paid very poorly. This contributes to the seeming inefficiency of the system because there are enough people to do all sorts of things – including the human conveyer belt of having workers going round collecting products.

We experimented with the workers making a sound for their own action, and putting the sounds together to create an overall soundscape. We discussed ways to reduce its volume, or slow it down, once the dialogue of the scene begins.

The suggestion of having a scene with Little King played out simultaneously on stage was raised.

For the hand-chopping episode we devised a simple action that made Xiaomei's right hand very visible as part of the action. Then when Sange cries out (as she sees it about to happen), Xiaomei quickly covered her hand as though gripping her arm in pain. We discussed the possibility of using red paint in a Brechtian-style version of the moment, using red ribbon as in Kabuki theatre, and the fact that the story of her losing her hand completely could be confirmed later on in the play, when she goes to see her father (using a sleeve and bandage for example).

The 'Nicrosoft Worb' scene was explored using a whole row of students, with Lotus arriving late and having to disturb them all to get to her seat, and then ask for a pen. It raised the stakes of her being there, and also made it clear that this opportunity is a privilege for these girls, so they were all irritated at being distracted.

Staging the Bigger Scenes with a Smaller Cast

We choreographed a version of the opening section of the play – inspired by the Beijing Olympic Opening Ceremony, as indicated in the stage directions. This included very orderly marching on to the stage in rows, turning to face the audience, and performing a very simple, Tai-Kwon-Do-style routine. It ended with everyone crouching before the sequence of phones ringing began. We experimented with different versions of this, including adding an idea that one person's phone goes off first, and everyone turning and staring at the unlucky individual. Anders commented that although this version was dramatic, he was more interested in the idea of everyone's phone going off at the same time, to give a sense of the collective identity he wanted to suggest reminiscent of the communist history of China.

We had about ten people in the group performing this opening section, but because they moved in unison, and were fairly close together for the phone-ringing sequence, it meant that the sense of chaos was in clear contrast to the orderly, choreographed beginning.

For the protest scene towards the end of Section One, Anders pointed out that the reference to 'dancing' in the stage direction should be treated carefully – there is something serious and sombre about it, and it should appear politically motivated rather than a big party.

Can the Play Support a Brechtian style?

We looked at some stylistic choices that could be made in the final scene, and possibly earlier in the play too. As the final scene includes all the characters from the story in small episodic sections, it might be possible to have multiple scenes take place on stage together (but not simultaneously). Each time a scene section ends, for example after the section when Xiaomei goes to see her father and he hits her, the actress playing Xiaomei stayed on stage, in a frozen position reacting to the hit, for the rest of the play, until the final moment when the crowd scene develops and all the actors on stage surround Li for the final lines. It was quite effective to have Lotus watch Xiaomei visit her father – it read as though she was imagining it happening to her. However it also worked well to have Lotus and Johnny frozen for that section.

It also worked to find a way to 'overlap' the video section of the opening scene with the rest of the scene: the actors in the video could surround Li and Zhang, stand to the side of them as in a separate scene, or come and clear the previous scene in order to use the entire stage. We discussed whether Li and Zhang might freeze during this section, or watch the action. We also discussed the options of having the protesters shout to Li and Zhang, or out to the audience.

In this way, the play lends itself to inventive and experimental staging: this scene could also have been staged by dividing each scene and having actors leave the stage for each section.

The Brechtian element of the script could be most strongly exemplified in the final speech by Li. Angus suggested the actor read it with such urgency that it meant he could only turn out to the audience to share his message – because he felt so passionately about it. The earlier scene with Li's father's speech could also work in this way.

The use of sound: live percussion, recorded factory sounds, or voices of the actors (this is more difficult to sustain over a prolonged period), could all be used to support the noisy factory location in particular, especially in the absence of a set, in a 'poor theatre' aesthetic.

Suggested References

Leslie T. Chang, *Factory Girls: From Village to City in a Changing China* (2008).

'The Beijing Olympic Opening Ceremony' video can be found on YouTube.

Dancer in the Dark (2000, dir. Lars von Trier), with reference to ideas about how to stage the factory location.

Blind Shaft (2003, dir. Li Yang), based on the novel *Shen Mu* (*Sacred Wood*) by Liu Qingbang.

From a workshop led by Angus Jackson,
with notes by Ellen McDougall

The Grandfathers

Rory Mullarkey

Characters

Kol
Tol
Val
Kost
Stas
Dim
Lev
Sash
Zhen

Roles may be played by actors of either gender.

Scene One: Kol

Kol   When I wake up I don't know where I am.

A hillside in Central Asia. Gunfire, explosions. The section is pinned down, behind a wall of sandbags. **Kol** *opens his eyes. He is heavily wounded.* **Zhen** *is holding him.*

Zhen   Look at me, Kol, stay with me.

Kol   Zhen . . .

Zhen   I'm here Kol, look at me mate.

Sash   Kol!

Zhen   Kol look at me, mate, fucking look at me.

Kol   What the fuck am I looking at?

Zhen   What?

Lev   Taking heavy fire.

Kol   What the fuck am I looking at?

Dim   Kol.

Zhen   Me, Kol, you're looking at me.

Kol   No, what the fuck are you looking at? What the fuck are you looking at, Zhen mate, what the fuck are you looking at?

Zhen   What? Stay with me, Kol!

Kol   Haha, you remember, Zhen? What the fuck are you looking at? Haha! You're crying, Zhen!

Stas   He's delirious.

Kol   Crying! You're crying!

Zhen (*his hands are putting pressure on* **Kol**'s *wound*)   I don't have a free hand here, someone fetch me a tourniquet! Anyone!

Kol   Haha, why you so concerned about me?

Sash   Everyone stay down!

Kol   If you receive this letter, Sash! Sash, think about the letters going home.

Val   Machine guns, snipers, we're completely pinned down!

Tol   Mortars soon, too, that means. We'll need to fall back!

Val   We can't, Sarge, we can't, we're completely pinned down!

Lev   This wall won't hold, Sarge!

Kol   In terms of defence, Lev, there's nothing better than a wall! Haha!

Zhen   Stay with me, mate!

Kol   What the fuck are you looking at? Haha, you remember, there's nothing better than a wall!

Tol   Return fire!

Dim   They'd shoot my head straight off, Sarge, I can't even – And Kol, Sarge, and Kol –

Kost   Mortars!

Dim   Sarge, we have to get Kol out!

Kol   For fuck's sake, Dim, we're trying to get some sleep over here!

Zhen   Don't close your eyes, Kol!

Kol   You're keeping us all awake, Dim, we're on parade in the morning!

Zhen   Stay awake!

Stas   Grenade!

Val   We're pinned down!

Stas   Grenade!

Kol You named him Hector, Stas! Haha, you named him Hector but he's only a baby!

Dim What about Kol?

Tol Just keep him talking!

Kost I don't think we'll have a problem doing that.

Kol I can see my face in your boots, Kost. All shiny and new, haha, they're like mirrors!

Tol We've got machine guns at twelve and two, snipers at eleven and one.

Kol Scoff at six and PT in the morning, haha!

Val There's too much fire!

Zhen Count for me, Kol, count to ten!

Kol Val, what makes the grass grow?

Zhen Don't look at your wound!

Stas Incoming mortars!

Lev Heads down!

Kol Val, what makes the grass grow?! What makes the grass grow?!

Lev Heads down!

Zhen Count to ten, Kol. I'm here, don't close your eyes, count to ten!

Kol One. You're crying!

Zhen Count!

Kol Two.

Sash Stay down!

Kol Three.

Lev Heads down!

Kol   Four.

Dim   Is he going to make it?

Kol   Five. I can't feel my legs!

Stas   Grenade!

Kol   Six.

Kost   We have to fall back, Sarge!

Kol   Seven.

Val   We're completely pinned down!

Kol   Eight.

Tol   Mortars!

Kol   Nine.

Zhen   We're losing him. I think we're losing him!

Kol   Five hundred and forty-seven! What the fuck are you looking at?

Zhen   He's going cold – oh God, Kol, please don't die!

Kol   Hahaha! Five hundred and forty-seven! Five hundred and forty-seven!

A large explosion. The sandbag wall is destroyed.

Five hundred and forty-seven days!

Scene Two: Tol

Tol   Five hundred and forty-seven days. Your country called you up, and you came.

A barracks room. Months earlier. **Tol**, *a non-commissioned officer, is speaking to the conscripts, who stand fresh, green, in a line.*

When men in suits fuck up, the soldiers get sent in. You ask me why you're here, I tell you someone, somewhere, made a right royal pig's ear of things. There's a high chance that you're going to get sent to battle. There's a high chance that you're going to end up on a hill in some shithole cursing the God that made you young. You ask me why you're here, I tell you so you don't get your arse shot off as soon as you land. You ask me why you're here, I tell you: training.

Lights change. The conscripts are doing press-ups.

Tol What do you call that, conscript?

Zhen A press-up, Sarge.

Tol Very good. And what do you call that, conscript?

Val A press-up, Sarge.

Tol Very good. And what do you call that, conscript?

Stas A press-up, Sarge.

Tol Very good. And what do you call that, conscript?

Kol A press-up, Sarge.

Tol A what?

Kol A press-up, Sarge.

Tol That is not a press-up, conscript, that is a mediocre impression of a snake having sex with a doughnut. Look over there. (*Indicates* **Zhen**.)That, conscript, is a press-up. Watch him. Now you try.

Kol *does a better press-up.*

Tol Very good. The press-up is your lover, the press-up is your friend. Those burning arm-extensions are the closest thing you'll get round here to a hug. The ache of your chest muscles in the morning is the closest thing you'll get to a broken heart. You can even kiss the floor if you like, while you're down there. Do you like press-ups, conscript?

Sash Very much so, Sarge.

Tol Well, you've come to the right place.

Lights change. The conscripts are on a jog.

The average teenager nowadays has the constitution of a seventy-year-old man. Generally, the most strenuous exercise he is able to perform is reaching to turn off his Xbox before bed. His diet has all the nutritional value of the smell that comes out of a tramp's arsehole on a lazy Saturday afternoon. Would that be fair to say, conscript?

Lev   Not at all, Sarge.

Tol   Then prove it.

Lights change. The conscripts are doing star-jumps.

This is not just your job now: this is your life. You sleep when I say, you go to scoff when I say. There isn't a bead of sweat that falls from your nostril without my say-so. You've met your maker, conscripts, and it's me. You are moulded in my image, so you'd better mould good because I'm proud of myself. Forget personal liberty, forget personal space, erase the word 'personal' from your vocabulary. It was never even there.

Lights change. The conscripts are crawling across a field.

Think of me as your centurion. If you hate me, it is only because I love you too much. It is only because I know that if you want to fight easy you have to train hard. Train hard.

All   Fight easy!

Tol   Train hard.

All   Fight easy!

Tol   I want you to suffer. When you lie in bed at night I want you to be in pain. And in the morning we do it all over again.

Lights out.

We wake up!

Lights. The conscripts are doing press-ups.

Tol What do you call that, conscript?

Dim A press-up, Sarge.

Tol Very good. And why are we doing press-ups?

Dim As a punishment, Sarge.

Tol Speak up, conscript, I don't have supersonic hearing.

Dim As a punishment, Sarge.

Tol Correct, conscript. A punishment for what?

Dim I didn't make my bed properly, Sarge. The sheets weren't straight enough.

Tol What do we do to test the tautness of the sheets?

Dim We bounce a coin on them, Sarge.

Tol And what did the coin do on your sheets, conscript?

Dim It rolled off, Sarge.

Tol Correct, conscript. It rolled off.

Lights change. The conscripts are on a jog.

Tol You are part of a large conscript army. Your term of service is five hundred and forty-seven days. After that term is up, victory or none, you go home. Cross the days off on a calendar, count them backwards in your head, it won't make them go any quicker. And when you're old and stupid and look back over your life, you might even remember these days fondly. You might even smile. You might even think to yourself, 'They made me who I am.' That won't make them feel any better now, though. They feel like hell, and they're supposed to.

Lights change.

Occasionally, you may be given short periods of recreation time, for chatter and the like.

Kol Did you see the football last night?

Zen   Well, obviously not.

Tol   That's enough!

Lights change. The conscripts are doing star-jumps.

Tol   You did not choose to be here. But you will never forget that this is now your life. One!

Val   Two!

Kost   Three!

Stas   Four!

Dim   Five!

Lev   Six!

Sash   Seven!

Zhen   Eight!

Kol   Nine!

Tol   Ten! And in the morning we do it all over again.

Lights out.

We wake up!

Lights. The conscripts are doing press-ups.

What do you call that? One!

Val   Two!

Kost   Three!

Stas   Four!

Dim   Five!

Lev   Six!

Sash   Seven!

Zhen   Eight!

Kol   Nine!

Tol   Ten! We train hard!

All   We fight easy!

Tol   We train hard!

All   We fight easy!

Tol   And in the morning we do it all over again.

Lights out.

We wake up!

Lights.

And in the morning we do it all over again.

Scene Three: Val

Val   I'm not sure I'd describe myself as happy. You get used to it, I suppose. I guess happiness is something different nowadays: waking up with a start but realising I've still got an hour left in bed before reveille; that occasional Friday at scoff when they get the custard just right. So I guess what I've done is, I've changed the meaning of the word happiness. It wasn't actually that hard to do. It's just a word, after all.

A field. **Val** *is standing motionless in front of a life-size dummy, his bayonet fixed to his rifle.*

Tol   What makes the grass grow?

Val   I can't.

Slight pause.

Tol   Right.

Slight pause.

Well, we're not going anywhere until you do.

Slight pause.

Tol   Conscript.

Val   It's just, it's its eyes, Sarge. I feel like it's looking at me.

Kost   It doesn't have any eyes, Val. It's a fucking dummy.

Val   It's just, well, you know what I mean, don't you?

Kost   Not really.

Val   It's looking at me. What's inside it?

Zhen   Meat. Pig guts.

Dim   He's joking.

Lev   It's just sand.

Val   It's just, it's not like on the range, is it? It's not like with a rifle, a bullet, you're not asking us to pull the trigger dead cold like, you're asking us to stab, with our arms and our strength, it's a stab you're asking me to do. Get right close and stick it in the guts.

Lev   In the sand.

Val   But still. It's what it means.

Tol   Well, we're not going in until you do. We'll stand out here through to dark, if that's what it takes.

Kol   Come on Val, mate, it's cold.

Val   This doesn't happen a lot, does it, I mean like, up close?

Zhen   Well, who fucking knows, mate?

Val   But like with, you know, bayonets. Even the word sounds old, savage. Makes me think of trenches.

Kost   For fuck's sake, Val!

Val   I'm sorry!

Kost   Fucking Zhen over there, he twatted the shit out of it, left his looking like a crocodile'd been at it.

Zhen   I just got carried away.

Kost   He's a regular fucking Rambo.

Kol   You nearly had my eye out, mate.

Zhen   Sorry.

Kol   You should be.

Zhen   Well you shouldn't stand so close then.

Kol   I wasn't close I was –

Kost   Oi save the lovers' tiff for later, yeah? Come on Val, its not that hard, just imagine it's him or you. Just imagine he's fighting back.

Val   But he's not.

Kost   Just imagine it.

Sash   See it in your head, mate, it's him or you.

Lev   You're at the front.

Sash   You're deep behind enemy lines.

Stas   You're in a corridor.

Zhen   A long, dark corridor in a bombed-out house.

Dim   One of those ones with dirt on the floor, you know, grass sticking through the floorboards.

Kol   In the mountains. High up.

Zhen   In the mountains.

Lev   And suddenly, he's there.

Stas   He strafes out from an obscured door frame.

Kol   And he's there.

Zhen   And it's him or you, at that moment, cos if you let him, he'll stick you where you stand.

Lev   And if he gets away, he could stick any of us.

Stas   Any of us.

Sash   He could be the one who kills your brothers.

Zhen   And he's not even looking at you now, but he could be the one, if you leave him.

Lev   A bomb in the road or a sniper's round screaming towards our heads.

Zhen   And you could be the one who lets your brothers die.

Kol   It is not justice, it is not politics.

Dim   It is animal.

Zhen   So do it, for fuck's sake.

Stas   For us and for you.

Kol   Do it.

Kost   Do it.

Stas   Do it.

Dim   Do it.

Lev   Do it.

Sash   Do it.

All   Do it.

Slight pause. Without much force, **Val** *sticks the bayonet into the dummy.*

Tol   Good. But now again. Mean it. Kill him. What makes the grass grow?

Val *sticks the bayonet into the dummy again.*

Tol   What makes the grass grow? When the enemy practise this they use the rotting corpses of our troops. What makes the grass grow?

Beat.

Val   Blood, Sarge.

Tol   What?

Val   Blood, Sarge.

Tol   Speak up, conscript, I don't have supersonic hearing.

Val   Blood, Sarge.

Tol   Yes. What makes the grass grow?

Val   Blood, Sarge.

He sticks his bayonet into the dummy with more force.

Tol   Yes. What makes the grass grow?

Val   Blood, blood, blood. (*He begins stabbing the dummy on each beat.*)

Tol   What makes the grass grow? If you don't kill him he will kill your brothers. What makes the grass grow?

Val   Blood, blood, blood.

Tol   What makes the grass grow? It's either him or you. What makes the grass grow?

Val   Blood, blood, blood.

Tol   WHAT MAKES THE GRASS GROW? LOOK HIM IN THE EYES! WHAT MAKES THE GRASS GROW?

Val   BLOOD, BLOOD, BLOOD!

All   WHAT MAKES THE GRASS GROW?

Val   BLOOD, BLOOD, BLOOD!

All   WHAT MAKES THE GRASS GROW?

Val *closes his eyes and repeatedly stabs the dummy. Eventually, breathless, he subsides.*

Tol   What makes the grass grow?

Val   Blood, Sarge. Blood.

Scene Four: Kost

Kost   When it comes down to it, I just really love twatting stuff. So it's kind of the perfect job for me, really. If it wasn't for this war I'd probably still be twatting stuff, just I wouldn't be wearing a uniform. Makes no difference to me, I just love twatting stuff. Some of the other shit they make you do, though, you know what I mean? Gets right on my tits.

The barracks room. The conscripts are cleaning their boots.

'So I can see my face in them?' I mean, what does that even mean? I mean, literally, what does that mean? I mean what possible fucking reason could I ever possibly have for wanting to see my own face in a pair of combat boots? There's a mirror on the fucking wall!

Lev   No mirrors in the field though, mate.

Kost   And why exactly, Lev, do you think I'd need a mirror when I'm out in the fucking field?

Lev   On account of your extreme vanity, I'd imagine.

Kost   Oh, fuck off. I mean literally, so I'm out in the field yeah, I'm pinned down taking heavy fire from several machine guns and snipers, my mates are being blown up all around me and God knows if I'm gonna get out alive, so I know what I need to do right now, I need to check my fucking quiff. I mean literally. Bullshit mate, bullshit.

Lights change. The conscripts are ironing their combats.

I mean, it's camouflage, for crying out loud. Why do I need to put perfect creases in my camouflage? Where am I gonna be hiding, Burton bloody Menswear? Do you really think our ability to combat insurgents is directly proportional to our velocity at ironing? Sarge takes me aside the other day, he says:

Tol   Are you disrespecting our country?

Kost   Of course not, Sarge, I say.

Tol   Then why does the crease on your jacket not go directly through the centre of the flag badge on your arm?

Kost   He asks me, I mean fucking hell.

Stas   We remember, Kost.

Sash   We all did the press-ups.

Lights change. The conscripts are polishing their belt buckles.

Kost   I mean, I'm the best rifleman in the section.

Zhen   Second best.

Kost   Well, that's debatable.

Zhen   I mean it's not.

Kost   I'm the second best rifleman in the section, I have the fastest sprint time in boots –

Zhen   Well –

Kost   One of the fastest sprint times in boots, put me on the range and I'll own, give me a bayonet and I'll take you to town, I'm just great at twatting stuff essentially, but I keep getting brought up cos I'm not some kind of domestic fucking goddess.

Lights change. The conscripts are making their beds.

I mean, it's just gonna get slept in again tonight.

Lights change. The conscripts are doing press-ups.

Tol   Discipline. Integrity. Respect. These values do not just extend to others, they extend to yourself and to your appearance. You are a unit, a machine working in perfect synchronicity, a sleek, beautifully ironed, nicely polished aesthetically pleasing machine. You keep yourself in order, you keep your life in order, you follow your orders and you keep your life. Do you understand me, conscript?

Kost   Yes, Sarge.

Tol   He is your responsibility and you are his. Do you understand why you are being punished, conscripts?

All   Yes, Sarge.

Tol   One.

Val   Two.

Kost   Three.

Stas   Four.

Dim   Five.

Lev   Six.

Sash   Seven.

Zhen   Eight.

Kol   Nine.

Tol   Ten. Attention!

They stand to attention.

Quick march!

They march off.

Kost   You guys just wait till I get in the field.

Scene Five: Stas

Stas   The worst part is always now. The old men say the worst part is always now. They say every part is the worst part. And then, looking back, they say parts they once said were the worst are now the best. And the worst part is always now. But what do we care for 'they'? We have no use any more for they or he or she or you or I. For now, it is only we. Now, in the worst part, in the very worst part, it is only us.

The barracks room. **Stas** *and* **Sash** *are crouched over a cardboard box.*

Sash   What are you gonna do with it?

Stas   Dunno.

Sash   Well, you can't keep it.

Stas   Why not?

Sash   Well, just because.

Stas   Because what?

Sash   Just. Because.

Enter **Kol**.

Kol   What are we looking at? (*He sees what's in the box.*) Oh.

Stas   We're trying to work out what to do with him.

Sash   So it's a him now?

Stas   Well.

Kol   Well, you can't keep it.

Sash   That's what I said.

Kol   Sarge'll burst a blood vessel.

Sash   He will. He'll burst a bloody blood vessel.

Kol   How'd he get in?

Enter **Dim** *and* **Lev**.

Dim   Alright.

Lev   Fuck are you doing? (*He goes over and looks in the box.*) Fuck is that?

Kol   It's a bird, Lev.

Lev   Yes, no, I realise it's a fucking bird, Kol, but what the fuck is it doing in our barracks room?

Stas   He flew in through the window.

Dim   When?

Stas   Just before. But he hurt his wing in the flying in, see, and now he can't fly, so we're working out what to do with him.

Dim   Well, you can't keep him.

Sash   Exactly. Exactly.

Enter **Zhen**.

Zhen   Hey. What's going on?

Kol   Zhen, there's a bird.

Zhen   Shit, where? Has anyone got any deodorant?

Kol   No, not like a bird, a bird, like – (*Points inside the box.*) A bird.

Zhen   Oh. Right.

Stas   He's only a baby.

Sash   So he's a baby now?

Stas   Well, yeah, he looks like a baby.

Sash   He's not a baby, he's just small. You're just saying he's a baby cos he's small but he's just a small bird.

Stas   He's a baby.

Sash   He's just a small bird. All birds are small.

Stas   But he's –

Dim   What about ostriches?

Sash   Well, no, yes, not ostriches.

Kol   Or flamingos.

Sash   Okay –

Lev   Flamingos are definitely gay.

Dim   What?

Lev   Definitely.

Sash   I don't think that's the issue here.

Lev   Going around in pink like that, I'm sorry, but: gay.

Dim   I don't think they choose to be pink, mate.

Lev   I don't think you choose to be gay.

Sash   Look –

Enter **Val** *and* **Kost***.*

Kol   What about female flamingos?

Val   What's going on?

Lev   We're discussing whether flamingos are gay or not.

Sash   No, that isn't the issue here.

Kost   Definitely gay.

Lev   Thank you.

Sash   There's a bird.

Val   What? Where?

Sash   Stas found a bird.

Stas   He flew in here but he hurt his wing in the flying in, and now he can't fly. I don't really know what to do with him but I think I'm going to keep him.

Val   Well, you can't keep him.

Sash   Exactly.

Stas   Yes I can. I'm gonna nurse him back to health.

Val   Well, you can't.

Stas   Yes I can. I've already named him Hector.

Sash   Oh, for God's sake.

Lev   Hector?

Stas   Yeah, Hector. I like the name, I think it suits him.

Dim   It actually does kinda suit him.

Kost   Let me have a look. (*He has a look.*) I'm sorry mate, but we're going to have to twat him.

Stas   What?

Kost   We're in a barracks, yeah? It's a military position.
That bird just made a clandestine incursion into the sovereign
territory of this country.

Stas   He flew in through the window.

Kost   It's still an incursion, mate. It's fine, I'm happy to
twat him for you if that helps.

Stas   We're not gonna twat him.

Kost   He's infiltrated –

Stas   He's a bird!

Kost   But still –

Stas   A bird!

Pause.

Kol   Kost is kinda right though.

Stas   What?

Kol   Hector's really not supposed to be in here. If Sarge
finds out he'll go mental. He'd burst a bloody blood vessel.

Sash   Exactly. He will.

Stas   He won't find out.

Kol   And anyway. Look at him. He's wounded.

Stas   He'll get better.

Kol   That wing is fucked, mate. And what's a bird gonna do
without a wing? Flying's like the main thing they do.

Zhen   So we should kill him just because he's wounded?

Kol   Well –

Zhen   If you were wounded, would you want to be killed?

Kol   Depends where I was wounded, I suppose.

Zhen   So you'd be happy if I killed you just because you were wounded?

Kol   Well. Maybe.

Zhen   Don't expect any help from me, then.

Kol   Fine.

Kost   Just in case it helps, my offer to twat the bird still stands.

Stas   No one's gonna twat him.

Val   Well, we'll have to put him outside then.

Stas   What?

Val   He's not one of us. He's only our responsibility cos he flew in here. If we put him outside he's not our responsibility. He's not on our terrain, then.

Zhen   But he'll still be wounded.

Val   But that's not our responsibility.

Stas   Why not?

Val   Cos he's not on our terrain. I'll take him over to the woods.

Stas   So that's all we should do then, is it? Look after our own.

Val   That's all we can afford to do.

Lev   Val's right.

Stas   So we shouldn't help him?

Dim   We can't. He's not one of us. He belongs outside.

Sash   We need to leave him. We need to forget about him. If shitloads of wounded birds came in you'd just help them all, would you?

Val   Outside.

Stas   But there aren't shitloads of wounded birds, there's only one.

Dim   Outside.

Lev   Outside.

Stas   There's only one.

Zhen   Outside.

Sash   Outside.

Stas   But –

Val   Outside.

Kost *has taken off his boot and tries to drop it into the box on to the bird.*

Stas   No, Kost, fuck off. No!

He tries to pull the box away.

The boot misses.

Stas   Fuck off!

Kost *picks up his boot and tries to hit the bird.*

Stas   Fuck off!

He grabs **Kost***. A struggle ensues.*

The conscripts pull **Stas** *and* **Kost** *apart.*

Val   Hold him back.

He picks up the box, and moves off.

Stas   No, Val, no, fuck off, there's only one! Hector!

Kol   It's for the best, mate.

Stas   Hector! I'm sorry, Hector.

Lev   He wasn't one of us.

Stas   I'm sorry, Hector.

Dim   He wasn't one of us.

Stas   I'm sorry, mate.

Sash   He wasn't one of us, mate.

Kol   He wasn't one of us.

The conscripts let go of **Stas**. *He is crying a bit.*

Stas (*to* **Kost**)   What are you looking at? You can fuck off and all.

He goes to leave. **Zhen** *blocks his way. He turns back. He sits on his bed, his head in his hands.*

Scene Six: Dim

Dim   The night always seems a bit brighter when there are other people in the room. Have you noticed that? It's as if we give off light.

The barracks room. After lights out. The conscripts are in their beds.

Do you guys ever get scared?

Lev   Fuck off, Dim.

Dim   Seriously –

Lev   No.

Sash   We're trying to get some sleep, Dim.

Dim   Fine.

Pause.

But don't you, ever, just a bit?

Sash   Fucking hell!

Val   Just shut up!

Dim   Like now, when we're all lying here awake.

Kost   Dim!

Stas   Dim, I swear – Dim.

Dim   Okay.

Pause.

But this is the time, isn't it, when these thoughts come to you?

Kol   For fuck's sake, Dim.

Stas   We've got fucking parade in the morning mate. And I swear –

Dim   No just – Just hear me out.

Lev   I'm not even listening to this.

Zhen   Just shut up.

Dim   Okay. Okay.

Pause.

I don't think I've ever actually seen any real blood.

Sash   AAARGH!

Dim   No, I don't think I have, I mean like, you know, real blood real actual blood not like the blood on telly or dressing-up blood vampire blood, not even like beef, you know, meat blood, I've seen that obviously, and nosebleeds too, I guess, and papercuts, yeah, lots, but I mean actual blood like from a whatcha called, an artery, is that it? Yeah, like a lot of blood all flowing out or spurting or whatever it does after a proper cut or like a gunshot depending and I was wondering if the colour was different cos I feel like it might be, you know, darker I feel like it might have more of thickness to it, that kind of blood.

Kol   For fuck's sake.

Lev   Just don't even bother. Just don't even bother listening to it.

Slight pause.

Dim Nights I wake up I think I'm covered in it. Mine, or someone else's, I can't be sure.

Slight pause.

Because that's what they say, isn't it, that when you're wounded that deep, when it really hits you bad that it doesn't actually feel of anything really, that you just feel, I dunno, kind of light and wet, obviously, from all the blood. There are other things that people can do, to make you feel the pain much more.

Slight pause.

Do you think about being captured? I do. Sarge says everything you can imagine has already been done, he says try and imagine something and it's happened, and that there are people whose job it is to imagine the worst thing and then to do it and these people have way worse imaginations than any of us. A wire round the testicles, a loop which lops them off, being nailed to things, having my eyes popped like balloons and then the dogs lick them out, my testicles in my mouth and all my skin going down my gullet, that's what I imagine, so that means it's been done and that there's people to imagine worse. Sometimes I think it's better not to think. But they've done it, in the past, when it was just land that they wanted, just land that we wanted, but now the people that fight us and we fight have different ideas to us and we can't take their ideas off them like we took their land, we can cut off someone's nose but we can't drill into their head and cut out their ideas, so that just makes me wonder if it will ever ever end.

Slight pause.

I saw a video where they cut off a journalist's head. It wasn't as bad as I thought it would be. It was cleaner.

Slight pause.

And that'd be an alright way to go, maybe, well at least that'd be an end to it, at least that moment would be the worst moment of all, but I do worry more about other people, and what they'd say when they heard, how they'd feel, and whether that would be the worst moment for them too. My mum, you know, my mum particularly, because I love all my family of course I do, but I like really really like my mum. Cos just my dad, he – And my granddad. But my mum.

Slight pause.

And I know we've got parade in the morning, but still, these things. They're always there.

Pause.

Are you asleep? Is everyone asleep?

Scene Seven: Lev

Lev   I keep having dreams that I'm a Roman soldier. I've got a sword and a shield and I'm wearing one of those skirt things you didn't get teased for wearing cos everybody wore them, and this wave of enemy are coming at me. Tribesmen, like. And they've got swords and shields too and we stand in the middle of the field and we hit each other. And that's all there is to it. Hitting each other with swords and shields. No IEDs, no RPGs, no Apache attack helicopters, no Dragunov sniper rifles, just swords and shields. And hitting each other. And it just seems way more fair like that.

A field. The conscripts are building a wall out of sandbags: passing the bags along a line, laying them out, straightening them up. Their movements are deft, together.

In terms of defence, there's nothing better than a wall.

Slight pause. The conscripts are working.

Bloody hard work to build, though. There's a rumour going round we're getting deployed. That true, Sarge?

Slight pause. The conscripts are working.

Sarge?

Tol   Eh?

Lev   There's a rumour going round we're getting deployed, Sarge. That true?

Tol   I am unable to confirm or deny any speculation on that front.

Beat.

But yeah. It's true.

Val   Fuck.

Kost   Woohoo!

Zhen   Well that wasn't exactly the world's best-kept secret.

Kol   Yeah, HQ have been tiptoeing around, looking at us all shifty-like for weeks.

Lev   Any idea where, Sarge?

Tol   What's that?

Lev   Any idea where?

Tol   None as of yet.

Sash   Some shithole, I suppose.

Stas   Some sweaty, guff-smelling, foreign, why-is-there-a-desert-we're-half-way-up-a-mountain shithole.

Tol   I wouldn't be surprised.

Pause. The conscripts are working.

Lev   We'll finish up our terms out there, I suppose. Then back home.

Dim   Telly.

Sash   Trainers.

Kost   Mum's food.

Stas   Privacy. Holy fucking privacy.

Val   My bedroom.

Zhen   Safety.

Kol   Sleep.

Pause. The conscripts are working.

Lev   Then I'll have to find a fucking job.

Tol   Yeah, good luck with that, conscript.

Slight pause. The conscripts are working.

Lev   When the Romans got back from campaigns they'd get given land. Villas in the countryside. Horses, slavegirls, gold. Not like that any more. There's fuck-all any more. My granddad got back and drunk a hole in his liver. Mate of mine ended up on the streets. They risked their lives and there's fuck-all for them. People can be ungrateful fucking bastards.

Pause. The conscripts are working.

Here, Zhen. Can you carry two sandbags?

Zhen   You what?

Lev   Two at a time. You reckon you could do that?

Zhen   Could have a go.

Lev   Bet you can.

Zhen *lifts two sandbags on to his shoulders.*

Zhen   Easy as pie.

Kol   Here, let me have a go.

Lev   No way could you do that.

Kol   You wanna bloody bet?

Lev   Go on then.

He tries. He can't lift them.

Haha. Told you.

Kol   Fuck off. I can do it.

Lev   You just bloody tried.

Kol   No no I can do it.

He tries again. He puts the sandbags on to his shoulders. He topples slightly.

Zhen   Careful!

Kol   No, I'm – Arrgh.

He falls over under the weight of the sandbags.

Zhen   Bloody hell, Kol. Are you alright?

He helps him up.

Kol   Yeah, I'm fine, I'm fine, argh.

Zhen   You bloody idiot. You sure you all right?

Kol   I'm fine. Why you so concerned?

Zhen   I'm not.

Kol   Why you so concerned about me all of a sudden? Thought you said you'd just let me die. Why you concerned about me?

Zhen   I'm not.

Pause. The conscripts are working.

Kol   You concerned about me?

Zhen   I'm concerned about the section. I'm concerned about the productivity of the section. We're a team and if one of us is incapacitated it puts us all at risk. We're a team, you know, so I'm concerned about everyone.

Kol   You're concerned about me!

Zhen   Shut up.

Kol   Haha, you're concerned about me!

Zhen   Shut up.

Kol   You bloody softy.

Pause. The conscripts are working.

Lev   What's the weather like where we're going?

Tol   Let's just say you'd better pack your sunblock.

Lev   Well, at least it'll be warm.

The conscripts finish building the wall.

There. Perfect. That'll hold. Good work.

Scene Eight: Sash

Sash   Something always matters more when you know it is going to end.

The soldiers are at bus stops, at airports, on station platforms, in front gardens, in hallways, saying goodbye.

I used to count the days through in my head. My favourite parts of the day were the parts that would pass as quickly as possible.

Val   The time at scoff, those extra hours of sleep.

Sash   I often just wished this time –

Kol   This five hundred and forty-seven days –

Sash   Would pass entirely. I just wanted to age. Fuck it, you know, I'd much rather be old and safe than be young and be sent off to die.

Stas   They say the worst part is always now.

Sash   But then the time came before deployment and I just wanted time to slow down.

Stas   Is always now.

Sash   I was at home on leave but I just started doing press-ups in my bedroom because I knew that periods of intense physical exercise have the ability to make time pass incredibly slowly.

Tol   What do you call that, conscript?

Sash   Something I learnt from my training days. Nights I'd lie awake completely unable to sleep.

Lev   At home.

Val   In my bedroom.

Kost   In my bed.

Dim   Do you ever get scared?

Tol   And then in the morning we do it all over again.

Sash   And my dreams –

Lev   A Roman soldier.

Dim   Covered in blood.

Sash   When I did get to sleep, were the worst I'd ever had.

Kol   When I wake up.

Sash   I know that whether I'm different now –

Val   I guess happiness is something different nowadays.

Sash   Or exactly the same –

Kost   I just love twatting stuff.

Sash   That these days.

Tol   That they have made me who I am.

Sash   I'm part of something bigger than myself.

Tol   Erase the word 'personal' from your vocabulary.

Zhen   I'm concerned about the section. I'm concerned about the productivity of the section.

Tol   A sleek, beautifully ironed, nicely polished aesthetically pleasing machine.

Sash   And I'm proud of that. I'm intensely proud of that.

Tol   We trained hard.

All   We'll fight easy.

Sash   We trained hard and I hope with every part of me that we will fight easy.

Stas   But it is only us.

Sash   And it doesn't always work like that.

Stas   In the very worst part –

Dim   Everything you can imagine.

Stas   In the very worst part –

Lev   We're completely pinned down.

Quietly at first, the sound of gunfire and explosions begins to underscore.

Sash   It is only.

Kol   Ever.

Zhen   Us.

Kol   One.

Tol   Two.

Val   Three.

Kost   Four.

Stas   Five.

Dim   Six.

Lev   Seven.

Sash   Eight.

Zhen   Nine.

Kol   Us.

Sash   And they made me sit down and they made me write. And if you receive this letter.

Zhen   And if you receive.

Kol   If you receive this letter.

Tol   If you receive.

Val   If you receive.

Sash   Then you know that the worst.

Stas   In the worst part.

Dim   And if you receive.

Lev   If you receive.

Sash   Then you know that the worst has happened.

Kol   The worst has happened.

Zhen   The worst has happened.

Val   We're completely pinned down!

Tol   And if you receive.

Stas   Grenade!

Zhen   If you receive.

Tol   Heads down!

The sounds are louder now.

Kol   If.

Kost   If you receive.

Lev   If you receive.

Sash   We're completely pinned down!

Tol   Grenade!

Val   If you receive.

Stas   Grenade!

Dim   If you receive.

Kol   And I have a terrible feeling.

Sash   If you receive.

Kol   When I wake up I don't know where I am.

Zhen   If you receive.

Val   What makes the grass grow?

Kol   And the thunder closes in.

Tol   If you receive.

Kol   And I see omens in everything.

Sash   If you receive.

Dim   If you receive.

Stas   The bird with the broken wing.

Sash   And if you receive.

Val   What makes the grass grow?

Tol   We're completely pinned down!

The sounds are deafening.

Dim   If you receive.

Kost   Grenade!

Stas   And now, in the worst part.

Zhen   If you receive.

Dim   Grenade!

Stas   In the very worst part.

Zhen   It is only.

Stas   Ever.

The sounds stop.

Kol   And if you receive this letter, then you know that the worst has happened.

Stas   And now in the worst part.

Tol   It is only us.

Kost   It is only us.

Kol   Will you be there to meet me –

Val   What makes the grass grow?

Sash   When I wake up?

Dim   When I wake up?

Zhen   Will you be there to meet me –

Kol   When I wake up?

Scene Nine: Zhen

Zhen   On the first day of training I was the first one to arrive at the barracks. I was so homesick and I was crying. (*He starts to cry.*) And you came in. And you saw me.

The barracks room, months earlier. **Zhen** *is crying.* **Kol** *enters.*

Kol   Wow, that train journey was a nightmare, had to stand the whole way, I can barely feel my legs now. I'm Kol, by the way.

Slight pause. He notices **Zhen** *is crying.*

Kol   Oh, sorry, are you alright?

Slight pause.

Are you alright?

Zhen (*through tears*)   Just fuck off, okay?

Kol   Erm. Sorry. Just. Okay.

Pause. **Zhen** *starts to busy himself.* **Kol** *is watching him.*

Zhen   What the fuck are you looking at? Stop looking at me. What the fuck are you looking at?

Zhen *looks at Kol.* **Kol** *is silent.* **Zhen** *goes back to busying himself by unpacking his things. Pause. The rest of the conscripts slowly trickle in, in silence. They start unpacking their things and making up their beds.* **Kol** *continues to watch* **Zhen** *for a very long time.*

The Grandfathers

*Notes on rehearsal and staging, drawn from a workshop
with the writer at the National Theatre, November 2011*

How the Play Began

Rory was invited to write a play for Connections with Russia
as the starting point, a country where he has lived and
travelled and whose language he has studied. Coming from a
family with a military background, Rory had been interested
in Russian national service for a while and wanted to explore
it further. All young people in Russia are called on to undertake
a year and a half of national military service, and Rory was
struck by the fact that conscripts beginning their service
routinely overlap with soldiers coming to the end of theirs.
Those more experienced soldiers are known as 'grandfathers'
and the culture of the service allows the grandfathers bullying
rights and seniority over new conscripts.

A research trip to Moscow on Russian Remembrance Day
and attempts to get access to Russian soldiers and the military
in Archangel left Rory with the impression of a closed culture,
suspicious of spying on the service. He also visited a British
army training barracks, where he spoke to officers, young
men who had come for interview and recruits in the middle of
their training. He was struck by the fact that for many of the
British soldiers deciding to sign up, the war in Afghanistan
and the prospect of active service had been attractive factors.
They were also drawn to the army by the desire to be part of
a team, to be one man in a section working as a unit – a
group of young men from a range of social backgrounds who
were buying into a sense of community in a society that often
feels its lack.

When he came to write a first draft, Rory was keen to write
something that might be performed and interpreted in a
variety of different ways. He wanted to write the play with
strong roles for its nine characters and so hit upon the

structure of each character taking the lead in one scene. In his words, he was not writing 'a play about national service, but about people alive in that situation'. Nor did he set out to write a play about masculinity or war or something with a political agenda: rather, the play explores the tension between each person and the group in a situation where people are forced to suppress their individuality for the good of the unit.

As well as reflecting the 'grandfathers' of Russian national service, for Rory the play's title echoes the fact that for most young people in 2011, their grandparents were the last generation to perform national service. The title also openly questions whether or not the characters will survive their deployment and live to be grandparents.

Ways to Begin Work

ORDERING

Exercises that start building the cast into a military unit are a good way to begin work on the play. Ask the actors to arrange themselves into height order silently and under time pressure, into order of their eye-colour from light to dark, by cleanliness of shoes or any other parameter you devise.

GROUP COUNTING

Ask the company to count from one to ten together in a circle, with one actor saying each number on their own and any mistake or overlap returning the count to zero. In the play, the conscripts check in using numbers and this kind of drill can help to develop the instinctive rhythm with which they operate.

This exercise can be extended by introducing a metronome or beat, with one actor saying a number on each beat. During the rehearsal process this exercise could be done at different speeds, encouraging the actors to develop an index of pace that can be used to set the heartbeat or tempo of each scene.

ONE-ON-ONE

In pairs, the actors count from one to three in a loop,
alternating between them for each number. As they do this,
you can alter the speed or ask them to perform the task with
no giggling or comments. You might add an acting note that
requires them to work as though they were bomb-makers
counting for their lives. Another variation gradually replaces
the number 'one' with a clap, then the number 'two' with a
stamp and then 'three' with a click.

These exercises can be built into a rehearsal drill that starts
making the company behave and cooperate like a training
unit. They also encourage good acting behaviour, battling
giggles and performance nerves while training actors to be
focused and physically alert. For a director they are an
opportunity to learn about the company, and to spot leaders
and those with a strong group mentality.

The World of the Play

The play imagines a fictional space that is neither modern
Russia nor contemporary Britain. The world of the play is
open to the interpretation of the director and actors and their
imaginations. Character names are based on shortenings of
Russian names, such as Dim for 'Dmitry', but that doesn't
mean characters must be played as Russian. The wars that
influenced Rory in the writing of the play were the coalition
war in Afghanistan, the Russian conflict in Afghanistan, the
first and second Chechen wars and the Vietnam War, but
none of these is the specific conflict into which the play's
conscripts are plunged.

The author laid out the following facts about the fictional
country or world of the play, most of which are derived from
the text:

- This is a country where conscription has been in place for
  generations and with a generation of grandparents who
  fought in a major war.

- This is a world with Burton's menswear, the Xbox and military technology including IEDs (improvised explosive devices) and RPGs (rocket-propelled grenades).

- The war described in the play is a central Asian guerrilla war that is just beginning at the start of the play and escalates through the course of the action. The war is complex and ideological rather than territorial.

- The conscripts in the play do not necessarily know exactly why they are fighting. For most conscripts, their training is the first time they have lived away from home.

- After training is complete and should they survive, the characters can return home and go to university or continue education if they want or are able to.

- The only exemptions to military service are for physical or mental disabilities.

- This is a world in which the writer has deliberately avoided ascribing a particular religious inclination to the conscripts or the enemy they are fighting.

The Characters

The play's characters can be approached in lots of different ways and these choices are in the hands of the actors and the company. The following pen portraits give a sense of how Rory imagined the characters as he wrote the play, but are not set in stone.

The characters were imagined as seventeen-year-olds, apart from Tol who is one or two years older than the others. However, a production might choose to imagine them at a different age. The play also avoids giving them particular backgrounds or dictating what class they come from. Both are left open to the group of performers.

KOL is the most optimistic of the characters. He doesn't think very deeply but lives moment by moment, focusing on the immediate consequences of his actions rather than on the bigger picture. He isn't the star of the group and may be the least naturally capable in terms of soldiering. However, he wants to be accepted and might be a role for an open and likeable actor.

TOL is clearly the highest-status member of the group. A professional soldier now, he is someone who has chosen to stay on after his national service. He is not a bully but a respected leader who trains the section hard because he wants them to be prepared. He is an intelligent and pro-active character who might suit an extrovert actor. It is important that other actors play and reflect Tol's status.

VAL is a strongly rational character with middling status in the group. He's calm, considered, intelligent and needs to know why he's doing something. He is independent-minded, as demonstrated by his questioning of why the conscripts need to bayonet a dummy. His frenzy at the end of this scene requires an actor who can let go and reach an emotional peak as well as keep control.

KOST is the most aggressive of the conscripts and inclined to talk back. There's a lot of bravado to him and he's not as well liked or as much of a star in the section as he might think he is. Kost was probably the naughty kid at school and he's a quick thinker with a bit of charisma as well. This is a role for a good comic performer.

STAS is sensitive and introspective. He might be called the 'poet' of the group. It is in his scene that the division between the individual and the group is really explored. The bird he tries to save is a symbolic cause for him, representing a personal emotional attachment. He is one of the youngest in the group, and his emotions are near the top of his skin.

DIM has a brain that works fast. He is imaginative and aware of the world beyond the barracks. Dim looks at the overall consequences of something, and his monologue demonstrates his awareness of what the conscripts might face. The scene isn't a comic riff on a character who won't stop talking while the others try to sleep; it's introspective and personal and asks an actor to sustain a train of thought.

LEV has a practical quality and is confident and well liked. He enjoys training and tasks like building the sandbag wall. He is a natural leader, with a 'head boy' quality to him.

SASH is a team player who is absolutely dedicated to the idea of the group and the unit as one. He's of middling ability as a conscript, but very committed. His scene might be approached as a monologue with other voices that interject around Sash's central train of thought.

ZHEN is the star of the section and the most naturally capable as a conscript without really trying. He is better liked than he thinks he is and he lacks confidence. In many ways he is the opposite of Kol and it's hard for him to express his emotions. He is a rock and very physically present.

Kol and Zhen have the key relationship in the play and are almost symbiotic in the way they feed off one another. Their scenes are the first and last, and complement each other directly. The characters should be cast for compatibility.

If the characters had a pecking/status order it would be: Tol, Lev, Zhen, Sash, Kost, Val, Stas, Dim, Kol.

Casting

The Grandfathers can be played by a company of female actors, a mixed company or a company of actors much younger than seventeen. The play is about a generation of young people going through the experience of service rather than the group's masculinity. Female performers should be encouraged to play the characters as women, changing or adapting the few gender-specific references in the text. With a mixed company, actors should be cast from personality rather than playing the most sensitive or weakest characters as women. A male–female pairing for Kol and Zhen should be avoided so as not to suggest an unintended romance.

The play cannot be performed with fewer than eight actors. With eight, Sash's scene should be given to Zhen and his other lines reassigned. For larger groups, a non-speaking ensemble should be avoided. One actor should take the leading character in each scene and Tol, Kol and Zhen should be played by the same actors throughout. Other lines within each scene should be distributed between other performers.

Rehearsal Exercises

CHARACTER

In a play with nine characters of the same age in the same situation, it's as important to make their individuality clear as their behaviour as a unit. Character work in rehearsals might involve creating top-trumps cards that mark them on their aggression, physical strength, ability to follow orders, academic achievements and selfishness or selflessness. Actors could also create a Facebook profile for their character.

The conscripts' dreams play a significant role in the play and actors might create a visual map of their characters' dream worlds using magazine cuttings and images. Once you've decided on a uniform or costume for the unit, each actor could be allowed one customisation that defines their character.

There are over thirty relationships in the play and a strong sense of the dynamic in each of them is important. You might ask each actor to complete the sentence 'I am . . . ' for their own character, and the sentence 'He/she is . . . ' for each of the eight other characters. These relationships can shift through the rehearsal process and help to give depth beyond the play's prominent relationships.

As actors get to know their characters, their instincts can be tested and developed by asking them to place themselves from left to right against a wall in response to different questions:

- How good a sleeper are they?
- How confident are they with members of the sex they find attractive?
- How healthy is their relationship with their parents?

- How dedicated are they to the unit or group?

- How healthy is their diet?

- How friendly are they on the street, or back in civilian life?

Actors can discover things through an immediate, physical reaction to these questions. It may also be revealing for the company to answer some questions from the perspective of one character.

STATUS   A good exercise to engage the actors in playing status involves assigning each actor a playing card to hold on their forehead, without knowing the value of the card. Actors are asked to interact with each other and to establish their status from the behaviour of others. With Tol, it's important not to give him status by separating the actor from the group or working with him or her to shape and instruct.

TIMELINE   The period of training in the play lasts fourteen weeks and we meet characters at selected moments in this period. Mapping their progress in terms of ability and their emotional journey can be a really effective part of rehearsal and a good way of keeping performers engaged and active in scenes where they only feature briefly. Another timeline could be built for the memory or dream life of each character, including the images that preoccupy them.

MILITARY UNIT   Alongside building up the set of drills suggested to start work on the play, the company could work on more physical training including circuit training, press-ups, sit-ups and squat thrusts.

In the play and in real-life military training, punishment for small mistakes from dirty boots to a badly made bed is common. There is a culture of 'beasting', where the entire unit is punished for one individual's infraction. This encourages a dependency on one another and a care for detail that might help soldiers save each other's lives in the field, in the way that Zhen attempts. Extra repetitions in an exercise for the whole group when one steps out of line might be a way of asking the company to engage with this.

Exercises that build an instinctive reliance on each other or fast co-operation among the group could also be useful:

- Ask the company to move together from one side of the room to another without touching the floor and without leaving anyone behind.

- Build a wall together like the conscripts in the play, but against the clock.

- Play ambush, where the group splits into two, and one half tries to pass the other and reach a wall behind them. Tactics are discussed before the game is played and a strategy executed.

- An exercise from the theatre company Complicite asks actors to stand in a straight line and move together towards a line four or five metres away. No individual should lead the group and the group only moves once they are all in tune with each other.

Key Moments

Each scene of the play is built around certain key moments or shifts and comes at a particular point in the fourteen weeks' training. Get each scene working with its own mood and tempo before running too much of the play, so they are distinctive as well as serving the whole. The play has a relentless pace that a company might struggle to maintain unless each scene is worked individually.

Drawing the shape of each scene in groups or with the whole company will help make them distinctive and dramatically effective. This could be done on large sheets of paper with a line that reflects the heartbeat of the scene or where tension/pressure mounts and relaxes.

SCENE ONE takes place on the first-ever foot patrol the section undertake when they arrive in the war zone. At this point they are only 140 days into their 547-day national service. The scene builds in intensity towards the explosion at its end, which leaves it unclear whether or not the unit survive.

SCENE TWO charts the first two weeks of the training, beginning from the second day. It is a scene that builds like a montage and registers the passing of time.

SCENE THREE comes four to five weeks into training when the conscripts move from general fitness to skills like bayoneting. The scene turns on the moment when the conscripts push Val to stab the dummy and builds towards his frenzy at the end.

SCENE FOUR is seven or eight weeks into training, when the novelty has worn off for the conscripts. The key event is Kost's slackness being overridden by the discipline of the rest of the section, who almost seem to leave him behind at the end of the scene. The scene is a reminder of how important humour is in the play.

SCENE FIVE sits at the centre of the play and comes ten to eleven weeks into training. A key moment in the scene comes when Kol announces, 'Kost is kinda right though.' The group discipline themselves and turn against the bird and Stas. Whether the bird dies or not is left ambiguous and Stas's exit might be played as a defiant attempt to save the bird or an emotional reaction to its fate.

SCENE SIX is set two weeks from the end of training. The conscripts are off to war soon and one of the key thoughts in Dim's monologue is the moment when he wonders whether the violence 'will ever ever end'. This is the closest a character comes to questioning the broader implications of what the soldiers are doing.

SCENE SEVEN takes place in the last week of training and turns on the moment when the conscripts discover from Tol that they are being deployed – and that they are heading somewhere warm.

SCENE EIGHT takes us from the end of the soldiers' leave at home once the training is finished right back into the foot patrol in Scene One. A rhythmic pattern of voices in the scene kicks in when they begin counting and it's here that the soldiers arrive back psychologically in the foot patrol.

SCENE NINE takes place on the first day of training, when
all the conscripts arrive at the barracks. It sits in opposition to
Scene One, the final image of Kol and Zhen apart from one
another contrasting with the opening image of Kol in Zhen's
arms.

Staging Notes

The Grandfathers could be staged in a range of very different
ways reflecting the ideas, imaginations and priorities of
different companies. The literal settings in which the play
takes place are a dormitory room at the barracks, a parade
square, a field near the barracks and the war zone itself.
However, these need not be represented in great detail (or at
all) and a very literal approach to space and location might
limit a production. This is a play that could be produced with
nothing at all, or with one very simple element of staging.

A number of ideas and challenges could shape the staging of
a production:

PSYCHOLOGICAL SPACE   Psychologically much of the
play takes place in a barracks environment and this could
prompt a company to set the whole play in a barrack room
or use the furniture and physical objects of the barracks to
present everything including the war zone. The play is
divided quite starkly between the public environment of the
training unit and the private dream space of the conscripts.
You might choose to reflect this psychological space in the
staging or physicality of the production, splitting the space or
blocking actors differently for public or private moments.

AUDIENCE RELATIONSHIP   Characters in the play often
appear to address the audience directly, particularly in the
monologues that head up each scene. How you stage this
relationship could shape your production. A very direct
production might choose to present all the characters out front
or on microphones, engaging the audience as individuals and
allowing the text to create the world of the play in the

audience's heads. Alternatively you might preserve the fourth wall and have characters share only their most private thoughts with the audience.

TRANSITIONS   In moving from one scene to another, it seems important not to impose a total blackout or break between scenes. There is a fluidity to the transitions that could be imagined in a number of ways.

Movement might be key, whether this means turning transitions into a soldiers' drill or something more poetic and patterned that responds to the web of memories and images in the play, including the bird and blood on grass.

While the text describes transitions using lighting cues, you might choose one lighting state and use sound or music to move the action between scenes or use the opening statement from each character to cover set changes.

SCENE STRUCTURE   The play's use of one character to lead each scene might also inform staging. Scenes could be announced by projecting or speaking the character name and each scene could have its own distinctive physical character.

The company might work from iconic images of soldiers at war, physical groupings that are used to shape each scene, with a camera on hand to record these. Whether abstract or literal, military shapes and formations are theatrically powerful, as are the moments where they are broken, interrupted or disturbed.

SWEARING   The swearing in the script is an accurate and conservative reflection of the language of soldiers. The writer would like directors and companies to have respect for the text and not to change it. However, he acknowledged that there would be times when teachers simply had to minimise the amount of swearing in a text.

Should you need to minimise the swearing, the following rules might be applied. The first and last uses of swearing in the play are important and these should be included whenever it is possible to do so – i.e., at the start, **Zhen**: 'Kol look at me, mate, fucking look at me,' and the last line of the play: 'What the fuck are you looking at? Stop looking at me. What the fuck are you looking at?'

Swearing in the play is usually used for escalation in an exchange or line of thought, for emphasis or as part of the way a character expresses themselves. Rather than just cutting, alternative words should be inserted to preserve the rhythm and care should be taken to ensure that any alterations preserve the intentions and keep the rhythm of lines.

Suggested References

Sebastian Junger, *War* (Fourth Estate, 2010).

Soldier Girls (dir. Nick Broomfield, 1981).

Black Watch Cast in Training (National Theatre of Scotland, 2010, video on YouTube).

Call of Duty: Modern Warfare series (video games).

Music: Rory listened to lots of First and Second World War soldiers' songs and folk songs while writing the play. You could find a song and learn it together as a company to encourage the group to work rhythmically together.

Image: *Sleeping Soldiers* by Tim Hetherington.

From a workshop led by Lyndsey Turner,
with notes by Sam Pritchard

Alice by Heart

book and lyrics by
Steven Sater

music by
Duncan Sheik

story by
Steven Sater and Jessie Nelson

Time and Setting

1940, an underground station, London; and late one summer afternoon in Wonderland. (The familiar storybook figures mysteriously appear, then melt away once more, as if part of some half-remembered dream.)

While the set of this show could be rather elaborate, I want to stress that the design could also be quite minimal. The entire underground station could be constructed of nothing but light and sound cues. It could also be a simple unit design which then transforms into Wonderland.

Wonderland itself may surely be suggested merely by imaginative costumes, the proper props, and a sense of play.

Song List

1 West of Words (*Alice and Alfred Hallam*)

2 Down the Hole (*All*)

3 Getting Bigger (*Mock Alice, Little Mock Alice, Another Mock Alice and Alice*)

4 Get Dry (*Mouse, Dodo, Duck, Magpie and Alice*)

5 Do You Think We Think You're Alice? (*Mouse, Dodo, Duck, Magpie and Alice*)

6 Chillin' the Regrets (*Two Caterpillars, Alice and Chorus*)

7 And When We're High (*Alice, Two Caterpillars, Cheshire Cat, Mouse, Dodo, Mock Alice, Little Mock Alice and White Rabbit*)

8 Manage Your Flamingo (*Duchess, Knaves of Hearts and Clubs, Ace of Hearts, Mock Alice, Little Mock Alice, White Rabbit and King of Hearts*)

9 Sick to Death of Alice-Ness (*Mad Hatter, March Hare and Dormouse*)

10 Isn't It a Trial? (*Queen of Hearts, Little Mock Alice, Another Mock Alice, and Knaves of Hearts and Clubs*)

11 What Have I Done with Me? (*All*)

12 Another Room in Your Head (*White Rabbit and Alice*)

13 And There You are (*Cheshire Cat, Alice and Chorus*)

14 Down the Hole – Reprise (*All*)

Characters

This play can be performed with as few as six actors or as many as desired. (Even the first scene can accommodate more voices — by adding characters to it and simply distributing some of the extant lines to those new characters.)

All the roles, except for that of **Alice**, *may be doubled, and the division of those roles can be made according to the production scheme and the particular actors' strengths. Certain roles, however, are written specifically to be doubled. Those I list here:*

Alfred Hallam, White Rabbit, March Hare

Red Cross Nurse, Mock Alice, Queen of Hearts

Dodgy, Duchess

Harold Pudding, Mad Hatter

Buxby, Duck

Angus, Caterpillar

Tabatha, Cheshire Cat

Mabel, Magpie

I've always imagined the actor playing **Nigel** *would also play the* **Mouse** *and* **Dormouse** *— but that could vary according to available casting.*

London, 1940.

*Lights rise on a ward of displaced young teens, encamped in an Underground station. Camp beds and hammocks stretch across the platform; coats and hats hang above; rows of shoes lie beneath; photos are tacked to walls. A frail teenage boy, **Alfred Hallam**, lies on a makeshift hospital bed. Down the platform, **Alice** sits on the floor, propped against her bed – as if beside her sister on the bank – immersed in a storybook.*

*In total denial of their surroundings, several besotted upper-crust youths – **Ada**, **Dodgy**, **Nigel** – attempt a night-time high tea. Meanwhile, **Mabel**, **Buxby** and **Angus**, working-class teens, play cards.*

Beyond, wounded young soldiers on stretchers.

Note: the pace of this scene should be brisk. These characters have been living like family together, and are more than accustomed to finishing one another's sentences.

A siren sounds.

Dodgy *(that insufferable sound)* And just when all our hearts had grown so tired . . . !

Nigel The endless chain of days, you know.

Ada Cream?

Dodgy If you can call it cream – and calling makes a thing.

Nigel *(touches his teacup to his heart, then extends the cup)* In honour of our dear, departed cream.

A bomb sounds. The Underground shudders.

*Music sounds. Song light finds **Alice**. She looks longingly towards **Alfred** – no one else can hear her.*

WEST OF WORDS

Alice
> *There are moments when you dream*
> *About all you are –*
> *A world of pictures*

And songs you never heard,
West of words . . .

A **Red Cross Nurse** *trundles through, with a stretcher.* **Alice** *is directly in her path. Music continues quietly underneath.*

Red Cross Nurse   Alice?

No reply.

Alice – moving through.

Better button up that blousey, Mousey.

Alice (*covering herself, stepping aside*)   But it is – all buttoned. It's just grown smaller, really.

Red Cross Nurse   Funny how that happens, when the boys start growing bigger.

The **Red Cross Nurse** *presses on, towards the wounded.*

Alice
You're falling through the ground,
You're falling so,
The flowers calling out, to stop and know
All that yearns –
West of words . . .

Song light finds **Alfred Hallam**. **Alice** *and he sing in private worlds. But she hears him in her heart.*

Alice *and* **Alfred Hallam**
West of words . .

The lonely tortoise
Crawling onward,
A music heard,
West of words . . .

The song light dims on **Alfred Hallam**.

Alice
And something listens
Beyond the lawn,

You watch the pages turn –
West of words,
West of words . . .

The lights shift. **Harold Pudding** *– a young soldier who's lost his wits in the war – suddenly leaps from his camp bed.*

Harold Pudding   Shall we have a riddle?

Shall we? A riddle?

Mabel (*takes a card*)   Pudding. Harold Pudding.

Loses his wits on the front, then comes home to the Blitz.

Buxby (*like a quack*)   Whaaaaaaat?

Mabel   Just the way you lost your hearing, when the bomb went off there, dearie.

Buxby   *Whaaaaaaaat?*

Song light finds **Alice** *once more.*

Alice
And something whispers of something gone,
A little Cheshire purr . . .
West of words . . .
West of words . . .

Music out. The lights shift.

Nigel (*to* **Dodgy**)   Jam on your bun, ma'am?

Dodgy (*nabbing one*)   Can't bear buns.

Ada   Me, I shall never need another bun.

My Mum's coming for me today.

Dodgy   Oh she is?

Nigel (*pointing to the other youths*)   Just like mine – and yours – and his – and hers – and *theirs*, of course . . .

Alice *draws close to* **Alfred Hallam**.

Alice   Shall we go there, then?

I can read to you.

Alfred Hallam　No.

Alfred *turns from her.*

Alice　I felt you there, with me, only a moment ago.

Alfred Hallam　You're dreaming.

Alice　You were too.

A beat.

We haven't read it in so long – after all our endless, summer afternoons. Come with me.

You can run there, you can breathe there.

Alfred Hallam　No more.

Alice　But, you must.

You can't let them take this too.

It's what we have. It's Wonderland.

Alfred Hallam　There's no time left – you understand?

Just too late for all that now.

Alice　It isn't.

You can't . . . lose heart.

Alfred Hallam　Oh really? After everything else I've lost?

He begins coughing violently – blood on to his hankie. **Alice** *watches, stricken.*

The card game:

Mabel　I can use that Knave. Yes, thank you.

Angus　Bit of bacon – on that bun – says you can't.

Mabel　Bit of gun shell says I can.

Angus　Charming.

Tabatha *appears, as if from above. Orphaned at an early age, she's wise beyond her years.*

Tabatha   Is it?

Rationing out the world we had.

She disappears.

Determined to get through to **Alfred Hallam**, **Alice** *reads to him from the storybook.*

Alice   'Alice was beginning to get very tired of sitting by her sister on the bank . . . '

Alfred Hallam   I'm not listening.

Alice   'Once or twice she had peeped into the book her sister was reading . . . '

Red Cross Nurse   Alice Spencer – off! Off! Off!

The **Red Cross Nurse** *grabs the storybook from* **Alice** *– slams it shut.*

Alice   *Don't!*

It's mine. It's all that's mine!

Red Cross Nurse   I don't care if you've known that boy since birth. Catch that cough – he'll be your death.

The **Red Cross Nurse** *strides off, the book with her.*

Nigel   Appalling.

Tabatha *appears – high above – perched in the rafters, where the kitties crouch.*

Tabatha   *Is* it?

Nigel (*'yes'*)   Him, camping out, in the rubble that had once been home? Dining on filth and ash?

Dodgy   No coughing on *me*, thank you.

A beat.

Ada   More tea?

Dodgy   Hate tea.

The **Red Cross Nurse** *drags* **Alice** *to her bed.* **Alice** *sits, bereft.*

Tabatha   No worries, love.

The book you know by heart.

Alice   I do?

Harold Pudding   So then, shall we have the riddle?

Dodgy   Dear God, no.

Harold Pudding   'What goes on its belly in the morning – '

Angus   *Gin.*

Harold Pudding   'Sleeps in gold all day – '

Nigel   Love gin.

Harold Pudding   'Then, flutters off the tea tray through the night . . . ?'

Alice *rises.*

Red Cross Nurse   *OFF OF THAT BED!*

Alice *jumps up on her bed, clamps her hands over her ears, entering her imagination. No one else can hear her. As her voice rises, their chatter continues quietly. Only* **Alfred Hallam** *can hear her.*

Alice   Stop! Stop! You – and you – and you!

Off with all your high-tea heads!

Music rises: 'Down the Hole'.

Alice (*to* **Red Cross Nurse**)   I'll show you. (*To* **Alfred Hallam**.) I'll *bring* you. I know it all by heart.

Alice *and* **Alfred Hallam** *lock eyes – somehow he can't resist her.* **Alice** *enters her imagination. The chattering recedes.*

Alice (*from the storybook*)   'And so, with nothing to do, Alice was considering *what* to do, when suddenly . . . '(*Pointedly, to* **Alfred Hallam**.) 'A white rabbit ran close by . . . '

Alfred Hallam *rises from his bed, no longer ailing. The Underground set transforms, as . . .*

He sings, donning a waistcoat, pocket watch and gloves, and becoming the **White Rabbit.**

DOWN THE HOLE

White Rabbit
>*Just some summer book,*
>*God, and it was hot too.*
>*Who knew where to look,*
>*What to do, and not do.*

>*Now some rabbit looms*
>*Like there's no tomorrow.*
>*How can I refuse,*
>*When he tells me follow?*

Alice
>*And now we're down the hole –*
>*And really on a roll.*

Alice *and* **White Rabbit**
>*And something on the shelves*
>*Holds something of ourselves.*

One by one everyone transforms into their Wonderland character. **Angus** *becomes a* **Knave of Hearts**.

Knave of Hearts
>*Down and down we fall –*
>*Now where have we wandered?*
>*Pictures, books and all,*
>*Tumbling from the cupboards.*

Tabatha *turns – a* **Cheshire Cat.**

Cheshire Cat

Hit the ground below,
Everything so tiny.

White Rabbit

Now, where did it go –
The world I left behind me?

Girls (Boys *echoing*)

For, now we're down the hole (Down the hole)
And really on a roll. (On a roll.)

God knows where we're at.
Should have brought the cat.

All

But now we're down the hole
And calling from the soul.

Girls

The walls are all so tall,
They're too small for the hall.

White Rabbit

These hands are not my hands –
So, is this Wonderland?

Alice

No rabbit can begin
To know the state I'm in.

Nigel *is a* **Dormouse**, **Harold Pudding**'s *a* **Mad Hatter**,
Dodgy *a* **Duchess**.

Mad Hatter

You meet a marble cake
Your heart begins to ache.

Duck

But once you start to eat,
You're too tall for your feet.

Duchess (**Girls** *echoing*)
    The bottle tells you Drink, (Tells you Drink)
    You never stop to think, (Stop to think,)

Queen of Hearts, **Little Mock Alice** *and* **Girls**
    How quickly you will shrink,
    The more and more you drink.

Alice
    But now you're down the hole –
    Now you're down the hole . . .

All
    Now you're down the hole,
    And calling from the soul:
    What happens if I can't
    Get out of Wonderland?

Suddenly, music out – everyone disappears but **Alice** *and the* **White Rabbit***. They stand, alone in Wonderland. A grown girl meeting a storybook character.*

Alice   So there you are!

White Rabbit (*proper, in his role*)   And there *you* are.

Alice   I'm just so . . . pleased to see you.

Here, that is.

White Rabbit   So pleased to see you too.

In brief: I'm late. You know?

Alice   Oh. I know. Sorry. It's all just been so . . .

White Rabbit   Of course. Of course.

Oh my ears and whiskers! I must go.

Alice   *No!*

Something's been punctured.

White Rabbit   What?

Alice   I don't know what. Honestly. It's just . . .

White Rabbit (*checks his watch*)   *What?* It's time – it's well past time – you know.

Alice   But . . . here we are.

White Rabbit   Yes – what? How long can we spend on this same page?

Alice   One moment. Please.

The **White Rabbit** *taps his watch, shakes his head, 'No'.*

Alice   But why not? It's still the story. We're still here *in* the story.

White Rabbit   No. If we're here in the story, we must be *in* the story. And so . . . if so, I better go.

I mean, that *is* the story . . .

Alice   Is it?

Neither one moves. The **White Rabbit** *has no language but the Storybook's.*

White Rabbit   Perhaps you ate a bit more marble cake today, and you grew bigger?

Alice   And, is that so bad . . . ?

Pulsing chords of music begin: the intro to 'Getting Bigger'. The **White Rabbit** *lifts his paw, cutting her off.*

White Rabbit   The Queen will be just savage. If I've kept her waiting.

He holds out his gloves and fan.

I believe I . . . leave you these?

Unsure what else to do, **Alice** *nods, reaches for the gloves and fan. The* **White Rabbit** *disappears.*

And, a pool of tears appears before her. She looks into it.

Alice   Dear, dear. I'm huge! (*Catching sight of her newly developing body.*) Where have my shoulders got to? My poor dear hands – how is it I can't see you?

In a pool of light behind **Alice**, **Mock Alice** *appears, dressed just like* **Alice**. **Mock Alice** *looks as if she'd outgrown her outfit, her hair style's too girlish on her. She sings at* **Alice**, *mockingly.*

GETTING BIGGER

Mock Alice
> *Bite by bite –*
> *Oh you're getting bigger.*
> *Night by night.*

Another pool of light. **Little Mock Alice** *appears, looking too small for her Alice outfit, as if she still needed to grow into it.*

Little Mock Alice
> *Pool of tears –*
> *Aren't you looking bigger.*
> *Year by year.*

Another pool of light. **Another Mock Alice** *appears. She's wearing a different-coloured Alice outfit.*

Another Mock Alice
> *Feeling all the things one mustn't say –*
> *Does she really have to act this way?*

A seeming set of mirrors appears. Everywhere **Alice** *looks, there are* **Alices** *and* **Mock Alices**.

Alice
> *Butter pie with a friend, and some orange gorgeous muffin,*
> *Tarts without end – with no repercussion.*

Mock Alices
> *It was easy . . .*

Alice
> *Running, hiding with friends – doing pantos and dress-ups.*
> *Days without end – with no fear of lessons.*

Mock Alices
Wasn't it easy?

Little Mock Alice
Just don't even start –
With this getting bigger.

Another Mock Alice
You'll break your little heart –
Gosh, you're getting bigger.

Mock Alices
Aren't you getting bigger?
Don't we love the figure!
Bigger bigger bigger . . .

Aren't you getting bigger?
Don't we love the figure!
Bigger bigger bigger . . .

Mock Alice
Bite by bite –

Little Mock Alice
Don't we love the figure!

Another Mock Alice
Dress so tight.

Mock Alice
Garden door,

Little Mock Alice
Alice can't fit in here,

Mock Alices
Anymore . . .

Alice *turns. It's as if she's had enough – and suddenly flipped the page.*
The mirrors melt into a radiant pool which fills the entire playing space.
Immediately, a **Mouse** *swims on: 'Get Dry'. The* **Mock Alices**
disappear.

Alice   Oh! My Mouse!

Monseigneur Mouse! Do you know any way out of this pool?

Mouse (*French accent*)   You don't poo poo this pool.

>*It's just so queer,*
>*Swimming here.*
>*We'll never get out of your pool of tears.*
>*We'd swim in a bit of your pity – but why?*

The **Mouse** *continues off.*

Alice   But wait – Mouse, dear . . . ! I can explain!

The **Dodo** *appears.*

Dodo
>*What to do –*
>*Two of you.*
>*You look in the mirror, and ooh boo hoo!*

Dodo *and* **Mouse**
>*We'd swim in a bit of your pity –*

Alice
>*But why?*

The **Duck** *appears.*

Duck
>*You've got to love the sort of duck*
>*Who sucks it up like me.*
>*This got so old in London –*
>*Or do you disagree?*

Mouse, **Duck** *and* **Dodo**
>*'Do you disagree?'*

Alice *considers.*

Dodo   Well, I do.

Alice   Dodo?!

Duck (*hard of hearing – a quack*)   Whaaaaaat??

The **Magpie** *appears.*

Magpie (*the diva*)   I'm singing. Please!

The Dodo grins
As we swim . . .

The **Mouse** *appears.*

Mouse
And now with the Magpie fallen in . . .

Dodo, **Duck**, **Magpie** *and* **Mouse**
We'd pity your pity – we'd never get dry.

The song concludes. Note: this scene too unfolds at a brisk percussive clip.

Alice   Well, well.

Magpie   Well done?

Dodo   We're done?

Alice   I mean, I'm just so terribly pleased to be here.

Mouse (*blasé*)   Hear hear.

Dodo   Ho ho. Hear, hear. Terribly here.

Duck   Whaaaat?! Shut up!

Alice   Please!

I mean, I'm *pleased.*

Magpie (*not buying it*)   Oh please.

Alice   So pleased. To be back here with all of *you.*

Dodo   Ho ho. Terribly.

Alice   Please!

Duck   Enouuugh! We've done that beat.

Magpie (*to* **Alice**)   Yes yes – you must be – you – terribly – pleased.

Who wouldn't be?

Mouse   *I* wouldn't be.

Dodo   I couldn't pee.

Magpie   So terribly –

If I had spent so long a time as you away from me.

Mouse   Apparently.

Dodo   So pleased.

Duck   Shuuut up!

Magpie (*to* **Dodo**)   Do. (*To* **Alice**.) So . . . Reading other books, were you? And meeting other Magpies?

Alice   No no, Miss Magpie, no –

Magpie   Then, you've met some other Magpie.

Don't mind me.

Alice   But, I assure you: there is no other book. No other Duck. No other Magpie!

Duck   Some other Duck? Whaaat?

Dodo   Some Duck? Ho ho – remind me.

Alice   Never, never! You're the only –

She breaks off – seeing the **White Rabbit** *dash past.*

White Rabbit   Oh! The Queen! The Queen!

Alice   White Rabbit!

No reply.

Alice   *White Rabbit!!*

But he's gone. **Alice** *sighs.*

I think he might've said hello.

Magpie (*busting her on her 'crush'*)   So.

Mouse   So.

Dodo   Ho ho. Terribly. So.

A beat.

Magpie (*to* **Alice**)   Well, if you'd rather thump thump thump, don't mind us.

Alice   Oh no.

Absolutely. No.

A beat.

It's just that, as you say, I've spent such time away . . .

Has he met some other girl to give his gloves?

Magpie   Only the mere thousand who come tumbling down each hour.

Mouse   Double that, on Sundays.

Alice   But I thought I was his only . . .

Duck   Nooooot!!

Music begins:

    DO YOU THINK WE THINK YOU'RE ALICE?

Magpie
> *Do you think we think you're Alice –*
> *You're some one and only Alice?*

Mouse
> *And we're nothing when you're not here.*

Duck
> *And so something once you've got here?*

Dodo
> *Do you think we think, 'Oh duckie!'*

Mouse
> *'Now you're here, we'll all go punting!'*

Duck
> *Like, we're waiting till you turn the page*

Magpie
> *To pop out of our dismal beige?*

Duck
> '*Cause Wonderland was silent,*

Dodo
> *Till some visit from Your Highness –*

Magpie
> *Everything just waiting here in place?*

Duck, **Dodo**, **Magpie** *and* **Mouse**
> *A hopeless place . . .*

Alice
> *Well, I think I think I'm Alice.*

Duck (*echoing*)
> *Well, she thinks she thinks she's Alice.*

Magpie
> *Oh you do? The only Alice?*

Mouse (*echoing*)
> *Oh she does? The only Alice?*

Alice
> *I fell down the hole to get here.*

Mouse
> *Do you think that means you're it here?*

Magpie (**Duck** *echoing*)
> *Do you think we missed the whisper*

Magpie (**Dodo** *echoing*)
> *How you bored even your sister –*

Duck
> *With some book you always took to bed,*

Mouse
> *The rabbit rooming in your head?*

Duck *and* **Dodo**
> *Oh, Wonderland was deadly,*
> *Till you sang your little medley,*

Magpie
> *Till you found us here and brought us there.*

Duck, **Magpie**, **Dodo** *and* **Mouse**
> *Like, we care . . .*

Magpie, **Duck**, **Dodo** *and* **Mouse** (*double echo*)
> *Do you think we think you're Alice?*
> *You're some one and only Alice?*

Alice
> *Well, I'm here!*

Magpie
> *Never fear!*

Duck *and* **Dodo**
> *Wow, you're here!*

Mouse
> *Now, you're here!*

Alice, **Magpie**, **Duck**, **Dodo** *and* **Mouse**
> *Wonder where . . .*

The **Dodo**, **Duck**, **Magpie** *and* **Mouse** *disappear.*

A mushroom rises from the earth beside **Alice**, *and towers over her. The* **Caterpillar** *appears, smoking a hookah. For our young* **Alice**, *it is like the first time a sexy, older boy has hit on her. Throughout the scéne, the* **Caterpillars** *are playfully coming on to the young, innocent* **Alice** – *the humour of the scene depends on that dynamic. These* **Caterpillars** *are a well-oiled team, lending a lively pace to this scene.*

Caterpillar   Whooooo are yooooou?

Alice   Well, once upon a time, I knew. But, I've changed so many times today.

Caterpillar   Do you mean – you've changed your mind?

Alice   And body too.

Caterpillar   Oh don't I know.

Then, whooo are you?

Alice   I'm afraid I'm new to me.

Caterpillar   Well, you are new to me –

Caterpillar 2   No matter really who you are to you.

Alice *looks. Another head has appeared – another handsome head – from the* **Caterpillar***'s tail.*

Alice   But . . . who are you?

Caterpillar 2   Come, look.

Alice   But, are you part of him?

Caterpillar (to **Alice**)   Or, is he part of you?

Alice   Now, how would that be?

Caterpillar 2   Whose head's in the book?

Not his.

Caterpillar   Or his.

Alice   Now, I'm confused.

Caterpillar   You?

Caterpillar 2   Or the new you?

Caterpillar (*to* **Alice**)   You you you must put put down that book . . .

Caterpillar 2   Yes, do.

Caterpillar   Then, come look.

Alice (*to* **Caterpillar 2**)   But, you . . . you're not even in the book.

Certainly not in the pictures.

Caterpillar 2   A boy can't change the pictures?

Caterpillar   Can one know a book by its pictures?

Caterpillar 2   Any looking-glass will tell you:

Caterpillar *takes a puff from the hookah.*

Caterpillar   'Who's appearing in the pictures . . . '

Caterpillar 2 *takes a deep puff.*

Caterpillar 2   'Depends upon who's peering in the pictures.'

Caterpillar *offers* **Alice** *the hookah.*

Caterpillar   One puff . . . ?

Alice *hesitates, shaking her head.*

Caterpillar 2   Stops time, it does.

Alice   It *does?*

Caterpillar   To whom time may concern, it does.

Alice (*an idea dawning*)   But, does it work on . . . other creatures too?

Caterpillar 2   Let's start with you.

A beat.

Alice   I have a friend, you know, spends so much time *pursuing* time.

I merely thought . . .

Well, if there *were* room in the picture . . .

The **Caterpillars** *exchange a look. Then:*

Caterpillar   You mustn't tell your sister!

Caterpillar 2   We won't.

Caterpillar   Set it down a minute.

Music in:

CHILLIN' THE REGRETS

Alice   What?

Caterpillar   The scripture.

Caterpillar 2   In your head, that is.

Caterpillar   It doesn't always go the way it's scripted.

Caterpillar 2   Just too many trials in Wonderland.

Caterpillar
Hey, cool – saw this Caterpillar,
Looked at me so blue
I could have looked at him forever.

He puffed upon his pipe and kind of stared me down.
Drew me to his bluer shroom and even bluer cloud . . .

Ohh . . . even bluer cloud . . .

Caterpillar 2
He said: Where have you gone –
Or have you been there yet,
Where the soul gets down,
Chillin' the regrets . . .

Caterpillar *and* **Caterpillar 2**
O, the wind is wonderful –
O, really, when it greets the rain . . .

It tells you who is who,
Whenever you are you,
As if it let you in whoever's dream –

Caterpillar *and* **Caterpillar 2**
Chillin' the regrets . . .

Chillin' . . .
Chillin' the regrets . . .

Chillin' . . .

The **Caterpillars** *pass round the hookah.* **Alice,** *who's been tempted and conflicted, gamely takes a puff.*

Caterpillar 2
I thought: where have you gone –
Or did you get there yet,
Where the soul goes south,
Chillin' the regrets . . .

Alice *takes a puff from the hookah.*

Alice *and* **Caterpillars**
> O, the wind's so wonderful –
> No, really – just as sweet as rain;
>
> It tells you who is who,
> Whenever you are you,
> As if it met you in some other dream . . .
>
> Chillin' the regrets . . .
> Chillin' . . .

Caterpillars, **Alice** *and* **Cheshire Cat**
> Chillin' the regrets . . .
>
> Chillin' . . .
> Chillin' the regrets . .
>
> Chillin' . . .
> Chillin' the regrets . . .

Alice
> Chillin' the regrets . . .

As the song concludes, the **Caterpillars** *draw the stoned* **Alice** *to them, as if to kiss her. The* **White Rabbit** *appears, surprising her – anxious to claim what's his. He clears his throat, interrupting the moment.*

White Rabbit   I believe you have my gloves . . . ?

Alice (*out of it*)   I do?

White Rabbit   Well, yes. I've been waiting for that crash of broken glass.

You know the bit – ?

Off her blank look.

The page you skipped?

Alice   I did?

White Rabbit (*'duh'*)   When your hand is just so big, you knock down my entire house . . . ?

And, I call you 'Mary Ann' . . . ?

Alice (*finally getting it, with a wild laugh*)   And send me off to fetch your gloves and fan . . .

White Rabbit   I'm frantic for them, actually.

We'd rather expected your hand, there.

Alice   Of course. So sorry. Sorry. I suppose I . . .

Caterpillar   Got distracted?

Alice   Yes.

White Rabbit (*pulling her back*)   So, shall we?

Alice   Yes!

The **White Rabbit** *grins, takes a grand thespian 'moment' – finding his character – then assumes his most* **White Rabbit** *manner and enters the storybook 'scene'.*

White Rabbit   'Oh Mary Ann!

Mary Ann!

Fetch me my gloves, this instant.'

Mock Alice, **Little Mock Alice**, *and* **Another Mock Alice** *appear to* **Alice**.

Mock Alice   But, is that really why he's come? To fetch his gloves?

Little Mock Alice   And fan.

Another Mock Alice   Oh please.

Mock Alice   As if you meant no more to him than random Mary Ann.

The **Caterpillars** *lean towards* **Alice**, *offering part of the mushroom.*

Caterpillar   Oh Mary Ann . . . ?

Caterpillar 2   Back a bit, where *we* began . . .

Alice *considers. Oh what the heck? She takes a deep bite. The* **White Rabbit** *watches, tempted.*

Alice (*in her own world*)   Oh. Oh . . . !

My head . . . free at last . . . !

White Rabbit   Oh my white paws!

Alice *takes another taste.*

Alice   Whoooooaaaa . . .

Now, who knows where I am.

And, who is Mary Ann?

The **Cheshire Cat** *appears to* **Alice***, hovering on high.*

Cheshire Cat   Who knows or cares?

Alice   Cheshire Puss – a moment, please.

Cheshire Cat   'Please' and 'Puss'? I like that.

Alice (*scared but excited*)   My head! Will I ever get it back?

Cheshire Cat   Then, do you want it back?

It took so long to lose it, as it is.

Alice   True. And still, I'm so very accustomed to . . . having it.

Cheshire Cat   High time, then, you find out how to do without it.

Alice   But how do I do *that*?

Cheshire Cat   Lose *yourself*, with *it*.

The way, some say, a lover disappears into the kiss . . . ?

Alice   Well, when you put it that way . . .

The **Cheshire Cat** *disappears.* **Alice** *turns back to the* **White Rabbit***, offers him a bit of mushroom.*

Alice   Come. Shall we . . . disappear?

White Rabbit   Oh, my dear fur and whiskers!

The Queen! The Queen!

She'll have my head – you understand? As sure as ferrets are ferrets!

Alice (*sceptical*)   Will she?

White Rabbit   Yes. Oh yes.

Dear, dear! We've missed the crash, the Broken Glass, the big 'Alas' . . . !

Music begins. **Alice** *bursts with frustration –*

AND WHEN WE'RE HIGH

Alice
Well, it just gets too boring
When you're neither here nor there,
And you wake up in the morning
In some pool of tears.

Caterpillar
When you wake up in some story
And it all just gets too weird,

Caterpillar 2
Tell the fools to just stop talking
Or you're out, you're out of here.

Cheshire Cat
When your wits are not the driest,
And you feel like someone else,

Alice
And that someone's not the nicest
And you can't forget yourself,

The **Caterpillars** *rise high into the air.* **Alice** *follows – joining the* **Cheshire Cat** *as well.*

Alice *and* **Caterpillar 2**
Take a leap into the silence
And let heaven ring your bell,

Caterpillar *and* **Cheshire Cat**
Tell the crowd to keep on walking,
'Cause you know their world too well.

The **Mouse** *and* **Dodo** *enter and watch* **Alice** *and the*
Caterpillars *fly.*

Caterpillar *and* **Caterpillar 2**
Oh, you know it well.

Cheshire Cat
They do dull so well.

The **Mouse** *and* **Dodo** *join* **Alice** *in the air.*

Alice, **Caterpillars** *and* **Cheshire Cat**	**All**
And when we're high,	*High*
And when we're gone,	*Gone*
We'll dry our eyes, sing a song,	*Eyes*
And carry on . . .	*Carry on . . .*
We'll climb so high,	*High*
We'll spill the dawn,	*Dawn*
We'll fly so blind, far beyond,	*Blind*
And carry on –	*Carry on –*
And carry on . . .	*Carry on . . .*

Alice *takes the* **White Rabbit**'s *hand and swings him playfully from the ground, as she flies.*

Alice
Well, some may call it living,
To be always sitting still,

White Rabbit
When there's nothing much beginning,
And there's nothing much until.

Alice
Guess some girls would take up knitting –
But I swear I never will,

Alice *gestures. The* **Mock Alices** *rise into the air and fly with her.*

Alice, **Mock Alice** *and* **Little Mock Alice**
> *'Cause my heart will not stop looking,*
> *And I'll never get my fill.*

Alice, **White Rabbit**, **Magpie** *and* **Cheshire Cat**
> *And I never will.*

Alice, **White Rabbit**, **Cheshire Cat** *and* **Mock Alices**
> *Never ever will.*

All
> *And when we're high*
> *And when we're gone,*
> *We'll dry our eyes, sing a song,*
> *And carry on . . .*
>
> *We'll climb so high,*
> *We'll spill the dawn,*
> *We'll fly so blind, far beyond,*
> *And carry on –*
> *And carry on . . .*

Alice
> *Carry –*

An alarm suddenly sounds. The **White Rabbit** *checks his watch – no issue there. He tears open his vest, frantically yanking out one watch after another till he finds the culprit. He shuts it off.*

White Rabbit   Oh my sweet white ears!

I am late! Soooo late!! So much – such a muchness – still to finish . . .

Alice   Just . . . please. One minute more, on this page.

White Rabbit   This page?! *What* page?! We're not even on a page!

Alice   We can change what's on the page.

White Rabbit   No, no. *You* can change. The page can't change.

And so, I'm late!

Alice   Please! One minute.

White Rabbit (*at a rapid, manic pace*)   Oh we all know about minutes. How they start out, merely minutes – *seeming* minutes . . .

Soon, each second, it's a minute, and the minutes run like seconds till they're hours – running, slipping – gone, gone, gone . . .

Alice   But they're not. Not *here*, they're not.

White Rabbit   *I'M* LATE, I'M LATE, I'M LATE!!

Alice   For what? Croquet? I'll come.

White Rabbit (*dropping his guard, with a raw urgency and empathy*)   Stop. Please. This isn't just some silly game.

I have no time left. Not for this.

Alice   There's time. There's always time.

White Rabbit   No. If you knew time as I do . . .

The **White Rabbit** *disappears.* **Alice** *calls after.*

Alice   We'll stop time.

We can. We will!

The **Duchess** *appears, in an enormous bonnet and more enormous dress.*

Duchess   Now, now.

This Little Piggie just could not stay home.

Alice *turns.*

Alice   The Duchess . . . ?

Duchess (*warm, maternal*)   Now, you. Now, Piggie, come to Duchess.

The **Duchess** *pulls* **Alice** *on to her lap and dandles her.*

Duchess   All grown up, are you?

Alice   No. I'm not. At all.

Duchess   Not what I hear.

Alice   From whom?

Duchess   From *youm* – wallowing through the afternoon, trailing bunny tails and doing shroooms?!

Alice   But I wasn't.

Duchess   Were.

Alice   I wouldn't.

Duchess (*busting her*)   I can see it in your eyes, Pig.

I can smell it in your hair.

Alice   But the Caterpillars –

Duchess   Blaming insects, dear?

*She smacks **Alice**'s bottom.*

Alice   Ouch!

Alice *breaks free. The* **Duchess** *withdraws a truncheon from her skirt, circles after.*

Duchess   Now, now. You must look to your snout: the more that comes out, the more to talk about.

The more that goes in, the porkier the chin.

But ohhhh, Piggie got so big!

Ohhhhh, she had to puff and grin to keep that pigtail in!

The **Duchess** *smacks* **Alice** *with her truncheon.*

Alice   *Ouch!!*

Duchess   So, now you're all too big to be my pig!

Alice   I never was your pig.

Duchess   Pig! You made yourself too big.

Alice   OUCH!

Duchess (*the words pouring from her in a frenzy*)   Grew yourself such breasts and hips, my lovelies sagged, just watching them.

You ripped the plumpy from my rump and left me this fat belching gut.

You broke my heart, you selfish tart, and now my day's just fart fart fart!

And now my cheeks just leak! Leak! Leak! You made my bed a dripping sink!

And so I'm left – with no one left.

You stole my soul and made me old, you pig!

You stripped the sheets and robbed my sleep and left my youth a dream! I'll see you at the trial!

You PIIIIIIIIIIIIIG!!!

Alice   *You* PIIIG!

Duchess   PIIIIIIIIIGGGGGGG!!!!

Alice   PIIIIIIIIIIIIIIIIIIIGGGGGGGGGGGG!!!!!

Duchess   'Tis so.

'Tis so.

And thus, 'tis *is*!

(*Self-satisfied.*) I shall make you a present of everything I've said. Just . . .

The **Duchess** *gestures. Music begins:*

MANAGE YOUR FLAMINGO

As the **Duchess** *sings, a gazebo-cum-croquet ground drops from above.*

Duchess (*to* **Alice**)
   Manage your flamingo,
   If you'd play croquet, dear.
   When you play croquet, dear,
   You have to do the do.

A **Knave of Hearts** *glides to* **Alice** *and deftly sets a flamingo in her arms.*

Knave of Hearts *and* **Duchess**
> *You tuck him down low,*
> *From feet to the chin,*

Duchess
> *Then batter your hedgehog again and again.*

Mock Alice *steps in and leads* **Alice** *to an* **Ace of Diamonds**.

Ace of Diamonds
> *Ohhhh, manage your flamingo,*
> *Like the Queen is passing.*

Ace of Diamonds, **Duchess**, **Mock Alice** and **Little Mock Alice**
> *When the Queen is passing,*
> *You have to do the do.*

A **Knave of Clubs** *approaches, and leads* **Alice** *away.*

Knave of Clubs (**Duchess** *and* **Knave of Hearts** *echoing*)
> *You plant a rose white,*
> *You'd best paint it red.*
> *Or soon as she passes, it's off with your head.*

The **Knave of Hearts** *smoothly drops a hedgehog at* **Alice**'s *feet. She attempts to batter at him.*

Alice   Poor thing, he's frightened!

Knave of Hearts (*ironic*)   Off with his head!

The **Duchess** *leads* **Alice** *away.*

Duchess
> *Knaves lose their faces,*
> *The Duchess must die.*

Duchess (**Knave of Hearts** *echoing*)
> *Fives club their Aces,*
> *Diamonds ask why . . .*

Duchess (**Knaves** *echoing*)
> *Don't they ask why . . .*

Knave of Hearts, **Duchess** *and* **Alice**
> *Don't they ask why . . . ?*

The **White Rabbit** *looks up from some Wonderland version of his camp bed.* **Alice** *stops in her tracks.*

White Rabbit
> *Ohhh, manage your flamingo,*
> *Or it's done for you, my love.*

The **Duchess** *leads* **Alice** *away. The* **White Rabbit** *goes off.*

Duchess (*to the* **White Rabbit**)
> *Oh, she's done with you, my love.*

Knave of Clubs (*'indeed'*)
> *Unless you do the do . . .*

The **Mock Alices** *lead the* **Ace of Diamonds** *back to* **Alice**.

Ace of Diamonds (**Knaves** *echoing*)

> *And tell her how fine*
> *A day for croquet.*

Duchess *and* **Knave of Clubs**
> *Then, who but a Queen could conceive such a game?*

The **Knave of Hearts** *takes* **Alice**'*s arm.*

Knave of Hearts
> *Gather your hedgehog,*
> *Set him on the green.*

Knave of Clubs (**Knave of Hearts** *echoing*)
> *Swing your flamingo –*

Knave of Hearts *and* **White Rabbit**
> *God save the Queen.*

Alice *stands, completely confused by all these seeming allegiances.*

Duchess (**Knaves** *echoing*)
Will God save the Queen?
Will God save the Queen?

Alice
Will God save the Queen?

A bomb sounds – all Wonderland shudders. As **Alice** *ducks,
instinctively, everyone else disappears. Bits of plaster fall from the sky – or
ceiling.*

The next moment, a long table begins descending from above. The **Mad
Hatter**, **March Hare** *and* **Dormouse**, *all crowded at one end.
Hair thick with dust. Note: this scene rapidly escalates to a frenetic pace –
as if all those at the party have had way too much caffeine.*

Mad Hatter (*to* **March Hare**)   Do we see that little tweeb
down there?

March Hare (*can't control himself, to* **Alice**)   My dear, what
have you done to your hair?

Alice   Don't be rude.

Mad Hatter   Then don't offend us – with that hair.

March Hare   Sorry – no room.

Alice   There's plenty of room.

Dormouse   Not here.

Mad Hatter (*to* **March Hare**)   You give the goon some
room, the next thing that you know she wants your chair.

Dormouse (*to* **Mad Hatter**)   Can't bear these chairs.

Alice *takes a seat at the table.*

The **Mad Hatter** *moves a place away from her. The* **March Hare**
nudges her to where the **Mad Hatter** *was, the* **March Hare** *steps
where she was*)

Mad Hatter (*in the midst of all the nudging and moving about, to*
Alice)   I'll have another cup.

Alice   Of tea?

Mad Hatter (*'indeed'*)   A clean cup.

A bomb sounds. Wonderland shudders. The **Mad Hatter** *examines his cup — in the wake of the explosion.*

Another chip.

March Hare   Rationing out our wits in bits.

Mad Hatter   More fish and chips?

March Hare (*to* **Alice**)   One place on, please.

Alice *obliges.*

March Hare (*to* **Mad Hatter**, *about* **Alice**)   Did you hear how mean she was to Mary Ann?

Dormouse   Love Mary Ann.

Alice   I wasn't. She was. Mean.

Mad Hatter   Then, you should say what you mean.

Alice   But I did.

March Hare   One place on, please.

Mad Hatter (*to* **March Hare**)   She means: she means what she says.

March Hare   It was mean what she said.

Mad Hatter   And did.

March Hare   But then, that's how she is.

Dormouse   Hate how she is.

Another bomb sounds. The **Mad Hatter** *empties plaster from his cup.*

Mad Hatter   Another. Mad.

Turns to **Alice**, *sweetly.*

Mad Hatter   More tea?

March Hare   One place on. And more tea, please.

Alice   But why do we keep moving on − ?

In truth, there are no places, plates, or tea.

Mad Hatter   In truth, she wants more tea.

March Hare (*to* **Mad Hatter**)   So now we all explore: the Girl Who Wanted More.

Alice   But, I haven't had *any* yet.

So, how could I take *more?*

March Hare   No. How can you take *less?*

Mad Hatter   It's simple to take more.

March Hare   That is, when you've had *none.*

(*To* **Mad Hatter**.) But then, that's how she is. Correcting us. Rejecting Mary Ann.

Dormouse (*to* **Alice**)   You Smarty Pants!

The **March Hare** *rises, like a thespian, and recites:*

March Hare
   We have measured out our life with you in spoons,
   And never heard the music from the further room . . .

Alice *looks again. The* **March Hare** *is the* **White Rabbit**.

Alice   You . . . ?

White Rabbit   You too.

Alice   But . . .

White Rabbit   Just − please.

The **White Rabbit** *gestures: 'No more.' And he's the* **March Hare** *once more.*

Mad Hatter (*to* **Alice**)   You can't sit still, or spoon a spoon, or even steal a spoon, now can you?

Alice   Yes. I can.

Dormouse   Then, give it back.

Alice   I shan't. (*Turns to the* **March Hare**, *pointedly*.) I mean, you're all so mean!

March Hare   We do that.

Alice   Must we?

March Hare   You tell me.

You keep coming back for more.

Mad Hatter   Shall we have a riddle?

Alice   Yes.

Mad Hatter   Now, she wants a riddle.

March Hare   That, and tea.

Mad Hatter   *More* tea.

Dormouse   Loathe tea.

Mad Hatter   All right, then. Since you insist: why is a raven like a writing-desk?

Alice (*pointedly, to the* **March Hare**)   You tell me.

Mad Hatter   I haven't the faintest idea.

March Hare   She knows that.

And yet, each time we see her, she still asks it.

Alice   No. *You* ask it.

Mad Hatter (*to* **March Hare**)   And always and forever, she insists I give her the same answer.

Alice   That there *is* no answer.

(*To* **March Hare**.) I think *you* might do something better with your time than waste it asking riddles with no answer.

Dormouse   You're the one who's asking.

Mad Hatter (*with a look to the* **March Hare**)   If you knew Time as we do, child, you wouldn't talk of wasting it.

Alice (*to* **March Hare**)   You waste time by not spending it.

Dormouse (*'spare us!'*)   Oh. Dear. Me.

March Hare (*to* **Alice**)   I dare say you have never spoken to Time.

Mad Hatter   We, we've spent so many years with him, and you, you are just meeting him.

Dormouse   So, prithee: pass the scones.

March Hare   Time for you to riddle yourself home.

Dormouse   Leave us alone.

Alice   No, I won't.

It's you who talk in riddles.

Mad Hatter   Come, we live in riddles, child, and sometimes there's no answering them.

March Hare (*with heightened reverence*)   Indeed.

Dormouse   Indeed.

An unaccustomed silence, to allow this truth its moment. Then:

Mad Hatter (*to* **Alice**)   More tea?

Alice   Yes. Please.

March Hare   She, and her incessant need.

Mad Hatter   For cream.

March Hare   And sugar.

Mad Hatter   Ham.

March Hare   Smoked ham.

Mad Hatter   And jam.

March Hare   Cold jam.

Dormouse   And cheese.

Mad Hatter   Butter on her every sad sardine.

March Hare   The next thing you know, she'll be demanding herbal tea.

Alice   I don't like herbs.

Dormouse   Or Herb?

Mad Hatter   Oh please.

Music rises:

SICK TO DEATH OF ALICE-NESS

Mad Hatter
> *So you tell us now you've got a thing for tea,*
> *Wander through the world, as if it were your dream.*
>
> *Wasn't long before before, before you started seeing things,*
> *Talking animals and nasty, acid, vicious Queens.*
>
> *How do we put you back to bed?*

Mad Hatter, **March Hare** *and* **Dormouse**
> *Take this, take this cup from us of everything you've said.*
> *No more sucking up to us – we don't want in your head.*
> *We're sick to death of Alice-ness.*
> *Yes, we're sick to death.*

Mad Hatter	**Girls**
You're such a boring pain!	*Sick to death*

Dormouse	
Such a boring pain!	*Alice-ness*

March Hare	
You're such a boring pain!	*Sick to death*

Mad Hatter, **March Hare** *and* **Dormouse**	
Such a boring pain!	*Alice-ness*

Dormouse
> *So, you think you've got the hang of Wonderland,*
> *Telling riddles now as if you understand . . .*

March Hare

Time to get back above the ground –
Not that they know you're not around.
Not that they wanna hear a sound from you.

Mad Hatter, **March Hare** *and* **Dormouse**

Not a sound from you . . .

Stop the analysing of everything you've read.
No more making nice with us – we don't want in your head.
We're sick to death of Alice-ness.
Oh, we're sick to death.

	Girls
You're such a boring pain.	*Sick to death*
Such a boring pain!	*Alice-ness*

Take this, take this cup from us of everything you've said.
No more sucking up to us – we don't want in your head.
We're sick to death of Alice – yes.
Oh, we're sick to death.

You're such a boring pain.	*Sick to death*
Such a boring pain!	*Alice-ness*
You're such a boring pain.	*Sick to death*
Such a boring pain!	*Alice-ness*
You're such a boring pain.	*Sick to death*
Such a boring pain!	*Alice-ness*

And, we're boooooooorrrrred . . . !

As the song concludes, the **Mad Hatter**, **Dormouse**, *and the table disappear. As the* **March Hare** *is disappearing too –* **Alice** *reaches for him. He fixes her with a look and is gone.*

Alice *casts about – searching one way, then the other. A flurry of white tail, there – a pink nose peeping out, there . . .*

Alice   White Rabbit? My White Rabbit?! . . .

The **Cheshire Cat** *appears.*

Alice   Cheshire Puss – help me please. He was here. Just here. And now . . . he's disappeared.

The **Cheshire Cat** *begins disappearing, from tail towards her head.*

Alice   Not you, too!

The **Cheshire Cat** *pauses – only her head remains.*

Alice   Can you tell me, please, which way I ought to go from here?

Cheshire Cat   That depends a good deal on where you want to get to.

Alice   In truth, I'm now so lost . . .

Cheshire Cat   Then does it matter, really, which way you go?

Alice   Yes, it does. Of course it does!

Cheshire Cat   Well, I'm sure you'll wind up somewhere.

Alice   *Where?*

It all keeps disappearing. The pages turn so quickly . . . !

The **Mock Alices** *appear.*

Mock Alice   All the pictures.

Little Mock Alice   All the lovely conversations . . .

Another Mock Alice   They never stay.

Mock Alice   No. Where's the time?

The **Mock Alices** *disappear.*

Cheshire Cat   It isn't how much time. It's how we use the time.

Alice   But he's always out of time.

Cheshire Cat   Perhaps he hasn't much to give.

Alice, pause, and let the picture in.

A beat.

To be *there*, Puss, that's to be in Wonderland.

*The **Cheshire Cat** disappears. **Alice** reaches for her, but she's gone, leaving her grin upon the night air.*

A sudden trumpet sounds.

An immediate frenzy. Characters race madly across the stage – dropping and donning costumes, shifting frantically into one character after another – assembling for the trial.

*In the midst of the frenzy, **Alice** stands, unmoving. A garden of white roses rises and blooms beside her.*

Assorted Characters   The tarts! The tarts!

Hubbub continues underneath.

Mad Hatter   Who stole the tarts?!

Another Mock Alice   The trial – the trial!

King of Hearts   The wig! My wig! (*Searching his head for it.*) Good God, the wig!

Duck   Whaaaat?

Duchess   Idiots!

*The **White Rabbit** dashes on, dressing himself in his official costume as herald.*

White Rabbit   Quick! Quick! The clock!

*He halts, seeing **Alice**.*

White Rabbit   Alice?

She turns, remaining still. The hubbub quiets down a bit.

*The **White Rabbit** crosses to her, speaking as rapidly as possible. Over the course of the next few lines, everyone runs off, leaving **Alice** and the **White Rabbit** alone.*

White Rabbit   Alice! Come!

Alice   No. I know what's next.

White Rabbit   Then, *please*. We're late.

The Trial!

Alice   I'm staying here. There cannot be a trial without me there.

White Rabbit   Come, come, we must turn these pages quickly, or we'll never finish.

Alice   I shall never turn this page.

We'll simply stop the story here.

White Rabbit   I caaaan't.

Alice   You can. We can. For ever. Here.

The **White Rabbit** *begins coughing. All the white roses suddenly turn red.*

Alice   Nooooooooooooo!!

The **White Rabbit** *lifts his paw, silencing her.*

White Rabbit   *Please!*

Alice   But, your roses . . . !

White Rabbit   Yes.

They are as roses are. As roses, here, must be.

Alice *takes this in. Looks imploringly to the* **White Rabbit***.*

White Rabbit   I've got to reach the end.

Just this once more.

A beat.

Alice   I thought that when you knew a book, you had the chance to have it as you always want to have it in your head . . .

White Rabbit   It doesn't always end as books would end.

A beat.

Perhaps we were never really meant to . . .

Alice   Yes, we were.

We *are*. We still can be.

White Rabbit (*'no, we weren't!'*)   I'm a rabbit in a waistcoat, really. Running out of time in Wonderland.

Alice *leans near – to touch the* **White Rabbit**.

Immediately, an air-raid siren sounds. Instinctively, **Alice** *starts to duck. And . . .*

Queen of Hearts   OFF WITH HER HEAD!

The **White Rabbit** *leaps frantically into position as the herald.*

White Rabbit   Silence in the Court!

The Queen! The Queen!

Queen of Hearts   A page too late for all that, I'm afraid.

In a tremor, in a trice, the entire Court assembles, the **King of Hearts**, *the* **Knaves of Hearts** *and* **Clubs** *among them.*

Queen of Hearts (*to* **Alice**, *'how pathetic!'*)   Love love love love love – make me puke!

The **Queen of Hearts** *turns privately to the* **King of Hearts**.

Queen of Hearts   At least she's brought her head.

King of Hearts   That's good.

Alice *approaches the* **Queen of Hearts**.

Alice   Your Majesties.

Queen of Hearts (*to* **Alice**)   You shameful girlish thing.

You hate the part that's tiny still in you. And yet, you want to hide within the child in you.

Alice   I don't. I won't.

Queen of Hearts   You can't, you mean.

You can no longer *not* know what we mean.

The **Queen of Hearts** *snaps her fingers. Music begins:*

ISN'T IT A TRIAL?

Queen of Hearts
Talk and talk and talk,
Still, you're never not you.
All the same old wants –
Now where have they brought you?

Shuffle all your hearts,
Play like Sister taught you.
No one wins at cards –
Or plays like they ought to.

Queen of Hearts (Little Mock Alice, Another Mock Alice *and* **Knaves** *echoing)*
Isn't it a trial,
To try and stay a child?
When everything you've read
Swells your little head.

Queen of Hearts
Shall we have a song
For the Girl Gone Naughty?

Little Mock Alice
Somehow feels so wrong
Now to have that body.

Queen of Hearts
Rabbit got so big –
What's his mama fed him?

Another Mock Alice
Though you feel a pig,
Still you want to pet him.

Queen of Hearts (Little Mock Alice, Another Mock Alice *and* **Knaves** *echoing)*
Isn't it a trial
To try and stay a child?

The world no longer fits,
And still you're stuck in it.

Oh, isn't it a trial?
No child can stay a child.

Queen of Hearts
God knows what you did,
But now you're not a kid.

Knave of Hearts
So, now you have a past,
And no one understands.

Knave of Clubs
Just turn another page,
My dear, you look your age . . .

Queen of Hearts (Little Mock Alice, Another Mock Alice and **Knaves** *echoing*)
And isn't it a trial,
To try and stay a child?
And no one, no one knows
The way out of the hole?

Isn't it a trial?
No child can stay a child
The story never told,
How Wonderland grows old.

Queen of Hearts
Oh isn't it a trial?
Isn't it a trial?

As the song concludes, the **King of Hearts** *gestures. A trumpet sounds.*

White Rabbit (*barrelling through his text*)   'The High Court of Her Majesty Against the Heartless Alice – '

Alice (*to* **White Rabbit**)   *Please!*

White Rabbit   Not *me*.

The **King** *and* **Queen of Hearts** *and the* **Duchess** *close in on* **Alice**.

The **White Rabbit** *unrolls a scroll and intones the allegations against her. Note: the* **White Rabbit** *speaks as quickly as possible, his urgent need to finish the book driving the pace of the scene.*

Queen of Hearts (*snapping her fingers, prompting the* **White Rabbit**) Item.

White Rabbit 'Item. She went reading, then proclaimed she'd dreamed us.'

Alice Who did?

Queen of Hearts *You* did. (*To the Court.*) *She* did.

(*To* **Alice**.) Pay attention when your Rabbit's reading.

Turns to the **White Rabbit**, *snaps her fingers.*

Queen of Hearts Item.

White Rabbit 'Item. First she bragged she'd brought us here – '

Queen of Hearts Louder!

White Rabbit 'First she bragged she'd brought us – '

Queen of Hearts Funnier!

White Rabbit 'First she bragged she'd – '

Queen of Hearts Faster!

White Rabbit Yes!

Alice You don't mean that!

Queen of Hearts Guilty!

Alice (*to the* **White Rabbit**, *privately*) Well, this certainly *is* a trial.

White Rabbit For you and me.

And it's late! So late. The items –

Duchess   Pig! Pig! PIG!

*The **Mad Hatter** steps forward.*

Mad Hatter   She added a big 'un' to everything 'important'.

Queen of Hearts   Off with her head!

Snaps her fingers.

Item!

Alice   Why *these* items?

Mad Hatter   Now, she wants to *choose* her items.

White Rabbit   Faster!

King of Hearts   Mad. She's mad.

Alice   I'm not!

Mad Hatter   You're *here*. We're all mad here.

Alice   Not me.

Little Mock Alice   Oh please.

Queen of Hearts   Guilty!

Snaps her fingers.

Item!

White Rabbit   'Item. She rewrote the tale – '

Alice   But, I didn't mean –

Duchess   Tit tot. You tart.

You girl without a heart!

(*To the world.*) She was my pig – I loved my pig! –

And then she got so mean and big!

Alice   I *didn't*!

Duchess   Did.

Little Mock Alice (*to **Alice***)   You wish.

Mad Hatter   Go fish!

Alice (*to the* **White Rabbit**)   I only meant to offer you a place again – a place we could belong again . . .

Queen of Hearts (*snaps her fingers*)   Item!

White Rabbit (*doing his lines as quickly as possible*)   'She made Wonderland her garden, breeding Lobsters out of Card-Men – '

Alice (*to the* **White Rabbit**)   It wasn't like that. You know that.

Knave of Hearts   Well, she certainly held my hedgehog, and wriggled my flamingo.

Queen of Hearts   Child, I never!
Acting as if she were some mock me?

Another Mock Alice *steps forward.*

Another Mock Alice   A mockery!

Mad Hatter   The riddle? She could barely even read it.

Queen of Hearts (*snaps her fingers*)   Item!

White Rabbit   'Item. She – '

Alice   Who's *she*?

Mad Hatter   You's she. You little tweeb.

Queen of Hearts   Guilty! Guilty! Guilty!

(*To* **Alice**.)   Now we shall decide if you can leave here.

Alice   Do you mean you'd keep me here?

King of Hearts   Every dream would love to hold its dreamer.

It's the dreamer who can't bear to know she's dreaming.

Alice   But I'll know! I'll know.

I know the dream – by heart.

This *is* my heart. My dream.

King of Hearts   Oh do you think?

Then who, and what, are we?

Alice   Part of it.

King of Hearts   You think?

Then, where are we, when you're not here?

Queen of Hearts   You think we just appear, because you see us?

King of Hearts   The truth is, we are here, and sometimes we let you into our dream.

Alice   I won't believe you.

Queen of Hearts   Do you think our dream needs *you* to dream it?

King of Hearts   You, who are no longer you?

Queen of Hearts   You no one.

Alice   I'm not no one.

Queen of Hearts   No one!

Alice   No no – you, and you, and you are! Watch what happens when I close the book.

Queen of Hearts   No – please!

King of Hearts   Noooo!

Duchess   My precious Piggie!

Alice   Try and stop me.

White Rabbit   But we have to reach the end!

Alice (*from the storybook*)   ' "Stuff and nonsense!" Alice said loudly.'

A desperate panic sets in.

Little Mock Alice   No – please!

Mad Hatter   Take my tea!

Another Mock Alice   The songs we'd sing!

Mad Hatter   My cream! It's steamed!

Queen of Hearts   Here – play the King!

Alice   'You're nothing but a pack of cards!'

Queen of Hearts   Play *me*!

Alice   No more King or Queen! No Duck or Duchess, Pig or Fig!

White Rabbit   And me . . . ?

Alice *waves her hand – 'Enough!'*

Music begins:

WHAT HAVE I DONE WITH ME?

Alice
Sure, there are moments I won't regret.
But this is surely the hottest mess I've ever left.
No matter how you insulted me,
I always tried just to trust the ride and do the dream.

It's like you talk without hearing it.
Or like you've drained all the wisdom from experience.
And when I trust and I turn to you,
It's like you put every word up for absurd review.

All (*except* **Alice**)
But what are we to do,
When you are just so rude?

Knave of Clubs
And where oh where's the love?

Duchess
After all we've done for you?

All (*except* **Alice**)
For you . . .

Alice *and* **Chorus**
No more caring for you no ones,
What's this supposed to be?

No more tearing my heart open.
What have I done with me?

Alice
I've seen the nothing behind your grins,
I've watched you turn every thought into some non-event.
There's nothing left here to understand –
I've watched you run all the wonder out of Wonderland.

All
When all is said and done,
The players had their fun.

Duchess *and* **Knaves**
So, to close the show,
Off you go –
This can't go on.

This can't go on . . .

Alice *and* **White Rabbit**
No more caring for you no ones.
I've done the lonely dream.
No more tearing my heart open.
What have I done with me?

Alice
And when the longing comes calling me,
Just let me sleep

Alice *and* **Female Chorus**
In some solitary reverie.

All (*except* **Alice**)
Well, what are we to do,
When you are just so rude?

Boys
> *And so, we'll close the show,*
> *Off you'll go.*
> *Enough of you.*

All (*except* **Alice**)
> *Enough of you.*

All	**Alice and Little Mock Alice**
No more caring for you no ones.	*La . . .*
What's this supposed to be?	*La la la la . . .*
No more tearing my heart open.	*La la la la la la . . .*
What have I done with me?	
No more caring for you no ones.	*La . . .*
What's this supposed to be?	*La la la la . . .*
No more tearing my heart open.	*La la la la la la . . .*
What have I done with me?	
No more caring for you no ones.	
What's this supposed to be?	
No more tearing my heart open.	
What have I done with me?	

As the song concludes, everyone disappears. **Alice** *stands, once more, alone. Nowhere in Wonderland. But wait – the* **White Rabbit***'s there too.*

Alice   You.

White Rabbit   Still here.

Alice   Somehow.

White Rabbit   Yes.

An awkward beat.

Alice   I suppose because I can't . . .

I still can't let you go . . .

The **White Rabbit** *nods.*

White Rabbit   I can't tell you what it's meant, to come here once again – to run here once again . . .

Alice *nods, holding back tears.*

White Rabbit   I hope you will remember how it was . . . ?

Alice *nods.*

White Rabbit   In the story, there's no moment of farewell, you know.

This lands.

White Rabbit   And so . . .

The **White Rabbit** *starts to go.* **Alice***'s words stop him.*

Alice   But how shall I be here without you, now?

A silence. Neither moves. Music begins:

ANOTHER ROOM IN YOUR HEAD

White Rabbit
What will you do, when I'm not here with you,
And you sit here and you're not with me?
How will you do, finding something to do,
When there's so much you thought that we'd see?

Alice
What will you do, when I'm thinking of you –
All the things I'll be thinking you'd say?
How will I do all the things we would do,
When I'm thinking of you through the day?

As the music swells, a **Chorus** *gathers – unseen, but heard, by* **Alice***.*

White Rabbit
Oh, will you find another room in your head?

White Rabbit *and* **Alice**
Lose your mind in another room in your head?

White Rabbit, Alice *and* **Chorus of One**
Left behind in another room in your head . . .

White Rabbit

Will I still sleep in some part of your mind,
In some way I may never know?

Alice

Will I still dream that you're here and you're mine,
And I never have to let you go?

White Rabbit *and* **Alice**

Oh, will you find another room in your head?

White Rabbit, Alice *and* **Chorus of Two**

Spend some time in another room in your head?

White Rabbit, Alice *and* **Chorus of Four**

Wondering why in another room in your head?

White Rabbit

Will you dream it's like always – haunting as always,
You still there, wanting my love?

Alice

Will you dream I'm still watching, full of such longing?
Wanting so much still, my love?

White Rabbit *and* **Alice**

In my dreams, when I'm falling – falling and falling,
You'll be there, wanting my love . . .
In my dreams, you'll be calling – calling with longing,
Nothing there, haunting our love.

White Rabbit

You still there, wanting my love.

What will you do, when I'm not here with you,
And you sit here and you're not with me?

Alice

What will you do, when there's nothing to do,
And there's so much we thought that we'd see?

White Rabbit *and* **Alice**

When there's so much we thought we would be?

White Rabbit, Alice *and* **Chorus of Three**
Oh, will you find another room in your head?

White Rabbit, Alice *and* **Chorus of Four**
Spend some time in another room in your head?

White Rabbit, Alice *and* **Chorus of Five**
Wondering why in another room in your head?

White Rabbit (*wailing above*)
In another room in your head . . .
In another room, another room in your head . . .

As the song concludes, the light, the sound, of a tube train shuttering past.
In the moment, the **White Rabbit** *is gone.* **Alice** *stands, alone.*

The shadowy form of the Underground station slowly fills in around her,
like a dawning realisation. The first light of morning filters through.
Alfred Hallam's *bed lies empty.* **Alice** *stares blankly at it. Everyone*
else in their beds. Except, that is, for **Harold Pudding**, *who's*
jumping about.

Harold Pudding   Give up, then? On the riddle?

Alice (*about* **Alfred**)   So, he's . . . ?

Dodgy   Miss Cross, she took him off.

Mabel   In a better place, he is.

Alice *takes this in.*

Angus   Amen, then.

Ada   Nothing to be done.

Angus   For him, that is.

For me, I'll have another bit of bun.

Alice *realises she has something in her hand – the* **White Rabbit**'s
pocket watch. She crosses to **Alfred Hallam**'s *empty bed.*

Alice (*concluding the story*)   ' "Oh, what a curious dream I've
had," Alice said . . . '

Mabel   There she is – still reading to him.

Alice   'And she told her sister, as best she could remember, all her strange adventures . . . '

Buxby   Nooooot.

Angus   Let's be done with that, love.

Ada   Boy is gone.

Alice   He wanted so to . . . finish it.

(*To the departed* **Alfred**.) '"Such a curious dream," Alice said.'

A glimmer of light reveals the enigmatic grin of the **Cheshire Cat**, *hovering high in the dark. Only* **Alice** *senses her.*

Cheshire Cat   '"But wonderful."'

Harold Pudding   Give up? On the riddle?

Nigel   On its belly in the morning, was it?

Harold Pudding   Oh yes. Belly. Ping.

As the riddling continues, music rises.

Dodgy   Sleeps in gold all day?

Ada   Flutters off the tea tray through the night?

Dodgy   Harold, come, we all give up.

Harold Pudding   Well, it's a butter-*fly*, of course.

Nigel (*aside, to* **Dodgy**)   Appalling riddle.

Dodgy   Thoroughly.

AND THERE YOU ARE

Cheshire Cat
> Stars of blue on autumn nights,
> Through the windy western sky;
> Half a moon, there on high . . .
> With a whisper, with a sigh,
> Still the evening shuts its eyes,
> Fading blue through the night.

Nothing comes or goes without a shadow.
Somewhere in the soul you hold the candle.
Let the sorrow go, it's half the battle.
Down the hole you go, to where you are.
Down the hole you go, and there you are.

Alice

There are rooms you leave behind,
Other wounds of other times.
Other songs fill your mind.

Rabbits lead you for a while,
Picture books and sister's smile,
Summer drifts, like a child.

All

Oooh . . .

Nothing comes or goes without a shadow.
Somewhere in the soul you hold the candle.
Let the sorrow go, it's half the battle.

Cheshire Cat

Down the hole you go,

Alice

To where you are.

Cheshire Cat

Down the hole you go,

Alice

And there you are.
Down the hole you go, and there you are.

CURTAIN CALL

White Rabbit

Just some summer book,
God, and it was hot too.
Who knew where to look,
What to do, and not do.

White Rabbit and **Alice**
Now some rabbit looms
Like there's no tomorrow.

Alice
How can I refuse,
When he tells me follow?

Alice *and* **Knave of Clubs**
And now we're down the hole –
And really on a roll.
And something on the shelves

Alice, **Knave of Hearts** *and* **White Rabbit**
Holds something of ourselves.

Knave of Hearts
Down and down we fall –
Now where have we wandered?

Knave of Hearts *and* **Little Mock Alice**
Pictures, books, and all,
Tumbling from the cupboards.

Cheshire Cat
Hit the ground below,
Everything so tiny.

White Rabbit
Now, where did it go –
The world I left behind me?

Girls (**Boys** *echoing*)
For, now we're down the hole –
And really on a roll.
God knows where we're at.
Should have brought the cat.

But now we're down the hole
And calling from the soul.
The walls are all so tall,
They're too small for the hall.

White Rabbit
> *These hands are not my hands –*
> *So, is this Wonderland?*

Alice
> *No rabbit can begin*
> *To know the state I'm in.*

Mad Hatter
> *You meet a marble cake,*
> *Your heart begins to ache.*

Caterpillar
> *But once you start to eat,*
> *You're too tall for your feet.*

Duchess
> *The bottle tells you 'Drink',*
> *You never stop to think*

Queen of Hearts, **Little Mock Alice** *and* **Girls**
> *How quickly you will shrink,*
> *The more and more you drink.*

Alice
> *But now you're down the hole –*
> *Now you're down the hole . . .*

All
> *Now you're down the hole –*
> *And really on a roll.*
> *Just tall enough to see*
> *You're smaller than the key.*
>
> *'Cause now you're down the hole,*
> *And calling from the soul:*
> *What happens if I can't*
> *Get back to Wonderland?*

Alice *and* **White Rabbit**
> *Now you're down the hole . . .*

Alice by Heart

Notes on rehearsal and staging, drawn from a workshop
with the writer held at the National Theatre, November 2011

The Conception

Alice by Heart is a brand-new musical, with the book and lyrics
written by Steven Sater and music by Duncan Sheik. Steven
wanted to create something specifically for young people
about the experience of growing up. Set in London in the
1940s during the Blitz, the familiar world of Wonderland is
reinvented to tell the story of the challenges of leaving
childhood behind.

Themes and Areas of Research

Refamiliarise yourself with the original book *Alice's Adventures
in Wonderland*, by Lewis Carroll. It will be useful to identify the
moments that appear in the musical, and how the musical
reinvents and reimagines them.

The play is set in a very specific time and place – London,
1940, an underground station during the Blitz. Time could be
spent researching the world of the 1940s, and deciding with
your company how and why this particular moment and
place in history is relevant to you, to your own location, to
your audience. Consider how the environment and the context
of the Blitz can inform Alice's personal journey and what
Wonderland is – i.e., a world in danger, on a precipice, where
the threat of death, grief and loss is a continual reality and a
place where young people have nothing but their imaginations.

Themes include:

- Loss, grief, the challenge of letting go and learning how to
  leave someone behind.

- The rites of passage from childhood to adolescence.

- Innocence vs experience.

- Sexual awakening.
- The search for identity.
- Imagination, fantasy, escapism.

Directing a Musical

The genre of the musical should be embraced and celebrated. It is not just a 'play with songs'. It is called a musical for a reason. Directing a musical is challenging, exciting, exhausting, demanding and, ultimately, hugely rewarding. As directors (and you might also be your own set designer, lighting, sound, costume designer), allow yourself to go on flights of fancy, let your imagination run away with itself, feel empowered to own the story and create the world you want to create. You are the leading interpretive artist, so be playful, think big and bold and visually, let the music and the story lead and fire up your sense of spectacle.

Know who you are making the show for. Who is your audience? What will they respond to? Don't make work that is in a timeless vacuum – you are making it *now*, so let whatever is happening in the world that year, even that day, inform the work. Know where you are putting the musical on – your specific location. What is the city, space, demographic, etc.?

Have complete respect for the text and don't change a word without permission from the writer, but don't be slaves to the stage directions. Let them be a starting point and if they are not useful, remove them. Your job is to help your audience understand the story, so don't allow them to stifle your own imagination. Interpretation is your job and privilege.

Listen to the music at every available opportunity. Immerse yourself in it. Let the music direct you. Put it on your iPod and let the music get under your skin, into your blood, let it become as familiar to you as breathing. Let it work on your brain, your heart, your subconscious. Trust it and let it lead your instinct. Understand the style and rhythm of the piece. Don't just focus on the words. You don't always need to be intellectual in your connection. Sometimes by forgetting the words and giving your full attention to the music you can unlock something. Often the music will lead a scene and your understanding of it. If there is conflict between the words and the music, the music will always win.

The basic structure of a musical is that all the time you are building to a song and coming out of it. Keep this in your mind and know where the songs come and what they are doing. Text and song must walk hand in hand, and this bridge between the two is the constant quest in terms of a consistency in tone and style.

Use underscore at your discretion. At certain points, it is clearly written when a scene is underscored and at what point the music starts and finishes. There is a reason and a desired effect that you must not ignore. At other points, it will be up to you, so use it with caution and only if it is serving the scene.

Directing *Alice by Heart*

Alice by Heart is elliptical and ambiguous. It can mean any number of things. Some of the above themes and areas of research might be useful, or you might discover a different connection to it and find different ways in. Work with your company to decide what the play is about for you.

It could be done with a cast of six or of sixty. It could be done with just a piano and a guitar, or a full orchestra. It could be done with unlimited resources or with nothing but your actors. Decide what scale is fitting for your particular group. Whatever scale you are working towards, let your performers be at the centre and work with what you have, not what you wish you had. Find a way to keep the music live. A recorded soundtrack is infinitely less interesting and more problematic.

A certain level of proficiency is required from your singers, but more importantly performers need to feel comfortable and confident in expressing themselves musically.

Whether you use microphones will depend on the size of your theatre, the size of your band, the strength of your singers.

Protect their voices and be wary of pushing young voices too hard. If you are using drums in your band, you will need microphones or your singers will be drowned. Don't overpower the vocals with the music. Use your musical imagination to keep everything in proportion.

A straight read-through might not be the most useful way to begin rehearsals. Without the songs and the music, you cannot get a grasp of the rhythm and momentum of the piece as a whole. The story will be incomplete and unsatisfying, so allow your company time to get to know the music first.

Characters and Doubling

While there are some obvious male and female roles, you could be using an all-male, or all-female cast. You must keep to the doubling of Harold Pudding and the Mad Hatter and of Alfred Hallam and the White Rabbit. Other suggestions of doublings are included in the text, but there is room for manoeuvre. There is also room to expand certain chorus moments and to distribute the lines of songs to accommodate more voices. One example could be when the Mock Alices appear to taunt Alice and her changing body. There is the potential for having lots of Mock Alices appear. You can reallocate lines to fit their number, as long as they act as a chorus. You could do a similar thing with the Caterpillars.

However, make sure that your decisions have a clear logic and do not confuse the storytelling. Some passages are very clearly meant to be sung by a certain character.

You might have to consider transposing certain songs to cater for different vocal ranges.

Accents

Although the musical begins in London, don't get hung up on accents as they can be restrictive and time-consuming. It is more important that performers feel confident in their characters and in the world of the musical than in their ability to perfect a London or an RP accent. Individual accents will bring a texture and a truth to the piece. If you did want to explore the possibility of different accents, perhaps the accents in the world of the Blitz are different to those in Wonderland? Perhaps you could explore singing in one accent and speaking in another? Make sure that whatever you decide has a logic, that you are consistent and that performers feel comfortable with what they are doing.

Style

This is very much an ensemble piece. While Alice's journey is at the heart of the story, there is something universal in her journey of growing up and letting go. If you are working with a large company, find ways of using everyone onstage.

The musical style is that of pop rock. It can sound free and improvised, but is actually very precise. Pay attention to the tempos suggested by the score. They are given for a reason. Be wary of the rehearsal-room piano and of speeding up within songs. Once other instruments are added, a consistent tempo has to be maintained for a song to work.

Pace and energy are crucial to the rhythm of the piece. It hits the ground running and does not stop.

There are two worlds that co-exist within the story: that of the underground station and that of Wonderland. Both worlds are heightened and in high definition, and one should inform the other. There are glorious moments of fantasy and nonsense that should be embraced and celebrated. Ride the nonsense and don't over-analyse it. Trust the text.

However, nonsense for nonsense's sake is boring and unsatisfying to watch. Steven has written a strong, truthful and emotional through line that provides the backbone for all the nonsense and fantasy and spectacle. So make sure that you and your company invest time and thought in understanding the individual and collective character journeys within the play.

It is vital to decide what Wonderland is for you and how you want to represent it. Be playful, inventive and bold. Wonderland at the beginning symbolises for Alice escapism and childhood – a place of dreams and fantasy where anything can happen. Her journey within the play is psychological, as she comes to realise that Wonderland is actually a place inside herself.

Structure

The structure of the piece has been very carefully crafted. Before you start rehearsing, break the piece down into workable units/sections. Each section is about something Alice learns. Find the main event in each section, identify what Alice wants and what is stopping her from getting it.

Ensure that the storytelling is clear for you and for an audience. There are key lines of text that need to land in order for the story to maintain an emotional resonance. There are some exciting images and visual opportunities, but don't get bogged down in these or you risk losing the text and creating an empty production. Keep the story and the emotional through line taut and clear and at the front of your mind.

The flow of the piece should be fluid and continuous, with songs and scenes weaving in and out of each other. There should never be a moment where characters enter 'song mode'. Characters need to keep their integrity and truth through the songs.

Language in Scenes and Songs

The vernacular of the characters is not how modern young people communicate, yet sheds light on what it is like to be a young person growing up today. Characters have their own way of communicating that are unique to this theatrical world, and the style of language is key in holding the two worlds of London and Wonderland together. Encourage your performers to embrace the theatricality of the language, trust the poetry and own it.

Imagination is key. Invite your company to engage their own imaginations and connect on a personal level to the language and music of the piece.

Often the feeling of the music is the feeling of the scene, so look at the songs within the context of the scene, not in isolation. One always informs the other.

Treat the lyrics of the songs with respect. Make sure everyone knows what they are singing and why they are singing it. Spend time with your singers deconstructing the meaning and finding the emotional truth within each song. Encourage them to engage imaginatively and let the images come to life in their heads as they sing.

What are they singing about? Very often a song gives time for characters to chase a thought, to express what is in their minds, to work out what they are feeling. There is always a need. Take care that songs are focused outwards and are shared with the audience. The moment an emotion is internalised or indulged, the meaning becomes empty.

Staging

Everyone onstage needs to have a motivation and a reason for being there that sheds light on Alice's central journey. With a large cast, could the ensemble be made up of displaced youths who are sheltering in the underground station? There is plenty of scope for individual characters and activity within this context.

Establishing a physical language that supports the style of the music is vital. Fluidity and speed are key, so this needs to be reflected in the movement and choreography. Match the stylisation of language with bold, heightened, sharp physical moments. Are there moments where the ensemble move/ transform as a unit?

Consider practically how you are going to make the shifts from the 'real' world of the underground to the fantasy of Wonderland. It has to happen quickly and easily. Find the moment where Wonderland is introduced. For example, by the end of the song on page 327, Alice has to have arrived in Wonderland.

Have the courage and confidence to keep playing and exploring the staging possibilities, and don't set things too early. Know the point where you need to stop playing around and when decisions need to be made. Once you have reached this point, then set it to within an inch of its life.

How do you move in and out of songs? Consider moments of transition first. The most important question is how you will get from A to B. These moments can take time to discover and will inform how the scenes themselves are played. It might be useful to think of each transition like the turning of a page.

Motivate the beginnings and ends of songs. Does the end of a song have a punctuated ending? Or does it leave you hanging? Look to the music for staging clues. Does the music lead the action, or does the action lead the music? You can control where the focus needs to be by where you place people, and how people enter and leave the stage.

Design

Try and think beyond the fourth wall in your design ideas. This is a piece that feels immersive, that could really lend itself to a shared experience in which performers and audience can co-exist. There is an intimacy and an immediacy that is exciting. Think beyond the proscenium arch. Think unconventionally. Is there potential for promenade? Or audience on two sides? Play with the performer–audience relationship. Can performers be in and around the audience, with the potential to appear, disappear and surprise? Can you use a traditional space in a non-traditional way? Can you transform a non-theatrical space?

There are several design challenges that need to be met. How are you going to create a pool of tears? How will white roses turn red? How can a table float down from the ceiling? How are the two worlds created? Is there potential for object manipulation? Do you want totally to transform from one world into another, or are there always elements of both? Be wary of projections – playfulness and appealing to the imagination is far more exciting than literal representation.

From a workshop led by Timothy Sheader and David Shrubsole,
with notes by Kate Budgen

Generation Next

Meera Syal

Character Notes

Nina, nineteen. A savvy young woman, street-smart rather than book-smart, who has no idea how funny her motormouth can be. Has a canny edge which comes from growing up without much money and feeling it. Willing to make pragmatic rather than romantic decisions to get a better life.

Anita, eighteen. As idealistic as her sister is practical, she burns with the fire of injustice, and her desire to change the world sometimes means she's blind about herself. Fiercely intelligent and impatient for change, like a lot of intellectuals she's not so hot at personal relationships. Men confuse her, frankly.

Kiran, eighteen. The only Indian-born character, she's always the outsider and never feels she belongs. She moves from sweet innocent abroad to someone darker and manipulative but never forgets she has feminine wiles and beauty and will use them whenever necessary.

Raj, sixteen. Nina's baby brother starts off as the most immature of the bunch. Too young to handle his relationship with Sally, too influenced by his yobby friends, he grows in maturity and ambition as the play progresses.

Vip, eighteen. Smart, easygoing and ambitious, she carries a confidence that comes from growing up with a loving family and easy money. He is in turns fascinated and confused by Anita, and realises too late in the play that what he felt for her all along was love.

Rikki, nineteen. A bloke's bloke, he reflects the easy sexism of his peers as it's easier to fit in. His struggle is about being brave enough to ditch the patriarchal shit and connect with Nina. As the play progresses, he moves from average Joe to a high-flyer who knows his worth.

Vikram, twenty. Starts off as a bad boy, using his considerable wits to duck and dive in all sorts of illegal gang business and considers himself the daddy of the friends. His weak spot is Kiran, and as the play progresses the balance of power shifts between them, with him trying to own her, then please her and failing. Too late, he realises she never thought him good enough in the first place.

Dave, seventeen. Dave's easygoing manner masks a deep desire to belong somewhere. First he hangs out with the Asians, then finds religion and finally drugs. He doesn't say much but when he does, you realise he's saying it for everyone.

Sally, sixteen. Sally and Raj dance around each other for the whole play. She is in turn fascinated and repelled by him. She's young too but smart enough to know when to protect herself. She hates the feeling she sometimes gets that she's not good enough to join this gang.

Characters

Nina, *the Bride*
Anita, *the Bride's sister*
Kiran, *the Bride's best mate*
Raj, *the Bride's brother*
Vip, *the Bride's brother's mate*

Rikki, *the Groom*
Vikram, *the Groom's best man*
Dave, *the Groom's mate*
Sally, *the Groom's mate's girlfriend*

Setting

Each act takes place in Southall at a Punjabi wedding, in the years 1979, 2005 and 2035 respectively.

Sets should be minimal, with interiors and exteriors suggested by lighting.

Notes

Each cast member plays the same character in each act.

Don't attempt the accent if it feels forced or uncomfortable. Better to play the truth of the character than end up sounding like a bad curry advert.

Where you see the forward slash / this indicates the point of overlap in dialogue.

For the set dance numbers, any number of actors can be called upon and used, the more the merrier. Learning to bhangra is huge fun and not complicated: it's a hearty harvest dance meant to be rough around the edges and celebratory – once you've got the basic steps down, anything goes. So go for it.

Scene One

Southall Community Centre, 1979. A hall set for a Punjabi wedding. Mid- to backstage suggests the hall interior. A spotlit single table is decorated with helium balloons with the inscription CONGRATULATIONS TO THE HAPPY COUPLE! *It is set with plastic compartmentalised food trays and the centrepiece decoration of a bottle of whisky, a bottle of Coke and a carton of orange juice.*

Front stage suggests the back exterior of the hall. An alley with overflowing dustbins and a sign declaring SOUTHALL COMMUNITY CENTRE: STAFF PARKING ONLY.

As lights snap on, the stage is invaded by wedding guests, including core cast members, all dancing to the iconic bhangra hit, 'Rail Gaddi'. Costumes are gaudy and traditional, the energy and joy should lift the roof.

The song snaps off suddenly, lights dim as all exit except **Nina** *and* **Rikki** *in half light.*

Loud radio static plays in, giving way to a radio news reader, continually interrupted by a fading signal.

Announcer   . . . since the Shah's overthrow three weeks ago on April the first, the newly formed Islamic Republic in Iran . . . Tanzanian troops overtook Kampala forcing dictator Idi Amin to flee . . . Hundreds of police expected in Southall today as the National Front say they will march through the mainly Asian-populated town on St George's Day . . . US President Jimmy Carter is recovering well after being attacked by a jack rabbit whilst fishing three days ago in his home town of White Plains, Georgia . . .

A spotlight snaps on to **Nina**, *eighteen, dressed in traditional red and gold bridal sari. She can barely move due to the heavy embroidery and the bunches of mini-coconuts and good-luck amulets hanging from her wrists.*

Simultaneously, a spotlight on **Rikki**, *nineteen, equally dolled up in a traditional bridegroom's suit, with a huge glittery turban, at the front of which is hanging a veil of tinsel. He removes this at some point.*

Both speak with that first British-born generation accent of West London blended with Punjabi glottals and expletives. They both speak very quickly.

Nina   I mean, course you think about it, hena? I mean, you're brought up that way innit? What with singing lovers leaping into the bushes in the Bollywood movies and your aunties yapping in your ear as soon as you can roll a round chapatti, it's not like you can say no or anything. I mean, you can say no if you don't like the fella, I mean if he's like too short or too greasy or a bud-bud just off the boat, I mean, have I got British passport tattooed on me arse or what? Don't take me for no fool, innit!

Rikki   I never really thought about it yaar, I mean you spend more time thinking about not being caught practising if you know what I mean . . . not on apne curie, our girls, cos everyone knows you mess with the princesses, you got to marry them. And your knob falls off. Fact. But no one hangs the sheets out after the wedding night to prove the boy's been a good boy, in fact you're expected to be a bad boy until you settle down and then be a good husband and forget you ever did any of that shit cos for sure, you ain't going to be doing it with your wife cos she's a good girl. And even if she wasn't, no bloody way she's gonna let on cos what would I think of her then? (*Beat.*) I'd bloody kill her.

Nina   Or, save me bhagwan, you might end up with a mummy's boy who's gonna throw you to your mother-in-law like a masala lamb chop to a starving jealous tiger as soon as the wedding gold's packed away. I mean, some of my mates, right, day after the wedding off come the coconuts and you're suddenly cleaning the toilet and trimming grandad's nose hair and sod off leaping into bushes cos you're probably doing the bleeding gardening as well.

Rikki   So this is the weird thing, yeah, you're both like, pretending to be something you really ain't right from the wedding night, you swallow down the lies with the laddoos but at least you got someone there who ain't gonna get up off the back seat of your car, put her knickers back on and say buy me a kebab before you drop me home. (*Beat.*) Me mate Vikram said, get a girl from back in the pind, the village, like he did. Cos you know with the imported girls, they're like, pure. And not as mouthy. And do as they're told. And I said, yaar, what you looking for? A wife or a household pet? And he says, I'm having a wife-flap fitted to me front door. He's a nutter, Vikram, he kills me.

Nina   So you think about it and you watch your parents worry themselves into wrinkles and grey hair saving for the big day cos of course, the bloke don't pay for nothing cos everyone's just so grateful some bugger's gonna take you off their hands and at least you ain't one of the saddos who end up at thirty still being touted round the temples and the matchmakers while everyone whispers, 'Well if she's not married yet, there must be something wrong with her . . . See what happens to these career women? Too much thinking makes your ovaries dry up, no man wants to plant his son in a desert . . . ' I wish I'd finished me college course though.

Rikki   Yeah, it was arranged, families knew each other and all that, so what? I could have said no. But I was ready. I mean, it's time to grow up. Be a man. And once I'd finally passed my business studies re-re-re-retake, I'd run out of excuses. Plus Nina has in fact got a great arse.

Nina   I could have said no. But our parents, look what they've given up for us. They want to see us settled so they know the long journey was worth it. It's about family, not just me. I know I'm lucky really, getting Rikki.

Spotlights snap off, full lights on **Raj** *and* **Vip**, *who enter laughing.*

Raj   Oh man, thought I was gonna die laughing!

Vip   Did you see when he /

Raj   / When he went straight into that crowd of aunties . . .

Vip   / Was like an explosion in a sari factory, ptaak!

Raj   Did you see Toupée Uncle . . . trying to . . . trying to catch its tail!

Vip   Hear him? 'Hat hat Frisky! Hat hat!' Like he's herding an elephant!

Raj   What a headline – 'Groom Trampled to Death Hours Before Wedding'!

Vip   Oh man, what a great start. Whose idea to put Rikki on a white horse? (*Beat.*) Did you say 'Toupée Uncle'?

Raj   Don't tell me you missed it. It flaps when he runs.

Vip   But which one is he? What's his name?

Raj *gets out a packet of ten Embassy and lights up.*

Raj   Fuck knows. Too many of them to remember their names, man. Hence Toupée Uncle, Bosoms Auntie, Existential Uncle . . . don't get talking to him, you'll be there for hours . . .

He jumps as **Anita** *and* **Kiran** *enter, stubbing out the fag in his hand, burning himself.* **Kiran** *has a strong Indian accent and is dressed very traditionally.*

Raj   Bloody hell! Can't you like . . . knock or something?

Kiran   Oh Raj. You're not smoking now? That is so 'basti'. At a religious function as well.

Raj   Chill out, mataji. It's just a fag . . . Don't people smoke in India?

Kiran   Not at their sister's wedding. If anyone sees you . . .

Anita   She's right, you oolloo. What if Mum had come out here?

Raj   I'd say it was Vip's and I was holding it for him. Everyone knows these private-school kids do all the hai-hai chi-chi dirty western things!

Vip *catches* **Raj** *in a headlock, they mock wrestle.*

Vip   Take it back, sala!

Raj   The suit, man! Mind the suit!

Anita   Grow up, you two!

Raj   Where is Mum anyway?

Anita   Going mental cos of Rikki nearly being crushed by that stupid horse and half his guests not here cos of the road blocks.

Raj   Road blocks?

Anita   Maybe if you watched the news occasionally little bro, instead of re-runs of *Happy Days* . . .

Raj   Heyyyy! No one disrespects the Fonz . . .

Kiran (*giggling*)   Actually that's quite good! I love that show . . .

Vip   Is it bad out there?

Anita   What, a bunch of fascists marching through our town being protected by the same police who don't give a shit when our people are attacked and abused every day? Yeah, I'd say it was quite bad.

Vip   I was only asking . . .

Raj   Don't get her started, she does my brain in . . .

Anita   Don't you care?

Vip   Yeah, I do, I . . .

Raj   I'd care more if you didn't yap on about it all the time.

Anita   Paki-bashing is a legitimate phrase now, they say it on TV. We're a national sport!

Vip   Listen, I know what –

Kiran   It's true. What she's saying. Someone spat in my face in the Spar. All I did was squeeze an aubergine. I mean, back home, we squeeze everything, hena? Otherwise how can you tell what's ripe? I told Vikram. He told me stick to the

Indian shops. I said it's like being in India anyway round here. Apart from the cold. And the spitting. And the loneliness.

An awkward pause. **Anita** *gives* **Kiran** *a sisterly squeeze.*

Anita   Vikram being an arse, is he?

Kiran   Oh no. He's . . . just very busy.

Anita   Dunno how you do it. Married off at sixteen, shipped over here, ending up with bloody Vikram . . . I'd have said no.

Raj   No one asked you, sis. That's why Nina's getting married before you, innit?

He laughs at his own joke. No one else does, though. He trails off, embarrassed, absentmindedly scratching his head.

Anita   Yeah, scratch your head for a change and give your balls a rest.

Kiran (*gasps*)   Anita! You are too much!

They all explode into laughter, except **Kiran** *who holds her ears and does the 'warding off the evil eye' sign.* **Raj** *gathers his dignity.*

Raj   I'm gonna see what's going on. Supposed to be the Milni now, innit?

Kiran   Oh I love the Milni! Ours was so cute, when the dads from each family welcomed each other with garlands and presents, and then our mums, and then our sisters and then our brothers and then our cousins and then our thayas and thayees and then our chachas and chachees and then our mamas and mamees and then our masis and masers and then our nieces and nephews . . .

She trails off as everyone is looking at her.

It went on for forty minutes. Longest recorded Milni in Southall.

Anita   No boy's side here, no Milni. We're already two hours late.

Raj (*to* **Kiran**)   Coming?

Kiran   Okay. But don't touch me anywhere. If Vikram smells smoke on me, he'll go crazy . . .

They exit, leaving **Vip** *and* **Anita** *alone.*

Vip   Indian time or English?

Anita   What?

Vip   Two hours late you said. In English time?

Anita   Indian.

Vip   So four hours. That is late. Well 'besti' in fact.

Anita *finally cracks a smile.*

Anita   Don't try and talk street, doesn't suit you, private-school boy.

Vip   Why not? Grew up on the same street as you.

Anita   Not any more. How is the pebble-dashed mansion in Harrow?

Vip   It's mock-Tudor actually . . . and it's . . . good. It's quiet and green.

Anita   White, don't you mean?

Vip   So what? So I have to live in the ghetto to prove I'm a proper Indian?

Anita   Well, yeah. Especially on days like today because people like you should be fighting with us . . .

Vip   That's okay. Just let me know when the rioting starts and I can get my dad to drop me off in his Roller.

Anita   You've got a Rolls-Royce? I *knew* it!

Vip (*laughing*)   Bloody hell . . . course we haven't . . . You are . . .

Anita   / When one of our lot gets successful what's the first thing they do . . .

Vip   . . . / like some bloody mental wind-up toy . . . Crank her up and off she goes . . .

Anita   They move out and move on and don't care . . .

Vip   Of course we do! We move out and move *up*! Cos that's why we're here, Anita! We're immigrants! Our parents didn't come here to watch some Shakespeare and party with the fucking Beatles! They came to make money so we could have the choices . . . /

Anita   / It's not just about money . . .

Vip   Why do you think Kiran married Vikram? He may be a nutter, but he's a rich nutter, compared to who she'd get over there. (*Beat.*) Do you know how good it feels to be in a school where people don't think you're a knob because you might actually want to learn something, make something of yourself?

Anita   No. I don't know.

Vip   You'd fit right in, you know that? Clever passionate girl like you . . .

Anita   Woman . . . I'm a woman. Eighteen. At Southall Technical College where they think I'm a mong because I don't wear mascara to lectures. But your parents can afford to pay . . .

Vip   / They go without so I can have . . .

Anita   / And mine can't because . . .

Vip   / I can move up . . . no holidays, no meals out . . .

Anita (*shouting over him*)   And mine can't because they have spent all their savings on this sodding wedding!

A beat. **Vip** *wants to say something,* **Anita** *is begging him not to. This is way too shameful. The silence is broken by* **Vikram**, **Dave** *and*

Sally *arriving.* **Sally** *is wearing an inappropriately short revealing dress.*

Vip   Vikram! You're here.

Vikram *(mockingly checks himself)*   Fuck me, so I am. No flies on you, Mr Coconut.

Vip   Pardon?

Vikram   And so polite too, va va!

Anita   Leave it, Vip. Where's Rikki, he okay?

Vikram   Yeah. Hello Anita, I'm fine thanks. Apart from having his nuts crushed from riding bareback, Rikki's cool. Still waiting for his lot from up north to get here. Pigs everywhere man, like a war zone.

Vip   What's that mean, the coconut thing?

Anita   Never mind, Vip. Listen Vikram, we can't hold up the wedding much longer!

Vikram   Listen back, woman, you're bloody lucky Rikki made it here alive. Good job some of my lads were around to keep an eye.

Anita   Aah. Still playing street gangs, are we?

Vikram   Good job you're not a bloke. Yet.

Anita   If I was, I'd be out there, not in here serving samosas.

Vikram *(laughs)*   Oh we are out there, believe me. Soon as I seen me best mate married, we'll give them white trash something to think about. No offence, Dave. That's Dave, by the way.

Dave   None taken, mate.

Vikram   Think we're pushovers, don't they? Ah, bless 'em, nice quiet Asians open all hours, some bottom-burning curry with your lager, sir? Maybe you'd like to bugger me with that naan as well because I'm just so fucking grateful to be here. (*Beat.*) Wind blows, you'll stick like that.

Anita (*shuts her mouth*)   Only thing you've ever said that's made sense. I didn't think . . .

Vikram   Best not, sweetheart. Turns a woman ugly. Seen my Kiran anywhere?

Anita   She's inside, helping Mum.

Vikram   Good girl, she is. Knows her place.

Anita *snorts loudly.* **Vikram** *grins, enjoying winding her up.*

Dave   Well scary it was out there though. Thought we weren't gonna make it.

Vikram And then they go and put Rikki on a horse . . . I mean, don't get me wrong, I'm all for tradition, but unfit Indians with massive hangovers ain't the best cowboys.

Dave   That was well cool. You lot make an effort innit? My sister's wedding we had a finger buffet for thirty down the local pub. And she made me dance to Abba afterwards. Something died in me that day.

Sally (*laughing*)   Silly sod!

Dave   Oh yeah, this is my plus one, Sally.

Sally/Anita   We've met.

Dave   She's never been to an Indian wedding before. This is my eighth. In two months.

Anita (*staring at* **Sally**)   Only turns up for the free food.

Dave   Know the difference now between a laddoo and a lassie.

Sally (*staring back at* **Anita**)   It's 'lussi', a cooling yoghurt drink that can be salted or sweetened, often topped with crushed pistachios. Lassie's the shaggy dog who pulls kids out of burning buildings.

Dave   If I wasn't so confident in my massive sexual presence, I'd think you were trying to undermine me, Sally.

Sally   Sorry, I'm good on the food. Just don't get invited to the weddings.

Anita (*glancing at* **Sally**'s *short dress*)   Well, nice to see you're dressed for it. I'm gonna see if Mum and Dad are okay . . . 'Scuse me.

The guys watch **Anita** *stalk off. In the distance, sirens sound.*

Vikram   Whhoo! Catfight catfight! God, wish there was a bit of mud we could push you both into . . . make all my dreams come true . . .

Dave (*laughing*)   Told you, he's a nutter! He kills me!

Vikram   She's only jealous, sweetheart.

Sally (*embarrassed*)   She don't have to be. She's well pretty.

Vikram   Until she opens her mouth . . .

Vip   Leave it, Vikram.

Vikram   Plus there's the shame, see? Cos her sister's getting married . . . /

Vip   / Vikram, that's enough . . .

Vikram   / and she's actually the eldest. Her parents have begged in three different continents and they still can't find . . .

Vip   SHUT IT, WILL YA!

A tense pause. **Vikram** *squares up to* **Vip**. *There's something dangerous about him, coiled. He puts his hand inside his coat, indicating he has a weapon. The sirens are nearer, louder.*

Vikram   You didn't just raise your voice at me? Did you? Yaar?

Vip   I've worked it out, by the way.

Vikram   Is it still speaking? Why is it still speaking?

Vip   Coconut. Brown on the outside, white on the inside.

Vikram   So your knobhead posh school not a total waste of time then.

Vip   Which makes you a . . . a . . . rabbit dropping.

Vikram   A what?

Vip   Hard on the outside, shit on the inside.

A beat. **Vikram** *laughs and thumps* **Vip** *on the back, laughing.*

Vikram   Sala! And I thought you had raisins for bollocks. Maybe I won't cut you today.

Vip   Might put a dampener on your best mate's wedding.

Vikram   Innit though.

Vip   What have I ever done to you, Vikram? Is there a problem?

Vikram   Yeah Mr Coconut, too bad you don't know what it is. But it can wait, man. I got time.

Raj *comes running on breathless, looking distressed.*

Raj   Vip! . . . Vip! . . .

Vip   Breathe yaar! What's the matter with ya?

Raj   It's all kicked off. There's like . . . rioting . . . fighting . . . Toupée Uncle tried to ask the police if they could let our guests through . . . They . . . just whacked him, man! He's like down, covered in blood . . .

Vip   / You're joking . . .

Raj   So a few of the lads got involved . . . all got arrested . . . then the mums waded in all hysterical . . . hitting the police with their glittery wedding handbags . . . till they got hit back . . .

Vip   / No . . . they can't do this . . .

Raj   / There's kids out there! Grannies throwing chilli powder at the police dogs . . . old geezers with medals pinned on their turbans waving kirpans . . . It's . . . I dunno what it is . . .

Vikram   Whatever it is, it's started. (*He grins at* **Vip**.) You might want to stay here, nice boy like you. Might get messy. What about you, Dave? Bit awkward innit?

Dave   Like a beefburger-at-a-Hindu-wedding sort of awkward?

Vikram (*laughs*)   Ain't your battle.

Vip   We going out there, then?

Vikram   Sure it's yours?

Vip   I'm not the enemy here, Vik.

Vikram *smiles, nods at* **Vip** *and leaves with* **Dave**. **Vip** *hesitates. Sirens constant now, sounds of crowds shouting, moving.*

Vip   Can you tell Anita . . . Never mind.

He runs off, leaving **Raj** *facing* **Sally**. *He reels back in shock.*

Raj   Sally? What . . . what you doing here?

Sally   I came with Dave. I had to see you, Raj.

Raj   At my sister's wedding? . . . And what you wearing?

Sally   I thought you'd like it. You always liked me in . . . dresses.

Raj   No, look, I told you . . .

Sally   I know what you said. But after a whole year you can't expect me /

Raj   / This is not great timing, Sally . . .

Sally   / Expect me to just . . . disappear. Like some dirty little secret . . .

Raj   Well it was. Not dirty. I mean, you knew the score . . .

Sally   So I'm not good enough for you. In public.

Raj It's just . . . I mean, we were never gonna get married or anything so why . . .

Sally So why did you say you loved me then? Just to get into my pants?

Raj We're sixteen for fuck's sake! It was supposed to be a bit of fun, innit?

Sally You knew I was a virgin!

Raj (*trying to cover her mouth*)   You gone mad? Shut it!

Sally Don't see any of your lot trying it on with Asian girls. Cos we're here to practise on, is that it?

Raj Yes . . . I mean no! (*Beat.*) I mean, you could have said no. An Asian girl would have said no.

Sally You little shit . . .

Raj I didn't mean . . . I can't deal with this . . . I've gotta go, see what's happening –

Sally / I'm gonna tell your parents. (*Beat.*) I'll tell them. What their good little boy's been up to. With a dirty white girl.

Raj (*hardening*)   Go ahead. You'll just prove what they already think about someone who . . .

Sally What?

Raj Turns up to an Indian wedding in a dress like that.

Sally That make me a slag, does it? There's only two kinds of women for you lot, innit? The nice girls that you marry and the rest of us, the slags. Well, boys can be slags as well you know.

Raj You calling me a slag?

Sally You're not any better than me!

Raj I've got to go.

Sally You come back here, you slimy bloody Pak . . .

A beat. **Raj** *turns to face her, both in shock.*

Raj   Go on then. Say it. It's always there, innit? It's always gonna be there, Sally. That's why you shouldn't have come.

Raj *leaves.* **Sally** *bursts into tears.* **Kiran** *runs on.*

Kiran   Where is everybody? Where's Vikram? (*Beat.*) Hello, I'm Kiran.

Sally   Leave me alone.

Kiran   I know, it's a bit scary, all of this. My papa says it's nothing compared to Partition, though. He saw some terrible things. He thought I'd be safer over here. (*Beat.*) Aren't you feeling a bit cold in that dress?

Sally   Yeah. Freezing actually.

Kiran   I've got four shawls with me. The pink pashmina will look lovely on you. (*Beat.*) Some of the ladies are praying inside and there's hot chai. Would you like . . . ? Chai, I mean, not praying. Chai means tea by the way.

Sally (*faint smile*)   I know.

As they exit one way, **Nina** *in full bridal gear runs on from the other.*

Nina   Kiran? . . . Kiran! Where is everybody? Why is this happening to me? It's NOT FAIR!

She lets out a loud scream. **Rikki** *comes on, holding his crumpled wedding turban. He looks exhausted. There are red stains down his bridal jacket.*

Rikki   Do you have to?

Nina *sees him and screams again, trying to hide herself.*

Nina   Don't look at me, don't look at me! We're not married yet! It's really bad luck! (*Beat.*) What's that on your suit? Ohmigod, ohmigod . . . Is that . . . blood?

Rikki   'S okay. Not mine.

Nina *screams again.* **Rikki** *covers his ears.*

Nina   What we gonna do? Everything's ruined!

Rikki   We'll have to cancel it. Do it another day.

Nina   We can't.

Rikki   Nina . . . half the guests ain't here, the other half are chucking stuff at skinheads or dodging the fuzz . . . it ain't happening, babe.

Nina   But . . . we have to. Today.

Rikki   Ah. Can't wait to get yer hands on me, eh, my little laddoo?

Nina (*snaps*)   My parents can't pay for this again. They just can't.

Rikki   Not my fault, is it?

Nina   But it is *our* problem. Isn't it?

Rikki   Vikram was right. We're not even married yet and you're already . . .

Nina   What?

Rikki   Bossing me, woman! I didn't make this tamasha happen outside, did I?

Nina   But it's happened. And shit is gonna happen. Is this how we're gonna deal with it? Me having an idea and you thinking I'm 'bossing' you?

Rikki   You've changed. That isn't supposed to happen till at least six months after we're married. Then you can nag me and get fat. That's allowed.

Nina   But it's all gone mad, ain't it? There's no . . . rules out there today. So . . . what about . . .

Rikki   See, you're doing it again!

Nina   What if . . . we make our own rules as well?

Rikki   What you on about?

Nina   Come on, Rikki, you know how we're supposed to do this. I could play all the good-wife games, right? Pretend you're a god and I'm grateful and you're the first and only and the best . . .

Rikki   Wait a minute . . .

Nina   And you can strut around shouting, so everyone knows you rule the house and get me pregnant as quickly as possible just to prove you're a man . . . Or –

Rikki   What?

Nina   We could just . . . work things out ourselves. Decide what we think is best. We don't have to tell anybody else. Be our secret. (*Beat.*) I'm scared. Aren't you?

Rikki (*bluffing*)   Nah.

Nina   My parents, they can't afford . . .

Rikki   I heard you, woman.

Nina   I think the priest is still here. (*Beat.*) Rikki? Do you still want to do this? Still want me? (*Beat.*) Think I should go and find the priest and get this marriage done?

Rikki (*beat*)   I do.

Nina *walks off in one direction.* **Rikki** *dusts off his turban and exits the other way. A beat later,* **Anita** *enters, carrying bags of red chilli powder. The noise of the rioting gets louder behind her.*

Anita   Guys? . . . Vip? . . . Raj! Chilli powder! I've got chilli powder!

Realisation sets in, they have left her behind. She takes her chunni (traditional scarf) and ties it around her body like a warrior ready for action.

Blackout.

Scene Two

*July 2005. The same set, except the spotlit table now supports an
expensive floral centrepiece, crystal glasses and place settings and an
impressive chocolate fountain. In the back alley, the bins are gone, the
sign now reads:* SOUTHALL BANQUETING SUITE − EXECUTIVE
PARKING ONLY. CLAMPING IN OPERATION!

*The same wedding guests run on and dance to Jay Sean's 'Eyes on You'.
This time the bhangra has morphed into something more like house/hip
hop fusion stylee thing. The clothes are still traditional but designer
Indian wedding couture, ostentatious wealth on display in the jewels and
accessories. But the same joy and energy prevails.*

The dance ends with the lights snapping to dim, **Nina** *and* **Rikki**
*again left in half light as the same radio news broadcast plays in, intercut
with static.*

Announcer   . . . Last Tuesday's terrorist attacks on
London's transport network which left fifty-two dead and
more than seven hundred injured. More details are being
released about the 7/7 bombers who . . . Overshadowed the
celebrations the day before when London was named as the
host of 2012 Olympics . . . Islamic Jihad have claimed
responsibility for the July twelfth bombing of a shopping mall
in Netanya, Israel . . . Said the concerts on July second had
achieved their goal of raising global awareness of crippling
Third World debt and that the Make Poverty History
campaign would now go on . . .

Spotlight up on **Nina**, *in a stylish wedding outfit, not a coconut in
sight. Spotlight also up on* **Rikki** *in a similarly chic Indian wedding
suit − no tinsel, more catwalk. They both speak into mobile phones.*

Nina   . . . Well, I don't know if the chocolate fountain is
vegan-friendly, do I? . . . Chocolate's got milk in it, hasn't it,
so probably not . . . Right, so you tell Bimla Auntie as we paid
for her to fly over business class with her three fat kids for the
wedding, if she doesn't like it, she can buy her own bloody
pudding . . . Oh, stay there, I gotta take this call . . .

Rikki   . . . If he doesn't sign by the end of the day, plenty of other people waiting who want the property . . . Nah mate, no worries, we're cleaning up on repossessions, we're so liquid, we're the bleedin' Indian ocean . . . Yeah, today. Yes, it's today! I'm about to jump into the traditional white Mercedes with the plastic still on the seats . . . Hang on, got another call coming through . . .

Nina   Oh, I wish you were here too, darling! . . . I miss you too . . . but the baby's too little to travel . . . You know what, you sound American already, I swear . . . No, I went for the ice sculpture in the end . . . Me and Rikki, life-size, gorgeous . . . Waiter service, bhangra disco leading on to cheesey 'eighties stuff and the dancing eunuchs are coming to sing us off to the airport . . . Well, they're trannies really, can't get the visas for the proper Indian eunuchs . . .

Rikki (*loudly throughout phone call*)   . . . Hanji! . . . You're on a mobile? . . . In India? Okay, cell phone, you Yankee lick-arse. What's it run on, cowshit like everything else out there? . . . Yeah man, good to hear you . . . Listen, work is work, don't apologise, anyway I can email you the wedding pictures, only be about five thousand of them, plus the Bollywood epic Nina's got them filming . . . What 'new life adventure'? She's been living in my house last six months . . . not officially, but our parents ain't gonna say anything . . . One, cos we've paid for everything and secondly, they're just grateful neither of us are marrying blondes . . .

Nina   . . . No, we're all fine . . . I know, horrible, awful, the whole of London just shut down, mobiles went down . . . My sister's mate got trapped on one of the trains . . . No, he's okay, but . . . I know . . . We'd love to, free trip to California! . . . You did well, getting an American Indian . . . I should have . . . (*Laughs.*) You know what kind of Indian I mean! Well, I better go and marry Big Chief Tricky Rikki . . . Course I'm happy. I just wish . . . you were here . . .

Rikki   . . . How much? . . . Gurgaon? How far's that from Delhi central? That's peanuts, mate, that much land for . . .

Peanuts! Cheap! . . . Yeah of course cheap for me, lots for you, but if we go in together . . . Listen, can I call you back when I'm married? . . .

They both hang up simultaneously as the lights snap off.

Lights up as **Anita** *sneaks out and lights a cigarette. She jumps as* **Kiran** *enters.*

Anita *is dressed in a sari but wears trainers underneath.* **Kiran** *looks like a Bollywood star, dripping with jewels.*

Anita   Bloody hell, Kiran! Keep a lookout, will you?

Kiran   Give me a drag first then, sweetie.

She takes a drag, then sprays her mouth with breath-freshener.

Why are you wearing lesbian shoes with such a nice sari?

Anita   Is that how you spot the lesbians in India then? By their trainers?

Kiran   No, silly. By their moustaches. (*Checks her mobile.*) How's uni?

Anita   Great, yeah. Just got my dissertation approved – the rise of female vigilante groups in rural villages. There's so much anger out there cos of the rapes and bride-burning and acid attacks that finally these women, you know, really poor uneducated women, / they're rising up to say enough is –

Kiran (*screams excitedly*)   / Ohmhigod, I got that casting!

Anita   Pardon?

Kiran (*waving her mobile*)   For that advert I went up for last week!

Anita   Congratulations.

Kiran   The director says, listen to this . . . 'Only you could say "Mummy's Mango Pickle" with such a sexy twinkle in your eye!'

Anita   / Really –

Kiran   / I mean, I know it's just an ad but this guy, he's going places. He wants me for this movie, the lead role and everything! The script is really challenging! In the first scene –

Anita   Let me guess. You've just got out of the shower to answer the door and there's a plumber standing there holding an enormous tool . . .

Kiran   / What?

Anita   And then a big gust of wind blows your towel right off and . . .

Kiran   Oh. I see. Yes, very funny. The single girls have to be nowadays. Bridget Jones and all. Can't get a man so make a joke.

Anita   Believe me, no woman *needs* a man . . .

Kiran   But jealousy really doesn't suit you, darling.

Anita   I'm not! . . . I'm just saying be careful because . . .

Kiran   Because what? I might end up famous and you'll still be stuck here in your lesbian shoes writing about women in my country who would sell their grannies to get a part in a Bollywood film?

Anita   Wow. Marriage really suits you, doesn't it?

Kiran   Vikram does as he's told. Least he can do for dragging me over here . . .

Raj *and* **Sally** *enter.* **Sally***'s dressed in a smart Indian suit.* **Raj***'s speech is more Mockney-street than Indian now.*

Raj   Boiling in there, guy. I could murder a beer . . . Sal?

Sally   Want me to get you one? I could say it's for me . . . Anita?

Anita *shakes her head.* **Sally** *exits as* **Vikram** *enters.*

Vikram   There you are, baby! I was worried . . .

Kiran (*baby voice*)   Don't you worry about your baby, she's just got that advert!

Vikram (*sweeping her round*)   Vaidhaiya (*'congrats'*) princess! Hear that, Anita?

Anita   I heard.

Vikram   We'll do a launch when it's on, yeah? At one of my clubs. Have it showing on a big screen, few drinks, get the press in . . .

Raj   Sounds massive, guy. What is it?

Anita   A mango-pickle advert.

Kiran   Shown on three continents. That means Hollywood, Bollywood . . .

Anita (*to* **Raj**)   Hounslow . . .

Kiran   And the *Big Brother* auditions are next week . . .

Sally (*entering with beers*)   Oh I love *Big Brother*! God, don't people realise what complete arses they make of themselves? I mean, talk about desperate. You know the producers actually bribe people to shag around just cos of the ratings? I mean, I know I'm sad watching it but it's like driving past a motorway pile-up, you don't wanna look but you just can't help it.

Vikram   You're not doing *Big Brother*.

Kiran   Sweetie, don't be silly . . . Don't you trust me?

Vikram   It's other people I hate. Not you. You're class. We'll make it to the top the proper way.

Anita   Talent?

Vikram   Publicity. Loads of it.

His mobile rings.

Speak to me, bro . . .

He walks off to answer it. **Kiran** *turns on* **Sally**.

Kiran   Thanks a lot, buddhoo!

She stalks off.

Sally   I'm guessing that's Punjabi for be-ach.

Raj   Stuck-up cow. She think she better than any of us, always complaining, 'Back home we had servants . . . Daddy gave me my own driver . . . ' She don't like it, she shouldn't have come here should she?

He sucks his teeth loudly. **Anita** *stares at him.*

Raj   What you look 'pon, sis?

Anita   My brother, who looks brown, speaks black and sounds like Nick Griffin.

Raj   Who's Nick Griffin?

Sally   By the way, you hear about Dave?

Raj   Only he ain't called Dave any more . . .

Anita   What do you mean?

Dave *enters. He is dressed in a smart Pakistani suit and cap, and carries a prayer mat.*

Dave   *Salaam aleikum*, Anita. I was looking for somewhere to do namaaz?

Anita *just stares, speechless.*

Raj   It's like rammed in there, Dave man, every room's got some wedding shit going on in it . . .

Dave   Jamal. It's Jamal. Sorry.

Sally   Course it is, we knew /

Anita   / When did this happen?

Dave   Pardon?

Anita   I mean . . . when I saw you, like six months ago . . . at that party in your college bar? You were . . .

Dave   I was a mess, yeah.

Anita   Well . . .

Dave   I was a mess. (*Beat.*) Do you know why we do it? Our generation?

Anita   What?

Dave   Why we think the only way we can have a good time is to get off our tits and then put it on the internet so we can feel real? Cos we're so insecure we gotta know that someone is watching us, that we've got an audience? Why is it that it's not a good night out unless you're so pissed you can't stand, you're so high you can't feel . . . anything?

Raj   It *is* so we can't feel anything, innit blood?

Dave   Yes! Yes, my friend! Because when the shit wears off, there's nothing. A black hole. Cos we don't have anything to believe in, to strive for. We ain't poor or hungry or squashed, like half the world, like our parents were. We buy stuff we don't need, we think being famous is a job, we pity anyone who looks old cos we think the old are useless and irrelevant. A mess, right, so, one day, I looked inside my black hole . . .

Sally (*snorts*)   Sorry! . . .

Raj (*supressing a laugh*)   Sally, man!

Dave   See this is what I'm talking about . . .

Anita   / Raj! Shuttit . . .

Raj   It's cos he said . . . his black hole!

Anita   / Go on, Dave . . .

Dave (*making to leave*)   Excuse me . . .

Anita   No, Dave, wait up a sec . . .

She grabs **Dave***'s arm. He pulls away like he's been scalded.*

Dave   Don't!

Anita   What? I . . .

Dave It's disrespectful to me. And you. Any physical contact between unmarried men and women.

Anita Oh, please . . . It's me, Anita! How long have I known you?

Vip *has entered, unseen. He has a bandaged wound on his neck. He watches.*

Anita Don't tell me you're one of those /

Dave / One of those what exactly?

Anita I respect so much of what you've said but . . .

Dave You're gonna go Muslim-bashing now like everybody else?

Anita Show me a fundamentalist man of any religion and I'll show you a man who hates women!

Raj Dave's not a fundy, are you?

Sally (*prodding him*) Jamal . . .

Raj Jamal, yeah. I mean, like those terrorist nutters, I mean, you're not . . . are you?

Dave They weren't 'nutters' . . .

Vip What were they then?

They all swing round to face **Vip***.* **Anita** *goes to him.*

Anita Vip. I wasn't sure you'd make it.

Vip Said I'd be here. Didn't want to let you down.

Dave I heard what happened. Terrible. Are you okay?

Vip Fine, yeah. Little cut. Bit of buzzing in my ears cos of the blast. Not sleeping much. Few images in my head I wish weren't there . . . but I'm one of the lucky ones, aren't I?

Dave Thank Allah you're okay.

Vip Allah didn't save the Muslims who were killed though. And Hindus, Jews, Christians . . .

Dave   I do need to find somewhere to pray. We can talk later. Excuse me . . .

Vip   Gonna pray for me? Cos I could do with a bit of help right now.

Dave   Look, I've come to a Hindu wedding, to celebrate with all of you. If I'm not welcome now . . .

Raj   Leave it out, guy. We're mates, ain't we? I mean, we're all just people at the end of the day or whatever, right? I mean, we never took much notice about who was what religion. Like Mum and Dad, they're cool about me and Sally, and she's Welsh Baptist apparently.

Dave   Maybe we should take more notice.

Vip   Of what? Of what we have in common? Or what makes us different? /

Dave   / We all need to believe in something . . .

Vip   / Because I don't see what right anyone has to . . . kill people just because /

Anita   / Guys, people are looking at us! Keep it down . . . guys . . .

Vip   / – their government does some shitty colonial stuff /

Dave   / You think we are all the same? We think the same? Is that it? Do you know what that makes you, Vip? A racist! You fucking racist!

A beat. **Dave** *trembling, with his finger right in* **Vip***'s face.* **Anita** *gently takes* **Dave***'s arm and pulls it down. He does not pull away from her this time.*

Anita   Please. It's my sister's wedding. Look at us.

Vip (*staring at* **Dave**)   I'm looking. And I still don't believe it.

Dave   I'm not the one being aggressive here . . .

Anita   Listen! My Asian lecturer told me that in the seventies . . .

Raj   / Oh here we go . . .

Sally   / Shut up, Raj –

Anita   / She called herself Black, cos we were all part of the worldwide Black struggle. Then we all called ourselves Asians –

Sally   / Not all of us –

Anita   / Cos we were one people standing together against the racists. Now suddenly we're Hindu, Muslim, Baptist . . . and fighting each other.

Vip   That's progress for you.

Anita   The mess is still gonna be here tomorrow. So today, can we just pretend . . . it's not 2005?

Nina *enters, carrying garlands of marigolds.*

Nina   What the hell you doing out here? The Milni's supposed to be starting? This is not my job!

Anita   Sorry, Nina, we were . . .

Raj   Here . . . (*Takes the garlands.*) One each, is it?

Nina   You know the drill, how many weddings you been to? The parents have all got theirs . . . Anita, you'll be garlanding Rikki's sister . . . Raj, his younger brother . . .

Raj   The fat one, the squinty one or the one who wears really tight trousers?

Nina   The spotty one.

Raj   Great . . .

Nina   Vip, your equivalent on Rikki's side is I guess Dave so you guys exchange garlands right after Uncle Kapoor and Rikki's uncle from Vancouver. Got it? Vip? Dave?

Dave   Yes. That's fine.

Nina　*Love* your suit, by the way. Glad someone's making an effort. It's so . . . authentic! (*Her mobile rings.*) . . . Jaz! . . . Lost? How can you lose a bus full of transvestites?

She exits, leaving **Dave** *and* **Vip** *facing each other.* **Raj** *hands them each a garland and exits with* **Sally**. *After a beat,* **Dave** *follows them out, passing* **Vikram** *on the way, who does a double take when he clocks* **Dave**.

Vikram　Was that . . . ?

Anita / Vip　Jamal.

Vikram　Good timing, walking around London looking like that. Only needs a rucksack and he'll be sorted. Never have to wait for a seat on the tube again.

He delivers this whole speech to **Vip**, *challenging him.*

Anita　Vikram! Don't you know . . . ?

Vip　Course he knows. His idea of a joke, eh, Vik?

Vikram　Gotta laugh, eh? Cos pricks like Dave make it harder for the rest of us. You think when we walk down the street, anyone's gonna ask us what religion we are before they spit on us? We're all Muslim now, mate.

Vip　As long as we're not all like you. Mate.

Vikram (*to* **Anita**)　He's still in shock obviously . . .

Vip　Dunno what turns my stomach more, psychopaths playing God or you playing Donald Trump.

Vikram　Jealous I'm making more a month than our parents scrape in a year? Then stop your student sponging off the state and get a proper job.

Anita　Job? You call it a job? I know about the so-called nightclubs you help run . . .

Vip　Anita . . .

Anita　They're brothels, full of girls, *our* girls, you've drugged and pimped off the fucking street!

Vikram Says who?

Vip Everybody.

Vikram Never been raided once. My boss is a respectable family man who got an OBE last year for his services to the community. Come down one night and see for yourself.

Anita I didn't want you here. My parents didn't want to offend your parents.

Vikram Got to love the old ways.

Anita No. Not if the old ways are the bad ways. After today, I never want to see your smug sick face again.

Vikram Have a lovely wedding, you two.

He exits. **Anita** *is trembling so much,* **Vip** *takes her in his arms.*

Anita Sorry. I should learn to keep my gob shut.

Vip Never.

Anita I was so worried about you. For a few hours when I didn't know if you'd even . . . made it, the whole world went . . . dark.

She chokes back tears. **Vip** *wipes one away, surprised.*

Vip Hey, come on! You're Anita. Fiery goddess of oppressed women everywhere! Righter of wrongs! Scarer of men! Crushing testicles wherever she goes!

Anita (*laughing*) Yup, that's moi! (*Beat. Suddenly serious.*) Do these trainers make me look like a lesbian?

Vip I like them. They're . . . you.

Anita Because I'm not. Not that there's anything wrong with being . . .

Vip When everything else is going . . . upside down and wrong, you're still out there, believing it can change. Get better. The world needs people like you.

Anita And people like me need people like you.

She goes to kiss him. **Vip** *leans back, shocked.*

Anita   Did I do something wrong?

Vip   No! No it's just that . . . well, we're friends. Best mates. I wouldn't want anything to change that.

Anita   Mates. (*Beat.*) Yeah, course. Dunno why I did that! Wedding stress, eh? Sort of infects you. Next thing I'll be picking out names for our kids!

They both laugh with relief. A loud cheer comes from inside the hall accompanied by a banging of Dhol drums.

Vip   Looks like the Milni's started. Maybe we should . . .

Anita   Yeah, cool! I've just got to . . . er, change into my shoes, yeah? You go in, just be a moment.

She keeps the smile pasted on until **Vip** *exits. Then buries her face in her garland as the lights snap off.*

Scene Three

Southall 2035. The same set, with the same table and decorations from 1979. Except the whole table is now encased in Perspex, like a museum exhibit, which it is. The gallery sign tells us this is a TYPICAL INDIAN WEDDING TABLE SETTING CIRCA 1979. *The back alley is the same, but litter-strewn and shabby-looking. A faded sign says* SOUTHALL HERITAGE MUSEUM: HYBRID VEHICLE PERMIT HOLDERS ONLY.

The wedding guests run on and start dancing in complete silence. Everyone is wearing headphones attached to their mobile phones – this is a silent rave. Their clothes, though wedding themed, are dowdy-looking, second-hand. There is poverty here. During the dancing we hear the news announcer's voice again.

Announcer   . . . Many areas suffered a mass PBC meltdown when the network serving the population's Personal Brain Chips malfunctioned causing chaos in homes and offices . . . Confirmed that India now had the third highest

GDP in the world, second only to China and the US. At today's Indo-Arab Alliance Conference, India's president Gita Rao said . . . Iceland announced that its last remaining petrol pump closed yesterday, making it the world's first nation to run solely on hydrogen-fuelled transport . . . More rioting in Scotland due to fuel and food shortages, with fears this may spread to . . . A Staffordshire man has blamed his wife's PBC hologram for the breakdown of his marriage. Kevin Watson from Wolverhampton claims the problems started when his wife, Susan, chose Hollywood star Matt Daniels to be her virtual PBC announcer. 'I knew something was up when she kept locking herself in the toilet for the news updates,' he said . . .

Towards the end of the above, **Nina** *enters in a muted wedding suit and sits carefully on a hi-tech-looking chair. She places her mobile phone into a compartment in its arm and dons a discreet pair of headphones with attached microphone. Lights fade on the wedding guests and come up on her. She addresses the audience as if she's being interviewed, which she is.*

Nina   Nina Cho . . . (*She clears her throat.*) Sorry I'm a bit nervous, you are getting me okay? . . . Yes sorry, my PBC went down yesterday, everyone's did round here, that's why I couldn't . . . (*Beat.*) Nina Chopra. 134, Lady Margaret Close, Middlesex. Date of birth, fourteenth of March two thousand and sixteen. (*Beat.*) Why am I wearing . . . ? (*She looks down at her clothes.*) It's . . . my wedding clothes. (*Beat.*) Well, actually, it is today. In about an hour. But honestly, I put my Indian residency application in over eighteen months ago, I thought . . . (*Beat.*) I know, I know how busy it is. It's become. I thought by now . . . Anyway, I know this is my final interview, isn't it, so you could let me know today, couldn't you? If I've got it? (*Beat.*) How did I meet my fiancé? . . .

Spotlight up on **Rikki**, *in a similar chair, mobile in compartment. He's smartly dressed in a designer Indian wedding suit and speaks in a faux-American/Indian accent. He also addresses the audience as if speaking into a screen.*

Rikki   No, Mama, I'm in London now, in the hotel! . . .
Yes, journey was fine, the usual queues at Immigration but . . .
No, the venue's just a few minutes from here so . . . Mama, sit
on a cushion or readjust your chip, all I can see is the top of
your head . . . Ramlal! Get madam a . . . that's better. What's
the point of having twelve servants when none of them . . .
Never mind. Just make sure you're comfy by the time the
wedding starts . . . Yes, everyone's hooked up, Raju in
Sydney, Leela in Hong Kong . . . they'll all be online and
streamed in . . . *Streamed!* Forget it. Just ask Ramlal to push
the right buttons, okay? (*Beat.*) Are you kidding? No way
would I have let you come, you'd have been mugged or sick
within minutes of landing . . . Apparently you can't even
drink the tap water any more anywhere outside London . . .
and the beggars . . . (*Beat.*) I can hear the peacocks. Behind
you, Mum. Monsoon must be on its way.

Nina   . . . So after Rikki went back to India we just stayed
in touch and . . . (*Beat.*) No, he was allowed in because his
parents kept their Indian citizenship, mine had to choose so
they chose British . . . It's all in the application form . . . (*Beat.*)
Yes, I know we were only eleven when he left but we knew
then . . . (*Beat.*) Sometimes you do know, we never forgot each
other, he came over to see me, we never stopped . . . (*Beat.*)
Marriage of convenience? Yes, I know what it means. (*Beat.*) I
know a lot of people are trying it on . . . (*Beat.*) No, if I hadn't
met Rikki I'd be quite happy to stay in London. Honestly.
(*Beat.*) Economic refugee? Me? (*Laughs.*) I'm a girl in love,
that's all.

Rikki   Yo, Vip, where you at, man? Yeah, just landed a few
hours ago. God, so weird flying into London again. Told the
cabin crew I was flying in to pick up a bride, free champagne
all the way! (*Beat.*) Looks like you're in the venue . . . God,
what a dump . . . Still you told the priest, ten minutes max on
the ceremony, long enough to make it legal . . . Hey, I'm
paying for the whole damn thing, if I ask him to whistle the
national anthem with a coconut up his butt, he better do it . . .
(*Beat.*) Just spoke to Mum, she's got no idea . . . No, she thinks

it's sorted, how can I tell her I might be leaving tonight
without my new wife? . . . Tell me about it, India's shutting
her doors, man. They turned down Pot Belly Uncle's son last
week, he's a damn doctor. He said to them, 'I'm a damn
doctor, surely you need doctors?' And they said, 'Du-fao (*piss
off*) this is India, every second guy serving in McDonald's is a
damn doctor.'

Nina   Listen, you're Indian obviously, I mean you're in
India right now speaking to me and . . . were you born there?
(*Beat.*) I don't mean to be personal. I'm about to get married
and feeling a bit emotional and . . . Delhi? My parents are
from Delhi. Rajinder Nagar. Pusa Road, where they sell the
best milk barfi, am I right? (*Beat, she laughs.*) See, even though
I've never been, my parents . . . kept it alive. Told us we may
be here, but . . . it's what we still call ourselves. British but
Indian. We never thought we'd have to choose. And cos you
live there, you'll never have to, will you? (*Beat.*) I know why
you have to be strict. I'm just saying, I'm not asking to be let
in, I'm asking to be allowed to come back. With my husband.

Rikki   Vip . . . man, stand still a minute I'm getting dizzy . . .
So don't suppose you've heard . . . Shit! You are shitting me!
You got in? You got entry? On a scholarship? Where? (*Beat.*)
Top place in India, man. You brainy bastard! . . . So when do
you . . . that soon? What do your parents . . . (*Beat.*) Sure, so
would mine. Get out while you can. It's only going to get
worse. I'm just hoping that Nina can . . . She's left it so late . . .
(*Beat.*) Cancel the wedding? No point. I can argue her case
from there. In any case, not in a hurry to come back here.
(*Beat.*) If they say no? (*Beat.*) I haven't thought that far. I guess
I'll have to . . . I don't know, man. At least you'll be with me
over there, maybe we can . . . Shit. Have you told Anita?
(*Beat.*) Start praying, arsehole . . .

*Soundtrack of static mixed with chattering voices plays in as the lights go
up on the back alley where* **Anita** *sits sewing marigold flowers together
to make garlands.* **Raj** *exits with a plastic washing basket full of other
completed garlands. The background static continues low level under the
dialogue.*

Raj   Ten marigold garlands. Took me bloody hours. Look at my fingers. Slave labour, this is.

Anita   Cheaper than buying them ready made. They're so pretty.

Raj   Why you sitting out here? There's rats.

Anita   It's sunny. First time in ages. Mum said the summers here used to last months. And you didn't have to wear pollution masks. Wish I could remember that.

Raj   I dunno why we need this many garlands. Half of our lot aren't coming and all of Rikki's lot are virtual.

Anita   We have to do a Milni. It's traditional. Or the nearest we can get to it.

Raj   You talked to Nina?

Anita   She's blocked all incomings. I'm guessing she's being interviewed right now. Bastards. I mean eighteen months . . .

Raj   / We told her, we all told her takes two years at least . . .

Anita   / she's had to prove every time they've met, spoken . . . Surprised they haven't asked for virginity test to see if he's had her hymen off her.

Raj   God, do you have to . . . Such a potty-mouth . . .

Anita   They did that. In the old days. When we were all trying to get in here. I read it somewhere. Funny how we always seem to end up in the wrong place, knocking on someone else's door.

Raj   Yeah, that's the spirit! Let's get this wedding going! Whoo! What else can we point out? Crap venue? Check! Your choice . . .

Anita   I love this place! It's got . . . history!

Raj   Crap food? Check! Cos of course we had to hire the old blind widows' association to do the food cos you felt sorry for them . . .

Anita   We should always hire and buy locally. It's government policy!

Raj   Not when the groom's stinky rich and has offered to pay for it all!

Anita   That doesn't mean we take the piss, okay? Anyway he's getting Nina. That's precious enough.

Raj   Oh shuttup! You've already redecorated her room . . .

Anita   / That's not fair! There was mould in the wardrobe . . .

Raj   / Telling everybody your sister's jumping ship, like a rat deserting a sinking ship, you said . . .

Anita   / And I'm studying, I'm in a box room . . . I never said that!

Raj   I heard you. You streamed it to Kiran. And anyone else who was online at the time.

Anita   Did I? (*Beat.*) Bollocks. God, am I on now?

She gets her mobile out and, after a pause, dramatically switches it off. The background static stops. Silence. **Anita** *drinks it in, amazed.*

Raj   What's it like?

Anita   Shhh. (*Beat.*) It's so . . . quiet.

Raj (*shivers*)   Just the thought of it makes me feel . . . naked.

Anita   It's like . . . this huge . . . space just opened in my head.

Raj   Maybe it's a tumour.

Anita   Gee, thanks.

Raj   No, really, now they're saying *not* using a PBC could mess up your head. It's the panic you get when you realise all the stuff you might be missing. Right now!

Kiran *enters, panicking. She's dressed up but there's something defeated about her.*

Kiran   Anita? Oh, thank God . . . You just shut down I thought . . . It's not the network again, is it, because I'm live . . .

Raj   She disconnected.

Kiran   On purpose?

Raj   Nutter. I give it five minutes, she'll be shaking like a junkie.

Anita   No. I'm offline until Nina's married. That's my . . . present.

Kiran   Can't you get her a toaster like everyone else?

Anita   My present to me. (*Beat.*) Do you know how quiet it is without all that traffic inside your head?

Kiran   I like the traffic. It's better than . . . (*Glancing at her phone.*) Vikram's arrived. Couldn't find petrol. He had to / leave the car in Ealing . . .

Vikram *enters with* **Dave** *and* **Sally***. They are all sweaty, messy and pissed off.* **Sally** *sits down heavily and removes her shoes, rubbing her feet.*

Vikram   / Leave the car in Ealing and walk. I'm gonna buy a horse, I swear.

Raj   It's the future. Four legs and the open road.

Vikram   In India the groom's supposed to arrive on a horse. Old Rikki could have paid for that. Did you ask him, Anita?

Anita   No, Vikram. He's your mate, did you?

Raj   I'll get you guys some water . . . Sally?

Raj / Sally   Bottled only!

Sally   You remembered.

Raj   It's a wedding. We got loads in.

He exits. Anita watches **Dave** *out of the corner of her eye as he pops a pill from a foil packet.*

Kiran (*running to* **Vikram**)   I was so worried . . .

Vikram   You worry too much.

Kiran   In London there's an assault every two minutes thirty seconds . . . (*Checking her mobile.*) According to my Muggers' Map App . . .

Vikram   You wanna get rid of that. (*Glances at his mobile then up at* **Anita**.) You're disconnected.

Anita   But amazingly still alive.

Sally   Some lowlife nicked my mobee on the tube. Cleared out my holiday fund and sent pictures of his arse to my entire address book. And you know the worst thing, some people thought it was *my* arse? I mean, why would my mates think I'd do a thing like that? They know me!

Anita   They don't. Just cos we're in touch with hundreds of people all the time doesn't mean we know each other.

Vikram   Thanks for that, Mahatma.

Dave *giggles loudly, in his own world. They clock him a moment and move on.*

Kiran (*checking her mobile*)   There's been another earthquake in Japan.

Vikram   I know. (*Beat.*) Any news from Nina?

Kiran (*checking*)   She's still offline, so . . .

Anita   She might not hear today.

Vikram   She probably will. I did, on my third interview. Hadn't even left the chair and . . .

Kiran   No. They said no.

Vikram   I know that too, Kiran.

Kiran   The country I was *born* in. Just because / he didn't have anything useful to offer . . .

Vikram   / Leave it will ya?

Kiran   / He even took Hindi at school! Vip doesn't speak Hindi! So how come . . .

Vikram   Shut it now!

Anita   How come what? (*To* **Sally**.) What?

Sally   I dunno.

Vikram   I told you, I've got applications in for the States, Canada . . .

Kiran   Canada's full . . .

Vikram   Sweden . . .

Kiran   Sweden! What do you know / about Sweden . . .

Vikram   / As much as I know about anywhere else you want me to apply! What's wrong with staying here?

Kiran (*laughing*) How can you . . . Are you blind? It's dying here! And we're dying with it. I want a future!

Vikram   There's opportunities here. I'll try anything . . .

Kiran   Yes, you have already! All your stupid dodgy schemes and plans and none of them worked! Maybe if you'd bothered to get a decent education . . .

Vikram   God, not that again! I couldn't afford one, okay? Now there's no decent free education and when they cancelled my parents' pensions . . .

Kiran   You had to work, / I've heard this so many . . .

Vikram   / And I work fucking hard! May not be the brightest boy on the block but I'm street-smart. I told you all this when we got together. I told you . . .

Kiran   Yes. You told me. (*Beat.*) My sisters live like queens. They joke about sending us food parcels. That should have been me.

Vikram   Go back then! If that's what you want . . .

Anita   Guys, come on, let's / all calm down . . .

Vikram   / You can go back! You were born there. We got married far too young anyway, stupid, who gets married at nineteen anyway?

Kiran   My sisters did!

Vikram   Fine. So why don't you just piss off back to where you came from?

A beat. **Kiran** *rushes off sobbing. After a moment,* **Vikram** *exits the other way.*

Dave (*singing*)   'I'm getting married in the morning! Ding dong, the bells are gonna chime! . . . '

Sally   It's alive.

Anita   The pills kicked in then?

Dave   Oh yeah. Prescription only. I don't do the nasty stuff.

Sally   Just the boring stuff. It makes you so bloody *boring*! Know that, Dave?

Raj *enters with bottled water. He and* **Sally** *stand apart from the others.*

Raj   Sorry, had to wrestle a few grannies to the floor for these.

Sally   Thanks, Raj.

She takes the bottle from him, brushes his hand. They exchange a look: there's history there, but **Raj** *pulls his hand away.*

Raj   Everyone's waiting to do the Milni. Rikki's here, all his family logged in waiting . . . Mum and Dad are really panicking . . .

Anita   Nina?

Raj   Still offline. Might be a good sign then, eh? If they're like chatting. Maybe she's booking her plane ticket out of here right now . . .

Sally   I'm gutted my holiday money's gone. Me and Dave were planning . . .

Dave   I didn't want to go really, anyway.

Sally   What? Why?

Dave   I mean what's the point? It took us two hours to get here.

Sally   The point is, don't you want to see a bit of the world?

Dave   See everything online. I could take you round the Taj Mahal blindfold, done the virtual tour so often.

Raj   They're brilliant, those tours. I know Peking like the back of my hand.

Sally   Yeah, but it's not the same is it . . . ?

Dave   The world's in here, Sally . . . (*He taps his head.*) You want to sort this out first, the world in your head. Then everything else makes sense.

Sally (*rising*)   You ain't making sense . . . as usual. Where's the loo?

Raj   *She-shui hua-hu gaan-she niin du-di guan-shu.*

Sally   Pardon?

Anita   He's top in Mandarin in his class.

Sally   Really! And what did you just say?

Dave   Piss off, you're really embarrassing me?

Sally   Funny, was gonna say the same thing to you. Off your head at your mate's wedding. You ain't seen him for months, he's in there now and you haven't even bothered . . .

Dave   / Chill out Sally.

Sally   He'll be going back tomorrow. God knows when he's next coming over. Could you just . . . (*Beat.*) It's like . . . you're not here half the time.

Dave   I suppose . . . I'm a bit out of practice.

Sally   Then start practising. I chose a boyfriend, not a hologram . . .

She storms off, upset. **Raj** *follows her, they stand apart from the others.*

Raj   You okay?

Sally   What do you care? (*Beat.*) I know you want a girl from India so you can get out of here. Kiran told me. (*Beat.*) God. It's true then?

Raj   We're sixteen. Who knows what's gonna . . . ?

Sally   Is that why you broke up with me?

Raj   If I don't get 95 plus in my uni entrance, I'm not going anywhere.

Sally   But choosing some stranger from five thousand miles away just cos you want a passport, that's sick.

Raj (*laughs*)   That's always how you've seen us, isn't it? My grandparents were introduced through their families, devoted till they died. Nothing sick about them. It's all a gamble, Sal. I just want better odds.

Sally   Sorry I was a bad bet.

She leaves. **Anita** *clocks this exchange.*

Anita   Raj? Can you go and check on Nina, find out what the hell's going on?

Raj *picks up the basket of marigolds and goes to exit, bumps into* **Vip** *entering.*

Raj (*hugging him*)   I heard! Congrats, bro! Gonna get some tips off you, yeah? You promise?

Vip   Any time, Raj.

Raj *exits.* **Vip** *and* **Anita** *stare at each other a moment.*

Anita   You're late. Indian time late.

Vip   Your network's down.

Dave   It's a silent protest. Switched off her phone. Imagine if we all did that. Digital suicide. We'd have to actually walk to people's houses to talk to them. Wild.

Vip   I sent you . . . several messages. So you don't know . . .

Anita   Know what?

Dave (*rising*)   I think I'm gonna go and be real inside. Make Sally happy. I reckon with a bit of concentration . . . (*Beat.*) No. It's gone.

He exits. **Vip** *shuffles awkwardly under* **Anita***'s gaze.*

Anita   Well?

Vip   Well . . . actually shouldn't we be going inside? Everyone's just standing around waiting . . .

Anita   For Nina. Nothing's going to happen without the blushing bride. Or the hysterical snot-covered bride, depending on what happens . . .

Vip   Can't believe she got her final interview today. Crap timing. For everybody.

Anita   I'm assuming you got the scholarship then?

Vip (*wrongfooted*)   Yeah. (*Beat.*) Yeah, I did. I sent you . . . You didn't get it.

Anita   I'm happy for you. Really. Worth all our missed dates and cancelled dinners.

Vip   You've been so amazing . . . I couldn't have done it without . . .

Anita   When do you leave?

Vip   Well, it's for the new term, September, so . . .

Anita   That soon. (*Beat.*) Your parents must be . . .

Vip   Come with me.

Anita   What?

Vip   I've thought it all out. I'm an S-one entry, top grade, I'm secure. It takes two years, right, so apply now, finish your degree, get top marks as you will do anyway and . . .

Anita   I don't want to go, Vip.

Vip   Sorry?

Anita   To India.

Vip   You don't want . . . /

Anita   / Mum and Dad are getting on and . . .

Vip   / But why? There's nothing here for . . .

Anita   We keep running away! Or running towards something we think is better . . .

Vip   It is better! Better than here . . .

Anita   But if we just keep moving . . . if we don't ever just stay and try and make it better . . . where we are . . . if all the good people just keep leaving, then how is anything going to change?

Vip   That's what people have always done! Move on . . . move up . . .

Anita   My parents still call India home and they haven't been for ten years! I've been once and I felt like . . . a tourist. My cousins laughed at my clothes! Nothing new there I suppose but . . . /

Vip   / I get what you're saying but . . . /

Anita   / Let me finish, cos I might not ever be able to make sense of this again! (*Beat.*) Everyone says, oh the world is so small now . . . we're all connected, we're all . . . together. But we're not. There's the ones going up, and the ones left behind.

Vip   That's what I'm saying. You don't have to be.

Anita   You don't get me at all, do you? It's about trying to be happy . . . where you are. There's so much to do here / and I want to be part of it.

Vip   / It's not your job, Anita! Why is it always your job?

Anita   It's everybody's job! That's why we're in this mess because we . . . we never thought ahead! Should have seen it coming . . . all that time we were recycling and saving the whales . . . We should also have tried to be kinder to each other . . . tried to be happy with less stuff and made more time to . . . (*Beat.*) What?

Vip   I feel like we've spent our whole lives . . . missing each other. (*Beat.*) You won't change your mind?

Anita (*shakes her head*)   Got to be someone left here to switch off the lights. Or light some new ones.

Vip   You'll forget me.

Anita (*smiles*)   We've always got these . . .

She waves her mobile, notices it's off.

Forgot this was off. How about that? . . .

Nina *runs on, upset, her mobile in hand.*

Nina   Anita! You've been disconnected! Oh Nita! . . .

She throws herself into **Anita***'s arms, crying.*

Anita   Oh God . . . what happened? What did they say?

Rikki *comes running out, mobile in hand.* **Nina** *rushes to him and they hug.*

Rikki   It's okay, baby. It's okay . . . it's all over. It's all over.

Anita   What? What happened?

Nina   I got entry. I'm leaving with Rikki tonight.

Vip *shouts with joy, he and* **Rikki** *backslap and hug.* **Anita** *walks over to* **Nina** *and takes her hand.*

Anita   Congratulations, sis.

Nina   I'm all messed up. I've got to pack, say goodbye . . .
(*She breaks down.*) I can't do it!

Anita   It's what you've wanted for years. Just . . . be happy
now.

Rikki *checks his mobile and laughs.*

Rikki   My mum's fallen asleep. In her dinner. It's late in
India. Shall we go and do this wedding thing, then?

Nina (*nods*)   And then . . .

Rikki (*grinning*)   And then?

Nina   Take me home.

*They wander in together as a ragged cheer goes up. Dhol drums start
thumping in celebration.* **Anita** *and* **Vip** *are left alone for a moment.*
Vip *offers* **Anita** *his hand, she takes it and they exit together.*

Fade to black.

*Curtain call: should be done as a dance number in the style of the very
first wedding dance back in 1979, celebratory, rough and ready bhangra,
reminding the audience the future isn't yet written, so today, we dance.*

Generation Next

*Notes on rehearsal and staging, drawn from a workshop
with the writer held at the National Theatre, November 2011*

How the Play Came to be Written

Meera feels that a lot written about the Asian community in
the UK has been from one angle: fundamentalism. She feels
that young people are not aware of the history of how they
got here, and their community's struggle in the 1970s. She
quoted Bob Marley: 'If you know your history then you would
know where you coming from.' Each character represents a
different aspect of the British Asian experience. She wanted to
write about 'who we were, who we are, and who we may be'.

Meera talked about watching the Southall uprising as a teenager and thinking, 'Finally.' She said that Asians were seen as
a soft touch, and no one thought they would fight back. The
Southall uprising was an iconic moment.

She is interested in the fact that the country that the parents
or grandparents of today's young British Asians left for a
better future: it has now become the future. Young people
who were born in the UK are now taking Hindi classes and
emigrating to India.

Meera stressed that the play has to work on an emotional
level first, and a political level comes after. She wants us to
get to know a group of friends over the course of the play.

Ways to Begin Work

In the first week of rehearsals, you could give each actor a
short research task to come back and share with the company,
so that they understand key events that happen in the play,
such as the Southall uprising and the 7 July bombings. For
example, is it true that during the Southall uprising women
chucked chilli powder at police dogs? It might be interesting
to find out more about the two main gangs, who came

together to fight during the riots, the Holy Smoke and the Tooti Nungs.

In order to start to develop characters, you could do an objects exercise. Ask the actors to bring in an object that is important to their character. Then hold 'psychiatry sessions', in which the director is a psychiatrist who interrogates the character as to why that object is important. This is a good way of starting to build a back-story for the character and a timeline of their life.

Characters

They are the same characters in each scene, but they have been dropped into different moments in time. How might the characters retain the essence of themselves, even though their circumstances are different? How can we make it clear to the audience that they are the same people? This is the biggest challenge of the play, and the company needs to spend some time thinking about it.

VIKRAM AND DAVE   Vikram plays high status. How might the others support or undermine this? In the first scene, Dave is Vikram's mini-gangster, who buoys him up. In the workshop, we tried having Dave react to Vikram's lines with laughter or encouragement, which made this scene really funny.

RAJ AND SALLY   Raj and Sally genuinely have feelings for each other. They should both be shocked when Sally almost comes out with the word 'Paki'.

NINA AND RIKKI   In the first scene, Nina's suggestion that they make their own rules and work things out themselves is an important moment. It is a big thing to ask Rikki to start their married lives as equals and prioritise their personal understanding over a conventional wedding ceremony.

KIRAN AND ANITA   Their scene should not be too catty; it should be about two confident women trying to persuade each other that their views are right.

VIP   In Scene Two, Vip should hold on to his emotion. He is in shock and he can't process it.

KIRAN   Kiran's experience changes from Scene One to Scene Two. In Scene One she has come from a village, and she is like a rabbit in headlights. In Scene Two she is a middle-class girl who is used to having servants and a driver in India. She therefore feels she needs to grab back the status that she has lost since coming to the UK.

RIKKI   In Scene Three Rikki should have a slight Indian accent.

VIP AND ANITA   In the workshop we decided that Vip came to see Anita with the intention of asking her to come to India. This amounts to a proposal, and we did a subtext exercise in which the actor playing Vip had to say 'marry me' before each of his lines.

All the characters in Scene Three have had it tough. They are worn out.

Rehearsal Exercises

In the workshop, we did exercises to help build an ensemble and to start to develop the characters.

Ask everyone to leave the room. Bring them back in and sit them down. Now ask them to remember every detail since they entered the room, send them out again, and ask them to come in and replay their entrance with all those details. (Who was in front of you/behind you? Who did you touch? Talk to? Where did you sit? How did you walk in?)

Split the group in half. One half stands in front of the other half. The half that are standing up are observed by the half that are sitting down. Each observer watches one actor closely. They must then get up, take that actor's place and imitate their partner exactly. Swap round the observers and the observed and repeat.

Split the group into threes. One actor is the clay and two are the sculptors. In the workshop, we did this exercise twice, choosing to 'sculpt' the three versions of Vikram and then the three versions of Kiran as they appear in Scene One, Scene Two and Scene Three. Start by asking the actors to shout out adjectives that describe each version of the character they are sculpting (e.g., in Scene One Vikram is a gangster, cocky, arrogant . . .).

In silence, the sculptors must make a still picture of that character, using the 'clay' actor. They should think about where the character's weight is, how their feet are positioned, what their facial expression is. Once the sculptures are finished, the group walks around them and looks at them from different angles. Then discuss what the sculptors' main ideas were and how the 'clay' felt being in that character's skin.

In small groups, appoint someone to be a narrator. They must start to tell a story, and the other actors must jump up and play the characters. First ask the actors playing the characters to be silent, then allow them to make noises but not speak, then allow them to say only the lines of dialogue the narrator feeds them, and finally allow them to speak the scene. You can also do this exercise with two narrators, sharing the storytelling.

Put a collection of objects in the middle of the room. Appoint two actors as 'artists' with competing visions for an installation. They must get the installation how they want it and undo the rival artist's work, without physically restraining them. Count down for the last thirty seconds of the installation and see whose vision wins out. Repeat the exercise allowing them to use sound. Repeat it again, secretly giving each actor opposing objectives.

Staging and Production Notes

There are lots of moments in the play when the characters interrupt each other and talk over each other. In the workshop, we found it took some practice to get these moments right.

Iqbal encouraged the actors to be really confident about getting their character's point across and not to wait for the interruption – the messier the better. We also worked on making the arguments tight and taut, rather than allowing the actors to shout.

You could use multiple actors for the radio. Each piece of news could be read by a different presenter, and in a different style (e.g., serious newscaster, MTV gossipy . . .). What would a radio announcement in 2035 sound like?

There might be an underlying buzz in Scene Three, which represents the PBC technology. The first few times PBC is mentioned it needs to ping out so that the audience can get used to this new idea.

Glossary of Punjabi Terms

Apne   Our.

Barfi   Indian sweets, often eaten at times of celebration.

Basti   Shameful.

Bhagwan   God.

Bud bud   Someone who's just arrived from India.

Buddhoo   Idiot.

Chachas   Father's younger brother.

Chachees   Father's younger brother's wife.

Dhol drums   Traditional large and loud Indian drums.

Du fao   Slang – 'Get lost!'

Hai hai chi chi   Slang – something really dirty.

Hena   Know what I mean?

Kirpans   Ceremonial dagger worn by traditional Sikhs.

Laddoo   A round, sugary Indian sweet.

Lussi   Yoghurt-based drink.

Masers   Father's sister's husband.

Masis   Father's sister.

Mataji   An elderly woman.

Milni   Part of the Hindu ceremony in which the bride and groom's family meet each other.

Namaaz   Muslim prayers, usually performed five times a day.

Oolloo   Literally an owl, regarded as stupid in India.

Pind   An Indian village.

Ptaak   The sound of an explosion.

Sala   Insult – idiot.

Salaam aleikum   Muslim form of greeting, 'hello'.

Tamasha   Confusion, trouble.

Thaya   Father's older brother.

Thayees   Father's older brother's wife

Vaidhaiya   Congratulations.

*From a workshop led by led by Iqbal Khan,
with notes by Jane Fallowfield*

So You Think You're a Superhero?

Paven Virk

Characters

ZeeBoy
Gary B
Sparkles
Smiley (*never actually smiles*)
Spikey
Slowboy
Sorted, *a Paralympics student who is in a wheelchair*
Kalina, *Bulgarian, Marvel's sister*
Marvel, *Bulgarian, Kalina's brother*
Reporter
Camera Person
Mindy
Beryl, *international student, her country can be chosen*
Crush, *an international Paralympics student who is in a wheelchair*
Score Card Student
Referee
Lippy Lilly, *make-up girl*
Glam Greg, *make-up boy*
Olympic Hero One
Olympic Hero Two
Olympic Hero Three
Olympic Hero Four / Rapper
Fan One
Fan Two
General Zero
Queen Zola
Zen

The stage is black.

Music: a montage of well-known Superhero theme tunes play full blast.

Sound effect: patter of running feet.

A spotlight comes up on **ZeeBoy** *running on the spot. He is wearing a full superhero outfit with a matching gold eye-mask and gold trainers. On his wrist is a Zola watch. He looks back.*

Lights come up on three evil nemeses: **General Zero**, **Queen Zola** *and* **Zen***. They are wearing similar outfits and eye-masks to* **ZeeBoy***. A chase is taking place. The nemeses run on the spot behind* **ZeeBoy***.*

Queen Zola   You cannot escape us, ZeeBoy!

General Zero   Planet Zola made you and we will not stop until we capture you!

Queen Zola   There is nowhere further than the planet border!

ZeeBoy   Yes, there is!

General Zero   Your General Zero is demanding you stop!

ZeeBoy *closes his eyes and repeats over and over again.*

ZeeBoy   Watch! Take me somewhere, anywhere . . . now!

Just as **General Zero** *and* **Queen Zola** *are about to catch up with* **ZeeBoy***,* **Zen** *slows down and shouts.*

Zen   General Zero? Can we, er, slow down a bit?

Queen Zola   Follow the pace of your leader, Zen!

Zen   But Queen Zola, I've got a stitch. Oh, it's a bad one. Must've been the Zola Pops – cocoa flavour – give me the runs, been on the loo all night.

General Zero   Take leave, Zen.

Queen Zola   General Zero, we are on a mission . . . together!

Zen *stops running, almost relieved.*

Zen   Think I've missed the last bus. Can I get the Zola hovercraft home?

General Zero   Yes.

Zen *exits.*

Queen Zola   You are too kind to young Zen. His language is poor, he is a disgrace and he must learn to –

ZeeBoy   Invisible mode activate!

He dives in the air. Everyone freezes.

Blackout.

ZeeBoy *exits.*

Queen Zola *and* **General Zero** *are alone on stage in the dark.*

Queen Zola   Now we have lost him?! General Zero, activate your night-vision goggles.

General Zero   I cannot.

Queen Zola   Why ever not?

General Zero   I kind of damaged them.

Queen Zola   How?

General Zero   Some girls from Planet Zania came to my fancy-dress party. The theme was 'come as a celebrity'.

Queen Zola   Celebrity?

General Zero   A form of human. Zania girls have this obsession with Beyoncé, so they have all had butt implants. Anyway, my goggles are on the sofa, they sit down . . .

Queen Zola   I get the picture. Follow me!

General Zero   Wait . . . I do not like the dark . . .

Queen Zola   Tough!

Did my party invite get lost in the post?

General Zero   You are not jealous, are you?

Queen Zola   No! By the way, girls with butt implants fart a lot!

General Zero   You are jealous.

They stumble off the stage.

Sound effect: loud crowd cheering.

A pair of running feet land on the ground as the lights come up. **ZeeBoy** *is running on the spot. This time he is wearing a pair of running shorts and top. His trainers and superhero eye-mask are the same as before. The faster he runs, the louder the cheering gets.*

ZeeBoy   I said leave me alone!

He looks around, still running.

Where am I?

Lights come up on seven **Teen Runners** *who are also running on the spot. First is* **Gary B** *then* **Sparkles, Smiley, Spikey, Slowboy, Kalina** *and* **Beryl.**

The **Teen Runners** *are all ahead of* **ZeeBoy**. **ZeeBoy** *soon catches up and runs past each one.*

Two **Sports Students** *stand on opposite sides of the stage, holding a finish line ribbon.*

A **Student** *with a scorecard flashes it at the audience, then turns the card round: it reads 'Cheer'. The audience and crowd cheer.*

Next to the finish line stands a **Teen TV Reporter** *and* **TV Crew, Mindy** *(teen TV assistant),* **Camera Person, Lippy Lilly** *(make-up girl) and* **Glam Greg** *(make-up boy, assistant to make-up girl, who doesn't speak but follows her around at all times).*

ZeeBoy   Where am I !?

He can't be heard for the noise of the crowd.

He raises his arms in the air as he runs through the ribbon. **Gary B** *comes in second place and* **Kalina** *in third.* **Referee** *places a trophy in* **ZeeBoy***'s hands. The crowd cheer and gather round* **ZeeBoy**, *lifting him up on to their shoulders.* **Kalina** *exits, upset.* **Fan One** *and* **Fan Two** *are hanging around.*

Reporter   We have our champion! Why haven't we seen this masked hero before? Teen TV reporting live from the BO Sports Academy, that's the British Olympic Sports Academy, where we have found our Academy champion! In twenty-four hours, our champion will be the only student from the Academy to take part in every game in Olympics 2012 and have a shot at winning the Madidas main race, in which the winner receives a Madidas sponsorship deal! By the looks of our sports hero, he is set to win! Now, time for a joke from a loyal Olympic fan!

Fan One   Why can't Cinderella play soccer?

Scoreboard Student *flashes card at audience. It reads 'I don't know'.*

But the **Reporter** *shoves* **Fan One** *out of the way before she gets a chance to finish her joke.*

Reporter   Out the way! Here come the runners-up!

Gary B *and his mates charge over as* **ZeeBoy** *is placed back on the ground and shove* **Reporter** *and* **TV Crew** *out of the way.*

Gary B   Out my way!

Scoreboard Student *flashes card at audience. It reads 'Boo'.*

Reporter *and his* **TV Crew** *trip and all land on the floor in a pile on top of each other.*

Reporter   Back in five, when we will chat to our future Olympic hero!

Reporter *and* **TV Crew** *exit.*

ZeeBoy *(to himself)*   What's an Olympic hero?

As the crowd disperses, we reveal **Marvel** *(the youngest and shortest student at the Academy). He is sitting on the floor reading a Superhero comic. A couple of international students,* **Beryl** *and* **Crush***, remain* *training.* **Crush** *is practising tennis shots.* **Beryl** *is doing some air boxing. Throughout the scene more students enter and start to train.*

Gary B *looks* **ZeeBoy** *up and down.*

Gary B   Who is he!?

Sparkles *removes* **ZeeBoy**'s *face-mask.*

Sparkles   Sponge Bob?

Everyone looks at him, shaking their heads.

I meant . . . Square Pants?

Slowboy   Sponge Bob and Square Pants are the same person.

Sparkles   Really?

Gary B   Can we get on with things?!

Smiley   Gary asked . . .

Gary B   Gary B.

Smiley   Gary B asked who you are.

Spikey   He don't look like he's from (*insert name of city or town*).

Sorted   D'you think he's a refugee?

ZeeBoy   Yes, I am . . . one of them!

Slowboy   Where you from then?

ZeeBoy   I can't say.

Gary B   So you're a R – E – F – U – G – E – E!

Spikey   Are there four Es in 'refugee'?

Gary B   Yeah, course.

Slowboy   So, what's your name?

ZeeBoy   My . . . my name is . . . is . . .

He looks around, panicking. They move in closer.

Smiley   Is what?

ZeeBoy   It's . . .

Beat.

Freeze mode activate.

Everyone except **ZeeBoy** *freezes. He paces up and down, then speaks to his watch.*

ZeeBoy   Watch. I need a history of Olympic heroes.

Enter **Olympic Hero One**.

Olympic Hero One   Olympic hero Polydamas of Thessaly. One of the most famous Olympic winners of 408 BC. Known to kill a lion with his bare hands and grab the feet of a raging bull and swing it around. King Darius of Persia sent his men with gifts and persuaded him to fight three of the best Persian wrestlers. Polydamas easily killed two of them and the third one ran away.

ZeeBoy   Freeze mode off!

Everyone unfreezes.

ZeeBoy   My name is Polydamas of Thessaly.

Slowboy   Poly-what?

Gary B *moves in closer to* **ZeeBoy**.

Gary B   What are you on about?

ZeeBoy   Freeze mode activate.

Everyone freezes.

Watch, I need another name of an Olympic hero!

Olympic Hero Two *enters.*

ZeeBoy   Diagoras of Rhodes. A champion boxer in 464 BC. His style was unique. He never tried to avoid a blow from his opponent and followed the rules strictly. His sons also became Olympic winners, one in boxing and the other in the *pankratium*.

After their win, the sons carried their ageing father on their shoulders around the cheering stadium. Suddenly, someone advised him to die at that moment, Diagoras dropped his head and died instantly.

ZeeBoy   Freeze mode off!

Everyone unfreezes.

I am Diagoras of Rhodes.

Smiley   Is he speaking English?

Gary B   He's trying to be funny with us.

Sparkles   Sponge Bob is funny, Square Pants is funnier though.

Slowboy   How many times do I have to tell you, Sparkles? Square Pants is Sponge Bob! Gary . . .

Gary B   Gary B.

Slowboy   Gary B, can I sort Sparkles out?

Gary B   We've got bigger things to sort out, like this – (*Pointing at* **ZeeBoy**.) wannabe champ.

Smiley   Yeah, who does he think he's fooling?

Sorted   Making up stupid names.

Spikey   He can't even do that properly. Check our names out. I'm Spikey. That's Smiley, Slowboy, Sparkles and Sorted, cos he's always sorted.

Slowboy   Gary B is gonna ask you once more.

Sorted   What's your name?

Gary B   Yeah, Gary B is asking you, what's your name?

ZeeBoy   Freeze mode activate!

Everyone freezes.

ZeeBoy   Please, give me a name they will understand!

Enter **Olympic Hero Three**.

Olympic Hero Three   Charlotte Cooper of the United Kingdom. Olympic champion in 1900. The first fem –

ZeeBoy   Thank you!

Olympic Heroes *exit.*

ZeeBoy   Freeze mode off.

Gary B   What you got for us?

ZeeBoy   Charlotte Cooper.

Beat. They all look at each other then start to laugh loudly.

Sparkles   I get it. He's not allowed to use his real name, so he uses a girl's name!

Smiley   That is funny. Funnee!

They laugh some more.

Sparkles   Yeah, funnier than Sponge Bob and Square Pants!

Slowboy   That's it. Come here, you!

Slowboy *chases* **Sparkles**.

Sparkles   What did I say?!

He clocks **Marvel** *still sitting nearby and grabs his comic.*

ZeeBoy (*points at comic*)   I'm from here . . . !

Slowboy *stops chasing* **Sparkles** *and turns his attention to* **ZeeBoy**.

Slowboy   That's a comic book?

Smiley *snatches it off* **ZeeBoy** *and gives it to* **Gary B**.

Gary B   So you're from – (*He reads.*) Planet Zola? Yeah, right.

Spikey   What bus route is that on?

ZeeBoy   Minus 4X. Due to strikes, it doesn't run as often as it used to.

Spikey   Wait, wait, I've got one. You related to Bananaman?

ZeeBoy   I do not know of this Banana-person.

Spikey   Eric is Bananaman.

ZeeBoy   And who is Eric?

Spikey   A schoolboy who leads an amazing double life. When Eric eats a banana an amazing transformation occurs, he becomes Bananaman, ever alert for the call to action. (*He strikes a superhero pose.*) Do you know him?

ZeeBoy   No.

Smiley   What about Superman?

ZeeBoy   Not directly, but a family member is thinking of marrying Superman's long-lost niece so that could indeed qualify as a relationship in the making . . .

They are all bent over laughing now.

Sparkles   Oh that's too funny.

Spikey   I think I've wet myself.

Everyone stops and looks at him.

Not like, for real.

Sorted   Seriously, where you from?

No reply.

Gary B   Dog got your tongue?

Spikey   I think it's . . .

Gary B   What!?

Spikey   Nothing.

Sorted   Welcome to your worst nightmare.

Smiley   We're the Fantastic Four and we're gonna . . . Eh, you lot, what do the Fantastic Four do?

Sorted   One's got killer bogeys – once they're flicked at you, you've had it. The other's got killer farts – once he quacks one, that's it. Then there's killer breath – she just has to say hello and you're knocked out. And the last one, killer zits, filled with pus that . . .

Gary B   We get it.

Slowboy   Anyway, there's five of us.

Smiley   Oh yeah.

Sorted   As I was saying, we're your worst nightmare.

They all start repeating and chanting while circling **ZeeBoy**.

Gary B   R – E . . .

Sparkles   F – U . . .

Smiley   G – E . . .

Spikey   E . . .

Sorted   E!

Kalina *enters and storms over.*

Kalina   Eh! What's going on?

Gary B   We're just trying to help the needy.

Kalina   Needy, eh? Who's holding the trophy?

They all look at each other, then at the trophy which is in **ZeeBoy**'*s hand.*

Sorted (*points at* **ZeeBoy**)   He is . . .

Kalina   Right. So he's hardly 'needy', is he?

Gary B   Whatever.

Spikey   She's got a point.

Gary B   What?!

Spikey   Nothing.

Gary B (*to* **ZeeBoy**)   Oi, you ain't planning on beating me in the main Olympic race – the Madidas Run – are you?

ZeeBoy   No. No plan to do that.

Gary B   I'm serious.

ZeeBoy   So am I.

Gary B   I want that Madidas sponsorship deal. I want my name and my face all over the place!

ZeeBoy   Here. Take the trophy. I'm practically made of this stuff . . . this metal stuff.

He hands the trophy to **Gary B**.

Kalina   Don't be silly.

She snatches it and hands it back to **ZeeBoy**.

Kalina   You won that race fair and square.

ZeeBoy   Race?

Kalina   Boys, don't you have Olympic training to get to?

Gary B   Kalina, don't tell us what to do. Boys, let's go, we've got Olympic training to get to.

Gary B *and his boys eye up* **ZeeBoy** *and exit, except* **Spikey** *who nervously approaches* **Kalina**.

Spikey   Do you have a map?

Kalina   Er, no.

Spikey   Cos I keep getting lost in your eyes.

There is an awkward pause.

Spikey   What do you call a chav in a box?

Kalina   I don't know.

Spikey   Innit. (*Beat.*) That's a joke.

There is another awkward pause.

Spikey   So you fancy flying back to Poland in my dad's private plane?

Kalina   I'm from Bulgaria.

Beat.

Spikey   I knew that.

Awkward pause. **Kalina** *turns to face* **ZeeBoy**. **Spikey** *is still standing there, looking on.*

Kalina (*to* **ZeeBoy**)   You did really, really well out there.

Spikey *coughs loudly.*

Kalina   Is he still behind me?

ZeeBoy *nods.* **Kalina** *turns around to face* **Spikey**.

Spikey   Your mum not taught you no manners?

Kalina   I thought you'd finished.

Spikey   I have now. (*As he starts to exit, slowly.*) And don't even bother shouting my name, cos I'm not coming back.

He milks every step, looking back to see if she will shout for him.

Kalina   Don't worry, I don't even know your name.

Spikey   It's Spikey. I'm in the Blue Block, Room 233, but don't even try and remember it, cos I'm not interested. You're not even worth stalking.

He looks back once more.

By the way, you're out of milk.

He exits.

ZeeBoy   Hi.

Kalina   Hi.

Beat.

You just beat everyone. I wish I had your talent.

ZeeBoy   Who says you haven't?

Kalina   I always come in third place. Never won a single race.

ZeeBoy   I could help take you from third to first place.

Kalina   What? Train together?

ZeeBoy   Yes.

Kalina   I'd like that. You know I'm not bothered which country you're from.

ZeeBoy   Or . . . planet?

Kalina (*nervously carries on rambling*)   I mean I've never met a real refugee. It must be kind of weird for you, maybe weird's not the right word – tragic? Or maybe it's brilliant that you've kind of escaped? Or both? Tragic and brilliant, with a bit of weird thrown in there? (*Beat.*) I can be weird too!

Awkward pause.

(*Pointing at* **Marvel**.) That's my brother, Marvel, so I'm kinda used to geeks trying to be superheroes.

ZeeBoy   You have superheroes here?

Kalina   We have superhero worshippers. Take my brother: he's ten years old and changed his name to Marvel, after his favourite comic-book series.

ZeeBoy   And a comic book holds the life story to all superheroes?

Kalina   Yeah, suppose so.

ZeeBoy   What was everyone cheering for back there?

Kalina   Duh, for you?

ZeeBoy   Me? What do you know? What have I done? Are they here to take me away!?

Kalina   Hey, it's okay. You're safe here.

ZeeBoy   Am I?

Kalina   Yeah.

Pause.

ZeeBoy   Back home there's a war going on, our enemies have created a Super Enemy and everyone my age is being forced into the army to fight a war, but we just want to be . . .

Kalina   Kids?

ZeeBoy   Yes. I no longer want to be a Su –

Kalina   It's cool – you don't need to explain anything. Unfortunately this academy will train you as hard as the army, but at least there's no war to worry about. You got somewhere to sleep?

ZeeBoy   I have a twenty-four-hour battery. So I don't really need to sleep.

Kalina   You're kind of odd. I like you. Your battery will have to be at the max as you're our Olympic hero and tomorrow's the big day.

ZeeBoy   I am an Olympic hero?

Kalina   Do you know anything about anything?

ZeeBoy   Can I just go to the . . .

Kalina   Toilet?

ZeeBoy *walks to a quiet spot and speaks to his watch.*

ZeeBoy   Watch. Olympic history, please.

Music: classical.

Numerous **Olympic Heroes** *appear on stage, holding Olympic torches. As they speak, a brief history of the Olympics is acted out through mime, dance and sport.* **ZeeBoy** *watches.*

Four Olympic Heroes *step away from the routine.*

Olympic Hero One   The Olympic Games are a major international event, featuring summer and winter sports.

Olympic Hero Two   In which thousands of athletes participate in a variety of competitions.

Olympic Hero Three   The Olympic Games have come to be regarded as the world's foremost sports competition. They are held every four years.

Olympic Hero Four *grabs an Olympic torch as a mike and starts to rap.*

Olympic Hero Four   Change the track!

Music: classical music fuses with a hip-hop beat.

Let's liven this history lesson up! Hear me now, the Olympic Games are ancient, from 776 BC to 2012 UK. Twenty-six sports to drive you crazy. For every boy, girl there's a sport that will amaze you.

Archery, Athletics, Badminton, Basketball, Boxing, Canoeing, Cycling, Diving, Equestrian, Field Hockey, Fencing, Football, Gymnastics, Handball, Judo, Modern Pentathlon, Rowing . . .

Hold on a sec . . . just need to catch my breath.

He takes an inhaler out and inhales, then quickly puts it away.

Crowd! You still with me?!

Scoreboard Student *flashes card at audience. It reads 'Cheer'.*

ZeeBoy *looks puzzled.*

Olympic Hero Four   Sailing, Shooting, Swimming, Synchronised Swimming, Table Tennis, Taekwondo, Tennis, Triathlon, Volleyball, Water Polo, Weightlifting and Wrestling. The end!

Music stops.

Everyone exits.

ZeeBoy *walks up to* **Olympic Hero Four**, *who is on a high after his rap performance.*

Olympic Hero Four   What do you think of that?!

ZeeBoy   Interesting.

Olympic Hero Four   You not bored of information being told the same way all the time?

ZeeBoy   Not really.

Olympic Hero Four   You into rap? Hip-hop?

ZeeBoy   No.

Olympic Hero Four   You hated it, didn't you?

ZeeBoy   Pretty much.

Olympic Hero Four   ZeeBoy, I'm your information memory. You're not . . . gonna . . . sack me, are you?

ZeeBoy   No.

Olympic Hero Four   Cool, cos with the war going on in Planet Zola, I really need this job.

ZeeBoy   Just don't rap again.

Olympic Hero Four   Got it out of my system now.

He takes his inhaler out and inhales, then quickly puts it away.

ZeeBoy   I didn't know you had asthma?

Olympic Hero Four   It's just the time-travelling. The air's not as clear as it used to be.

ZeeBoy   Your job involves a lot of time-travelling.

Olympic Hero Four   You know, asthma is pretty common in top athletes, especially in sports like cycling, long-distance running and even mountain biking, so really I'm just as fit as this lot.

ZeeBoy   Good answer. You may be excused.

Olympic Hero Four *exits.*

As **ZeeBoy** *walks back to* **Kalina**, **Marvel** *blocks his path.*

Marvel   You're not from around here?

No reply.

See this comic? (*Shows comic to* **ZeeBoy**.) It has a cartoon of superheroes that look just like you when you had that mask on.

ZeeBoy (*nervous*)   Does it?

Marvel   I've a good memory. Know all sorts of stuff. Stuff kids my age don't know. If you fart consistently for six years and nine months, enough gas is produced to create the energy of an atomic bomb. A cockroach will live nine days without its head, before it starves to death. Turtles can breathe through their butts. That kind of stuff.

ZeeBoy   With great power comes great responsibility.

Marvel   That's not a fact, that's Peter Parker.

ZeeBoy   The eye-mask . . . I . . . stole it from a . . . kebab shop.

Marvel   Do you know what a kebab shop sells?

ZeeBoy   It takes a bit of time, but information and words slowly begin to make sense.

Marvel   I can't prove you're not for real, but I'm gonna keep my eye on you, cos over there is my sis, Kalina, and she needs protecting from other species.

ZeeBoy   But – you're shorter than her, and aren't you ten years old?

Marvel   From my height I could head-butt your . . .

ZeeBoy *looks down.*

ZeeBoy   Boxer shorts? You got me there.

Beat.

So now what?

Marvel   Dunno.

ZeeBoy   Are you going to attack?

Marvel   Dunno if I can be bothered, just had a footlong Subway.

ZeeBoy   So now what?

Marvel   If I find out you got some kind of superhero powers, I'm having them, right? And a date with Buffy, Elektra and Storm, and my own comic book and . . .

Mindy *runs on stage.* **Reporter** *and* **TV Crew** *follow.*

Mindy (*pointing at* **ZeeBoy**)   There he is!

Reporter *rushes over to* **ZeeBoy** *with* **TV Crew**. **Reporter** *trips over, falling flat on his face. He continues to speak from the ground.*

Reporter   Teen TV, reporting live from the BO Sports Academy in (*insert city or town*). Everyone here is competing for the Olympics 2012, but more importantly for the Madidas sponsorship for their new trainers called . . .

Scoreboard Student *flashes card at audience. It reads 'The Superhero'.*

Reporter   Yes, 'The Superhero', because there is a superhero in all of us!

Scoreboard Student *flashes card at audience. It reads 'Woop woop'.*

Lippy Lilly *rushes over and helps* **Reporter** *up on to his feet.* **Glam Greg** *is right behind her and bumps into her and they all fall on to the ground on top of each other.*

Reporter   I'm pretty chuffed to be joined by the hottest new talent in sport! The only student who will be competing in every game!

ZeeBoy   What's going on?

He works up to the camera, looking into the lens.

What's in there?

Reporter   You're live on Teen TV! And we're here, reporting live at this year's Olympics, which will take place in exactly . . .

Mindy *whispers time to* **Reporter**.

Reporter   Twenty hours!

ZeeBoy   I don't want any of this.

Reporter   Cut the camera! Out the way!

He pushes **Camera Person** *aside and faces* **ZeeBoy**.

Reporter   I need this interview! And you're the news right now. The world needs a superhero and you're it!

ZeeBoy   I don't want to be a superhero no more.

Kalina *rushes over.*

Kalina   Just leave him alone.

Beat.

Let's go.

ZeeBoy *and* **Kalina** *exit.*

Reporter   You'll regret this!

Mindy *rushes over with* **Beryl** *and* **Crush**, *two international sports students.*

Mindy   I've found some others!

Reporter   But that's the boy everyone wants to know about!

Mindy   We're live in five . . .

Reporter   Why can't anything go right for me, Mindy?

Mindy   Five . . .

Reporter   Being on TV really hasn't changed anything.

Mindy   Four . . .

Reporter   I still can't get people to listen to me.

Mindy   Three . . .

Reporter   Or girls to go out with me.

Mindy   Two. I'll go out with you. One!

Reporter   Cool!

He turns to the camera and beams a cheesy smile.

Welcome back to Teen TV, where our Sports Superhero has
gone to grab a protein drink. I'm joined by our international
students. As you know, this year every student has had their
names changed to their chosen superhero names. So please
welcome . . .

Mindy *whispers name to* **Reporter**.

Reporter   Beryl?

Mindy *nods.*

Reporter   Beryl from – (*insert name of a country*). Tell us why
you chose the name Beryl. Hardly the name of a winner, don't
you think?

Beryl   Where I come from that name is very exotic.

Reporter   So, what would the Madidas sponsorship mean
to you?

Beryl   The Madidas sponsorship would be something I
would accept so I could help pay for a new school in my home
village in – (*insert a country name*).

Reporter   Right, so it's not to buy a Porsche?

Beryl   I'm thirteen.

Reporter   They're a good investment.

Beryl   So is education.

Reporter   Yeah. Course. Totally. I mean, charity is more important than a –

Beryl   Porsche.

Reporter   Nah, I'd want the Porsche. So you're here to compete in the teen boxing. Don't you feel that girls should maybe . . . not box?

Beryl   I've knocked out fourteen of the best boys in my country to be here, what do you think?

Reporter   That girls don't look pretty with black eyes?

Beryl   Interview over.

Reporter   You're not gonna punch me, are you?

Beryl   I don't hit girls.

She walks off. **TV Crew** *is trying to hide their laughter.*

Reporter   Did she just call me . . . ?

Mindy   A girl.

Reporter (*embarrassed*)   It must be all the TV make-up.

Mindy   I think boy-liner suits you, Terry.

Reporter   Thanks, Mindy. Who's next?

Mindy *whispers name to* **Reporter**. **Crush** *approaches in his wheelchair.* **Reporter** *bends down to speak to him.*

Reporter   Crush from – (*insert a country's name*).

Music: famous sports champion music.

Crush *takes centre stage as the lights start to flash along to the music.*

Scoreboard Student *flashes card at audience. It reads 'Cheer and woop woop'.*

Crush *does a short sports-style wheelchair routine. When finished, he enthusiastically grabs* **Reporter***'s microphone from him.*

Reporter   Wow, Crush, that was . . .

Crush (*snatching mike*)   Hey, it's Crush here! Great to be in the UK! I'm so excited by you guys! The English girls are real pretty and it means so much to me and my family to be here. Competing in the Paralympics in London is a dream come true.

Reporter *tries to grab his microphone back but* **Crush** *continues talking animatedly to the camera.*

Reporter   Can I –

Crush   Another dream I've had for a long time is to be a world champion!

Reporter   Can I have –

Crush   Before my accident I could swim with the sharks in the deepest ocean, race a cheetah up the highest mountain, cycle through fire and jump through hoops made of ice. But now I'm all that and a lot more! I'm going to come first in rowing, athletics, fencing . . .

Reporter   I'm here to –

Crush   I'm the man!!

He lifts his arms in the air like a champion.

Scoreboard Student *flashes card at audience. It reads 'Cheer'.*

Crush   I am the man!

Reporter   I'm interviewing!

He grabs the microphone back from **Crush**.

Crush   Don't push me!

Reporter   I didn't.

Crush *gets close up to* **Reporter**.

Crush   Do you wanna know why I'm called Crush?!

Reporter   Here, have the mic back. It's all yours.

Crush   Ha! Got you! I ain't violent. I'm all about the sport, and winning!

He continues training.

Reporter *sits on the edge of the stage, depressed.* **Mindy** *joins him.*

Reporter   This is still Teen TV with no guest, no story, no promotion . . . nothing.

Mindy   They're a difficult lot.

Reporter   If I don't get a brilliant interview, I'm fired. And that would mean going back to my day job.

Mindy   Which is . . . ?

Reporter   School.

Mindy   Don't you watch any reality TV?

Reporter *shakes his head.*

Reporter   What do you call someone who doesn't own a TV?

Mindy   I don't know – what do you call someone who doesn't own a TV?

Reporter   Mindy, I wasn't telling a joke. I don't own a TV.

Mindy   Quick lesson, to get a good interview you have to get the public to laugh and cry and feel for the person you're interviewing.

Reporter   Yeah, people love a sob story.

Mindy   It's a winner. Try again on Crush whilst I find someone else.

Reporter *walks over to* **Crush** *with* **Camera Person.**

Reporter   Crush, earlier you said it means so much for your family for you to be here. Do you want to send a message to your family and friends back home telling them how much you . . . miss them?

Crush *stops training and looks at the camera screen.*

Crush   Yeah. I'd like to.

Reporter   In your own time. Feel free to cry.

Crush   If my family is watching I want them to know how much their support has helped me get to where I am.

Reporter (*whispers to* **Camera Person**)   We can go in for a close-up now.

Crush   I just want to make my baby brother proud and thank my mum who's worked three or four jobs to get me through college and my friends who gave up their weekends to help train me.

Reporter   Closer.

Crush   Mum, if you're watching, I'm going to make you so proud and the trophy I bring home will have your name on it!

Scoreboard Student *flashes card at audience. It reads 'Ahhh'.*

Reporter   Thank you, Crush. That was . . . emotional. Teen TV reporting from . . .

Mindy *grabs* **Marvel** *and brings him over.*

Mindy   Got another!

Reporter (*goes back to cheesy presenter mode*)   What's your name and where have you travelled from?

Marvel   I'm Marvel from Bulgaria.

Reporter   Did you get a plane here?

Marvel   I got the 33 bus. It's a bendy bus.

Reporter   How do you jump those hurdles? You're pretty short.

Marvel   I'm ten, give me a chance to grow!

Reporter   And that's all we've got time for. Thank you for joining me on Teen TV Olympics Special. Back soon!

Marvel   Was that it?

Reporter   The camera doesn't love you.

Marvel   What are you on about?

Reporter   You're a bit bland, hardly Sports Superhero material. Stick to reading comics.

Marvel   You don't know nothing. I'll show you. I'll show you all!

He goes back to reading his comic. **Gary B** *enters and balances on his head.*

Reporter   Who's next?

Mindy   What about him over there?

Reporter   Who is he?

Mindy   Gary B. No one wants to interview him. Bad-tempered, could be a winner, but lets his anger get in the way of a race. He balances on his head when he loses.

Reporter   Let's go!

They walk over to **Gary B**, *who is still balancing on his head.*

Gary B   Fifty, sixty, seventy. Yeah. Count in tens, that's what real champions do.

Reporter   I'm stood by Gary B. Gary B is on a training marathon. He has been balancing on his head for nearly two hours now. Gary B, how you doing?

Gary B *looks at* **Reporter**.

Gary B   Where's all the real press?

Reporter   I'm here reporting from Teen TV!

Gary B   I'm training as hard as the big boys, so I'm supposed to get real TV people like Ant & Dec, not some . . . How old are you?

Reporter   Twelve and a half, but you've got to start young in show business.

Gary B   You think that's young? Guess how old I was when I knew I had the talent?

Reporter   I have in my research . . . nine years old?

Gary B   Your research needs researching. I was four years old, four years old when I was balancing on my head.

Reporter   Any reason why you were balancing on your head?

Gary B   You know, you're kind of funny.

He stands up.

Reporter   Funny?

Gary B   Funny in a good way. You're hired.

Reporter   Hired? For what?

Gary B   To be a Madidas front man – I need my profile raising. I'm gonna need someone to film my journey. Get me my own TV show and crisp advert. Then I'll be taken seriously.

Reporter   That's a nice offer, Gary B, but . . .

Gary B   Listen, I'm not asking. I'm telling you.

Reporter   But I need a bigger story. I need that new boy.

Gary B   You make me a Sports Superhero and I'll get you the dirt on that newbie. Deal or no deal?

Reporter   I'll deal on that.

Sparkles *and* **Sorted** *enter.*

Sorted   Gary!

Gary B   It's Gary B, boys.

Sparkles   Gary B, *Neighbours* has started.

Gary B *looks around embarrassed.*

Gary B   Why you telling me for?

Sparkles   You told us to come and get you.

Gary B   Nah, nah, I . . . didn't. I mean . . . why would I?

Sorted   Cos you watch it every day, even the omnibus.

Gary B   I only watch hard stuff like *Saw*. *Saw* for breakfast,
Saw for lunch and dinner.

Sparkles   You've got *Neighbours* pyjamas.

Sorted   And your gran bought you a *Neighbours* duvet set last
year.

Sparkles   You even cried when it moved to Channel 5.

Gary B (*rushes over to them and whispers*)   Not so loud!

They walk off.

Reporter   Let's call it a day. See you tomorrow.

Marvel *has heard everything. He walks up to* **Reporter**.

Marvel   I heard you talking about that new kid.

Reporter   And?

Marvel   I can get something on him.

Reporter   I've got Gary B now.

Marvel   Gary B doesn't even know how to spell his own
name. What if I can prove he's not for real?

Reporter   What d'you mean?

Marvel   I can't say no more unless I get the deal. I want
teen power, I want teen superpowers.

Reporter   If he's a fake, I'll make you the face of Teen TV.
Everyone will know your name.

Marvel   Yes!

Reporter   One condition, it has to be before the Olympic launch.

Marvel   That's like, tomorrow?

Reporter   I know.

Beat.

Marvel   You're on. Tomorrow. Keep your eye out for flying objects.

Reporter   You're not taking this seriously.

Marvel   I am. I need a live link to Teen TV.

Beat. **Reporter** *paces up and down, then stops.*

Reporter   I can get you on air at eight a.m. and use your mobile phone for us to link live.

Twenty-four hours later. The Olympic launch.

ZeeBoy *enters alone. He is carrying his superhero outfit on a hanger. He hangs it up and talks to it.*

ZeeBoy   ZeeBoy, you don't need me no more, there's plenty of superheroes in Planet Zola.

Beat.

I won't be needing my ZeeBoy 'Z's.

He takes out some letter Zs and throws them away. They land on a student, who yawns and falls asleep.

Or flying dust.

He chucks some dust offstage and a flying object / person / animal flies from one side of the stage to the other.

Or two-trillion-year guarantee Zola watch.

He takes his watch off.

But without my Zola watch I can never return home.

He puts his watch back on.

If I don't fly around the planets rescuing people, what else do I do?

Beryl *enters in a superhero outfit.* **ZeeBoy** *quickly hides his* **ZeeBoy** *outfit.* **Beryl** *starts to train. She is air-boxing.*

Beryl   Where's your superhero outfit? We've all got to wear one for the launch.

ZeeBoy *(hiding outfit behind his back)*   In the wash. You can really box.

Beryl   I know.

ZeeBoy   Where you from?

Beryl   *(insert country name).*

ZeeBoy   I've been there.

Beryl *(stops boxing)*   Have you?

ZeeBoy   On a mission. Earthquake rescue.

Beryl   What . . . ?

ZeeBoy   Oops. Freeze mode activate.

Beryl *freezes.*

ZeeBoy   Watch. Rewind.

Beryl *goes back to boxing and* **ZeeBoy** *exits and re-enters minus the outfit in his hand.*

ZeeBoy   You can really box.

Beryl   I know. Have I spoken to you before?

ZeeBoy   Nope. You're from *(insert Beryl's country name)*. Do you miss home?

Beryl   Yes, but the academy feels like home now. I've been here since I was eight. You?

ZeeBoy   I miss my people, but . . .

Beryl   This is your home now?

ZeeBoy   Maybe. I don't know.

Beryl   If you feel like I once did, then it must be a shock to be here. When my uncle found out the academy was looking for new talent in (*insert name of country*), me and my uncle walked for two days to attend the open call and another day of queuing. I did not think I would have the energy to show them what I could do, but look, I made it!

ZeeBoy   Are you happy . . . here?

Beryl   Oh, my first year they had to send me back home twenty-eight times, I was so homesick, but then I went into a real boxing ring and my heart was beating so fast. I never asked to go back home again. This place is like no other. We are treated like adults, we are not here to play games, we are here to become great sporting role-models.

ZeeBoy   It seems hard.

Beryl   It is. We cannot get injured, we cannot show our weaknesses and we have one goal and that is to come first.

ZeeBoy   Then why continue such hardship?

Beryl   Because when we compete it is like being a superhero!

Beat.

You not happy here? You just won a big race. You've got the freedom to . . .

ZeeBoy   Freedom?

Beryl   Yes. Freedom to achieve whatever you wish.

ZeeBoy   That's it! I'm free now! Thanks, Beryl!

Beryl   What did I say?

ZeeBoy   I'm a normal kid, so I can . . .

Beryl   Eat pizza? Play Xbox?

ZeeBoy Become the fifth member of JLS!

Beryl That's hardly 'normal'.

All students enter wearing Madidas-sponsored superhero outfits except for **ZeeBoy***, who is in his same sports outfit, and* **Kalina***, who is also in normal sports gear.* **Marvel** *is not there.*

Reporter *and his* **TV Crew** *enter.*

Reporter *(shouting over the music)* I hope you can hear me! Welcome to Teen TV live at the Olympic launch! We have a sporting treat for you! The BO Sports Academy live launch. Take it away boys and girls!

Everyone starts to get into position for a sport routine. **ZeeBoy** *clocks* **Kalina** *standing by herself.*

ZeeBoy Kalina, thank you for rescuing me from that reporter yesterday.

Kalina I could tell you felt a bit like I do sometimes.

ZeeBoy You also wish to be . . .

Kalina Painfully normal, yes. I mean, what's with all this superhero stuff? No one in this academy is a real superhero!

ZeeBoy Kalina, I haven't been honest with you . . .

Kalina I mean, who wants to be a big-headed, big-ego, love-yourself superhero? Did you says something?

ZeeBoy No.

Kalina We're just kids that train really hard in hope one day to represent our country.

Beat.

And come first place.

They laugh.

ZeeBoy Best get training then.

Dance music kicks in.

A big sports training routine takes place to music. **ZeeBoy** *leads the training routine with* **Kalina** *by his side.*

Kalina *and* **ZeeBoy** *end the routine with a sporting duet.* **Kalina** *is focused and out-performs all the other students.*

Scorecard Student *flashes card to audience. It reads 'Cheer'.*

Everyone exits, leaving **ZeeBoy** *and* **Kalina** *alone.*

ZeeBoy   I knew you had it in you!

Kalina   Maybe, yeah.

ZeeBoy   You could beat anyone here.

Kalina   Yeah, right. Most of them have been doing this since they were born. I started when I got kicked out of school.

ZeeBoy   Where you come from, what's it like?

Kalina   If it wasn't for the surrounding fields, I wouldn't be good at sport. It's a small town and no one has ever left there, not until I got discovered and here I am . . . third place girl. Hardly something to write home about.

ZeeBoy   Where I come from, everyone's good at everything, it's kind of boring.

They laugh.

The Olympics happen every four years, right? You want to wait that long to show everyone how good you are?

Marvel *enters suspiciously, holding his mobile phone and wearing a superhero outfit similar to* **ZeeBoy***'s.*

Marvel   New kid, I need your help!

Kalina   Go on, see what he wants.

ZeeBoy *rushes over to* **Marvel***.*

Marvel   I need to rescue my mates. They're in serious trouble.

ZeeBoy   I'll call a taxi!

Marvel They're in Australia.

ZeeBoy How far's that?

Marvel You'd have to fly to get there in time.

ZeeBoy (*pacing up and down*) How serious is it?

Marvel It's bad.

ZeeBoy Watch. Invisible mode activate.

Everyone freezes. Blackout.

Marvel I can't see anything!

ZeeBoy Do you get travel sickness?

Marvel Yeah, badly.

ZeeBoy Then grab a bucket because this is a whole lot worse!

Space travel sound effects.

Marvel Where you taking me . . . ?!

ZeeBoy To rescue your mates in Australia.

Marvel You serious?

ZeeBoy A superhero never lies. Hold on tight!

Marvel So it's true . . . you're . . . you're a real . . .

ZeeBoy We'll be there in three, two, one . . .

Music: latest hit party song.

Lights up on a beach party in Australia on one side of the stage and the Olympic launch on the other side. Crowds gather at both events.

ZeeBoy *is wearing his superhero cloak and eye-mask. He looks around in shock.* **Marvel** *stands filming him on his camera phone.*

ZeeBoy A party? What's going on, Marvel?

Marvel   It's my pen pal's Olympic party . . . Smile, you're on Skype! I've been filming your every move, new boy. You're live on Teen TV and everyone saw you fly me to Australia!

Mindy   He's a real superhero!

Shock reactions from Academy students.

Scoreboard Student *flashes card at audience. It reads 'O.M.G.'.*

Reporter   Quick, camera on!

He grabs his **TV Crew***.*

Welcome to Teen TV, where I have breaking news! Do not turn over because what you're witnessing is like major news!

ZeeBoy *tries to cover his face.*

ZeeBoy   Marvel, you don't want to do this. My identity needs to be protected.

Marvel *continues filming him with his camera phone.*

Reporter   Yes, our Olympic Hero is in fact a real superhero!

ZeeBoy   Why did you bring me here, Marvel?

Marvel   So I can be the face of Madidas! Tired of everyone thinking I'm the Academy geek.

ZeeBoy   Am I live now?

Marvel   Oh yeah!

Reporter   Yes, you are live on Teen TV! Do you want to explain to everyone why you lied?

Kalina   He never lied. He said he didn't want all this!

Reporter   Breaking news: our Olympic hero is a fake! A superhero trying to take a human's championship away. What a story!

ZeeBoy *grabs the mobile and looks straight at it.*

ZeeBoy   I'm not after no Olympic win!

Reporter   A fallen hero. How were we to know our sports superhero was a fake?

Camera Person   Battery's low, Terry. We've lost Australia.

Reporter   Hurry up and change it then!

Camera Person *puts the camera down. The live Australia–Academy connection cuts out. The Australian party people slowly exit.*

Camera Person   Why don't you?

He walks off.

Reporter   Get back here, we're live! We're missing everything!

In Australia, **ZeeBoy** *takes his eye-mask off and drops it on the floor.*

ZeeBoy   Is that what you want? To be me? It's all yours, Marvel.

Marvel *(picks up the mask and lifts it in the air)*   Yes!

ZeeBoy   Something my cousin Spiderman told me, with great power comes great responsibility, and that's a fact.

ZeeBoy *storms off stage.* **Camera Person** *walks up to* **Reporter**.

Camera Person   You know something, Terry? I've never liked you. How many times do I have to flush to get rid of you?

Reporter   What's that mean?

Mindy *grabs the camera.*

Camera Person   It means you're a . . .

Mindy   I've changed the battery! We're live in five, four . . .

Camera Person *exits.*

Marvel *puts the eye-mask on.*

Marvel   No more Academy geek!

Marvel *exits.*

Mindy   Three . . . two . . . one!

The live Australia–Academy connection is back on. There is no one left on the Australian side.

Mindy   Where's everyone in Australia?

Back at the Olympic launch.

Reporter   Mindy, on me!

Mindy *turns the camera on* **Reporter**. *The camera is not properly focused and appears to be cutting off some of* **Reporter**'s *face.*

Reporter   More breaking news. With our real superhero now disqualified from the games, we have to rerun the race to find a new BO Sports Academy superhero to replace him. The Academy has chosen seven of their best to compete for this title and here they are!

Music: Superhero theme tune.

Each, except for **Kalina**, *steps forward when announced and strikes a pose.*

Referee   Gary B, Sparkles, Smiley, Spikey, Slowboy, Beryl and Kalina!

They wave at the crowd.

Scoreboard Student *flashes card at audience. It reads 'Cheer'.*

Reporter   But first, a joke from a loyal Olympic fan!

Fan One   Why can't Cinderella play football?

Scoreboard Student *flashes card at audience. It reads 'I don't know'.*

A bright light shines in everyone's face. It is almost blinding. **Reporter** *shoves* **Fan One** *out of the way before she gets a chance to finish her joke.*

Reporter   Out the way!

Everyone looks at the bright light.

Crush   What is it?

Beryl   Is it a bird?

Gary B   Is it a plane?

Sparkles   Is it Sponge Bob?

Marvel *appears wearing* **ZeeBoy**'s *eye-mask and a superhero outfit. He is laden with gold jewellery, rings, chains, etc., that match his gold eye-mask and gold outfit.*

Marvel   No, it's . . . Blingboy!

He flashes his bling jewellery. **Reporter** *runs over. He trips up and lands flat on the floor but continues speaking.*

Reporter   Blingboy, aren't you disqualified?

Marvel   I'm not here to race.

Fan One *rushes past* **Reporter** *to* **Marvel**, *nearly stepping on him.*

Fan One   Blingboy's here!

A crowd of screaming **Fans** *storm over to* **Marvel**, *also stepping over* **Reporter**.

Fan Two   Can we have your autograph?

Fan Three   I wanna fly away with you, Bling!

Marvel   One at a time!

Reporter   So Bling, what's next?

Marvel   I'm gonna see what offers I get.

Reporter   Are you going to make the world a safer place?

Marvel   Dunno.

Reporter   Blingboy, exclusive only on Teen TV!

Gary B *storms over to* **Reporter**.

Gary B   I got some dirt. He's a fake. So where's my deal?

Reporter   Is that all you've got?

Gary B   Yeah.

Reporter   Not good enough.

Gary B   We had a deal.

He moves in close to **Reporter**. **Reporter** *panics.*

Reporter   Gary . . .

Gary B   It's Gary B! I want the same attention as Blingboy!

Reporter   Gary B, no one actually cares about Blingboy!

Gary B   They look as if they do.

Reporter   No, no. Everyone's waiting to see who the BO Sports Academy Olympic Hero will be! A human hero will always be the true star!

Gary B   So?

Reporter   So the way you'll get your deal and attention is if you win the race.

Beat.

He gets in line to race. **Marvel** *is enjoying his new-found attention.* **Kalina** *overhears him.*

Marvel   Yeah, it was me and a hundred sharks, but this girl was drowning and I thought, 'I can live without my legs.' Luckily, I only had to look at the sharks and they swam away.

Kalina   Wait a minute.

Kalina *pushes through* **Marvel**'s **Fans**.

Kalina   Can I borrow you?

Marvel   Can't you see I'm busy, sis – Oh, I mean, don't disturb bling boy . . .

Kalina   Over here . . . now!

Marvel *and* **Kalina** *walk to a quiet area.*

Kalina   You have got to be joking?

Marvel   He doesn't wanna be one no more.

Kalina   You're not a real superhero!

Marvel   They don't know that.

Kalina   What is it with everyone? Trying to be something they're not?

Marvel   Sis, I'm no good at sport.

Kalina   Yes you are – how else would you get in to the Academy?

Marvel   I overheard Mum talking to the head.

Kalina   When?

Marvel   When we first got here. Head said cos you've got a sporting gift, they'll do our mum a favour and take the kid brother as well . . . me.

Kalina   Really?

Marvel   Yeah. Just let me be a superhero. Just for a day?

Kalina   Come here.

They hug.

Referee   Please take your places for the Madidas Olympic race.

Reporter   Teen TV reporting. The repeat race is about to commence, where we will crown our real Sports Superhero!

The seven **Runners** *line up.*

Referee   On your marks . . .

Kalina *walks up to the line.*

Referee   Get set . . .

Kalina *gets in position.*

Referee   Go!

Everyone except **Kalina** *runs. They run on the spot racing each other.* **Kalina** *walks away and sits down. Someone is hidden near her.*

Suddenly, the runners and crowd freeze. **Kalina** *is facing the other way from the race, so does not notice.*

ZeeBoy   Psst.

Kalina *looks round.*

ZeeBoy   Yeah, you.

Kalina *clocks someone reading a comic that covers his face. It is* **ZeeBoy** *dressed in* **Marvel**'s *clothes.*

ZeeBoy (*whispers*)   Over here! Under the comic!

Kalina (*walking over to him*)   You're not Marvel?

ZeeBoy   No, I'm . . .

He puts the comic down, revealing himself.

ZeeBoy.

Kalina   Oh, is that your real name?

ZeeBoy   Yes.

Kalina   I'm so, so, so sorry about my brother.

ZeeBoy   I think those superhero tights are getting too big for him. At least he didn't steal my name.

Kalina   Only my brother would come up with Blingboy.

Beat.

ZeeBoy   You're supposed to be winning a race right now.

Kalina   What's the chances of me beating that lot?

ZeeBoy   Same chance of me living as a normal kid.

Kalina   But you're not.

ZeeBoy   Who's to know? Marvel's doing a good job being me.

Kalina   True.

ZeeBoy   I thought you wanted to go from third to first?

Kalina   I do.

ZeeBoy   Prove it.

Kalina   I know what you're trying to do.

ZeeBoy   Fine. Wait another four years.

Kalina   I'll be well old!

Beat.

Apparently I have a sporting gift. Shame not to use it. Okay! I'm in!

Beat.

Oh no, I'm not. The race will be over by now.

ZeeBoy   Turn round.

Kalina *turns round and sees that everyone is frozen.*

Kalina   How did . . . What did . . . ?

ZeeBoy   Still got some powers. Emergency only.

Kalina   Wish me luck. Oh, you're not going to give me some kind of powers so I can win?

ZeeBoy   Nah, I think we've got enough superhero wannabes, don't you think?

Kalina *joins the race. Everyone unfreezes.*

Referee   On your marks, get set, go!

The whistle blows. The race takes place in slow motion. **Gary B** *is way ahead,* **Kalina** *is in third place. Soon everyone starts to race ahead of* **Kalina***, but suddenly she finds the strength and charges ahead. Everyone's jaw drops.* **Gary B** *and* **Kalina** *are head to head, either could win.* **Gary B** *waves goodbye at* **Kalina** *which winds her up and she finds the strength to pass* **Gary B** *and win the race.*

Reporter   We have a female Academy Champion. Kalina from Bulgaria is our Sports Superhero!

Scoreboard Student *flashes card at audience. It reads 'Cheer'.*

Kalina *runs over to where* **ZeeBoy** *was.*

Kalina   ZeeBoy, I . . .

ZeeBoy *is not there.*

Music: celebration.

Everyone is dancing and celebrating.

Kalina (*looking up at the sky*)   Thanks ZeeBoy, wherever you are.

ZeeBoy *appears from behind, eating a Subway sandwich.*

ZeeBoy   Just having a Subway sandwich actually. Meatballs . . . nice.

Kalina   I did it! I did it! Thank you for . . . well, you know. Being there for me.

ZeeBoy   You're missing the celebrations.

Kalina   What about you?

ZeeBoy   Might catch a film.

Kalina   Right, well, I better go.

They walk off in separate directions, then stop.

What film you watching?

ZeeBoy   *Batman 2*, maybe. Went to school with his kids.

Kalina   ZeeBoy, what's green and smells?

ZeeBoy   Don't know?

Kalina   Hulk's farts.

ZeeBoy   I don't think they smell that bad.

Kalina   It was a joke.

ZeeBoy   Just, he's a friend of my uncle's, and he's always had a weight problem and probably can't control his . . .

Kalina   It really was just a joke.

Beat.

I could join you? I've got Orange two-for-one.

ZeeBoy   I'd like that.

They walk offstage talking.

Kalina   I love a good sequel.

ZeeBoy   I don't. The problem with sequels is . . .

Beat.

Fan One *runs onstage. She stands staring at the audience.*

Fan One   Why can't Cinderella play soccer?

Scoreboard Student *flashes card at audience. It reads 'I don't know'.*

Everyone runs onstage and shouts 'I don't know'.

Fan Two (*shouts*)   Because she's always running away from the ball!

Fan One *chases* **Fan Two** *offstage.*

Music: classical.

Olympic Hero Four (*offstage*)   Change the track!

Classical music fuses with a hip-hop beat.

Olympic Hero Four (*enters, rapping*)   Let's liven this up!

Everyone enters as a grand sports dance finale takes place.

Hear me now! The Olympic Games are ancient, from 776 BC to 2012 AD. Twenty-six sports to drive you crazy. For every boy, girl there's a sport that will amaze you.

Archery, Athletics, Badminton, Basketball, Boxing, Canoeing, Cycling, Diving, Equestrian, Field Hockey, Fencing, Football, Gymnastics, Handball, Judo, Modern Pentathlon, Rowing.

Crowd! You still with me?!

Scoreboard Student *flashes card at audience. It reads 'Whoop and cheer'.*

Sailing, Shooting, Swimming, Synchronised Swimming, Table Tennis, Taekwondo, Tennis, Triathlon, Volleyball, Water Polo, Weightlifting and Wrestling. The end!

Blackout.

So You Think You're a Superhero?

Notes on rehearsal and staging, drawn from a workshop with the writer held at the National Theatre, November 2011

How the Play Came to be Written

The play came from Paven's love of superheroes and comic books, in particular how they deal with very human stories, often about what it's like to grow up. She had written a play for Hampstead Theatre's Heat&Light Young Company about superheroes in a school, and around the same time was researching sports academies, so it seemed an interesting fit to put the idea in that environment, since sports academies are places where dreams are made and shattered, and there is huge pressure from a very young age. Very often youth theatre focuses on the serious and intense, so Paven wanted to write something that offered the opportunity for great visual stuff to happen on stage with fun, crazy characters.

Starting Out

Before you start your work on the play itself, draw up a list of references that the play makes you think of. These can be from any medium (film, music, television), but it's useful to find things that really speak to you. These are some references from the workshop:

The Amazing Adventures of Cavalier and Clay • *Batman* in the 1960s • Ben 10 • Comic strips • *Despicable Me* • *Doctor Who* • *The Incredibles* • *Kick Ass* • Pop art (Lichtenstein) • *Scott Pilgrim vs the World* • *Spy High* • *Spy Kids* • *Superman* • Video games

In particular, *Scott Pilgrim* seemed a useful reference because of its bold colours, clever visuals and graphics, and because it's a story of someone overcoming obstacles they think are insuperable, just like many of the characters in the play.

It might also be a good idea to throw together a really rough staging of the whole play, rather than sitting round reading it. This will give you a much more immediate and dynamic sense of the play's structure, rhythm, shape and size, and also starts off a rehearsal period allowing everyone to be bad – this can take off the pressure and free everyone up.

The production offers an opportunity to be fast-paced, cartoony, colourful and heightened. However, be careful to define moments of shift and change, making sure that the pace isn't relentless and still reveals the more human moments. There's a risk that characters' stories become swamped by action. The key thing is to tell the story as clearly as possible. Make sure that the set pieces move the story forward and don't just exist for their own sake. Each set piece has a very specific part of the story to tell and you need to make sure that your first priority is to communicate that clearly.

Characters

ZEEBOY   Comes from Planet Zola, where he's effectively a normal boy because everyone has special powers. He's being pursued because the government are recruiting for war. He's been to Earth before when he saved people in Australia, but he's never been to this place. His powers incude being able to make people freeze or fly, and often he uses his watch to make this happen. His watch is also his link to home, so it's very important – find a way of making its power and the effect it has clear. He's made mostly of metal and has a twenty-four-hour hour battery. He has to be careful about using his powers because, as we all know, with great power comes great responsibility.

INTERNATIONAL STUDENTS   They're grateful for the opportunity they've been given. Their nationalities are up for grabs – find something that makes sense and suits your group. Kalina always comes in third place. She's ballsy and can stand up for herself and others. While she must have a fair degree of talent, she's not a favourite at the academy and everyone is surprised when she wins. Marvel is geeky, smart and people don't believe in him. He's only there because of his sister, so he's in the wrong world and has something to prove. Beryl is a boxer who won't hit people who are weaker than herself. Crush has an ego but also a softer side. He doesn't carry the baggage of the other characters – nothing gets him down.

THE MEDIA The Teen TV Reporter is depressed and thinks his task is unachievable. What is his relationship to Mindy? Does she actually want to go on a date with him, or is she just hurrying him up? How does the double act between Lippy Lilly and Glam Greg work? How can you show that the media team are disorganised and technically rather useless? The important part of their narrative arc is that they don't really like each other, and this comes to a climax – make sure they've got a journey to go on.

GARY B AND THE FANTASTIC FOUR Gary wants attention and attempts ridiculous things to get it (like standing on his head). He's got an anger problem. He has been training since he was four, and he's the student to look out for, so there's a lot of expectation. He could be a leader but he's not suited to teamwork and probably struggles at the Academy as a result. There's a conflict between his physical and emotional growth – how can you stay a big fish if you can no longer win?

NEMESES They're from Planet Zola and wear Superhero costumes. What is their status and relationship to each other?

PARALYMPICS STUDENTS Paven wanted to include some characters who are paralympians, partly to celebrate the Paralympics, but also because there is an opportunity to show a moment of incredible skill. In the script, two of the characters are written as being in wheelchairs, but the specifics of the disability are up for grabs. Spend time exploring disabilities to find out how they affect athletic events, use YouTube to enthuse the group about the Paralympics, and find a disability that suits your group and your production.

All of the groups in the play include characters who feel like outsiders, are singled out for being different, have lost their identity, and are trying to achieve something they fear may be beyond them. This is the basis for the main narrative arcs of the play – ZeeBoy: from a superhero to a normal boy; Kalina: from third to first place; Marvel: from an overlooked loner to Bling Boy; Gary B: from champion to low status.

Exercises

GAME I

Stand in a circle. A member of the group walks towards another member across the circle, being very clear who they are walking towards. This second member walks towards another, and so on, until everyone has crossed the circle, and the final member walks towards the first member. This creates a sequence which you repeat until you feel comfortable remembering it – you always walk towards the same person.

Now a second sequence is added by a member of the group bouncing a tennis ball to another member. As before, this second member bounces the ball to another person, and so on, until everyone has crossed the circle, and the final member bounces the ball to the first member. Once everyone is comfortable that they've mastered the two sequences (you only have to remember who you walk/throw to and who walks/throws to you), try and set both sequences off at the same time.

You can add more sequences using people's names (the first member says someone's name, who says someone else's name, and so on) or adding more balls or beanbags. If you build up your skill playing this game it can be very useful to find the rhythm of the group and to encourage picking up tight cues. It's crucial to listen to what comes before and after your line, and to respond accordingly. The game is deliberately complicated and difficult but gradually the group will get better at it.

GAME 2

Stand in a circle. A member of the group clicks their fingers
and indicates they're passing the energy of the click to another
member of the group. This member then passes the click to
someone else, and so on. Keep passing the click, and once
people are comfortable, change the quality of the click (fast,
slow, heavy, bouncy, etc.), so that it is given and received in
different styles. Once you've built this up you can then start
moving around so it's more difficult to follow the click, and
the group are forced to be even more aware of where the
click is at any one time. This also helps to find rhythms within
a group and encourages being playful with the delivery of
lines – just as you can change the quality of the click, so can
you change the quality of a line.

TRAINING

Every rehearsal could start with training exercises that you
build up over the rehearsal period. This will help with your
research into athletics, will build up the physical fitness and
dexterity needed to make the play really fly, helps start the
rehearsal with a focus, creates material you can use in the
production, and could be used as a way of handling entrances
and exits, and the general stage state. You could keep everyone
onstage at all times, and keep them training throughout when
they're not directly involved in a scene. When athletes are
training, every part of their technique is broken down into
tiny components that are practised rigorously and then put
back together. The journey of Olympics training is a lot like
the journey of putting on a play.

Moments in the Play

THE OPENING

The play moves very quickly – in the first two pages we have
a scene on an alien planet, a chase, a magical escape, an
Academy sports race, a new mystery runner winning the race,
and a swarming media crew – so make sure you've clearly

communicated each beat of the story. We need to see the superhero moment when ZeeBoy jumps into the air and vanishes, leaving the others behind and travelling to another world – make this feel as magical as possible. You could play around with the scene being performed with all the lights on, but with the General and the Queen playing the idea that they can't see. Or you could explore fun stories between them fumbling around in the dark. Is there a way of telling the story of ZeeBoy's journey from Planet Zola to Earth through the actors – perhaps doubling characters so that the guards chasing ZeeBoy turn into the runners? What's the most effective way of making the running stay alive and interesting to watch?

GARY B'S GANG

It's crucial that the gang is made up of individuals and that there's a sense of status between them. How can you make this work? Is there a style of movement that can express this fluidly? How can you establish the two worlds of the Academy pupils and the Olympic heroes economically? Could Gary B's gang become the Olympic heroes after being zapped by ZeeBoy's watch? How can you make the most of the moment the watch freezes them?

THE MEDIA

Again, make sure you've understood the dynamic and status of individuals in the group. What are the different ways you could represent the fact that things are being filmed – live feed, pre-recorded, a frame/box that an actor holds? The key thing is the story of the scene, the Reporter being the centre of the action, and being specific about where the focus of everyone's attention should be, line by line.

AUSTRALIA

How can you establish the two different worlds? One group showed three worlds – ZeeBoy and Marvel in Australia, the media crew filming, and another group watching it live on TV. What's the most exciting way of showing ZeeBoy flying? Spend some time researching how superheroes typically fly and find your own style. How does ZeeBoy carry Marvel? How is the watch used? Make sure that we can understand that ZeeBoy is controlling the superhero moments – there needs to be a clear connection between what he does and what happens.

It's important that Marvel's phone is part of the story. When should he start filming? When do we need to see it? What's the most efficient way of showing this (not necessarily the most accurate or realistic)? How can you keep the atmosphere of Australia alive once the initial surprise has been revealed?

From a workshop led by Lu Kemp,
with notes by Dan Bird

The Ritual

Samir Yazbek

translated by Mark O'Thomas

Characters

in order of appearance:

Joel, *Márcia's boyfriend, nineteen years of age*
Mauro, *Bianca's boyfriend, eighteen years of age*
Celso, *Ana's brother, fifteen years of age*
Ana, *Celso's sister, sixteen years of age*
Bianca, *Mauro's girlfriend, seventeen years of age*
Lia, *eighteen years of age*
Márcia, *Joel's ex-girlfriend, eighteen years of age*

With the exception of Márcia, all the characters in the play attend the same college.

Location

Various places.

Action

During the course of a month.

Scene One

A city square. **Joel** *is sitting with his mobile in his hand. He appears unsure whether or not to make a call. Enter* **Mauro**.

Mauro   Well, then?

Joel (*looking at his phone*)   Well, what?

Mauro   What are you doing here alone?

Joel   Thinking.

Mauro   Are you all right?

Joel   I am. Are you?

Mauro   Yep.

Joel   And how's it going with Bianca?

Mauro   She's doing fine.

Joel   What about you guys?

Mauro   What of it?

Joel   Are you doing all right?

Mauro   I think so.

Joel   You 'think'?

Mauro   What are you getting at, Joel?

Joel   It's just that it doesn't look to me like things are going so well for you right now.

Mauro   For me?

Joel   Yeah.

Mauro   Why's that?

Joel   You don't seem so happy with Bianca.

Mauro   But I am.

Joel   Are you sure?

Mauro   I'm not getting you.

Joel   I think that you trust Bianca too much.

Mauro   Are you trying to say you know something that I don't?

Joel   I just have this feeling about it.

Celso *and* **Ana** *enter.* **Ana** *looks as if she has been crying.*

Joel   Hi, Celsinho?

Celso   Hi.

Joel   I heard you joined the college drama club.

Celso   News travels fast.

Joel   Congrats.

Celso   Cheers.

Joel   It'll be good – help get you out of yourself a bit. (*Referring to* **Ana**.) Did something happen to your sister?

Celso   She had a fight with her boyfriend.

Ana   Celso!

Celso   Calm down.

Ana   I've told you not to go talking my business to people.

She exits.

Celso   The big bust-up continues.

Mauro   What did he do?

Celso   Cheated on her.

Mauro   Whoa.

Celso   She's gutted.

Joel   I can imagine just how she feels.

He paces up and down, agitated.

Mauro   What's up with you?

Joel   Let's meet up at my place tomorrow.

Mauro   What for?

Joel   I've got an idea.

Mauro   What kind of idea?

Joel   Something to do with all this love stuff. But I can only tell you about it tomorrow. You coming, Mauro?

Mauro   When have I never been interested in your 'ideas', mate?

Joel   What about you, Celsinho?

Celso   Do I really need to be there?

Joel   Of course you do.

Celso   I don't even have a girlfriend!

Joel   You don't know what I've got planned yet!

Celso   All right, then, I'm in.

Joel   And bring your sister, too. I think it'll be good for her.

Celso   I'll try.

Joel (*to* **Mauro**)   Can you ask Lia?

Mauro   Lia?

Joel   She'd be great for what I've got in mind. Right, then, let's get going. I've got some planning to do for our meeting.

He exits. **Mauro** *and* **Celso**, *unnerved by* **Joel**, *exit, too.*

Scene Two

Mauro's *bedroom. He lies on the floor, looks up at the ceiling.* **Bianca** *sits in a chair.*

Bianca   What happened, Mauro?

Mauro   Why?

Bianca   You're acting strange.

Mauro   It's just foolishness, Bianca.

Bianca   Do you want to tell me something?

Mauro   It's all right. (*Silence.*) Did you ever cheat on me?

Bianca   What a question!

Mauro   Answer me.

Bianca   Of course not.

Mauro   Are you sure?

Bianca   Why are you asking me this now?

Mauro   I told you it was foolishness.

Bianca   Did someone say something to you?

Mauro   It's just what I'm thinking, that's all.

Bianca (*leaving*)   I think I'd better go.

Mauro   Where are you off to?

Bianca   Home.

Mauro (*holding her*)   Wait.

Bianca   What is it?

Mauro   Stay a bit longer.

Holds her tighter. She breaks free and shoots him a look.

Are you pissed off with me?

Bianca   We'll see each other tomorrow afternoon.

Mauro   Tomorrow afternoon?

Bianca   Yeah, what's up now?

Mauro   I can't make it tomorrow.

Bianca   Why not?

Mauro   There's some kind of meeting at Joel's place.

Bianca   What, homework stuff?

Mauro   No, something else.

Bianca   Haven't you all stopped with all that meeting business?

Mauro   No, this time it's different.

Bianca   What's different about it?

Mauro   He wants to talk to us.

Bianca   Who 'us'?

Mauro   Our friends.

Bianca   What about?

Mauro   He didn't say.

Bianca   And it can only be tomorrow?

Mauro   That's when he called it.

Bianca   It's Saturday tomorrow, Mauro!

Mauro   Please, Bianca.

Bianca (*leaving*) You know what's best.

Mauro   Come back here.

She exits.

Scene Three

On a road. **Lia** *is passing by.* **Mauro** *talks to her.*

Mauro   Hi, Lia.

Lia   Hi, Mauro. How are you?

Mauro   Good. You?

Lia   Fine.

Mauro   Joel asked me to give you a message.

Lia   Message?

Mauro   He wants you to go to his place tomorrow afternoon.

Lia   Me?

Mauro   Not just you.

Lia   What for?

Mauro   He won't say. But it looks like it might be fun.

Lia   Oh, that Joel.

Mauro   You gonna go?

Lia   I suppose so.

Silence.

Mauro   And what about us?

Lia   What about us?

Mauro   You said you liked me one time.

Lia   God, that was ages ago!

Mauro   Don't you like me any more?

Lia   It's not that, Mauro. It's just that my life's changed so much over the past few years.

Mauro   How's that?

Lia   I'm not looking for a steady thing any more.

Mauro   Why?

Lia   I've been hurt too much by boys. Besides, aren't you still going out with Bianca?

Mauro   I am . . . But it's not going so well.

Lia   Why?

Mauro   I don't know.

Lia   Since when did all this happen?

Mauro   I don't know.

Lia   You don't know anything about it?

Mauro   That's about right.

Lia (*exiting*)   When you've really finished with her, we might talk, yeah?

Mauro   Really?

Lia   I've gotta go now.

Mauro   OK.

Lia   See you tomorrow – at Joel's place.

Mauro   See you tomorrow, Lia.

Lia *continues on her way.* **Mauro** *exits the opposite way.*

Scene Four

In **Joel**'s *garage.* **Joel**, **Mauro**, **Celso**, **Ana** *and* **Lia** *are all there. Some are seated in chairs while others stand or sit on the floor.*

Joel   OK then, well, you must all be wondering why I called you over here. I've come to realise that you are all walking around feeling bad because of this thing we all know as 'love'. I don't think it should be like this. Having analysed what it really means to be human, I can now see that the best thing is to never get involved with anyone in the first place. Go out with them for a bit and then drop them pronto. I want to think about this stuff and I want us to have somewhere we can all meet up and tell each other our own stories which will help lift our spirits. Our stories – things that no one else knows. If we can all recognise that feeling bad is kind of inevitable, then from now on we can make sure that it's us who make others end up feeling that way. We don't need to feel bad again, get it? So, Mauro, what do you think about it?

Mauro   Interesting.

Joel   Can I count you in?

Mauro   Course you can.

Joel   What about you, Celsinho?

Celso   Well . . . You know that I don't really get these things.

Mauro   Come on, mate.

Joel   You've got to man-up. And this is the perfect place for you to start.

Celso   Fair enough, I'm in.

Joel   Cool. What about you, Lia?

Lia   No need to ask.

Joel   There's a lot we can all learn from you. (*To* **Ana**.) What about you, babe?

Ana *starts to sob.*

Joel   What's up? What you crying for?

Ana   Can I go?

Joel   Already?

Celso (*to* **Ana**)   Stay a bit longer, Ana.

Ana   I can't stand it!

She exits.

Joel   What's going on, mate?

Celso   I don't know what's going on with her.

Mauro   Poor thing.

Joel   Poor nothing! She's responsible for her own actions. This is exactly what I wanted to talk to you all about. Let's use this to make something quite clear. Those who are in, are in. But if you're in, you can't run away. Right?

Mauro   You can't leave?

Joel   If we really want to lift our spirits, we need to be more radical.

Mauro   'Radical'?

Joel   You've got to trust me. If you don't, then you might as well leave now. (*To* **Mauro**.) Do you want to leave, Mauro?

Mauro   No way.

Joel   What about you, Lia?

Lia   Of course I don't.

Joel   Celsinho?

Celso   Nor me.

Joel   Great. What's really important in all this is that you understand that we are making a kind of pact against feeling low. By the force of our spirits!

Lia   So what are we going to call these meetings?

Joel   Do we need to give them a name?

Lia   I think so. Can I suggest something?

Joel   Go for it.

Lia   A 'ritual'. Let's make a kind of ritual that will help us all lift up our spirits!

Joel   Great! Let's make our ritual, then!

He turns to face the centre of the garage and opens up his arms, suggesting to the others that they do the same.

Now, repeat after me.

They all repeat each phrase separately.

I / swear / to be faithful / to the ritual / for the good of our group / and my own being.

He gets closer to them still.

By the force of our spirits!

All   By the force of our spirits!

They all exit except for **Joel** *and* **Mauro**.

Mauro   Can I have a word?

Joel   What's up?

Mauro   I'm worried about Bianca.

Joel   Why?

Mauro   Don't you think she could come along to these meetings?

Joel   Looks like you still don't really get it. We need to feel really free here. You don't know what might happen and you want to start bringing your girlfriend?

Mauro   It's just that she's pissed off with me.

Joel   If you're that bothered about her, then you're not ready for this.

Mauro   You think so?

Joel   Don't you think you're a bit too young to get involved in this kind of thing?

Mauro   Not at all.

Joel   With so many girls out there, you're just wasting your time.

Mauro   Maybe you're right.

Joel   Of course I am.

Mauro   And what about you?

Joel   What about me?

Mauro   Don't you like Márcia any more?

Joel   That was all over a long time ago. Right, I've got stuff to be getting on with.

Mauro   Fair enough, mate. See you later.

Joel   Later.

Mauro *exits.*

Scene Five

Ana*'s bedroom.* **Celso** *is sitting next to her.*

Celso   Why did you have to go and leave like that?

Ana   He's totally lost it.

Celso   What do you mean?

Ana   All that talk – it's craziness.

Celso   I don't think so.

Ana   I'm not going to waste my time going to those meetings.

Celso   It would do you good to take part in the ritual.

Ana   Good?!

Celso   I'm worried about you.

Ana   Why?

Celso   You've been sobbing your heart out for a month now.

Ana   Do you think it's easy going through what I've been through?

Celso   That guy doesn't want anything to do with you any more. Get over it.

Ana   Don't start, please.

Celso   I just want to help.

Ana   Well, you're not helping. (*Silence.*) You don't know what he promised me.

Celso   You mean no one should ever get dumped?

Ana   Not cheated on, no!

Celso   What's the point going on about this now, Ana?

Ana   Of course there's a point! He's got to learn that he can't go around treating people like that.

Celso   And that's what you're going to teach him, is it?

Ana   He'll see what I'm capable of.

Celso   Ana . . .

Ana   Everyone'll see.

Celso   You're scaring me.

Ana   Good, that's what I want.

She exits.

Scene Six

On a street. **Joel** *and* **Lia** *are in conversation.*

Joel   Thanks for coming over the other day.

Lia   You know I'm crazy about you.

Joel   Likewise, babe.

Lia   A lot of people won't even give me the time of day.

Joel   Hypocrites! They're full of self-deception! You can help people really start to live their lives.

Lia   I'm only starting out myself!

Joel   But you've got your feet on the ground.

Lia   Yeah, maybe.

Joel   I just want you to be yourself at our meetings.

Lia   Cool. (*Silence.*) So, what about you and Márcia?

Joel   What do you mean?

Lia   Have you forgotten, then?

Joel   Completely.

Lia   Good for you.

Joel   The truth is that she doesn't deserve anything I ever did for her.

Silence.

Lia   Right, well, I better go now.

Joel   Sure.

Lia   We'll chat later.

Joel   Cool.

Lia   Later, Joel.

Joel   See you, Lia.

She exits. **Joel**, *a little stunned, takes out his mobile phone, tries to make a call, but doesn't manage to talk to anyone.*

Scene Seven

On another street. **Mauro** *and* **Bianca** *are talking.*

Mauro   No way, Bianca.

Bianca   Why not?

Mauro   It's not right – you getting involved in these things.

Bianca   Am I not your girlfriend?

Mauro   That's got nothing to do with us going along together.

Bianca   So what do you actually do there?

Mauro   Talk.

Bianca   You don't want to tell me – is that it?

Mauro   I can't, that's all.

Bianca   Why not?

Mauro   We made a pact.

Bianca   A *pact*?

Mauro   It's a secret.

Bianca   And you want me to sit back and accept all this?

Mauro   You could at least have a go.

Bianca   I really don't know you any more.

Mauro   Don't make it so complicated, for God's sake.

Bianca   Fine, Mauro. I'll stop making it so complicated for you.

She exits.

Scene Eight

Joel's *garage. The place is set up for a meeting of the ritual. Four chairs are laid out in a semicircle facing the audience.* **Joel**, **Mauro**, **Celso** *and* **Lia** *are seated with their eyes closed. After a while,* **Joel** *opens his eyes and gets to his feet.. He opens out his arms and they all rise, moving towards him.* **Lia** *starts to move around the space in an exotic kind of dance. The others follow suit. After some time, they take their seats once more.*

Joel   You start, Lia.

Lia   Me?

Joel   It's easier for you.

Lia   You want me to tell . . .

Joel   Anything that shows the true force of your spirit.

Lia   OK, I'll try. And you tell me if it's OK, right?

Joel   Sure.

Lia   Last week, I met this guy in a café near to where I live.
He was sitting there eating this sandwich on the other side of
the counter, facing me. To be honest, I had no interest in the
guy at all but I decided to have a bit of a laugh. So I wrote
down my phone number on a napkin and got the waiter to
take it over to him. Anyways, after that he starts to call me
every day. To begin with, we'd chat about so many different
things. But then it started to heat up a bit. I asked him for his
mobile number and told him I'd call him back that day. But
we arranged it for me to call him when he was laying down in
bed, ready to go to sleep like.

Joel   You broke the mould, Lia.

Lia   You like it?

Joel   Loving it.

Lia   So let me get on with it, then! Anyways, he did exactly
as I asked. At the time we'd arranged, I rang him up and he
was there, freshly bathed, under the sheets.

Mauro   You really went to town on this one, didn't you?

Lia   You ain't heard nothing yet. When I asked him where
his hands were, he said under the sheets. That's when I
started coming out with all this crazy shit – the kind of stuff
that would make even the phone-sex girls go red in the face.

Joel   What happened then?

Lia   The next day he rang me up forty-eight times, and I
conveniently forgot to pick up my phone. Then he goes and
sends me twenty-odd texts which I did not reply to and leaves
me ten voicemail messages which almost made me piss myself
laughing!

Mauro   What did he say?

Lia   I can't repeat it. (*Silence.*) I hope you liked my story.

Joel (*getting to his feet to clap*) Bravo! What an amazing spirit
you have! I always knew we had much to learn from you, but

I never thought it would be this much. (*He sits back down. To* **Mauro**.) Your turn.

Mauro   Well . . . I don't know if this is really to do with what I've done or what I'm about to do.

Joel   What you're about to do?

Mauro   I'm gonna dump Bianca.

Joel   Really?

Mauro   There doesn't seem to be much point in carrying on with it.

Joel   What's brought you to that decision?

Mauro   I think I've been kidding myself that Bianca is the big love of my life when all it's really been is just some teenage crush.

Joel   That's exactly when the spirit starts to weaken.

Mauro   I know.

Joel   But you're taking action at the right time. Well done, Mauro! You will start to feel better soon.

Mauro   That's what I'm hoping for.

Joel   Your turn now, Celsinho.

Celso   I don't have anyone to talk about.

Joel   Think carefully.

Celso   I don't know anyway.

Joel   And you can't be bothered?

Celso   No.

Joel   Don't lie.

Celso   I'm not.

Joel   Don't lie to me.

Celso   I just don't like to talk about these things.

Joel There can be no secrets here.

Celso Don't tell my sister that, then.

Joel We won't.

Celso It's just that my story's just like hers.

Joel Something bad happened at home?

Celso I like this girl but she just makes me feel bad about myself.

Joel And you allow yourself to feel that way?

Celso I can't help it.

Joel (*to* **Mauro** *and* **Lia**) You see what a weak person we have here? Like a worm that anyone might stamp on. He is something that we must never accept. (*To* **Celso**.) Listen, Celsinho, here's a little detour I want you to take before we meet again. You've got to start to change the way you are with this girl.

Celso Change how?

Joel That's something only you can discover for yourself. But you can't carry on feeling like this. Next time you come here you've got to tell us how you got over it, OK?

Celso OK.

Joel Great. I think that's enough for today. Does anyone want to say anything?

All No!

Joel Right, then, I've got a present for you all.

He takes out four differently coloured bracelets. He gives one to each of them and puts one on his own wrist.

These bracelets come from America. A friend brought them back for me. Let's use them to symbolise the unity of our group. As long as we're together, no one can ever remove them from our wrists, OK?

All   OK.

Joel   Cool. Now let's do the closing ceremony. Do you remember how it goes?

Once again, he turns to the centre of the garage and stretches out his arms, indicating to the others that they do the same.

By the force of our spirits!

All   By the force of our spirits!

Everyone exits except for **Joel**. *He takes out his mobile and dials a number. As no one picks up, he leaves a message.*

Joel   Hello, Márcia? You not taking my calls? I really need to talk to you. Please, Márcia. Can you call me back?

He rings off.

Scene Nine

Outside a cinema. **Bianca** *waits. Enter* **Mauro**, *slowly.*

Bianca   Take your time, Mauro.

Mauro   Eh?

Bianca   You're half an hour late!

Mauro   Sorry.

Bianca   I've missed the film now.

Mauro   Isn't there anything else on?

Bianca   I wanted to see that one!

Mauro   We can come back tomorrow.

Bianca   Are you taking the piss?

Mauro   Course not. (*Silence.*) Bianca, look, I think we need to take a break from it for a while.

Bianca   What?!

Mauro   We just don't get each other any more.

Bianca   What are you talking about?

Mauro   You know full well what I'm talking about.

Bianca   Up until yesterday it was all fine and now today you come with this bombshell.

Mauro   I just think we fight all the time, that's all.

Bianca   'Fight'?

Mauro   I don't mean 'fight'.

Bianca   What do you mean, then?

Mauro   I don't trust you any more. You're not the same with me.

Bianca   Me?

Mauro   Fair enough. It's not your fault. It's what I feel. Or maybe what I've stopped feeling. Do you really think it's worth us carrying on as we are?

Bianca   Have you gone mad? What's happened to you? It's like you've become someone else! This is all Joel's doing. That so-called friend of yours.

Mauro   Don't talk about him like that.

Bianca   What did you all talk about at his place?

Mauro   Nothing much.

Bianca   Tell me, then.

Mauro   What do you want to know for?

Bianca   What's that on your wrist?

Mauro (*dodging the issue*)   Nothing.

Bianca   Are you trying to say that your friend is more important to you than us?

Mauro   It's not that.

Bianca   Don't worry, I'll find out for myself.

Mauro   Whatever, Bianca. Just leave me out of it.

He exits.

Scene Ten

A square. **Lia** *is waiting.* **Bianca** *enters.*

Bianca   I'm sorry for asking you to come over like this, Lia.

Lia   No worries.

Bianca   It's just I'm so worried about what's happening.

Lia   I get it.

Bianca   Everyone's going on about it and I just don't know what to think any more.

Lia   Just don't tell anyone you were talking to me, right?

Bianca   What do you do at these meetings? Is it true that it's some kind of ritual?

Lia   It's a bit like a ritual. But it's just chatting really. At least that's how it all started.

Bianca   But what do you all chat about, then?

Lia   The idea is to strengthen our spirits.

Bianca   How does that work?

Lia   You have to be there really.

Bianca   Can you try to explain it to me?

Lia   The idea is that talking to each other allows us to have them strengthened, especially talking about our love lives. So by the end, we learn how never to rely on anyone else.

Bianca   Never rely on anyone?

Lia   Yeah.

Bianca   I can't believe what I'm hearing. Whose idea was this?

Lia   Joel.

Bianca   It had to be him.

Lia   It's not a bad thing, Bianca.

Bianca   Not for you, maybe, because you're on your own. Not for Celso who's still a baby really. Not for Joel who must be getting something out of it all. But for me, who has just lost my boyfriend, it might well be.

Bianca *exits.*

Scene Eleven

Márcia *waits in a bar. Enter* **Bianca**. *They hug each other warmly.*

Bianca   Long time! I thought I'd never see you again!

Márcia   You never managed to get over here.

Bianca   You live so far!

Márcia   You reckon?

Bianca   It took me more than an hour to get here!

Márcia   I needed to get away from it all.

Bianca   How's the new college going?

Márcia   It's all right – I'm getting on with it.

Silence.

Bianca   Look, Márcia, I really need your help right now.

Márcia   What's up?

Bianca   It's Joel.

Márcia *winces.*

Bianca   I know you don't want to talk about him but there's so much stuff going down and you're the only one who can help me.

Márcia   What's happened?

Bianca   Joel's been organising these meeting kind of things that they all call 'the ritual' but it's not really a ritual at all. It's just a bunch of people talking about things and trying to raise each other's spirits.

Márcia   Raising their spirits?

Bianca   That's what I know.

Márcia   Who told you that?

Bianca   Lia. The group's still quite small. Apart from Lia and Joel, there's Mauro and Celso. Ana went once but didn't go back. But there's a lot of people now wanting to join. The problem is that Joel's encouraging them all not to have any real relationships any more.

Márcia   How?

Bianca   By breaking up with people. Mauro's already dumped me.

Márcia   No way.

Bianca   Way. And I know it's because of these meetings.

Márcia   Has Joel totally lost it?

Bianca   It looks like it.

Márcia   He wouldn't stop calling me and now this.

Bianca   What do you think he really wants?

Márcia   When we first ended it, he started to change. At times he started to act in ways that made me really afraid. He'd started chatting nonsense . . . He thought that I'd fallen for someone else. But it wasn't true. I just stopped being in love with him; nothing else. Once he told me he would do something really bad.

Bianca   Really bad like what?

Márcia   He said he had a bad childhood and he never wanted to suffer like that again.

Bianca   But what does that mean?

Márcia   I don't know. All I know is that he tried to kill me once.

Bianca   Are you serious?

Márcia   Why do you think I'd move to my uncle's place? I ran away. Ran away before something really bad happened. I haven't told a soul about it. I was scared of being in that relationship with him. So the best thing was for me to get right away from him. Even so, not a day goes by without me worrying that he might find me here. But now it looks like we've got other things to worry about.

Bianca   This is what I thought.

Márcia   'Raising spirits'? The only spirit Joel's worried about is his own.

Bianca   What do you think we should do now?

Márcia   Please don't tell anyone you came here and found me. You've got to warn Mauro.

Bianca   He won't believe a word of it.

Márcia   You've got to try.

Bianca   This is a nightmare.

Márcia   That's exactly what my life has become. You've got to try to convince Mauro to leave that group. Tip off the college if you need to. There's nothing Joel isn't capable of.

They hug each other.

Scene Twelve

A square. **Joel**, **Mauro** *and* **Lia** *are talking.*

Joel   All done, then?

Mauro   It was all for the best really.

Lia   You're free now.

Mauro   True.

Lia   I hope you get a spicy story out of it for our next session.

Mauro   Does it have to be spicy?

Lia   Didn't you get turned on by my story? Well, I have needs too!

Mauro   Let's see what I can do.

Enter **Celso** *looking forlorn.*

Celso   Have you heard?

Joel   Heard what?

Celso   Ana's killed herself.

Lia   What?!

Mauro   Don't talk like that.

Lia   How?

Celso   She locked herself in the bathroom.

Lia   Oh my God! Why?

Joel   Don't you know?

Lia   How would I know?

Joel   Think about it.

Celso   Because of that guy that dumped her.

Joel   What else could it be?

Celso   She left a note saying that she loved us all but she couldn't carry on living like that.

Joel   You see? What did I say?

Mauro   What?

Joel   Ana topped herself because she was the weakest one of all of us. Can you now see what's happening? If it weren't for our meetings, we'd all end up like her.

Lia   Heaven forbid.

Joel   Not you, Lia. You're more secure than any of us. (*To* **Celso**.) Sorry, mate. We can't allow life to do to us what it did to your sister.

Joel *exits.*

Celso   Do you think I have to keep coming to the ritual?

Lia   Why stop, Celsinho?

Celso   I'm not really into it.

Lia   You need to protect your spirit now more than ever.

Mauro   Yeah, now's not the time to leave the ritual.

Celso   All right . . . I've got to go. I can't leave my mum on her own.

Lia   Be safe, Celsinho.

Celso *exits.*

Lia   Poor girl.

Mauro   That's enough of that.

Lia   That's what happens when you get involved with people.

Mauro (*approaching her, seductively*)   Lia . . . Now that I'm officially single . . . What do you think if we . . . ?

Lia There's a time and a place, Mauro.

Mauro Eh?

Lia Ana just died!

Mauro (*trying to kiss her*) That's what I mean – we don't have much time on this Earth.

Lia (*breaking away from him*) Stop it!

Mauro What's wrong?

Lia What if you get back with Bianca?

Mauro I'm not getting back with no one.

Lia That's what they all say.

Mauro 'They' who?

Lia Men!

Mauro (*moving on her again*) Come on, Lia, you promised me.

Lia (*breaking away from him completely*) I said I'd think about it. But for now we need to focus on the ritual. If not, we'll end up together.

Mauro But this is what I want.

She exits followed by **Mauro**.

Scene Thirteen

Joel's *bedroom. He takes out his mobile and dials a number. As no one picks up, he leaves a message.*

Joel Hello, Márcia? It's me again. Are you sure that you can't pick up? You're going to get a shock. It's better that you talk to me.

He rings off. After a while, he calls another number.

Hi, man. (*Silence.*) Oh, come on! (*Silence.*) You know that thing I asked you to do. (*Silence.*) I'm going to need it done today.

(*Silence.*) Look, I can't wait any longer. (*Silence.*) Are you really sure you can get it for me? (*Silence.*) If not, I'd better find someone else. (*Silence.*) Fair enough. (*Silence.*) I'll wait to hear from you.

He rings off.

Scene Fourteen

A bar where **Mauro** *sits waiting. Enter* **Bianca**.

Bianca   Hiya.

Mauro   Hi. (*Silence.*) Sit down.

She sits down.

Mauro   What do you want?

Bianca   I wanted to ask you to stop going to Joel's house.

Mauro   You called me here for that?

Bianca   I was with Márcia.

Mauro   Márcia who?

Bianca   Joel's ex.

Mauro   What did you go and see her for?

Bianca   She's a friend of mine!

Mauro (*leaving*)   I better go.

Bianca   Stay, please.

Mauro   What do you want from me?

Bianca   Márcia told me some horrible things about Joel.

Mauro   I'd be surprised if she told you anything else.

Bianca   Did you know he tried to kill her?

Mauro   She said that?

Bianca And worse.

Mauro Worse than trying to kill your girlfriend?

Bianca Joel's a dangerous guy.

Mauro He's a good mate of mine – has been for years.

Bianca She said that he might do something.

Mauro Something like what?

Bianca I don't know.

Mauro Márcia's lost the plot if you ask me.

Bianca (*touching him*) Mauro, please believe me.

Mauro (*pulling away*) Don't touch me.

Bianca Why are you talking like that?

Mauro I don't want anything else to do with you.

Bianca Is that what Joel's done to you?

Mauro He hasn't done anything.

Bianca It's like I don't even know you any more.

Mauro Maybe you're right. I could say the same thing. I know that you cheated on me.

He exits.

Scene Fifteen

Joel's *garage. The same layout as in the previous meeting.* **Joel**, **Mauro** *and* **Lia** *are seated.* **Joel** *gets up and everyone follows him. They all do the same dance as before. At the end, they return to their seats.*

Joel (*to* **Mauro**) Today, you can begin.

Mauro OK . . . Once I ended it with Bianca, I finally did what I wanted to do.

Joel   And what was that?

Mauro   Took my powers of seduction to their ultimate conclusion with a girl. A girl, no. Three girls.

Joel (*clapping*)   Well done!

Mauro   That thing about 'don't do unto others as you would have done unto yourself' or whatever – I put that right out of my head. I played three of them along at the same time and told them exactly what they wanted to hear.

Joel   And what did you get out of doing all that?

Mauro   I bedded all three of them!

Lia   This story's a lot more spicy than mine!

Mauro   But I took it a bit further than that.

Joel   How come?

Mauro   I told each one that they'd been my guinea pig.

Joel   Seems a bit cruel!

Mauro   They were so revolted by themselves when I told them. I can hardly bear to think about it now.

Joel   You didn't need to go so far.

Mauro   Do you think I'm exaggerating?

Joel   We don't need to humiliate people in this way.

Mauro   Wasn't that what Lia did to the guy in the baker's?

Joel   Lia provoked him but she didn't turn the knife. What you did became an act of foolishness. (*To* **Celso**.) Your turn, Celsinho. How's it going with your lady friend?

Celso   A bit better.

Joel   Really?

Celso   I don't feel so bad any more.

Joel   She's stopped making you feel depressed?

Celso I won't let that happen any more.

Joel You need to stop being such a coward and start seducing this girl!

Celso I think she's getting pissed off with me.

Joel That's just a phase.

Celso Maybe.

Joel Ask her out to the pictures.

Celso I don't know how to do that.

Mauro We can help you.

Joel No one's going to help anyone!

Mauro Calm down, Joel!

Joel Don't ask me to be calm at a time like this! It's this guy's maturity that's at stake here. Do you want to be a man or not, Celsinho?

Celso Of course I do.

Joel So start doing what I tell you to do or you'll end up like your sister!

Celso *starts to sob but composes himself for fear of being told off.*

Joel And you, too, Mauro. Be careful with what you're doing.

Mauro What d'you mean?

Joel Dumping Bianca, bedding three girls and then trying to climb on top of Lia. And after Lia? Didn't I make it clear that no one in this group should get involved with anyone else, let alone someone from within the group itself?

Mauro Yeah, you did.

Joel Well, at least you admit it. (*Silence.*) Now, saving the best till last, let's have Lia.

Lia That's a big responsibility.

Joel   You're the only one who's up to it.

Lia   Well, it feels like I've passed some kind of test this week.

Joel   Test?

Lia   I think I came out of it OK.

Joel   Go on.

Lia   Well, imagine the love of your life.

Joel   OK . . .

Lia   Now imagine this guy blanking you completely.

Joel   OK . . .

Lia   And imagine that it's almost sending you round the bend.

Joel   What an imagination she has!

Lia   Well, that same guy found me the other day and started telling me that I was the love of his life.

Joel   This happens a lot.

Lia   Maybe, but my reaction to it doesn't.

Joel   What did you do?

Lia   I told him that I had changed and I wasn't the same any more. That I couldn't be the way I was before not for anything in the world. He didn't believe me but I did myself proud nevertheless.

Joel   We are all proud of you, Lia. What would we all be without your stories? And what would I be? I can see I've still got a lot to learn. I wish I had your strength, Lia, but I just haven't.

Lia   You will.

As on the previous occasions, **Joel** *turns to face the centre of the garage and reaches out his arms suggesting to the others that they follow suit.*

Joel   By the force of our spirits!

All   By the force of our spirits!

They all exit except for **Joel**, *who wanders around looking perturbed. Suddenly* **Ana** *enters.*

Joel   What are you doing here?

Ana   What's wrong?

Joel   You're dead.

Ana   I'm more alive than you.

Joel   I hate your cowardice.

Ana   Cowardice? Don't you think that I needed to have courage to do what I did?

Joel   Killing yourself to get someone to take some notice of you?

Ana   Maybe I was wrong to do it, but I couldn't help the love I felt.

Joel   If you hadn't left the ritual, this would never have happened.

Ana   The ritual's got nothing to do with it – not for you or anyone else. Why are you so ashamed of facing up to your problems?

Joel   I don't have any problems.

Ana   Your problem is thinking you don't have any. Leave those kids alone. Leave my brother out of it. He's about to lose it.

She disappears.

Scene Sixteen

Bianca's *bedroom. She seems distressed. Her mobile rings.* **Márcia** *is calling her from her place.*

Bianca   Hello?

Márcia   Hi!

Bianca   Who is it?

Márcia   Márcia!

Bianca   Hi, Márcia.

Márcia   Did you speak to Mauro?

Bianca   I got nowhere.

Márcia   Talk to him again.

Bianca   What's the point?

Márcia   To stop a tragedy happening.

Bianca   What tragedy?

Márcia   I've heard that Joel's gone and bought himself a gun. And a load of ammunition to go with it.

Bianca   Who told you that?

Márcia   His cousin.

Bianca   Oh my God . . .

Márcia   Something bad could happen any time. I'm going to another city and my cousin's going to go to the police.

Bianca   Police?

Márcia   Yeah.

Bianca   I can't believe it.

Márcia   Joel is going to do something really bad. And he's going to take you all down with him.

Bianca   I'm going to call Mauro.

Márcia   Do it. And be careful.

They ring off. **Márcia** *exits the scene.* **Bianca** *calls* **Mauro,** *who answers on his mobile.*

Mauro   Hello?

Bianca   Mauro?

Mauro   Hi.

Bianca   Mauro, you've got to listen to me. Márcia just called me and told me that Joel's bought a gun. He's getting ready to do something really bad. It might involve you guys! Please, warn everyone. I'm going to warn the college principal.

Mauro   Don't do that.

Bianca   Joel's cousin has gone to the police.

Mauro   What's it got to do with the police?

Bianca   What do you mean?

Mauro   Márcia really hates him, doesn't she?

Bianca   It was his cousin who told her about the gun!

Mauro   I know this cousin.

Bianca   And what's knowing him got to do with it?

Mauro   He's a gangster.

Bianca   That's worse! (*Silence.*) Mauro, do you have no feelings left for me at all?

Mauro   What a question.

Bianca   If you do, then do something.

Mauro   Let me have a think about it.

Bianca   There's no time to mull this over!

Mauro   You're driving me round the bend!

He rings off and exits the scene.

Scene Seventeen

Joel*'s bedroom. He takes out his mobile and dials a number. As no one answers, he leaves a message.*

Joel   Hello, Márcia? Still not taking my calls, eh? Well, listen to this one last thing. You don't need to call me back. I won't be waiting. I've been done over by loads of people. But no one went as far as you. So, I'm going to do something that will make you never forget me. It's for you to learn not to do that to anyone else.

He rings off.

Scene Eighteen

Joel*'s garage. The same layout as before but this time there are no chairs.* **Mauro**, **Celso** *and* **Lia** *stand while* **Joel** *watches them from a platform.*

Joel (*to* **Celso**)   You go first today, Celso.

Celso   Me?

Joel   We're all curious to hear how your story's going.

Celso   First off, I want to apologise to you all about the other meetings.

Joel   You don't need to do that.

Celso   It was shameful.

Joel   Get on with it, Celsinho!

Silence.

Celso   I killed someone.

Lia   You *what*?

Joel   How?

Mauro   You killed someone?

Celso   Yeah.

Joel   Who?

Celso   The girl who was making me feel so low about myself.

Lia   Oh my God . . .

Joel   But you said that she'd stopped making you feel like that!

Celso   Well, she started again more than ever!

Joel   Wasn't this the girl you were in love with?

Celso   That's the one.

Joel   I asked you to seduce her and you go and kill her?!

Celso   Did I do wrong?

Joel   And you're still asking me if you did wrong? You did very wrong! Is this really true? Did you really kill someone or are you trying to impress us?

Celso   I did kill someone.

Joel   Who do you think you are, taking someone's life away from them? What value do you place on life when you can go and just kill someone like that? What have you really suffered to make you go and do a thing like that?

Lia   Can I say what I feel about this?

Joel   This is serious, Lia!

Lia   But can I say something? When he said he'd killed someone, it made me . . . I can't explain it. It made me feel like I could kill someone, too!

Joel   No, Lia, no!

Lia   Why not?

Joel   You can't do that.

Lia   But I'd do it a different way. Not with a gun, but with an orgy where people could die from pleasure!

Joel   Shut up, Lia!

Mauro   Shut up, Joel!

Joel   What?

Mauro   I told you to shut up!

Joel   Have you totally lost it?

Mauro   You've gone too far this time.

Joel   What did I do?

Mauro   You're screwing us all up. And we didn't come here for that. We came here to have our spirits lifted! Wasn't that what you told us? Instead you've made us all mad, sick and weak! Look what's happening here now! What do you really want from us?

Joel   Do you really want to know?

He takes out a gun from under the platform. They all scream and go to run for cover. **Joel** *points the gun towards them all.*

Stay right there!

They all freeze.

Mauro   So it's true, then.

Joel   What is?

Mauro   Stop all this. At this rate, the police'll be on their way.

Joel   Who else knows about this?

Mauro   Someone must do.

Joel   No one knows a thing. You idiots! Bunch of tossers! (*To* **Ana**, *who has just appeared.*) Like that girl there!

Lia   Who are you talking to?

Joel   Celso's sister.

Celso   Liar.

Joel   You all calling this a 'ritual' – ritual of what?! Ritual for who? It's for me, that's who. The ritual of my life. The shitty little life that I'm still living! I'm tired of this world where everyone's out for themselves. People who think they're king of the whole universe. Well, now they're gonna see who's king. With an ending comes a rebirth! That's what I've always believed. I'm gonna show you what it really means to have a strong spirit!

Scene Nineteen

A square. **Mauro** *sits waiting.* **Bianca** *enters.*

Mauro   Sit down, Bianca.

Bianca *sits down.*

Mauro   Thanks for seeing me. (*Silence.*) You're still mad at me, aren't you?

Bianca   What do you think?

Mauro   Can you ever forgive me?

Bianca   Forgive you for what?

Mauro   For being so pig-headed.

Bianca   I'll try. (*Silence.*) I can forgive you for being so stubborn, for putting so many people's lives at risk, including your own. But what I can't change is what I feel for you.

Mauro   And what do you feel for me?

Bianca   Nothing.

Mauro   Meaning . . . ?

Bianca   You threw everything away.

Mauro   I know.

Bianca   All for this friend of yours.

Mauro   It wasn't because of him.

Bianca   What was it for, then?

Mauro   My ignorance.

Bianca   You were pretty stupid, then.

Mauro   I was weak.

Bianca   That too.

Mauro   Couldn't you give me another chance?

Bianca   I don't know.

Mauro (*taking the bracelet off his wrist*)   In case you want proof that I really mean it . . .

He throws the bracelet away.

Bianca   It's easy to do that now.

She makes to leave.

Mauro   Where are you off to?

Bianca   Home.

Mauro   Can I call you one of these days?

Bianca   Leave me alone, Mauro.

Mauro   Sure.

Bianca   I need to think about what's happened here.

She exits.

The Ritual

Notes on rehearsal and staging, drawn from a workshop with the writer and translator held at the National Theatre, November 2011

Thoughts from the Writer

The Ritual is a play about a group of young people who are totally disconnected from their parents and the world around them. They live without involvement from the adults in their lives and have no real sense of family. Although they don't discuss this openly at any point, they carry it through the play. In a way, *The Ritual* is about a breakdown of family values and the consequences of this breakdown.

When Samir arrived in the UK the first thing he asked was whether it was safe here. In São Paulo it is not safe to walk alone at night. Fear of crime and its impact run through everyday life, and it should underscore the play. It is not uncommon in Brazil for women to be murdered by their partners or expartners. *The Ritual* is in some ways a comment on this. Bianca is caught in the crossfire of Joel's anger, but Márcia is the catalyst for it, and therefore for the action of the play.

Locating the Play

The play was initially written about Brazil, and it strongly portrays life there, but neither Samir nor Orla O'Loughlin, who was leading the workshop, suggests that it need be the setting. Mark O'Thomas suggests that, as the translation is not 'localised', the absence of specificity allows a certain amount of freedom in terms of setting. The most important thing is that the logic of the world holds up. You might decide to set your production in any city or town, but there is a sense of 'otherness' in the characters, action and events which it is important to retain.

There are several things to note here:

- The characters must be somewhere where the murder Celso commits is in some ways unremarkable.

- In this world, middle-class young people can easily get hold of guns.

- Death is common in this world and it is also fetishised by young people.

- In this world the supernatural is natural. It is part of the fabric of everyday life, and therefore Joel is not surprised to see Ana's ghost.

It is crucial that wherever you choose to set the play, your chosen world can accommodate these points – if the events cannot be part of the fabric of this world then the action will not make sense.

Ways to Begin Work on the Play

CREATE A STRONG UNIT

Orla suggested that the 'group' or 'family' feeling of those taking part in the ritual is key. Try to find your own ways of making your acting company a strong, unified community. Experiment with different songs, games or exercises until you find something that feels right for your group. It should be something that helps create a bond between them. Things that can be repeated at the start of each rehearsal (almost your own company 'ritual') will probably be most helpful.

GETTING IT UP ON ITS FEET

Once you are ready to stand up and think about putting the play on its feet, Orla suggested a more active read-through. Line the actors' chairs up against the back wall. Start at the beginning of the play, with the characters in each scene entering, walking forward and standing in a line. All lines of text should be delivered straight out, and at the end of each scene everyone should exit, walk back to their seat and then re-enter if they are in the next scene.

This simple exercise can help you to unlock important information and enable exploration of each character's journey through the play. Mauro, for example, is in each of the first four scenes of the play, making him pivotal. This could indicate that *The Ritual* is, in fact, Mauro's story, in which case, this may have an effect on your choices of staging further down the line. Perhaps you might think about keeping Mauro onstage with the action moving around him.

HAPPINESS AND NORMALITY

There is a great deal of darkness in *The Ritual*, but Orla suggested that it is important to pick out the lighter moments, too. Try to identify what is normality and what is extremity in this world. There is a danger of playing the end at the beginning and you should work hard to avoid this. Samir suggests that the ritual itself begins as something fairly normal and escalates to an extreme. It is a joke that becomes serious.

The Characters

All the young people in the play are unused to having a voice. This is revealed by their surprise at their own power as they take control of, and end, relationships.

JOEL   His relationships with women are confused and complex. He is intelligent and has the power to lead, but he uses this power to negative effect.

The phone calls give an important insight into Joel's character and situation – they demonstrate that he feels a great need to maintain contact with people who do not want to speak to him – he must be in control. He has a strong violent streak and is angry when Celso steals his thunder by taking someone's life. Like a double-edged sword, Joel portrays himself as moral but is actually deeply violent. He is also extremely vulnerable, which is what drives him to seek power in the first place.

ANA   Ana is the only character who really resists Joel. Her return to torment him is a progression of this resistance and an important continuation of Ana's through-line. Ana wants to be loved, but her experience with relationships, her own parents and the ritual itself all undermine her hope. She is driven by a desire for revenge.

LIA Lia names the ritual, and she also creates the dance. She has a certain power, which comes from her overt sexuality. How aware she is of this power is a decision for each director and performer to make. Her dance is described as 'exotic', and this is not a cultural reference to South America but refers instead to Lia. The dance is character-driven and an expression of Lia herself. Lia is in love with Mauro.

BIANCA Bianca has not cheated on Mauro. She, like Ana, can see through Joel and understand the destructive drive behind his actions.

MAURO There is a fragility to Mauro that allows Joel to manipulate him. He has been with Bianca for a long time, and during the ritual he begins to think that he has never lived. He feels he's missing out on the excitement of single life and it is this, combined with Joel's lie about Bianca, that leads him to end their relationship.

CELSO It is very important that there is a clear age difference between Celso and the rest of the group. He is much younger than them, and he is always running after girls who don't like him.

MÁRCIA Márcia is not only the catalyst, but also the character through whom we see the truth. It is only when Bianca meets Márcia in Scene Eleven that the audience discovers how unhinged Joel is.

All the characters who take part in *The Ritual* follow a similar trajectory, with Joel being the most extreme. Samir suggests that it might be helpful to look at characters' counterparts, or 'echoes'. For example, Joel and Lia have definite similarities, as do Celso and Ana. However, less obvious but very important are Ana and Joel, who are both out for revenge in different ways.

Each character is filled with contradictions. For example, Ana could seem weak, but her dramatic act also takes strength. Orla suggests that the characters are almost musical in the way they go up and down. The silences within their arcs are particularly important, as they offer clues to each character's uncertainty. None of these people feels secure – they are uncertain of their place in the world from moment to moment.

It is useful to see how much information the text holds about each character's family background. All the adults seem to be either dangerous or broken – there is a hint that Joel's father was violent, and Celso's mother can't be left alone. This leaves our characters adrift in a world with no fixed points of security and safety. It is of their own making, and has no external boundaries, so they are making up the rules as they go along, and their worlds are filled with contradictions. Carefully consider how each character expresses the extent of their power, damage and vulnerability.

Suggested Exercises for Use in Rehearsals

IMPROVISATION

Orla recommends doing some work 'off the text' to help establish what is normal to these characters. Try exploring some of the following ideas through improvisation:

Bianca and Mauro's relationship   What was it like before Joel told Mauro that Bianca was cheating? (Although we never see them in this state, we need glimpses of it in order to understand what they stand to lose.)

The group's social life   What did they do before 'the ritual'?

Celso's love life   How does he try to approach the women he likes? And how does this lead to the murder?

Bianca and Joel   They never meet in the play, but their relationship is extremely important. Try exploring some scenarios in their recent past in which they meet.

INTERROGATING THE TEXT

There are several key moments in the text where it might be particularly beneficial to question a character's intention or motivation. One example is Joel's introductory speech in Scene Four. When the group gathers in Joel's garage, has Joel pre-planned his speech? How much has he considered what he will say? It might be useful to try two different versions of the speech – one in which he has pre-planned everything, and one in which it's more spur of the moment. How do these two different intentions affect the action? How does Joel come across and what implications does this have for his journey and the shape of the play?

CONNECT OR RETREAT

There are several duologues in the play, and this is a good exercise to try on all of them. Two performers stand several metres apart. They should read their scene from beginning to end, and on each line they can either step towards the other character, or away from them, or remain where they are, depending on whether they are trying to connect with the other person, or retreat from them or maintain their position.

Production Notes

In many ways *The Ritual* is a director's play, as there are so many important choices to be made when staging it. There are many subtle ambiguities in the play, and Samir is happy for each production to tackle these in their own way. You may decide that the ambiguity is important, or you may alternatively decide to make firm decisions about characters' intentions and actions. But be clear what the 'givens' are, as they will give you a secure place from which to interpret and make choices.

Consider carefully what the audience relationship to the action will be. The play comprises many short scenes – do you want the audience to view these end-on, or in traverse, or perhaps in promenade?

One way of exploring this might be to take a more complex scene, such as the first ritual, and experiment with different perspectives. How does it affect the action if we can see Joel's face but the rest of the group have their backs to the audience? What happens if you reverse this, or have them all at an angle? What do you gain or lose from each of these options?

Equally important to the audience relationship with the action is the characters' physical relationship to one another. How close are they, physically? It is particularly interesting to explore Scene Five. Ana and Celso are sitting in Ana's room together, which already indicates a closeness as siblings. Within this, play with how close or distant they are. What does the scene feel like if they are on opposite sides of the room? Or with Ana on the bed and Celso on the floor? Or sitting next to each other on the bed? Do they maintain eye contact, or does one or other of them look away? Take the time to play and explore each possibility and its implications.

PHONE CALLS

Joel has a conversation on the phone with an unknown character, from whom he is buying a gun. Decide what is being said on the other end of the phone and stick to it.

The phone calls could be staged in many different ways. It is also possible to explore different means of communication, such as Skype, iChat, email and Facebook. Conversations on the phone could be staged with one performer present and the other recorded, or with one character in the foreground and one in the background. Each of these different options has an impact on whose story you are telling, so explore all the possibilities.

REACTING TO THE CRISIS POINTS

Each character reacts differently to the news of Ana's death and later the murder Celso commits, and it is important to make sense of these differing and sometimes surprising reactions. In Scene Twelve, there is an element of shock –

none of them is prepared for this first death. It makes them think that anything is possible. The temperature of the play changes completely, and new, dangerous possibilities open up. Their reactions are also shaped by the fact that they are in a very public place. Mauro makes what seems like a totally inappropriate advance on Lia, but it's possible that he genuinely thinks that he has nothing to lose and his time may be limited.

THE END

In the penultimate scene, we see Joel waving a loaded gun at the other group members. The scene ends, and in the next scene, we see Mauro and Bianca discussing their relationship. At no point do we find out for certain how the gun standoff in the final ritual was resolved. Samir has no firm answers, but would instead prefer that each group makes its own decision as to how the ritual ended. You may choose to hint at this outcome in the transition between the penultimate and the final scenes, or you may like to leave the audience to make up their own minds.

From a workshop led by Orla O'Loughlin,
with notes by Kirsty Housley

Participating Companies

Aberdeen Performing Arts
Academy of Creative Training
artsdepot
Ashcroft Technology Academy
BSix Brooke House Sixth Form
  College
Bare Knuckle Theatre Company
Bedford College
Best Rest Youth Company
Bexhill 6th Form College
Blatchington Mill School
Bodens Youth Theatre
Bounce Theatre
Brentford School for Girls
Brewery Youth Theatre
Bridgend College
Brighton Hove Sussex 6th Form
Calderdale Theatre School
Callington Community College
CastEnsemble
Castleford Academy
CATS Youth Theatre
Chichester Festival Theatre
Chichester High School for Girls
Chickenshed
Christ's Hospital School
City Academy Norwich
Connaught School for Girls
Cotton Shed Theatre Company
Craigholme School
Deafinitely Theatre
Dig Deptford Youth Theatre
Dramarama Youth Theatre
Driffield School
Duck Egg Theatre Company
Easy Street Theatre Company
Elizabeth Garrett Anderson School
Exeter College
Explosive Arts
Felixstowe Academy

Flying High Theatre Company
Fortismere School
Fowey Community College
Glenthorne High School
Grand Youth Theatre Company
  (GYTC)
Gravesend Grammar School
Group 64 Youth Theatre
Guernsey Grammar and Sixth
  Form Centre
Haberdashers Aske's Knights
  Academy
Hammersmith Academy
Harris Academy Bromley
Havant Academy
Havering College of Further and
  Higher Education
High Jinks
Highly Sprung Performance Co.
Inspire Academy
InterACT Youth Theatre
ITW YT
John Cabot Academy
John Port School
Joseph Chamberlain College
Junk Shop Theatre Company
Key Youth Theatre
Kildare Youth Theatre
King Alfred School
Kingsley School
King's Lynn Academy
Lakeside Youth Theatre
Langley Grammar School
LightsDown Theatre School
Llanelli Youth Theatre
LOST Youth Theatre
  Company
Lyceum Youth Theatre
Lyme Youth Theatre in association
  with The Woodroffe School

Lyric Hammersmith
(Lyric Youth Company)
MProductions
Manchester Grammar School
Marine Academy Plymouth
Mark Rutherford School
Mill Hill County High School
More Pies Productions
New Hall School
Newent Community School
Notts Performing Arts
Odd Productions
ONE Theatre Company
Oval House Theatre
OX | Theater | Collective
Oxford Actors Company
Oxford Playhouse,
Magdalen College School
Padworth College
Perfect Circle Theatre Company
Platform Performance (Glasgow
East Arts Company)
Pump House CYT
PWAcademy
REDMAN@Greenroom
Reed's School
Ricards Lodge High School
Riddlesdown Collegiate
Roding Valley High School
Rotherham College of Arts and
Technology
Royal & Derngate
Sandbach School Theatre
SAVVY Theatre Company
Scarborough Youth Theatre
Shirley High School
Sindhi Association UK
Slow Theatre
South London Youth Theatre
South West Youth Theatre
South Wirral High School
Southwark College
St Catherine's School, Twickenham

St Dominic's
St George's Academy
St Monica's High School
Stephen Joseph Youth Theatre
with Fuse Youth Theatre
Stolti Delizia
Sudbury Upper School & Arts
College
The Amersham School
The Astley Cooper School
The Blue Coat School Oldham
The Boswells School
The Castle
The Crestwood School
The Customs House Youth
Theatre
The Garage
The Henry Beaufort School
The King's School, Ely
The Lowry
The Moat School
The Priory City of Lincoln
Academy
The Ravensbourne School
The Winston Churchill School
Theatre Royal Plymouth
Theatreworks
Thomas Tallis
Thomas Telford School
Trinity School, Teignmouth
Trinity School, Croydon
Trinity Youth Theatre Company
Tunbridge Wells Grammar School
for Boys
Upstaged Theatre Company
UROCK Youth Theatre
Walsall College
Walthamstow School for Girls
Warwick Arts Centre Senior Youth
Theatre
Waterhead Academy
Wellsway School
West Exe Technology College

West Lancashire College
West Yorkshire Playhouse
Wild Wing
Winterhill School
Wired Youth Theatre
Woodbridge High School

Yew Tree Youth Theatre
Young Persons' Theatre Company
Ysgol Aberconwy
Ysgol Morgan Llwyd
ZOOM! Arts
360 youth theatre

Partner Theatres

EAST
The Garage, Norwich
Norwich Playhouse

EAST MIDLANDS
Royal & Derngate, Northampton

LONDON
Arts Depot
Lyric Hammersmith
Rose Theatre, Kingston
Soho Theatre

NORTH EAST
Northern Stage, Newcastle

NORTH WEST
Brewery Arts Centre, Kendal

NORTHERN IRELAND
Grand Opera House, Belfast

SCOTLAND
Royal Lyceum Theatre, Edinburgh

SOUTH EAST
Chichester Festival Theatre
Oxford Playhouse

SOUTH WEST
Bristol Old Vic
Theatre Royal Plymouth

WALES
Canolfan Mileniwm Cymru/Wales Millennium Centre, Cardiff

WEST MIDLANDS
The Lowry Centre, Salford
Warwick Arts Centre, Coventry

YORKSHIRE
Sheffield Theatres
West Yorkshire Playhouse, Leeds

Performing Rights

*Applications for permission to perform etc. should be made,
before rehearsals begin, to the following representatives:*

For *Victim Sidekick Boyfriend Me*:
RGM Associates
64–76 Kippax Street
Surry Hills, NSW 2010
Australia

For *Journey to X* and *Generation Next*:
Rochelle Stevens
2 Terrets Place
London N1 1QZ

For *Little Foot*:
Attn: Adam Gauntlett
Peters Fraser and Dunlop (PFD)
34–43 Russell Street
London WC2B 5HA

For *Prince of Denmark* and *The Grandfathers*:
Casarotto Ramsay & Associates Ltd
Waverley House, 7–12 Noel Street
London W1F 8GQ

For *Socialism is Great*:
Attn: Ben Hall
Curtis Brown,
Haymarket House, 28–29 Haymarket,
London SW1Y 4SP

For *Alice by Heart*:
Attn: Olivier Sultan
Creative Artists Agency
162 Fifth Avenue, 6th Floor
New York, NY 10010, USA

For *So You Think You're a Superhero?*:
Alan Brodie Representation Ltd
The Courtyard, 55 Charterhouse Street
London EC1M 6HA

For *The Ritual*:
R. Paulo Orozimbo
503 #181, SP,
CEP 01535-000, Brazil

National Theatre Connections 2012 Team

Alice King-Farlow *Director of Learning Programme*

Rob Watt *Producer, Connections*

Anthony Banks *Associate Director, NT Learning*

Tom Harland *Programme Co-ordinator*

Paula Hamilton *Head of Programmes, NT Learning*

Katie Town *General Manager, NT Learning*

Sebastian Born *Associate Director, Literary*

Ruth Little *Script Adviser*

The National Theatre

National Theatre
Upper Ground
London SE1 9PX

Registered charity no: 224223

Director of the National Theatre
Nicholas Hytner

Executive Director
Nick Starr

Chief Operating Officer
Lisa Burger

Deputy Executive Director
Kate Horton